Social Semiotics as Praxis

Theory and History of Literature
Edited by Wlad Godzich and Jochen Schulte-Sasse

Volume 74. Paul J. Thibault *Social Semiotics as Praxis*
Volume 73. Hélène Cixous *Reading with Clarice Lispector*
Volume 72. N.S. Trubetzkoy *Writings on Literature*
Volume 71. Neil Larsen *Modernism and Hegemony*
Volume 70. Paul Zumthor *Oral Poetry: An Introduction*
Volume 69. Giorgio Agamben *Stanzas: Speech and Phantasm in Western Culture*
Volume 68. Hans Robert Jauss *Question and Answer: Forms of Dialogic Understanding*
Volume 67. Umberto Eco *On the Concept of the Sign*
Volume 66. Paul de Man *Critical Writings, 1953–1978*
Volume 65. Paul de Man *Aesthetic Ideology*
Volume 64. Didier Coste *Narrative as Communication*
Volume 63. Renato Barilli *Rhetoric*
Volume 62. Daniel Cottom *Text and Culture*
Volume 61. Theodor W. Adorno *Kierkegaard: Construction of the Aesthetic*
Volume 60. Kristin Ross *The Emergence of Social Space: Rimbaud and the Paris Commune*
Volume 59. Lindsay Waters and Wlad Godzich *Reading de Man Reading*
Volume 58. F.W.J. Schelling *The Philosophy of Art*
Volume 57. Louis Marin *Portrait of the King*
Volume 56. Peter Sloterdijk *Thinker on Stage: Nietzsche's Materialism*
Volume 55. Paul Smith *Discerning the Subject*
Volume 54. Réda Bensmaïa *The Barthes Effect*
Volume 53. Edmond Cros *Theory and Practice of Sociocriticism*
Volume 52. Philippe Lejeune *On Autobiography*
Volume 51. Thierry de Duve *Pictorial Nominalism: On Marcel Duchamp's Passage from Painting to the Readymade*
Volume 50. Luiz Costa Lima *Control of the Imaginary*
Volume 49. Fredric Jameson *The Ideologies of Theory: Essays 1971–1986, Volume 2*
Volume 48. Fredric Jameson *The Ideologies of Theory: Essays 1971–1986, Volume 1*
Volume 47. Eugene Vance *From Topic to Tale: Logic and Narrativity in the Middle Ages*
Volume 46. Jean-François Lyotard *The Differend*
Volume 45. Manfred Frank *What Is Neostructuralism?*

For other books in the series, see p. 304

Social Semiotics as Praxis: *Text, Social Meaning Making, and Nabokov's* Ada

Paul J. Thibault

Theory and History of Literature, Volume 74

University of Minnesota Press
Minneapolis Oxford

Published by the University of Minnesota Press
2037 University Avenue Southeast, Minneapolis, MN 55414.
Printed in the United States of America on acid-free paper

Library of Congress Cataloging-in-Publication Data
Thibault, Paul J.
Social semiotics as praxis : text, social meaning making, and Nabokov's Ada / Paul J. Thibault.
p. cm. – (Theory and history of literature ; v. 74)
Includes bibliographical references and indexes.
ISBN (invalid) 08166018658. – ISBN 0-8166-1866-6 (pbk.)
1. Semiotics – Social aspects. 2. Discourse analysis.
3. Intertextuality. 4. Nabokov, Vladmir, 1899–1977. Ada.
I. Title. II. Series.
P99.4.S62T4 1990
302.2 – dc20 90-39723
CIP

A CIP catalog record for this book is available from the British Library

The University of Minnesota
is an equal-opportunity
educator and employer.

For Enza and Ilaria

Contents

List of Figures

List of Tables

Preface

The conceptual framework of this book is a social semiotic one. It theorizes the relations between dynamic contextual processes and their textual products in the making, maintaining, and changing of systems of social meaning making practices. The textual analysis in this study is almost exclusively focused on Vladimir Nabokov's novel *Ada*. However, I propose this book as a contribution to the development of a critical neomaterialist social semiotic theory and practice. The book is divided into four parts. Each begins with several quotations from the principal intellectual sources of this study. The division into parts and the use of these quotations help to organize the eight chapters into a number of more general themes. Part I develops the conceptual framework and its implications for my conception of a social semiotics that is both a form of social action and a political praxis. These are outlined in chapter 1. I also attempt in that chapter to situate this endeavor in relation to the principal intellectual sources that I draw on throughout the book. These are the works of Mikhail Bakhtin/V. N. Volosinov, Gregory Bateson, Basil Bernstein, Jacques Derrida, Michel Foucault, Antonio Gramsci, Jürgen Habermas, and Michael Halliday.

Part II is a series of explorations around the dynamics of quoting and reporting speech and the relevance of these to metalevels of contextualization. Chapter 2 develops a sociosemantic analysis of the dynamics of quoting and reporting relations on the basis of Halliday's semantically oriented functional grammar and the account of the logico-semantic relations of projection at the level of the clause complex that is developed therein. This analysis is also used to develop a critique of the categories of "self" and "representation" through which semiotic forms and the social actions they realize are related to notions of an experiencing self that is, according to the folk-theoretical rationalization of these forms, "expressed" or "represented" in language. Chapters 3 and 4 further explore the dynamics of quoting and reporting relations by showing how their uses and various transforms (recontextualizations) index usually implicit information about "insider" and "outsider" categories and relations in the social semiotic system. I suggest that these may be able to teach us a good deal about the higher-order joint or hybrid contextualizations that are enacted whenever a theorist system interacts with the "object" of its theoretical practices.

Part III expands the focus of the earlier chapters by taking up the question of intertextuality. In chapter 5 I develop the concept of intertextuality in ways that can account for both the cothematic and coactional meanings through which meaningful relationships are constructed between texts. This is done in such a way as to avoid the reduction of this concept to a positivistic search for specific intertextual sources by focusing on the foregrounded copatternings of *typical* meaning relations that link particular texts to still wider systems of more abstract intertextual meaning relations. The categories of text and discourse are defined and elaborated in relation to the Bakhtin/Volosinov notions of dialogicity and social heteroglossia, which are necessarily implicated in all intertextual relations. Chapter 6 further elaborates these notions in connection with a detailed analysis of the lexico-grammatical resources through which cothematic and coactional intertextual meaning relations are made. I then try to show how specific foregrounded and backgrounded copatternings of lexico-grammatical selections realize two principal semantic orientations in these texts. These are the textual voicings of heteroglossically related sociodiscursive positioned-practices in the social formation. These semantic orientations are related to the differential access of discursive subjects/social agents to relations of power and knowledge in discursive practice. Intertextuality is here related to the ways in which particular copatternings of lexico-grammatical selections and the consistent semantic frames (textual voices) they realize are specialized to differentially distributed social semiotic coding orientations. The coding orientations thus provide an important link between the microlevel of actual textual productions and the higher-order social semiotic. These links are further developed in chapters 7 and 8.

In Part IV I try to construct a number of theoretical links between the problematic of the discursive subject and social meaning making practices. Chapter 7 begins with a critique of the concept of ideology. I then outline the foundational principles of a neomaterialist social semiotic theory of ideology and hegemony. Once again, this is a nonrepresentationist account in which systems of social meaning making practices enact a constant metastable dialectic of system-maintaining and system-changing relations and practices. Ideology is reworked in the social semiotic conceptual framework in terms of the system of disjunctions that both connects and disconnects social meaning making practices in regular and systematic ways at both the microlevel of specific textual productions and the level of higher-order systemic processes and contextualizing relations in and through which these are made. Chapter 7 anticipates a social semiotic account of the social agent/discursive subject relation, which is central in chapter 8. This final chapter is concerned with the multilevel hierarchical and dialectical systems of contextualizing relations among sociodiscursive practices, texts, metasemiotic "rules" of contextualization, social agents, and discursive subject positions. These multilevel systems of meanings and practices constitute the social semiotic resources that are potentially available to social agents in the maintenance and/or change of the social semiotic system or some part of it. The emphasis is on both the constituted and constitutive nature of these relations in our social meaning making practices. Social meaning making practices are both productive and constraining of what social agents can do and can mean in specific social activity-structures, texts, and their social contexts of use.

Chapter 8 also brings together and rearticulates the two principal themes of this book, namely, a concern with levels of relations and the dynamics of contextualization. As we shall see, it is not possible to discuss these two themes in isolation from each other. They intersect and mutually define each other in many complex ways. As a general statement about the design of this book, we can say that it is concerned with questions about levels of relations and contexts and with constructing adequate and responsible analytical representations and theoretical discourses about them. These concerns necessarily overlap because the social semiotic account of social meaning making practices and the textual productions that are enacted and made in and through them is primarily a relational one.

This book is itself a product of specific social practices. Its valorized final-product-like status helps to conceal the social functions it serves and the social processes in and through which it was made. We tend to talk about the individual "author" of the book and to acknowledge, according to the standard academic conventions, its intertextual relations with other academic writings. Its final-product-like status helps to mask the many different social discourses and social occasions that have constituted the social processes that are the real work of this book. I should like to take the opportunity in this preface of explicating and acknowledging the most important of those interactions that have enabled me to write the present book. Many of these cannot adequately be acknowledged in the conventional academic ways.

The preparation of this book has a history of friends and colleagues who have helped and often provoked me to shape and reshape the discursive construction of the "thinking" that I have tried to write into this book. In particular, I should like to mention the great support and encouragement of John Alexander, Manuel Alvarado (British Film Institute, London), Angela Andrisano (Dipartimento di Filologia Classica e Medioevale, Università degli Studi di Bologna), Gian Paolo

Caprettini (Dipartimento di Ermeneutica Filosofica e Tecniche dell'Interpretazione, Università degli Studi di Torino), Paolo Fabbri (Groupe de Recherches Sémiolinguistiques of the Ecole des Hautes Etudes en Sciences Sociales, Paris, and Facoltà di Lettere, Università degli Studi di Palermo), Roger Fowler (School of English and American Studies, University of East Anglia, Norwich), Michael Halliday (Department of Linguistics, University of Sydney), Noel King (Faculty of Humanities and Social Sciences, University of Technology, Sydney), Gunther Kress (Faculty of Humanities and Social Sciences, University of Technology, Sydney), Jay Lemke (School of Education, Brooklyn College of the City University of New York), Marc Lorrimar (School of Humanities, Murdoch University, Western Australia), Bob Lumsden (Department of English Language and Literature, National University of Singapore), Aldo di Luzio (Fachgruppe Sprachwissenschaft, Universität Konstanz), Alan Mansfield (School of Humanities, Murdoch University, Western Australia), Jim Martin (Department of Linguistics, University of Sydney), Radan Martinec (Department of Linguistics, University of Sydney), Bruce and Kathy McKellar (Casa Colina Hospital, Upland, California), Blair McKenzie, Stephen Muecke (Faculty of Humanities and Social Sciences, University of Technology, Sydney), Michael O'Toole (School of Humanities, Murdoch University), John Pellowe (Department of English Language and Literature, National University of Singapore), Gino Rizzo (Department of Italian, University of Sydney), Gabriel Sala (Istituto di Scienze dell'Educazione, Università degli Studi di Verona), Clive Thomson (School of French Studies, Queen's University, Ontario), Terry Threadgold (Department of English, University of Sydney), and Theo van Leeuwen (School of English and Linguistics, Macquarie University, Sydney). I should like to express my deep gratitude to all of these individuals, who have contributed in invaluable and often ineffable ways to the life and the work that inform this study.

I am also very grateful to Terry Cochran, at the University of Minnesota Press, and to Wlad Godzich, both for the interest they have shown in publishing this project and for their help and great patience throughout the preparation of the manuscript.

Enza Andrisano's humanity and her very special inspiration have helped me to complete this project. She has also provided me with great material and personal support as well as valuable help with the translations from Italian.

Finally, I should like to make a brief comment on the use of English translations. Unless I have indicated otherwise in the bibliography, all translations from original texts in French, German, and Italian are my own. In some instances, I have checked my translation against the most readily available English one. In several cases it seemed preferable to include the original text rather than a translation.

Part I
Introduction

It is very unlikely that one part of the semantic system would remain totally isolated from another; when new meanings are being created on a large scale, we should expect some changes in the fashions of speaking. It is far from clear how these take place; but it is certainly quite inadequate to interpret the innovations simply as changes in subject matter. The changes that are brought about in this way involve media, genres, participants and participant relations, all the components of the situation. New registers are created, which activate new alignments and configurations in the functional components of the semantic system. It is through the intermediary of the social structure that the semantic change is brought about. Semantic style is a function of social relationships and situation types generated by the social structure. If it changes, this is not so much because of what people are now speaking about as because of who they are speaking to, in what circumstances, through what media and so on. A shift in the fashions of speaking will be better understood by reference to changing patterns of social interaction and social relationships than by the search for a direct link between the language and the material culture.

Michael Halliday (1978: 77)

The philosophy of praxis is a reformation and a development of Hegelianism; it is a philosophy freed (or that strives to free itself) from every unilateral and fanatical ideological element; it is the full awareness of contradictions, in which the philosopher himself, understood individually or as an entire social group, not only understands the contradictions but places himself as an element of the contradictions and raises this element to a principle of knowledge and therefore of action. "Man in general," however he presents himself, is negated and all dogmatically "unitary" concepts are mocked and destroyed insofar as [they are the] expression of the concept of 'man in general' or of "human nature" immanent in every man.

Antonio Gramsci (1977a: 115–16; my translation)

Chapter 1
The Conceptual Framework of a Praxis-Oriented Social Semiotic Theory

Praxis and the Epistemology of Social Semiotics

Semiotics means very generally the study of signs, and in the "more rigorous definition" proposed by Umberto Eco (1976: 4) this is taken to include a definition of "sign-function" and "a typology of modes of sign-production." The conceptual framework of this book is a "social semiotic" one. The choice of the term *social semiotic* rather than *semiotic* is determined by my conviction that it is time the theory and practice of semiotics began to think beyond its idealistic foundations as the "science of signs" and hence beyond its self-identification with many of the foundational ideological assumptions of Western culture. These include the disjunctive oppositions meaning/reality, truth/falsity, signifier/signified, word/referent, material/ideal, interior/exterior, meaning/thought, mind/body, immediacy/mediation, and nature/culture. "Thinking beyond" should not be taken to mean that I am defining my own position negatively or as one of simple opposition to these and other foundational axioms and principles of our culture. It is, I believe, a question of taking a position in relation to these and the social meaning making practices in and through which they are constructed. This entails a social semiotics that is a social and political intervention in these practices as practices. A line of "radical deconstruction" extending from Nietzsche to Derrida and Foucault has exposed the metaphysical foundations and the antithesis of values on which these disjunctive oppositions are based. However, the "radical skepticism" that this critique has generated and the exposing of the complicity of this metaphysics in the relations of power and authority of the dominant social order have stopped short of developing an alternative theory and practice that can analyze the social functions of these without simply presuming them in our own practice as theorists of social meaning making and without merely defining them negatively with respect to these, that is, as "opposed to" or "against" these foundational axioms and assumptions.

"Social semiotics" is then proposed as an intervention in the theory and practice of semiotics. Such an intervention starts from the praxis-oriented view that our practice as analysts and theorists of the social meaning making practices and their textual products in our own and other social semiotic systems is itself a set of social meaning making practices just like those we study and analyze. We are not "above" or "external to" the meanings and social practices that constitute the "object" of our theory making. The kind of social semiotic theory and practice I want to develop fully accepts Derrida's (1978: 289) critique of totalization in the social sciences. Totalization enacts a form of metatheoretical contextual foreclosure that acts *as if* it were above or outside the social meaning making practices it studies. As Derrida argues, the very object of study—language, or more generally, all social meaning making—renders totalization impossible. This requires then that we reject the necessitation of teleological and causal explanations in our theory. As Hirst (1976: 18) argues, these "entail a teleology (a process with a definite direction, a necessary end) and some overall cause for that teleology" (see also Keller, 1985: 235). The psychosocial functionalism of speaker's needs, goals, and purposes is rejected as the basis for a theory of social meaning making. These folk-theoretical explanations of social practice have led to structural functionalism's totalizing account of a necessarily unified and coherent social order, taken as an ontological given, in which meanings and practices are rationalized on the basis of a general system's goals and purposes. In rejecting the ontology of a coherent and unified social totality in which the actions and purposes of agents are preservative of this order, this does not mean that we are rejecting the quite different functional basis of all semiotic forms. This calls for a functionalism that takes as its basis a given semiotic form's relations to other forms in some wider system of relations. This will be discussed further below in connection with Hjelmslev's concept of the sign-function (see also Thibault, 1986a: ii-iii). Our theories and analytical practices are a part of the contextual relations and dynamics of the social meaning making practices we analyze. To theorize about or to analyze these means to interact with them. Theory and analytical practice are never intransitive or unidirectional in their effects. Rather, what constitutes the "inside" and the "outside" of some theory is a result of the hybridization of the meaning making practices of the theory with those that are the object of the theory. As Jay Lemke (1983a: 1–4) has argued, the joint or hybrid meaning system that results can be recursively analyzed to produce representations of its own meaning making practices. "Outsider" or metapractices and the "insider" practices with which they interact are not givens that simply come together and interact. They are constituted by the interactions themselves. The dynamics of "insider" and "outsider" relations, their representations and deployments in the folk-theoretical accounts that are largely implicit in quoting and reporting relations, will be the major focus in chapters 3 and 4. A consideration of the dynamics of their contextualizing relations gives us some further important insights into the mechanisms for generating the recursive analysis of our own theory's meaning making practices.

Social semiotic theory does not, as I remarked earlier, place itself in a position of simple denial or of opposition to the culturally dominant foundational metaphysics, which has been radically deconstructed by Nietzsche and the poststructuralists. Nor can it be the epistemological guarantor of some transcendent ideological alternative, itself no more than a metaphysical illusion. Social semiotics, as a set of meaning making practices, is always immanent in the patterned exchanges and interactions of some wider social formation along with its regulatory and deregulatory functions. The concept of immanence, which derives from the pioneering work of Gregory Bateson (1973), has two principal consequences for our attempt to build a conceptually unified social semiotic theory and practice. First, immanence means that our theoretical and analytical practices are always constituted in and through the play of praxis to which Derrida refers. These are immanent in some system of differences, which is not, however, formally defined as a closed homeostatic system as in Saussure's ([1915] 1983: 108) metaphor of language as a form of game. Instead, Bateson (1973a: 286) has shown that a difference is a bit of information that makes a difference in a closed circuit of a transform of differences. A theory that sees itself as part of such a system of differences—a social semiotic system, for instance—participates in those processes that work both to maintain and to change the system of relations. In other words, a theory of social meaning making is always constituted in and through a given ensemble of social meaning making practices; yet, it can work to articulate alternative theories and practices, points of resistance to dominant cultural axioms, in ways that can destabilize them. This is a continual process of disarticulation of social meanings and practices and their rearticulation in the conceptual framework of a truly social semiotic praxis (see also Mouffe, 1979: 193). Second, the criterion of immanence means that this process of disarticulation-rearticulation aims to construct a unified theory and practice whose goal is not merely to expose and radically deconstruct the dominant cultural axioms and presuppositions. Instead, it is concerned radically to reconstitute, as Jay Lemke (1985a) puts it, those analytical strategies and traditions in the social sciences that can be of most use for the unified social semiotic praxis referred to here. I argue in chapter 8 that the differentialist rather than truly dialectical "textual politics" of poststructuralism has not succeeded in this task because the deconstruction of the formal and representational unity and coherence of textual meanings continues to act as if the text were the principal or, indeed, the *only* site of political struggle. Edward Said (1985: 147) has remarked on the alarming disjunction between this textual politics and the wider sociopolitical field of relations in which texts and their producers and users are situated. Now, these links are neither given nor straightforward, yet, the failure, for the most part, to theorize them arises, I believe, from the more general theoretical failure to link textual functions to their wider social functions in ways that do not simply reconfirm the folk-theoretical or commonsense rationalizations of social meaning making. This is a self-imposed limitation of any theory that is either viewed as a formal end in itself or whose theoretical axioms and assumptions remain merely implicit in the restricted practices of some theorist-community. For instance, the poststructuralist critique of the formal and representational criteria according to which textual meanings are evaluated by the dominant metaphysic does not recursively analyze its own textual practices to a sufficiently high order of contextualization in ways that permit its links with the wider social formation and its functions to be made and renewed. Consequently, a "decentered" notion of textual practice remains central in the sense that, say, authorial intention or a fixed relation between signifier and signified are no longer taken to be the epistemological guarantors of the meaning and authority of the text. However, this critique remains unable to develop a truly praxis-oriented conception. For a theory to be truly praxis-oriented in the way I defined above, it must be explicitly and self-reflexively connected to specific domains of social practice.

Thus, the notion of a *unified* theory and practice does not refer here to one that presumes to be "objective" or "totalizing." It refers to a unitary theoretical practice, which is able to construct meaningful and useful links between its own conceptual and analytical framework and specific domains of social practice in the service of an actional semiotics of social meaning making. This requires that we view our theoretical practices, the objects of our study, and their analytical approximations within the same unified conceptual framework.

The social semiotic conceptual framework is concerned with the systems of meaning making resources, their patterns of use in texts and social occasions of discourse, and the social practices of the social formations in and through which these textual meanings are made, remade, imposed, contested, and changed from one textual production or social occasion of discourse to another. The focus is on the material and dialectical interrelations of copatterned textual meaning relations and their uses in specific domains of social practice. It is a theory of *social meaning making practices*. The term *social semiotic* serves therefore to indicate that any semiotic or linguistic theory that takes the sign, sign-tokens, or typologies of these as its central or only concern will remain unable to move beyond a merely formal semiotics. Social semiotics therefore strives to be a critical, self-reflexive theory of the dynamics of these social meaning making practices. It is *critical* because it seeks to show how regular and systematic copatternings of textual meaning relations and their associated meaning making practices function in ways that enact, maintain, reproduce, and change the social semiotic system or some part of it. It is *self-reflexive* because it works to account for its own theoretical praxis within the same critical perspective. It works to define its own relations to other social discourses, its own positioning in the sets of intersecting and often conflicting relations among these, and the sociopolitical interests these serve. Furthermore, it is concerned with identifying potential areas of intervention and change in the dynamic interrelations between material matter-energy exchanges in the prediscursive physical and biological domains and the systems of social meaning making that constitute the discursive. Thus, social semiotics does not counterpose the social and the biological as two independent and reified domains of cause and effect. Neither the social nor the biological uniquely determines or defines patterned social semiotic behavior. Instead, this is defined by complex intersections and copatternings of the two domains in ways that covary with specific social and evolutionary conditions (see also Hirst and Woolley, 1982: 5–22). Nevertheless, the "social semiotic" is not reducible to some more essential biological domain and is therefore theorized on the basis of a conceptual and methodological framework that is specific to that domain (see also McKellar, 1988).

The social semiotic conceptual framework is also a *neomaterialist* one that is concerned with the multilevel hierarchically and dialectically related social semiotic processes and relations and their embodiment in the prediscursive material matter-energy exchanges through which the former are realized. Thus, textual productions, their contextualizations, and the social agent/discursive subject relations these produce are always immanent in some patterned transactions of matter, energy, and information. The neomaterialist perspective therefore has no need of the material/ideal distinction. It also rejects the reflectionism inherent in the duality of a symbolic superstructure and its material economic base. This requires that we abandon economic determinism and the causal primacy of the economic base, both of which have tended to function as the epistemological guarantors of some ultimate material referent in traditional Marxism. The political commitment of the present study draws instead on Antonio Gramsci's conception of *praxis*. The systems of multilevel contextualizing relations in the social semiotic are constituted in and through the typical context-types, social activity-structures, and the (inter)textual meaning relations through which the meaning potential of the social semiotic system, or some part of it, is enacted and maintained by social agents/discursive subject positions in nonrandom and differentially distributed ways. This book is concerned with the ways in which typical copatternings and intersections of (inter)textual meaning relations and discursive practices constrain in critical ways what social agents can do and can mean in specific domains of social practice. However, the semantic ambiguity in the modulation "can" (i.e., both "able" and/or "permitted") itself suggests that alternative meanings and practices are potentially available to social agents within the meaning making potential of the very same systems of relations that constrain all of us. There is potentially both selection and preselection at all contextual levels, which means that the patterned limits or constraints on the meaning making potential of social agents in a given social formation are never simply imposed or set from the top down as a one-way determinism.

This concern with levels and contexts entails a social semiotic account of the social agent/discursive subject relation. I shall be concerned in this connection with both the constitutive and the constituted nature of this relation, the ways in which these are differentially positioned and voiced, and the discursive functions of these positioned-practices and their textual voicings in the construction of the social semiotic. Our concern with levels, contexts, and the patterned constraints on the meaning making potential of social agents points, in the neomaterialist framework of this book, to the need to theorize the ways in which typical intersections of social agents with discursive subject positions occur in regular and limited ways from one text or social occasion of discourse to another. The typical and atypical intersections that occur are functional in both the maintenance and change of the social semiotic system. We shall be concerned therefore with the ways in which social agents are positioned and controlled as discursive subjects in specific domains of social practice. The principal concern here is with the wider social functions of such discursive subject positions in the maintenance and change of the sociodiscursive order. This requires a social semiotics able to go beyond formalism so that we can construct relevant and useful hypotheses about the social formations and practices in and through which texts are made and used by social agents. Social semiotics is therefore committed to the development and renewal of its links with social theory in ways that are able to articulate the links between semiotic forms and their social uses and functions.

The centrality of notions such as levels and contexts and our theoretical representations of the systems of relations that these entail raise the question of responsibility in our praxis as analysts and theorists of social meaning making. Volosinov (1973: 159) touches on this question, and I begin to articulate the relevance of questions of responsibility to a critical social semiotic theory and practice in chapters 4 and 8. This responsibility is social and political as well as theoretical, and it must be articulated and practiced on the basis of a praxis-oriented conception, such as the one developed by Antonio Gramsci. It is a question of both constructing adequate theoretical representations of the social semiotic system or some part of it and of critically intervening in appropriate and responsible ways in the ensemble of interacting subsystems that constitute the dynamic metastability of the social semiotic system. A critical praxis-oriented social semiotics is concerned with Real rather than Imaginary theoretical representations of the contextual relations through which relations of power, domination, and hegemony are enacted, maintained, and contested (see Wilden, 1981). This requires a praxis concerned with the possibilities of a critical intervention directed toward the exposing, challenging, and changing of those social meaning making practices that function to conceal and to maintain illegitimate and repressive relations of power and domination in the social order. Therefore, critical social semiotic theory is engaged in the play of praxis through which the meaning potential of the "yet-to-be-voiced," as Basil Bernstein (1982: 320–21) puts it, may come to receive its social voice. This book is a necessarily partial and incomplete attempt to construct just such a critical praxis-oriented social semiotics. It is concerned with texts as the products or records of specific social meaning making practices, rather than as the objects of a purely formal theory and analysis. Social semiotics, as I envisage it, is a mode of social action rather than a purely formal theory. Jay Lemke (1984c: 102) has shown us how such a theory can avoid the problems of self-consistency and completeness in theory building, which were first explored by Gödel in the area of metamathematics (see also Kosok, 1976: 341). A theory is itself a social meaning making practice, which always stands in some articulated relation to a given community of social practices. It is not "above" or "external" to these, but is immanent in them. All theory making is both constituted and constrained by the patterned meaning making practices of some community, just as it is potentially constitutive of alternative patterns of social meaning making. Our goal of a praxis-oriented social semiotics shares affinities with Habermas's ([1981] 1984) critical theory of language and communication insofar as he attempts to give voice to a critical practice that can provide a framework for the explanation of ethical and moral issues in social meaning making. Habermas seeks to reassert a critical model of language as social action whereby social agents can analyze and criticize social practices and their validity claims, as well as enact alternative meanings and practices. Communicative practice, for Habermas, is not simply something that is determined or constituted by static, abstract relations of production. Rather, it has a radical critical potential, whereby social agents can intervene in, challenge, and change social meaning making practices, conceived as modes of social action (see also Silverman and Torode, 1980: 340).

Alex Callinicos (1989: 104) points out that both Habermas and the poststructuralists recognize that the paradigm of subject-centered reason, which has dominated the Western tradition's attempt to ground a theory of rationality in the philosophy of consciousness, is exhausted. In opposition to the poststructuralists, Habermas claims that a theory of rationality can still be constructed, one which is based on the intersubjective structures of communicative action. I shall not discuss here the centrality of the speech act theorists Austin, Searle, and Grice to Habermas's enterprise (see, however, Thibault and Van Leeuwen, forthcoming, for a critical discussion). Yet, Habermas's criteria for the elaboration of a metaethics based on the differential validity claims that operate in the neo-Kantian domains of science, law and morality, and art remain *formal* criteria. In the first instance, this means that Habermas does not link these to material social practices in substantive ways. It also means that his theory does not generate any recursively analyzable relations between the systemic meaning potential of the social semiotic and its own formal criteria.

Texts, social occasions of discourse, and communicative acts are defined or identified as belonging in a structured system of alternatives. They are also defined in relation to or are identified *with* the text-specific meanings and transactions in which they are immanent (see chapter 5). But for criteria such as "intersubjectivity" to be possible, the system of alternatives must be able to be contextualized in situation-specific ways. Yet, the notion of "intersubjectivity" in Habermas does not refer to this systemic meaning potential—he shows that communicative acts *qua* acts can enact intersubjective structures, agreements, consensus, understanding, and so on. He does not, however, show how these acts are contextualized in and through specific and differential restrictions of the system's global meaning potential. This systemic meaning potential necessarily embodies contradictions, as Lemke (1984b: 84) points out, so as to maintain a reserve adaptive capability. But it is always contextualized in specific ways, and according to *which* specific social practices and relations operate. Habermas attempts to construct a globally consistent theory of communicative rationality. This is based on the differentiated neo-Kantian spheres of social life and their typical speech acts, but it is not *explicitly* connected to the partial hierarchies of global (systemic) meaning potential in the social semiotic. This may resolve conflict and contradiction *in theory,* that is, seen globally, from the outsider/theorist's perspective. It does not, however, contend with the fact that insiders—participants in concrete communicative acts—do not need to do so if local meanings and their folk-theoretical rationalizations are adequate and sufficient for the task of constructing, say, moralities and accounts of how agents in any given sphere are supposed to act. The explanatory power of such folk-theories is, of course, restricted to an explicit awareness of the most conscious, local, and automatized features of social meaning making. These folk-theories cannot construct more global explanatory frameworks, able to account for implicit, habitual (unconscious), and high-order contextualizing relations (see also Harré, 1983: 36; Silverstein, 1981). Moreover, specific textual productions, along with the socially defined positioned-practices they give voice to, are always *hybridizations* of specific and contradictory restrictions of the global meaning potential. This is rarely explicitly formalized by the theorist/outsider system of contextualizing relations, though it may ramify throughout its own praxis, which necessarily lies within the domain of the theorist's categories. Habermas does not address the issue of self-reference, which no theory of social meaning making can either avoid or restrict (Lemke, 1984b: 72). A notion such as "intersubjectivity" is too closely tied to the "insider" or folk-theoretical viewpoint, which is internal to specific social spheres and situation-types in the theorist's own insider culture. Its recursive and reflexive relation to the meaning making practices of the outsider/theorist system remains unanalyzed. In chapters 3 through 4, I shall sketch out an alternative account, which argues that a reflexive and recursive analysis of communicative rationality is not to be based on "intersubjectivity," but on the joint contextualizing relations – hybridizations – of insider and outsider positions and practices and their textual voicings.

The praxis-oriented social semiotics that I am attempting to write into this book begins, however, with Gramsci's commitment to the dialectical interpenetration of theory and practice. Critical social semiotics entails a political conception of its own theory and practice in relation to the cultural axioms and presuppositions, the social meaning making practices, and the textual productions that it analyzes. Gramsci's understanding of the links between language, culture, and the political in his development of the concept of hegemony thus provides one of the cornerstones of this project. I shall develop these links more fully in chapter 8. While the "systematicity of semiotic forms," the "semiotically plurifunctional" nature of their internal organization, and their function and distribution in higher-order structures are central (see Silverstein, 1985a), the present study also focuses on the dynamics of their contextualization processes and relations and the wider social functions of these. This dual focus requires not only a formal competence in the detailed microanalysis of the copatterned meaning selections in particular textual productions, but also the development and articulation of specific social, ethical, and political beliefs and commitments. It is an educational and political commitment, which strives to be more than a mechanical unification of "theory" and "practice." The praxis-oriented conception that informs this book endeavors to connect these to their wider social processes and functions in ways that resist and disarticulate commonsense cultural axioms and folk-rationalizations of semiotic forms and their uses. A critical praxis-oriented social semiotics, however, must also try to rearticulate these to its own critical goals so that potentially counterhegemonic social meanings and practices may be voiced.

Text, Social Meaning Making, and the Dialectic of Realization

What is the status of the concept of text in the theory? In this book, I argue that the dynamics of social meaning making practices cannot adequately be separated from the analysis of the textual products and records that are made and used in and through these practices. These textual products and records are always immanent in the patterned discursive exchanges and interactions that enact them. The neomaterialist social semiotic conceptual framework recognizes that these patterned exchanges and interactions are always materially embodied and enacted in and through the dialectical duality of prediscursive and discursive exchanges and transactions. The textual products and records of these transactions occur, as Lemke (1984b: 79–80) points out, in some relation of homology to the dynamic social semiotic processes that enact them. These relations of homology are neither given nor one-way in their effects, for the relations between texts and the social meaning making practices (semiosis) in and through which textual meanings are made are productive and dialectical ones. Nevertheless, the notion of some relation of homology between the two levels reminds us that both the type and the extent of this homologous relation are productive and nonarbitrary, therefore not totally fixed or determinate in their effects. This is because textual products and records and the copatterned meaning selections realized in them are always functionally related to the social semiotic processes and relations in and through which they are constituted and used. The dialectically dual nature of this relation has two important consequences for the conceptual framework of social semiotics. This entails a dual concern with both dynamic and formal analytical and theoretical criteria in our attempt analytically to reconstitute the functional relations between dynamic social semiotic processes and the formal patterns of realization of meaning selections in texts.

Central to the dynamic and formal criteria outlined here is Hjelmslev's ([1943] 1961: 40) notion of realization, which has been developed in Michael Halliday's (1978, 1985) systemic-functional theory of language as a concern with the formal copatternings of lexico-grammatical selections in and through which social meanings are realized in texts. I have argued elsewhere (Thibault, 1986f: 103) that realization is a productive dialectic rather than a top-down determinism, leading from the social situation to the formal copatternings of lexico-grammatical selections in texts. Meanings do not inhere in these formal patternings, but are made, produced, and construed in and through them in regular, systematic, and context-dependent ways. The latter refer to the productive discursive procedures and practices that enact specific, socially recognizable context-types. However, much recent work on these has taken place in ways that remain quite disjoined from the analysis of formal patterns of realization in texts. Threadgold (1986a: 28) has shown how the now widespread gap between semiotics and poststructuralist theories of discourse and discursive practice on the one hand and the detailed microanalysis of the patterns of realization of textual meanings on the other has arisen out of the suspicion on the part of the poststructuralists that such analysis in formal linguistic theory necessarily reproduces or is complicitous in the ontology of representation. This ontology has been critiqued by Derrida (1974) as a pervasive "metaphysics of presence" in Western discourses about the nature of the relations between language and the referentially given real world "out there." This critique has also been related to those made by both Derrida (1974; 1978) and Foucault (1974) on "totalization" in the social sciences. I shall have more to say in this connection in subsequent chapters. Let me confine myself to saying here that there is no doubt that these critiques have often been well directed, if not always well received or properly understood, in linguistics and the other social science disciplines. However, I would argue that the Saussurean and Hjelmslevian concepts of the sign and sign-function, on which much of this critique has been focused, permit quite a different reading, one that does not necessarily entail either a representationalist or a totalizing account of meaning. Of course, it remains the case that they have often been selectively read as if they do embrace the "metaphysics of presence" talked about by Derrida. This point has been well argued by Hasan (1987a), who provides a detailed account of both the Saussure and Hjelmslev texts in her interesting rebuttal of Derrida's position (see also Thibault, 1986e: 92–100).

Realization embodies the formal copatterned lexico-grammatical selections in textual productions in the sense that these textual productions are both the *realization* of something as the finished product and the process that enacts or *realizes* this product. The concept of realization is thus ambivalent in an important and suggestive way, which can be related to a further distinction Hjelmslev ([1943] 1961) makes between *system* and *process*. Here I draw on Michael Halliday's development of the original Hjelmslevian distinctions in his systemic-functional theory of language. The concept of system refers in this theory to the paradigmatic (systemic) meaning potential of the social semiotic, or some part of it. Systems are formally represented in systemic theory as networks of interrelated options in meaning, seen as a resource for the exchange of social meanings in specifiable semiotic environments (see Halliday, 1978: 17, 52, 192). Hjelmslev's *process* is interpreted in systemic-functional theory as *text* insofar as texts are the instantiation of this systemic meaning potential in the way described above. However, Hjelmslev's concept also incorporates the insight that textual meanings are made in and through the *specific* copatternings of meaning selections that they realize in their lexico-grammar. The ambivalence that is built into Hjelmslev's concept of text-as-process serves to remind us that textual meanings are not simply the outcome of a one-way determinism, leading from an abstract systemic meaning potential to the actualization of this potential in specific texts. Realization is, then, a productive dialectic in which the copatternings of formal lexico-grammatical selections in texts both realize, enact, produce, and index their situational contexts and their higher-order social semiotic by virtue of occurring just as much as they are realized or produced by these. Textual productions, viewed as forms of social action, can be either *accommodative* to or *creative* of their social situation-type (see Lemke, 1984b: 69). They may either maintain or creatively alter the situation by virtue of their occurring rather than some potential alternative social act from a structured system of alternatives. Realization, understood in this perspective, is, then, centrally concerned not with a static, one-way determinism, but with a productive social semiotics of action.

Texts are both the instantiation of some paradigmatic system of relations and the realization of context-dependent social meanings. Hjelmslev's dual focus on system and process requires the higher-level dialectical synthesis of the two former terms in ways that hypostatize neither the notion of system (cf. Saussure's *langue*) nor the semantics of the text. Linguistic pragmatics hypostatizes the latter when it postulates a situationally specific level of textual meaning, separate from the semantic level (i.e., pragmatic rules of use), which, however, never gets related back to the systemic meaning potential that makes text- and occasion-specific meanings possible. Pragmatics is a purely syntagmatically based semantics of the utterance or the text, without any basis in the paradigmatic (systemic) networks of meaning potential (cf. Hjelmslev's system) from which particular meaning options in texts are always selected. In other words, the ad hoc contextual or "pragmatic" criteria that are used effectively isolate the semantics of the single text from any theoretical representation of the system that makes a given instance possible.

It seems likely, as Hasan (1987a) suggests, that the poststructuralist critique of a representationalist "metaphysics of presence" in the Saussurean and Hjelmslevian conceptions of the sign is itself the result of what Whorf (1956) has called a "referential objectification" of the lexico-grammar of Standard Average European languages. Thus, the nominalizations *signifier, signified, expression, content,* and *realization* in the metasemantics of Saussurean and Hjelmslevian linguistics are "referentially projected" and objectified in such a way that they are perceived to correspond in a straightforward way to real entities "out there" (see Hasan, 1986: 141–42; Silverstein, 1979: 202–4; Thibault, 1986f: 103–4). (I shall further argue this point in chapter 8.) However, neither Saussure nor Hjelmslev can be said to provide a representationalist account of the sign, in which the signifier refers to something outside of itself, that is, something that referentially corresponds to the Real. Rather, signifier and signified or expression and content are functives whose reciprocal relationship produces the sign-function. The sign-function is not a simple, pregiven entity. It is, to use Hjelmslev's own term, a productive "solidarity" in which the functional relationship between signifier/signified or expression/content is productive of the sign-function. Hjelmslev puts the matter as follows:

> Up to this point we have intentionally adhered to the old tradition according to which a sign is first and foremost a sign *for* something. In this we are certainly in agreement with the popular conception widely held by epistemologists and logicians. But it remains for us to show that their conception is linguistically untenable, and here we are in agreement with recent linguistic thinking.
>
> While, according to the first view, the sign is an *expression* that points to a *content* outside the sign itself, according to the second view (which is put forward in particular by Saussure and, following him, by Weisgerber) the sign is an entity generated by the connexion between an expression and a content.
>
> Which of these views shall be preferred is a question of appropriateness. In order to answer this question we shall for the moment avoid speaking about signs, which are precisely what we shall attempt to define. Instead, we shall speak of something whose existence we think

> we have established, namely the *sign function,* posited between two entities, an *expression* and a *content.* On this basis we shall be able to determine whether it is appropriate to consider the sign function as an external or an internal function of the entity that we shall call a *sign.*
>
> We have here introduced *expression* and *content* as designations of the functives that contract the function in question, the sign function. This is a purely operative definition and a formal one in the sense that, in this context, no other meaning shall be attached to the terms *expression* and *content.*
>
> There will always be solidarity between a function and (the class of) its functives: a function is inconceivable without its terminals, and the terminals are only end points for the function and are thus inconceivable without it. If one and the same entity contracts different functions in turn, and thus might apparently be said to be selected by them, it is a matter, in each case, not of one and the same functive, but of different functives, different objects, depending on the point of view that is assumed, *i.e.*, depending on the function from which the view is taken. This does not prevent us from speaking of the "same" entity from other points of view, for example from a consideration of the functions that enter into it (are contracted by its components) and establish it. If several sets of functives contract one and the same function, this means that there is solidarity between the function and the whole class of these functives, and that consequently each individual functive selects the function.
>
> Thus there is also solidarity between the sign function and its two functives, expression and content. There will never be a sign function without the simultaneous presence of both these functives; and an expression and its content, or a content and its expression, will never appear together without the sign function's also being present between them. (Hjelmslev, [1943] 1961: 47 48)

The functional nature of the relationship between the two planes is one of *realization,* which we can avoid interpreting as a static, one-way determinism if this notion is dialectically reintegrated with the two key Hjelmslevian concepts of system and process. In this way, the ambivalence I spoke of earlier in the verb-process noun *realization* can help us to restore a much needed self-reflexivity to our own social praxis as semioticians. Words like *signifier, signified, expression, content,* and *realization* are not facts about language, just as they do not simply exist "in" language. They correspond to our ways of talking about language, which is itself no more than an act of semiosis, productive of these as meanings in specific, yet shifting, relations with other meanings. Meanings do not exist as more or less fixed correlations between the functives signifier/signified or expression/content. Nor do they, in Saussure and Hjelmslev, entail a longing for a "metaphysics of presence" by virtue of a putative referential conception of the sign-function. Textual productions are both the instantiation of the systemic meaning potential, seen as a resource for social meaning making, and the realization of situationally specific meaning relations (cf. text-as-process). This occurs in and through the social meaning making practices (semiosis) of the social agents/discursive subjects who make, use, dispute, and change textual meanings. It is the conceptual hypostatization of the signifier/signified and expression/content relation as an ontological dualism, seen in terms of an abstract *system* disjoined from *process,* that gives rise to the view that meanings simply *are* rather than *made*. To quote Eugenio Coseriu:

> The language which does not change is the *abstract language* (which, without doubt, is not unreal: the difference between concrete and abstract must not be confused with that between real and unreal). A grammar has never been seen which is modified by itself, nor a dictionary which adds to itself on its own account, and only the abstract language, deposited in a grammar and in a dictionary, is free from so-called "external factors." The language which changes is the *real language, in its concrete existence*. This language, however, cannot be isolated from "external factors"—that is to say from everything which constitutes the physicality, the historicity and the expressive liberty of the speaker—because it is found only in "the act of speaking": "The life of the language is not a general second life, which exists beside or above the speaker. [Hartmann, 1949, p. 219]." (Coseriu, 1981: 12; my translation; emphasis in original)

Coseriu's distinction relates to the one I make in this book between the internal functional organization and systematicity of semiotic forms, their (con)textual copatternings and distributions (cf. Silverstein's 1979: 206; 1980 $function_2$) on the one hand and the folk-theoretical or commonsense rationalizations (cf. Silverstein's $function_1$) on the other. The latter are deployed by social agents to rationalize or account for their uses of these forms. These work in ways that can either regulate or deregulate the sociolinguistic norms, assumptions, and practices of agents. Gramsci's (1977b: 248–51) distinction between "grammatica immanente" and "grammatica normativa" runs parallel to the one outlined here. Thus we have a perspective that is able to conceptualize the ways in which patterns of hegemony and ideology are not simply present in the internal functional organization and systematicity of semiotic forms. It is necessary to look at the socially constituted intersection of the two levels of relations postulated here (see also Bernstein, 1971: 122–23).

Poststructuralism, Callinicos (1989: 94) observes, calls into question the very possibility of such a metatheoretical enterprise, that is, one that proposes a rational and critical distance between, say, commonsense or folk-theoretical rationalizations and its own meaning making practices. But this is to sever the recursive and reflexive link between the meaning potential of the system and the activities of the theorist (see above). In so doing, the poststructuralists forget or deny that the goal of a critical and praxis-oriented theory is to produce practitioners (Lemke, 1984b: 72–73), and not theory per se. This would also amount to denying that, for example, the distinction Halliday (1983) makes between the grammar of a natural language—seen as a semiotic resource system—and its "grammatics"—our metagrammatical ways of formalizing and interpreting this—is valid or possible (see chapter 8, note 1). This view (correctly) presumes that the grammatics depends on the grammar, but in such a way that the latter totally presupposes and eclipses any potential for rational critique by the former.

But this succumbs to what Althusser ([1970] 1971: 128) eloquently refers to as the "tenacious obviousness (ideological consciousness of the empiricist type) of the point of view of production alone." The poststructuralists' denial of this critical potential forgets the recursive and reflexive nature of the relations between the two. Whorf's subtle deconstruction of the ideology of reference, as we shall see in chapter 8, better understood this point because he understood that such a grammatics is not, in the final analysis, above or external to the meaning potential of the grammar, but is constituted in and through it, and in ways that can renew it, along with the rational potential of critique itself. The poststructuralists' collapsing of the two implicitly accepts the "tenaciousness" of the production point of view of the insider/participant, when it attributes to it an empiricist consciousness that rightly belongs in the domain of the poststructuralists' own (reified) theoretical labor. This explains the emphasis on social meaning making practices in this study. This perspective, I argue, is possible only with a semantically oriented functional grammar of the kind developed in systemic-functional linguistics (e.g., Halliday, 1985). The clause, which is taken to be the fundamental analytical unit in the lexico-grammar, is functionally interpreted as a microlevel social act-type such that Halliday's functional grammar is, in effect, a grammar of microlevel social actions, their patterns of use, and their modes of deployment in their textual realizations. Texts are built up from copatterned lexico-grammatical selections, whose regularities and variations within single texts and across wider intertextual sets are functionally interpreted according to the semantic register-types, social activity-structures, and coding orientations that intersect in typical and atypical ways in specific textual productions. The lexico-grammar at all ranks (i.e., levels) from clause complex (cf. sentence) downward through clause to word and morpheme is functionally interpreted as being the simultaneous realization of semantic options from the three semantic metafunctions. According to the metafunctional hypothesis of systemic-functional linguistics, the lexico-grammar at all ranks encodes in a simultaneous, polyphonic fashion semantic options from the ideational, interpersonal, and textual metafunctions, each of which is realized in a structurally distinctive way in the grammar of the clause (see Halliday, 1979; also see chapter 6). The clause, viewed in this way, is not the representation of anything. It does not, for instance, represent underlying mental or cognitive processes, nor does it simply or straightforwardly refer to objects, events, and the like in the real world. In this connection, the contextual conditions on the plurifunctional nature of *referring* sign functions has been expressed in the following way by Michael Silverstein:

> Less obvious is the fact that the pragmatic dimension of referring, based as it is on the particular indexical relationship of presupposition–presupposition about the object of reference, presupposition about the code of reference, presupposition about the code of sense–is just one of any number of functional dimensions of a similarly pragmatic character. These involve indexical relationships between the token of language and the context in which it can be said to occur in one of two ways, *independent of the function of reference* organized in natural language by the basically Saussurean nature of structure. Either the linguistic sign token presupposes some aspects of the context in which it is used or, by virtue of the use of the linguistic sign token, the context in such-and-such configuration is entailed as a consequence. For analytic purposes, we may conceive of context as an organized, intersubjectively available and socially maintained configuration of factors of potential indexical relevance to linguistic form and meaning. [See Jakobson's (1960) schema of speech context articulated into communication-theoretic components.] Language use in context is the everchanging dynamic of indexical presupposition and indexical entailment between specific linguistic signs and specific aspects of the context in the speech event. To the extent that there are regularities of such, pragmatics is a realm of indexical Legisigns, of which there occur instances or tokens in actual language use. To the extent by contrast that usage is unique to the instant, it cannot be comprehended by systematic study, only "interpreted" as in the manner of ethnomethodology (see Cicourel, 1974, pp. 28–33, 84–88, 112, 124). (Silverstein, 1985a: 224)

Semiotics, as I observed at the beginning of this chapter, has tended to privilege the concept of sign, taken to be a discrete and static entity. The sign so conceived is founded on abstract, formal criteria that are disjoined from the material conditions and the contextual dynamics in and through which meanings are made. Doubtless, this has arisen in part on account of normative, structuralist accounts of grammar as in Saussure's *langue*. It would also appear to be a consequence of the dominance of the particulate, constituent-structure model of semiotic forms whereby meaning is digitalized (see Halliday, 1978: 139). The overdetermined, ambivalent, and "resonating" character of meaning relations is not reducible to digital notions such as those of identity, difference, and equivalence. Instead, the dynamic, open, contradictory, and plurifunctional nature of meaning relations requires that we account for both the continuous, analogue dimension and the overdetermined nature of meaning. Umberto Galimberti (1983) has proposed the suggestive notion of "ambivalence" as an alternative to the digitalization of the sign in semiotics. Galimberti acutely comments on the reductive, digitalized view of meaning that has privileged criteria founded on *difference* and *identity:*

> *Difference* . . . is not enough because it is on the inside of identity; here *ambivalence* is needed that splits identity in two, not to reassemble it, but to let live inside it that relationship of tension: A and not-A, which condenses the totality into one point. Nearness of the maximally distant, this is ambivalence; not meaning, [*senso*], but con-sent [*con-senso*], which has nothing to do with the consent that bodies throughout their history have been impelled to bestow on the only meaning that the despotism of the signifier distributed over all things when it assigned them a name. (Galimberti, 1983: 239; my translation).

Now, the clause in systemic-functional grammar is a microlevel social act-type, whose plurifunctional status does not privilege one particular kind of semantic function of, say, the propositional, experiential, or referring kind over any other. Nor does it siphon off the semantics of the clause to any single level of organization, for all ranks or levels from clause complex to morpheme and all strata from phonology and graphology through lexico-grammar to semantics are meaning making in the process of realizing textual meanings. As Jim Martin succinctly puts it in the following comment on the plurifunctional nature of this process, "Following Firth (1968: 174) it [i.e., systemic-functional linguistics] views each level as contributing a layer of meaning to text; it does not see language as a conduit through which thoughts and feelings are poured" (Martin, 1986: 226). This view of language assumes that linguistic and, less restrictedly, all semiotic forms realize a variety of different kinds of meanings and functions that are derived from paradigmatic systems of options, all of which, in the case of language, are structurally realized in different ways in the lexico-grammar. At each layer or stratum in the organization of text, selections are made from the systems of meaning making options that are represented paradigmatically as networks of options. Tactical relations organize the relations between items at any given stratum. Realization refers to the interstratal coding operations that map relations on one stratum to other strata in the organization of the text in a simultaneous, polyphonic fashion. Thus there is a constant dialectic between semiotic forms and their uses in the context of the systemic (paradigmatic) environments in which textual meanings are made. Halliday (1978: 139) has formulated this constant dialectic in the following way: "The ongoing text-creating process continually modifies the system that engenders it, which is the paradigmatic environment of the text. Hence the dynamic, indeterminate nature of meaning, which can be idealized out to the margins if one is considering only the system, or only the text, emerges as the dominant mode of thought as soon as one comes to consider the two together, and to focus on text as actualized meaning potential."

The unstable, indeterminate, and overdetermined nature of this dialectic requires a social semiotic account of the contextualizing relations and dynamics involved rather than a restricted focus on the sign as an abstract, isolated formal entity. This also requires an account of how social agents enact variability and change in the networks of systemic meaning potential in ways that may lead to the "semogenic" (Halliday, 1985: 251) reorganization of this potential. This will be further discussed in chapters 2 through 4, where I develop a dialectical and recursive model of the dynamics of the contextualization relations and processes that are involved in quoting and reporting speech. Such a model will be used to explore the ways in which the lexico-grammatical forms of quoting and reporting speech have "multiple indexical values" (Silverstein, 1985b: 256) for their users. These are selectively projected in their interpretation as being the determinants of the linguistic forms to which they are attributed. We shall see in chapter 2 how Banfield's (1973, 1978a,b) concept of the center of consciousness or SELF in free indirect discourse is a metaphor of structure reconstructed from a selective attending to linguistic forms as particulate, constituent structures that are then taken to "refer to" some a priori center of consciousness. My emphasis here on the concept of realization is translated in this book into a concern with the detailed microanalysis of copatterned lexico-grammatical selections in the text that is the object of this study. However, this does not entail a formalistic conception of the text. I shall not argue this point any further now for it will be developed throughout the chapters that follow. What I want to do here is suggest why such a concern with formal patterns of realization is so important for a critical social semiotics beyond the desire for analytical rigor taken as an end in itself, perhaps informed by a positivistic epistemology of scientific "objectivity" and "truth," which I reject. The connections between microlevel copatternings of lexico-grammatical selections in texts, textual analysis, and social meaning making practices are always produced or constructed; they are never given "in" the text, waiting to be "read off" with the right analytical tools. My starting point in this analytical act of construction is Foucault's (1974) definition of the statement as an analytical unit in a given enunciative field. As we shall explore in detail in later chapters, the following words of Foucault suggest that some powerful links can be constructed between Foucault's concept of the statement and the microanalysis of copatterned meaning selections in texts:

> I now realise that I would not define the statement as a unit of a linguistic type (superior to the phenomenon of the word, inferior to the text); but that I was dealing with an enunciative function that involved various units (these may sometimes be sentences, sometimes propositions; but they are sometimes made up of fragments of sentences, series or tables of signs, a set of propositions or equivalent formulations); and, instead of giving a "meaning" to these units, this function relates them to a field of objects; instead of providing them with a subject, it opens up for

> them a number of possible subjective positions; instead of fixing their limits, it places them in a domain of coordination and coexistence; instead of determining their identity, it places them in a space in which they are used and repeated. In short, what has been discovered is not the atomic statement—with its apparent meaning, its origins, its limits, and its individuality—but the operational field of the enunciative function and the conditions according to which it reveals various units (which may be, but need not be, of a grammatical or logical order). (Foucault, 1974: 106)

Thus, the analytical unit that Foucault calls the statement is concerned with what a particular meaningful act *does* in a particular enunciative field, that is, with its enunciative function. This is very close to our view of the lexico-grammatical resources of the language as microlevel social act-types, which are functionally interpreted in terms of what they *do* in a given (inter)textual field of relations. Furthermore, the statement, just like, say, the clause or any other lexico-grammatical unit in systemic-functional linguistics, is not given a meaning per se, but is related to its copatterning and distribution with other meaning relations and to the ways in which copatterned meaning relations are selectively foregrounded or backgrounded in the specific (inter)textual formations and social activity-structures in which they are used. The emphasis, then, is not on the meaning of textual patterns of realization per se, but on their regular, systematic patterns of use, their modes of deployment, and the social actions in and through which they are performed in and across their higher-order discursive formations (see also Fabbri and Sbisà, 1982: 596). It refers to what Foucault (1974) has called their *regularity in dispersion,* which is not relatable to some fixed, stable reality, identity, or rules "behind" their use, but rather to the metastable patterns of interaction through which the social semiotic system functions both to maintain itself as well as to change.

Foucault's criteria for the description of statements provide a valuable framework for the kind of detailed microanalysis that will be undertaken at times in the following chapters. I will not now attempt to amplify further the importance of Foucault for this project. This, too, will be developed throughout the book. Instead, I shall briefly outline the principal arguments in favor of the detailed microanalysis of copatterned lexico-grammatical selections in texts. First, the patterns of realization in texts and social occasions of discourse of, say, the lexico-grammatical resources of a natural language or any of the other forms of semiotic in and through which social meanings are made are, as Lemke (1985a) has pointed out, the only source and grounding of all our hypotheses about social meaning making. It is only on the microlevel of the realization of texts and social occasions of discourse that social meanings occur, are enacted, or are made. All social meanings are formally realized in some way by virtue of the systematicity and the plurifunctionality of semiotic forms, which I mentioned above. It is these patterns of realization that are, in the final analysis, the basis on which all our hypotheses and theories, either implicity or explicitly, are built. Our second argument is concerned with what Lemke (1985a) has identified as the disjunction between the macro- and the microlevels of analysis. Microanalysis is important in the analytical bid to bridge this gap, for it is essential that the two levels are dialectically rearticulated in relation to each other within the same set of terms or the same conceptual framework. The problem, as we shall see in chapters 3 and 4, is not one of size with respect to the various levels of analysis. It is a question of *meta*levels of analysis, the one articulated in relation to the other, in a hierarchy of contextual relations. A theory that is not founded on the explicit microanalysis of formal patterns of realization is unable adequately to articulate the macro- and microlevels in relation to each other. Third, this means that theories and hypotheses about the social semiotic system or some part of it that do not make explicit their connections with the formal patterns of realization of social acts *as* acts remain unable to confirm or disconfirm their own assumptions and hypotheses in practice. They are always protected by the self-validating claims and assumptions of macrolevel hypotheses and theories, which, however, remain purely speculative or conservative in their implications for praxis, for they are never explicitly articulated in relation to the level of social action. They are therefore "steady-state" theories, inclined only to react if perturbed from the "outside" and whose self-validating claims and assumptions frequently act as props for the almost pathological ramification of ideologically dominant folk-theoretical assumptions and rationalizations in the theory and practice of the humanities and social sciences (see Halliday, 1983; Reddy, 1979). This is convenient for those theorists and analysts of social meaning making who do not wish to have their hypotheses and assumptions tested in this way or who do not wish their investments in those positions of power and authority to which these assumptions defer to be put at risk. Finally, the detailed microanalysis of texts does not need to be an end in itself, but a tool of our praxis as theorists and analysts. This means that we are concerned with theory and analysis as a means of critical intervention in the forms of actional semiotic in and through which we are positioned and produced as specific kinds of discursive subjects from one text or social occasion of discourse to another. A praxis-oriented semiotics of social action must provide critical and self-reflexive criteria that social agents can use to intervene at the level of social action. Thus conceived, the microanalysis of the formal patterns of realization of social actions and meanings is a tool of a thoroughly political social semiotic praxis.

It should be clear by now that philosophical police, who seek to purify the concept of sign in an endless chain of historical revisionism, or a merely formal semiotics of signs, sign-tokens, and typologies of these, are inadequate for the task of constructing the praxis-oriented social semiotics that I have attempted to write into this book. This task can never be merely formal or complete, for its theoretical and analytical criteria depend primarily on the specific domains of social practice in which such a praxis-oriented social semiotics is made, used, applied, criticized, modified, exceeded, and discarded. The critical neomaterialist social semiotic framework has no need of the disciplinary and ideological boundaries that separate, say, semiotics, linguistics, sociology, philosophy, anthropology, literary theory, and so on. Nor does it have any need for the sociodiscursive practices that sustain these boundaries. However, this does not entail a sideways glance in the direction of the master or global theory, with its corollary of the master theorist. This would function to reproduce rather than resist the dominant ideological myth of the scientific subject-who-is-supposed-to-know (see Wilden, 1980: 30). Instead, a praxis-oriented conception must work toward the development of a unified theory and practice, which is a part of a still wider social and political project. Such a project endeavors to go beyond the "negative identification" (Wilden, 1980: 30) by means of which the deconstructionists place themselves in opposition to the axioms and values of the dominant social order. The radical skepticism of the deconstructionists has not succeeded in the task of both disarticulating and rearticulating useful elements from the humanities and social sciences so that we can reconstitute them in a truly critical, transdisciplinary, and praxis-oriented social semiotics.

A Brief Archaeology

An account of the domain of all the things said and read, the intellectual and personal encounters, the social occasions—the archive, in Foucault's words—that have contributed to the making of this book certainly exceed the generic functions of this introductory chapter. Yet, I believe that a shallow archaeology of the central reference points for the present study would be useful to the reader. In writing such an archaeology, I wish to recognize that this book, itself a textual product of a social process, is constituted in and through a series of interventions and exchanges whose boundaries can never be fixed or delimited in terms of a "history of ideas." I shall briefly nominate here the central reference points of the present study in the sense that these represent the principal points of connection in relation to which I attempt to construct a series of interventions, disarticulations, and rearticulations, which are the themes of my study. In so doing, these have at this stage no more than an indicative function, for their uses and definitions will be developed more fully in subsequent chapters.

The possibility of a critical social semiotic theory and practice is given in Michael Halliday's book entitled *Language as Social Semiotic* (1978). This important work is concerned with relating uses of language, the systemic potential of the meaning making resources deployed, and the higher-order social semiotic relations and processes that are both instantiated and realized in texts and social occasions of discourse. To use Halliday's own words:

> In investigating language and the social system, it is important to transcend this limitation and to interpret language not as a set of rules but as a *resource*. I have used the term "meaning potential" to characterize language in this way.
>
> When we focus attention on the processes of human interaction, we are seeing this meaning potential at work. In the microsemiotic encounters of daily life, we find people making creative use of their resources of meaning, and continuously modifying these resources in the process.
>
> Hence in the interpretation of language, the organizing concept that we need is not structure but *system*. Most recent linguistics has been structure-bound (since structure is what is described by rules). With the notion of system we can represent language as a resource, in terms of the choices that are available, the interconnection of these choices, and the conditions affecting their access. We can relate these choices to recognizable and significant social contexts, using sociosemantic networks; and investigate questions such as the influence of various social factors on the meanings exchanged by parents and children. The data are the observed facts of "text-in-situation": what people say in real life, not discounting what they think they might say and what they think they ought to say. (Or rather, what they *mean,* since saying is only one way of meaning.) In order to interpret what is observed, however, we have to relate it to the system: (i) to the linguistic system, which it then helps to explain, and (ii) to the social context, and through that to the social system. (Halliday, 1978: 192)

Halliday constructs a discourse that relates texts and their copatterned realizations of the lexico-grammatical resources of the linguistic system to their semantic register-types and through this intermediate level to their social contexts of situation and the still higher-order social semiotic codes that control and regulate the differential access of social agents to social contexts. Halliday has adapted this latter concept from the sociological work of Basil Bernstein (e.g., 1971, [1975], 1977). Halliday's systemic-functional theory of language thus provides a highly developed and well-articulated account of the links leading from the uses of copatterned lexico-grammatical selections in texts to the sociosemantics of their register-types. Bernstein's recent work in particular is most important, for it provides us with a framework that attempts to articulate macrosocial or higher-order coding orientations to their textual messages and voices and the subject positions these make available to social agents (see Bernstein, 1982, 1986a, b). I also use and develop the notions of voice, dialogicity, and social heteroglossia in the writings of Bakhtin (1973, 1981) and Volosinov (1973). Here, the concept of voice, which shares affinities with Bernstein's use of the term, is developed to show how specific intersections of social meaning making practices articulate or voice what I define as specific positioned-practices, corresponding to discursive subject positions (see Thibault, 1986g: 162). The systems of voices in the social semiotic, including potentially unvoiced meanings and practices, comprise the relations of social heteroglossia through which relations of alliance, consensus, opposition, conflict, and co-optation among voices are positioned and articulated in specific texts and intertextual formations (see also Lemke, 1985a, 1988a). The heteroglossic relations among textual voices can index a plurality of ideological and axiological positions, which can be realized within the bounds of a single utterance or textual production, thus defined as "dialogic" in the writings of Bakhtin/Volosinov.

Jay Lemke's work within the systemic-functional model of language develops the notions of intertextual thematic formation and social activity-structure, through which further important connections can be made with the above perspectives in the conceptual framework of social semiotics (see Lemke, 1983a,b, 1984, 1985a,b, 1988a). Lemke has also developed in this framework a concept of ideology as the system of disjunctions, which ramifies across the social semiotic system, systematically connecting and disconnecting social discourses and social meaning making practices in ways that function to maintain the overall *metastability* of the social semiotic system (see Lemke, 1985a, b). Lemke's use of this notion has close links with Foucault's (1971, 1974) work on the relations between discourse and power. Thus, Foucault's theorization of the analytical concepts of discursive formation, discursive practice, and statements and their enunciative functions provides us with a further set of critically important discourses and tools of analysis, which can be reconstituted within the conceptual framework and praxis of social semiotics. My attempt to develop a social semiotic account of discourse, ideology, and power within this general framework leads me to rearticulate Antonio Gramsci's conceptions of hegemony and *fascino-prestigio* (attraction-prestige). The critical importance of Gramsci's writings on language, the political, and the cultural for a social semiotic account of power and ideology remains seminal. The potential for such a linkage, to my knowledge, remains largely undeveloped; indeed, there is only one book-length sociolinguistic study that deals with the centrality of language in Gramsci's writings on hegemony (see Lo Piparo, 1979). The links I attempt to construct among the concepts of discourse, hegemony, ideology, and power are not to be thought of in negative terms as a question of simple repression, nor do these concepts entail a representationalist epistemology, which is the case with concepts like "false consciousness" and "mystification" in classical Marxism. My attempt to mediate between the former concepts and, thus, to reconstitute them takes place in the terms provided by Foucault. Power and ideology are productive relations in discursive practice, which function both to produce and position social agents in regular and systematic ways as discursive subjects. It is through our sociodiscursive practices that the system of disjunctions maintains the global metastability of the social semiotic system or some part of it in ways that constitute the relations of production of power, hegemony, and domination in a given social formation.

The concept of metastability derives from the work of Ilya Prigogine (e.g., 1976) and colleagues on thermodynamically open systems, namely, those systems – including biological and social systems – that engage in irreversible and nonlinear transformations under conditions that do not approximate a state of equilibrium. The relevance of the epistemology of dynamic open systems for social semiotics has been extensively argued in Lemke (1984a, c) and I shall not go into any detail here. Briefly, dynamic open systems are said to be metastable because the given system of relations, however stable it might appear, is constantly undergoing small perturbations. There is a constant dialectic between the conflicts, tensions, and disharmonies in the system (i.e., those relations and processes that can potentially change the system) and those processes and relations that work to stabilize or maintain the system of relations in a particular way. This constant dialectic is not simply regulated by the "external" environment; rather, the system has the potential to act back on its environment in ways which deregulate or alter the previously existing stability of the system. These processes are potentially irreversible and globally ramifying, which means that the system of relations cannot be returned to the prior state of equilibrium, for the entire system of relations has been transformed. Now, the use and adaptation of the concept of metastability in social semiotic theory is no mere rhetorical gesture. However, it is important that this is not done in a totalizing scientistic or positivistic framework that is unable to theorize the social and historical specificity of all social meaning making. The specificity of these metastable relations at the levels of text and social situation has been conceptualized by Halliday in the following way:

> The meaning of the text, for example, is fed back into the situation, and becomes part of it, changing it in the process; it is also fed back, through the register, into the semantic system, which it likewise affects and modifies. The code, the form in which we conceptualize the injection of the social structure into the semantic process, is itself a two-way relation, embodying feedback from the semantic configurations of social interaction into the role relationships of family and other social groups. (Halliday, 1978: 126)

The metastable system of connections and disconnections that ramify both locally and globally throughout our social meaning making practices – that is, the system of disjunctions – emphasizes in our theory and analysis, if not always in our daily social practice and our folk-theoretical rationalizations, that discourses are contradictory, overdetermined sites that enact and articulate both positive and negative effects. Gramsci's concept of *fascino-prestigio* is a useful tool for showing how the overdetermination of social meaning making functions to produce systematic effects of identification or binding of social agents to some social discourses and discursive subject positions rather than others in ways that enable globally ramifying hegemonic patterned meaning making practices to be articulated and maintained. A social semiotic account of hegemony, along with the detailed analysis of its articulation in relation to potentially counterhegemonic meanings and practices, is fundamental in a praxis-oriented social semiotics that is committed to the position that our social meaning making practices are a necessary site of power and struggle. It is a site requiring the positive transformative action of a critical and strategically conceived social semiotic intervention in our social meaning making practices. The overdetermined nature of the relations and processes through which hegemony is maintained and/or destabilized results in a constant dialectical tension between social agent/discursive subject relations and the wider system of disjunctions and the social functions these enact. This can mean that changes either within or among social activity-structures, (inter) textual meaning relations, contexts, voices, coding orientations, and discursive formations can potentially give voice to as-yet-unvoiced possibilities in the articulation and construction of social agents as discursive subjects.

Gregory Bateson's (1973) work on levels and metalevels of contextualization in all forms of communication, along with his development of the Russell-Whitehead concept of logical typing in this connection, suggests the critical importance of the adequate representation of the orders of contextual relations involved (see also Wilden, 1980). Bateson's work is central for our theoretical and analytical representations of the hierarchical and dialectical nature of the contextual relations and dynamics involved in social meaning making. Furthermore, Bateson understood that all acts of meaning are *immanent* in the patterned, redundant nature of the contextual relations involved, of which our own theoretical representations are always a constitutive part.

Finally, Jacques Derrida's (1974, 1978) critique of the pervasive "metaphysics of presence," which ramifies throughout both our folk-theoretical and scientific accounts of social meaning making, and his connecting this to the ontology of representationism as constituting the foundational ideology of "reality" and "truth" in Western culture help to give voice to our praxis-oriented social semiotic account of social meaning making. Derrida shows in numerous ways how this metaphysics of presence and the practices that sustain it extend throughout the humanities and social sciences in ways that continue to voice the dominant folk-theoretical assumptions and cultural axioms of our cultural order, thus maintaining the power, authority, and hegemony of that order. These deeply embedded assumptions and their associated sociodiscursive practices have effectively hindered the development of an alternative theory and practice that does not uncritically assume these and that provides resistance to them.

This book takes as its principal "object" of analysis a complex and protean narrative text, Vladimir Nabokov's novel *Ada*. This text is analyzed as the product of complex, shifting, and conflicting intersections of social meaning making practices in the historical and discursive field of transnational consumer capitalism. Why use a literary text which is itself the product of the sociodiscursive practices of the dominant bourgeois order? This book does not claim to be a work of literary theory or criticism. Most institutionalized literary and cultural criticism, including so-called deconstruction and many forms of Marxist criticism, fail to articulate the dynamic social processes at work in the production and use of texts as the products of specific, historically contingent social meaning making practices. More usually, literary and cultural theory and interpretation voice and sustain the social, institutional, and cultural norms within which the analyst is typically functioning. I would argue that this is equally true of many forms of so-called radical cultural and literary theory, which do not so much disarticulate and rearticulate the foundational ideological axioms and disjunctions mentioned at the beginning of this chapter, but merely articulate these from a position of their "negation" or "opposition." In so doing, the ideological disjunction of, say, "left wing/right wing" remains intact in ways that do not contribute to the development of a truly praxis-oriented theory and practice, based on the immanence of our own actions and meanings in still wider social relations and functions. This seems necessary if we are to avoid the restrictive consequences of what Broughton (1981: 407) designates as "the circumscribed domain of a theoretical or metatheoretical inquiry" within which a good deal of critical theory has operated. This brings home the importance of a critical social semiotic theory that is constructed in and through its relations with the specific material social semiotic processes and patterns of realization that it is attempting to theorize. It follows that the text that is the principal analytical focus in this book has helped to shape the theoretical critique in fundamental ways. This is, I would argue, the only way in which both theory and practice can be transformed in the service of a truly praxis-oriented social semiotics.

Part II
Contextualization Dynamics and Insider/Outsider Relations

Orientation of the word toward the addressee has an extremely high significance. In point of fact, word is a two-sided act. *It is determined equally by* whose *word it is and* for whom *it is meant. As word, it is precisely* the product of the reciprocal relationship between speaker and listener, addresser and addressee. *Each and every word expresses the 'one' in relation to the 'other'. I give myself verbal shape from another's point of view, ultimately, from the point of view of the community to which I belong. A word is a bridge thrown between myself and another. If one end of the bridge depends on me, then the other depends on my addressee. A word is territory shared by both addresser and addressee, by the speaker and the interlocutor.*

V. N. Volosinov (1973: 86; emphasis in original)

A bit of information is definable as a difference which makes a difference. Such a difference, as it travels and undergoes successive transformation in a circuit, is an elementary idea.

But, most relevant in the present context, we know that no part of such an internally interactive system can have unilateral control over the remainder or over any other part. The mental characteristics are inherent or immanent in the ensemble as a whole.

Gregory Bateson (1973a: 286; emphasis in original)

Chapter 2
The Sociosemantics of Quoting and Reporting Relations

It is commonplace in discussions of narrative discourse to refer to various features of narrative "representation" with the following classifications: direct, indirect, and free indirect speech and thought. The prevailing view is that in complex narratives these linguistic forms alternate throughout the text in order to establish a system of contrasting "points of view." The central difficulty with concepts like "representation" and "point of view" is that they tend to preserve the ideologically dominant myth that meanings and discursive subject positions lie "behind" language and necessarily correspond to some extralinguistic or extrasemiotic domain of "concepts," "consciousness," or "reality," whose relationship to language is a fixed, totally determinate, and referential one. Instead, I propose to develop, both in this chapter and in succeeding ones, the argument that meanings and discursive subject positions (cf. positioned-practices) are not transcendent in this way, but are immanent in the patterned relations and transactions that are regularly and systematically made and remade in and through texts and social occasions of discourse in the social semiotic system or some part of it. Indeed, concepts like "representation" and "point of view" are only construed as meaningful and derive their semiotic value by virtue of the patterned meanings and transactions that are enacted by the sociodiscursive practices of a given subgroup of theorists, along with their analytical and pedagogical practices in *our* social semiotic system (see chapter 8). Furthermore, as ideologically dominant ways of talking about linguistic practice they function to impose limits on our potential for constructing alternative meanings and theoretical practices in connection with these.

The notion of diatypic variation in language—"variety according to use" (Halliday, 1978: 35)—refers to the concept of register, which is a conceptual framework for attempting "to uncover the general principles which govern this variation, so that we can begin to understand *what* situational features determine *what* linguistic features" (Halliday, 1978: 32). It refers to the semantic potential that is typically realized in a given social situation-type. The notion of register is useful here, for it provides one of the intermediate levels of analysis in the conceptual framework of social semiotics for relating the textual voicings of discursive subject positions (positioned-practices) to their positioning in still higher-order intertextual and discursive formations (see chapters 7 and 8). A useful starting point for our discussion is Bronzwaer's claim that free indirect discourse cannot be formulated in purely linguistic or formal terms:

> If we define free indirect style as a rigid linguistic category, we are therefore likely to oversimplify the important problem of an author's subjective involvement in the object of his writing. Our definition of free indirect style should therefore admit of borderline cases and gradual transitions. On the other hand, in calling a certain passage free indirect reporting we should base ourselves on linguistic evidence as much as possible, either in the passage itself or in its immediate context. As we shall see, free indirect style is very often marked not by the presence of linguistic features that can be related to a set of rules but by deviations from and contrasts with contextual features. Although it cannot on this ground be called a linguistic category, it certainly is a linguistic phenomenon. (Bronzwaer, 1970: 50)

I shall return to Bronzwaer's insistence that free indirect discourse is a form of heightened empathetic involvement with the character by the author or narrator at a later stage. Bronzwaer's account is useful precisely because of his restriction of the notion of context to that of *co*text, thereby failing to relate the semantics of the text to the social situation-types in and through which the semantics of a particular text are made. Certainly, Bronzwaer is right to call attention to the need to consider "gradual transitions" among the various forms, though I should want to add that the linguistic evidence, as we shall see below, suggests that the situation is even more complex than that described by Bronzwaer. The problem really centers on the descriptive adequacy of the categories involved. I am not saying that we ought necessarily to discard classifications like "direct," "indirect," and "free indirect" speech and thought. Rather, these would be better regarded as ideal types that correspond to different points on a hypothetical scale or cline according to which the different categories are defined in terms of a typology of *types*. We shall explore this particular analytical strategy in functional semantic terms further on in this chapter. This kind of flexibility permits a considerable degree of subtle variation in the analysis of narrator and character discursive positions in narrative discourse. Even the category of free indirect discourse tends, I think, to be seen as functioning in more simple ways than is actually the case. For example, it is frequently claimed that free indirect discourse represents a character's speech or thought as he or she would express it. Banfield (1978a, b) cites the following arguments to support this view: in free indirect discourse the deixis is shifted away from reference to the here-and-now of the narrative speech situation; the personal pronouns are shifted away from first and second person to third person; and the tense is usually shifted from the present to the past. These arguments are used by Banfield to justify her claim that free indirect discourse is speech or thought attributable to a character rather than to a narrator. However, Halliday's (1985) semantically oriented functional grammar indicates, as we shall see further on, that a much more complex set of factors is involved. These factors are simply not allowed for in Banfield's formal restriction of grammar to immediate constituent structure, used as the basis for the semantic analysis of the "representation" of propositional content in sentences. The problems I have posed here can be related to a number of differing approaches in linguistics to the phenomenon of free indirect discourse and hence to the problematic of language and subjectivity. These approaches will now be discussed.

Banfield's Cartesianism: The Center of Consciousness in Narrative Discourse

Banfield (1978a: 296) defines the term *narrator* as the unique referent of the first-person pronoun, cotemporal with the present tense on the level of Performative time, that is, the time of the communication or speech act as distinct from Narrative time, which is the fictive level of the narrated events performed by the characters themselves. Banfield (1978b: 425) proposes a further concept of SELF, which refers to the *center of consciousness* at any given moment in the narrative. The center of consciousness is defined by Banfield as the narrative discourse participant to whom the expressive content (cf. propositional or experiential meaning) of an expression (E) is attributable. The center of consciousness is defined as the unique referent of the expressive elements (thoughts, perceptions, verbalizations, etc.) of some E in free indirect discourse. Banfield prefers the term *represented speech and thought* to the more usual free indirect discourse. This choice of terminology is itself quite revealing. In Banfield's terms, represented speech and thought imitates or represents the speech, thought, or perceptions of some center of consciousness. This formulation, I argue, merely reproduces the belief in a subjectivity or consciousness that is prior to and/or external to linguistic practice and that is "referred to" rather than constituted in and through linguistic practice. Banfield's characterization of the linguistic features of represented speech and thought can be schematized as follows:

1. Like direct speech, the sentences of represented speech and thought are nonembedded, independent clauses. They allow constructions that are not permitted in embedded sentences, and they are never preceded by subordinating conjunctions.
2. They may contain exclamations and other expressive constructions found in direct speech.
3. Questions retain their syntactically direct inverted form.
4. The expressive (propositional) content of sentences in represented speech and thought is to be understood as the point of view of the referent of the third-person pronoun in any E.
5. Only in represented speech and thought are the present and future time deictics not necessarily cotemporal with present and future tense. If the E of represented speech and thought has a first-person point of view, then it is distinguished from direct speech only by the simultaneity of the past tense and NOW. NOW is interior to represented speech and thought and no longer refers to the time act of the communication process, but to an act of consciousness.
6. Although represented speech and thought retains inversion in the question form, it does not show subjectless imperatives, namely, those that appear in main clauses.
7. Represented speech and thought does not tolerate (a) direct address, which is interpreted as part of the quoted speech; (b) sentence adverbials that are semantically predicated onto the I-you communication axis; (c) phonetic and syntactic indications of pronunciation, dialect, or language differences; (d) any second person or first person whose point of view is not represented; therefore the addition of a first- or second-person pronoun nullifies the interpretation of an E containing a third-person point of view.
8. What distinguishes represented speech and thought with a first-person point of view from direct speech is the absence of a second person to refer to the represented addressee/hearer and of the present tense referring to NOW.
9. Represented speech and thought is often typified by the use of mental and verbal processes.

Banfield bases her analysis on Chomsky's (1965) syntax-based model of transformational generative grammar. Language is thereby viewed solely as a set of syntagmatic forms, which are then interpreted by abstract semantic rules. Banfield's formulation of the center of consciousness in narrative discourse is founded on the Cartesian epistemology of the autoconstitutive subject, which informs Chomsky's rationalist criteria for linguistic theory. This epistemology receives its classic formulation by Descartes ([1637] 1963) in his "Discours de la Méthode." The Cartesian subject constitutes itself by identifying the thoughts and experience that it recognizes as its own. The Cartesian subject is a fixed, stable locus of knowledge and experience, whose unified identity and discursively prior existence merely "presuppose what it proves, having need of a subject already in place who then recognizes him/her self as a subject" (MacCabe, 1979: 296). The autoconstitutive subject is the "reality" whose "appearance" is expressed in language.

Banfield's formulation of the center of consciousness as the unique referent of some E in free indirect discourse presupposes this "subject already in place," which functions as a fixed center of identity and experience in discourse. The ontological primacy of the autoconstitutive subject becomes the determining principle of discourse. Banfield's account of the subject in terms of a presupposed center of consciousness is itself a discursive mechanism for deriving certain categories that are functional in capitalistic social relations. The center of consciousness is the *unique* referent of the thoughts, perceptions, and verbalizations of a given E in free indirect discourse. The experiences, thoughts, and perceptions, and so on, of the center of consciousness are made the determining principle of language (in the form of some E in represented speech and thought). The formulation of the center of consciousness as the unique referent of these properties and experiences reduces to the subject as the unique possessor of these. Banfield's formulation of the subject as the unique possessor of certain properties and experiences, which are then "expressed" in language, forecloses the possibility that the subject is a discursive construction from the overdetermined intersection of a heterogeneity of conflicting social discourses. Banfield takes the phenomenal appearance (the linguistic form of free indirect discourse) as the pure expression of a subjective essence that is prior to language rather than constituted in and through linguistic practice. This is reifying in a number of ways. First, there is no theoretical recognition of the historical character of the conditions, contexts, and relations of production that are the conditions of possibility of this particular form-meaning relation. Second, there is no self-reflexivity concerning the relations of Banfield's own conceptual framework and the practices this entails to the patterns of meaning making and the social actions of the particular theorist-community to which she belongs and the wider social functions these serve. Thus, the ideology of linguistic reference in Banfield's account maintains the disjunction between what is "referred to" by language, yet lies "behind" it, and what language does as a form of social action. This disjunction posits the center of consciousness as a transcendent reality obeying the autonomous and autoconstitutive laws of its own existence. The fact that it is no more than a specific form-meaning relation, which is immanent in some subensemble of our culture's social meaning making practices, is not accounted for. This reification of meaning relations and their articulation in social practice transforms social meanings and actions into autonomous, commodified "things," so that language is construed as no more than a phenomenal appearance, imperfectly expressing and reflecting the more essential reality that lies "behind" it.

Benveniste's Intersubjectivity: The Subject Constituted in the Categories of Language

In Section 5 ("L'homme dans la langue") of *Problèmes de linguistique générale, 1,* Benveniste attempts to define the subject/other relationship as it is constituted in language. Benveniste accordingly isolates the linguistic category of person as that part of the lexico-grammar where subjectivity is articulated. Benveniste proposes the distinction between *discours,* which is the subjective realm of I/you, and *histoire,* which is the objective realm of the third person pronouns. Benveniste recognizes an asymmetry between the realm of first and second person and the realm of third person. MacCabe (1979: 287) points out that Benveniste fails to avoid the subjective/objective division in his proposals concerning *histoire* and *discours*. For Benveniste, there is a gap between the subjective appearance of the speaking subject and the objective reality that is reflected in language. From this point of view, language is the site where intersubjective objectivity is recognized. Instead, the neomaterialist perspective of the present study argues that linguistic practice is the site of a plurality of conflicting social discourses and discursive subject positions (positioned-practices). We shall return to this argument below. Benveniste shows that the indexical resources of the personal pronouns have meaning because they work to invoke contextually specific features of some intersubjectively shared discourse. The meaning of the personal pronouns is always dependent on a specific context of use:

> The personal pronouns are the principal fulcrum for bringing subjectivity to light in language. Other classes of pronouns, which share the same status, are in their turn dependent on these pronouns. These are the deictic indicators, demonstratives, adverbs, adjectives, which organize the spatiotemporal relations around the "subject" considered as a marker: "this, here, now," and their numerous correlations "that, yesterday, last year, tomorrow," and the like. They have in common this characteristic of being defined solely in connection with the moment in the discourse where they are produced; that is, they are dependent on the "I" that enunciates them. (Benveniste, 1966: 262; my translation)

Frow (1986: 77) argues that Benveniste "restricts the process of the subject to the constitutive operation of formal grammatical structures (which he distinguishes sharply from the 'supralinguistic' realm of discourse)." However, a more careful reading of Benveniste will show that his formulation of subjectivity demonstrates the beginnings of a recognition of the situational specificity of the meaning of indexical items; that is, the act of speaking only has meaning in relation to some specific, intersubjectively available context, to which it "refers":

> The inscribing of "subjectivity" in language creates, in language and, we believe, just as easily outside of language, the category of person. It has, moreover, very varied effects in the actual structure of language, whether it is in the formal organization or in the relations of signification. (Benveniste, 1966: 263; my translation)

In both of the preceding quotations there are the beginnings of a recognition that the indexicals are always redundant with some feature(s) in the context of situation to which they refer and that they help to create by occurring. This amounts to a first tentative step toward the recognition of a hierarchy of contextualization, which would look something like the following: personal pronoun / indexical reference // context of situation. The contextualization principles entailed in this formulation mean that the use-in-context of a particular personal pronoun "redounds with" some indexed feature in the context of situation. In chapter 3 we shall see in some detail how the contextualization principles involved here can be developed in order to relate the forms of quoting and reporting speech and their various transforms to their higher-order contextual relations and dynamics in ways that can teach us a great deal about the constitution and articulation of insider/outsider relations in discourse.

This brief description of Benveniste's account of subjectivity in language is useful for our inquiry into the dynamics of quoting and reporting relations in a number of different ways. Benveniste's distinction between *histoire* and *discours* reproduces the classical division between the unified speaking subject and language as object. This division hinges on two different kinds of relations of the speaking subject to language, that is, the subject of enunciation and the subject of the enounced. Benveniste tried to show in his analysis of the asymmetry in the European pronoun system that the subject of enunciation is excluded from *histoire,* but is articulated in the subjective realm of *discours*. Similarly, Banfield's account of the relations between the center of consciousness (as subject) and the expression (E) as object maintains the subject-object split. Benveniste, as the preceding quotations show, was aware of the problem of subjectivity in language, yet he remained unable to develop an adequate theoretical account, one that does not simply maintain the subject-object dichotomy.

Speech Roles and the Intersubjectivity of Self and Other: Language as Expression and Communication

Banfield recognizes that free indirect discourse may contain exclamations and other expressive functions found in direct speech and that questions retain their

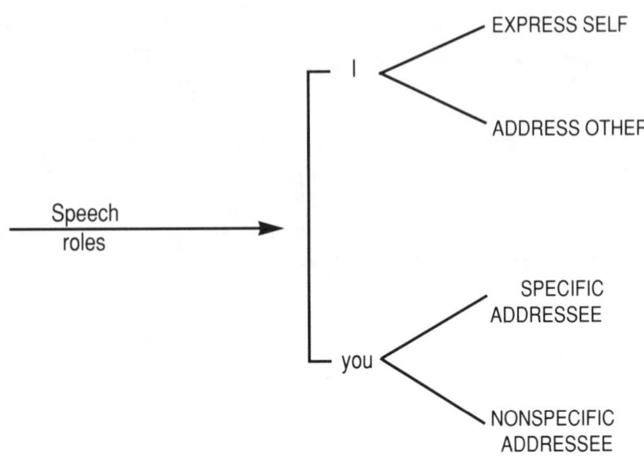

Figure 2.1. Speech roles; semantic functions

syntactically inverted form. This means that free indirect discourse retains the mood element of the quoted form, although it is a form of report in which time and person reference are shifted. Banfield's (1973, 1978a, b) formulation of free indirect discourse in terms of a formal transformational-generative model of syntax almost by definition places the burden of her description (interpretation) on the concept of linguistic *structure*. Her description is largely determined by syntagmatic criteria alone, which means that these form-form relations are then interpreted as having a given meaning. This restriction according to purely syntagmatic criteria does not adequately develop the fact that two distinct sets of semantic functions may be mapped onto the pronominal forms *I* and *you*. I would argue that it is more profitable to explore these semantic possibilities in relation to the meaning potential of the linguistic system, seen as a resource for social meaning making. The lexico-grammatical realization of the pronoun *I* has the potential simultaneously to realize two distinct, though related, semantic functions: EXPRESS SELF and ADDRESS OTHER. This distinction differentiates between utterances that are not necessarily oriented to a specific addressee and those that are (Martin, 1981: 59). Clearly, this distinction operates at a least delicate, hence situationally nonspecific, level of analysis. The lexico-grammatical realization of the pronoun *you* mirrors these semantic functions of *I* with the following functions: NONSPECIFIC ADDRESSEE and SPECIFIC ADDRESSEE. These are displayed diagrammatically in Figure 2.1.

Figure 2.1 shows that the lexico-grammatical realizations of "I" and "you" can simultaneously map the speech functions of EXPRESSION and COMMUNICATION. The terms used in Figure 2.1 may be explained in the following way: EXPRESS SELF is the verbalization of "inner" subjective consciousness, not necessarily oriented to a specific addressee; ADDRESS OTHER is the speaker (or narrator) in the communication, where the orientation is to a specific addressee; the NONSPECIFIC ADDRESSEE is the second-person recipient of some expression of SELF; and the SPECIFIC ADDRESSEE is the recipient of some act of communication. These are idealized categories, which may entail much variation and overlap among the semantic relations involved in any given instance of discourse. In all cases, these semantic categories are generalizable to individual, collective, or institutional subjects.

Now, Martin (1981: 59), from whom these distinctions are derived, makes a clear differentiation between the speech functions of EXPRESS SELF and ADDRESS OTHER by arguing that EXPRESS SELF utterances are not necessarily oriented to an addressee, while ADDRESS OTHER utterances are. I think this claim argues too strongly for a clear-cut distinction between the COMMUNICATION and EXPRESSION functions of the first- and second-person pronouns. I would argue that all utterances are other oriented even if the addressee is only implicit or presupposed in the discursive situation. This suggests the need for a framework that does not treat these semantic variables as if they are so clearly distinguishable in linguistic and discursive practice. Halliday (1985: 251) shows how the various independent variables involved in quoting and reporting relations may recombine in new ways, which enlarge and renew the meaning potential of the linguistic system. New patterns of *use* of the linguistic system may alter the meaning making potential of the system itself. Altered patterns of use of these resources can lead to "slippage" between the hitherto stable form-meaning relations that are regularly enacted in a given context-type. Halliday (1985: 251) defines this as a "semogenic" process whereby new meaning making possibilities are created. Halliday's own discussion of this phenomenon has centered on the way the various independent variables in the quoting and reporting relations are transformed and recombined to form free indirect discourse. Free indirect discourse is thus defined as a "projection space" (Halliday, 1985: 238 n.), which foregrounds the recombining and intersecting of the semantic functions of EXPRESSION and COMMUNICATION. My main point here is that it is in free indirect discourse that these semantic possibilities of recombination and transformation of the meaning potential embodied in the system of quoting and reporting relations are most fully exploited. The lexico-grammatical resources that are used will be discussed further below. These possibilities are in no way restricted to narrative discourse, although this will be the focus of the present study. Free indirect discourse is then a remodeling of the semantic potential of the system of quoting and reporting relations. It is a resource for the restructuring and transforming of the coded relations between, say, the reporting and reported contexts. The first step in the development of this line of thinking is to recognize that free indirect discourse is now fully coded as the bounded lexico-grammatical realization of these semantic resources. We shall examine in chapter 3 just how the semantic codes at work generate what Bernstein (1982: 306) has called specific recognition and realization rules in relation to the specialized textual voices (positioned-practices) and discursive transactions in which these forms are used. The specific semantic orientation of free indirect discourse was recognized by Volosinov (1973: 134) when he described this phenomenon as "half narration and half reported speech." However, Volosinov did not provide any detailed account of the lexico-grammatical realizations of these semantic functions. We shall undertake this task in connection with Halliday's (1985) semantically oriented functional grammar at a later stage in the present chapter.

Language and Intersubjectivity: A Neomaterialist Critique

Martin's (1981: 59) claim, which I referred to earlier, that EXPRESS SELF utterances are not necessarily oriented to an addressee reveals the individualistic ontology underlying this notion of the self. This self is an isolated monad, able to express its own inner essence or consciousness. I propose to develop in this book the alternative argument that self and other are not thinglike monads or fixed, individual centers of consciousness. Self and other are contextual relations, which are defined in the first instance in terms of the patterned meanings and transactions that connect self and other to each other. These metastable subsystem-subsystem transactions constitute the environments in and through which social agents are produced as particular kinds of subjects-in-process. There is then no single, unitary identity or consciousness that can be expressed through the representational medium of language. There is, to use the words of Marx and Engels (1976: 41–42), the "practical consciousness" of transformative human labor whereby social agents produce a second nature of social relations, social forms of the division of labor, and social meaning making practices. Yet, this dialectic is not merely the result of a "de facto situation" (Merleau-Ponty, 1983: 175) whose structures merely reproduce the given social order. Nor can it be reduced to a cryptonormative theology of the relations of production in the practical order, as in orthodox Marxism. This dialectic also embodies the contrary possibility whereby the activities of social agents may introduce counterfunctional tendencies through which this practical and communicative consciousness can be criticized and changed. We are therefore at one with the following words of Merleau-Ponty in his recognition of the dialectic of system-maintaining and system-changing functions in the practical and meaning making activities of social agents: "The human dialectic is ambiguous: it is first manifested by the social or cultural structures, the appearance of which it brings about and in which it imprisons itself. *But its use-objects and its cultural objects would not be what they are if the activity which brings about their appearance did not also have as its meaning to reject them and to surpass them*" (Merleau-Ponty, 1983: 176; emphasis in original). Now, in the neomaterialist framework of this study this entails the dialectic of both social agent and discursive subject relations. Therefore, we are required to reject (1) the intersubjectivity of interpersonal role relations and their expression in language, and (2) the economic determinism implied in the metaphor of cultural reproduction. Both of these will now be discussed.

Bourdieu's (1977: 81) strictures against "the occasionalist illusion, which consists in directly relating practices to properties described in the situation" are worth heeding here. The intersubjective individual-to-individual notion of self-other relations assumes a notion of self (subject) that is expressed in language (object). This intersubjectivist illusion entails the positivistic disjunction of subject and object whereby interpersonal role relations and functions are ascribed on the basis of individual-to-individual interactions in some social occasion of discourse. However, this fails to attend to the normative basis of the theory itself through which meanings are ascribed to or construed in linguistic and other semiotic forms. Therefore, language-as-object is conceived as being disjoined from the meaning-constituting activity of agents. It is regarded as belonging to an external domain about which observations and hypotheses are derived in an orderly, rule-governed way. These are rule-governed procedures that determine the validity and correctness of these observations and hypotheses in terms of analytically and referentially "true" statements, which are taken to *refer to* the designated external reality, which is the object of the theory. Bourdieu's critique serves to remind us that occasions of discursive interaction are constitutive of higher-order social semiotic relations and processes as much as they are constituted by them. This important and complex point will be a central and recurrent concern of this book.

The reductionism of the intersubjective approach conceives of this "practical consciousness" of social meanings and practices in terms of the interpersonal relations between the agents involved in some social occasion of discourse. These relations and the reductionism so entailed are conceptualized in terms of their social and discursive roles and role-functions. Role-theory and the related "occasionalist illusion" that Bourdieu writes about derive from the structural-functionalist sociological paradigm of Talcott Parsons (1964) and others. This paradigm is deeply entrenched in linguistics, where the "occasionalist illusion" leads to the disjunction of microlevel processes of social and discursive interaction from higher-order (macrolevel) social semiotic relations and functions (see chapter 8). The structural-functionalist paradigm presumes a normative and consensus-oriented conceptualization of the individual in relation to the social structure. The social structure so conceived is objectified as a spectacle in which social agents act out particular role-relations (Bourdieu, 1977: 96). The normative, consensus-oriented framework in which roles and role-relations are discussed commits three principal epistemological errors by virtue of which the relations of social agents to the social semiotic system or some part of it are mistyped.

First, the concept of role derives from a primary focus on the individual-to-individual conceptualization of social and discursive interaction. Individuals are said to act out particular role-relations on a given social occasion of discourse, which is defined empirically, as Bourdieu (1977: 81–82) points out, as a temporally and spatially bound "conjunctural structure" in which the individuals are assembled to enact specific social roles. This focus on the individual and the roles he or she performs is unable to theorize the material character of the wider social semiotic formations in and through which social agents are differentially positioned in the social order. Normative definitions of social and discursive roles thereby reduce the social to the individual through a restricted focus on the social situation or social occasion of discourse as the empirical setting in which individuals perform particular role-relations and functions. Such a theory can only adequately describe a restricted range of normatively defined role relations such as occupation (see Therborn, 1980: 21). However, such definitions are unable to theorize the relations of differentially positioned social agents to the means of production of a given social order. In Therborn's (1980: 21) words, there is "no normative definition of classes in capitalist society, no normative definition of surplus labour and surplus-labour extraction." This problem arises, for instance, in Hasan's (1986) linguistic study of the ideology of mother-child linguistic interaction, where the concept of social class is explicitly defined in terms of the socio-economic status of the father.

Second, interpersonal or social roles preserve the givenness of the social structure to which the particular role is assumed to relate. Thus, the differential positioning of agents in the social division of labor gets constitutively reduced to individuals who are responding to the demands of a de facto social situation, as mentioned earlier. This tends to assume a fixed, given correlation between role and social situation; yet, there is no adequate explanation of why this relation occurs in connection with wider issues concerning the maintenance and change of the social semiotic system. The empirical correlation that is established at, say, the level of social situation does not explain why or how the social division of labor into the categories of transmitters, reproducers, maintainers, legitimators, and challengers in a given social semiotic and the forms of the relations of social and cultural reproduction and change—compare Bernstein's (1982; 1986a) coding orientations—do not match or correspond in any such direct way. Roles get talked about in terms of their structural correlations with particular social and institutional situations. They are described in terms of typologies of assembled role-relations and their traits in their respective social situations. However, there is no adequate functional explanation of how and why particular role-relations are constitutive of the social formation at higher orders of contextualization.

Alternatively, I shall use the notion of positioned-practice throughout this study. This term is defined in relation to Bakhtin's (1981) concept of social heteroglossia and to the notion of semantic register in systemic-functional linguistics. Social heteroglossia refers to the strategic alignments, conflicts, and oppositions of social meaning making practices and their intersections in a given social formation and the ways in which these are articulated or voiced in specific textual productions. Register refers to the configurations of semantic selections that are typically made in a given social situation-type. These two concepts can be reconstituted in relation to each other and operationalized by the concept of voice, itself an adaptation of Bakhtin's original concept. This concept does not refer to the individual's speaking voice. Rather, I define *voice* as the textual realizations of specific intersections of heteroglossic varieties and semantic registers, seen as instantiations of some still wider system of heteroglossic relations in the social semiotic system or some part of it. Texts can be said to articulate or voice a plurality of conflicting discursive positions and values in relation to particular social practices. The resulting positioned-practices are articulated or voiced by distinctive configurations of these, which correspond to particular patterns of use and modes of deployment of the meaning making resources of the social semiotic. Thus, the related concepts of positioned-practice and voice can be used to show (1) the differential distribution of heteroglossic varieties and the differential access of social agents to these; (2) the differential principles of classification, framing, and semiotic regulation that can operate for social agents in the social formation (see Bernstein, 1982); and (3) how heteroglossic relations of alignment, opposition, and conflict among different positioned-practices and their textual voicings are functional in the dialectic of system-maintaining and system-changing processes in the social semiotic system (see Lemke, 1985a). Interestingly, Bernstein (1982; 1986a) explicitly replaces the concept of role, which was used in his earlier writings, with a notion of voice that shares many affinities with the mutually defining concepts of positioned-practice and voice in the present study. However, Bernstein's use of this term is not related to any notion equivalent to the system of social heteroglossia through which positioned-practices and their voicings are differentially positioned both in relation to each other and to particular semantic registers and their textual realizations. We shall further develop and reconstitute Bernstein's work, which is, I believe, critically important to social semiotic theory, in chapters 7 and 8.

The third reason for rejecting the concept of role is that it is a nondialectical concept (see also Therborn, 1980: 21). Therefore, normative concepts such as roles, role-relations, and conflicts between role-expectation and role-performance are unable to show us how, for instance, macrolevel categories such as social class are operationalized by social agents. Such operations occur by virtue of both the differential relations of agents and their practices to the material and discursive resources of the social semiotic system and the differential positioning of agents as subjects in relation to other subjects in specific texts and social occasions of discourse. The nondialectical character of the concept of role limits this concept to the givenness of particular roles in specific texts and social occasions of discourse. Yet, it does not show any more than that the performance of roles by social agents enact strictly local or microlevel relations to each other in some text or social situation. Roles, so defined, constitute a typology of possible macrolevel relations of agents to each other in a given text or social situation; hence the given, predetermined nature of these categories. Roles simply reproduce their macrolevel relations in a more or less direct way, as if there were some empirical correlation between a given role and some macrolevel category. There is, however, no dialectical account of how specific intersections of social meaning making practices in some text or social occasion of discourse are dialectically integrated into higher-order (macrolevel) relations. The concept of role is seen to operate at the local level of text or social situation, yet the macrolevel criteria for defining just what a given role is are not made explicit.

The notions of positioned-practice and voice provide an alternative, which can dialectically reconstitute both the discursive positioning of agents as subjects by virtue of their binding to or identification with regular, systematic copatternings of social meaning making practices and the ways in which subject positions are voiced and related to other subject positions in a wider system of social heteroglossia. Discursive subject positions (positioned-practices) are then specific typical intersections of social meaning making practices that social agents enact in relation to higher-order intertextual meaning relations, social semiotic codes, and discursive formations. The concept of voice is also essential so as not to reduce the concept of discursive subject to the social agent per se. Critical social semiotics seeks to provide a dialectical and relational account, which can show how specific heteroglossic relations of alliance, opposition, and conflict among voices in a given text can be related to macrolevel concepts such as the social division of labor and the uneven distribution of material and semiotic resources in the social semiotic system. These concerns are central in chapter 8.

Now, these latter notions derive from a Marxist sociological discourse of "social and cultural reproduction," whose principal exponents include Bernstein and Bourdieu. Critical social semiotic theory, however, rejects this reproduction model when it is taken to be an authoritative and transcendent organizing principle that privileges the discourse of economism. This easily reduces to a metaphysic of realism, as is manifested in Bourdieu's constant invoking of "objective conditions" (see Bourdieu, 1977). Social semiotics attempts to dislocate the problematic of stability and change from the discourse of reproduction and to relocate it in terms of the *dynamic metastability* of all social meaning making (see Lemke, 1984a, c; Prodi, 1977; Thibault, 1986e: 94). Social semiotics presumes a dialectical and systemic account that seeks to reconstitute and renew the relations of specific texts and social occasions of discourse to their metastable conditions of possibility in the higher-order social semiotic. We do not therefore simply envisage the "reproduction" of the former independently of the latter, nor do we propose the subordination of the social semiotic to the essentialism of individual experience, where these are conceived as two distinct orders of reality.

Both this chapter and the following one approach this problem in relation to the constitution of insider and outsider categories and relations through an analysis of the contextual dynamics of quoting and reporting relations and their various transforms or recontextualizations. We shall be concerned in chapter 3 with an analysis of the contextual dynamics of these so as to situate the above critique with respect to the reciprocal structuration and contextualization of insider and outsider relations. In this way the idealization of the subject-object split can be rethought so as to disarticulate the one from the other and to rearticulate them as a joint or hybrid context in which neither component of the subject/object or inside/outside dualities is a unique constituent but, rather, a component of a dialogic structure in which the one adapts and responds to the other. This requires a detailed analysis of the lexico-grammatical resources that constitute these relations and of the ways in which these functionally covary with the higher-order contextual relations in operation.

The Lexico-Grammar of Quoting and Reporting Relations: Halliday's Functional Grammar Account

Volosinov (1973) proposes a typology of the various types of quoting and reporting relations and their transforms. Volosinov mainly considers this type of discourse at the higher levels of its sociosemantic organization. He does not provide any detailed or systematic account of the lexico-grammatical resources that realize the sociosemantics of these forms. One of the main problems in proposing a classification of quoting and reporting relations is that there is no necessary one-to-one or biunique correlation between lexico-grammatical form and semantic function. However, my consideration of Halliday's (1985: chap. 7) account of quoting and reporting relations will show that the meanings that are realized in the lexico-grammar of this type of discourse are central for constructing any useful typology of these. I noted above that it is more useful to regard the transition from one type to another in terms of a cline or continuum. Bronzwaer is correct, in spite of the limitations of his view of context, to insist on the importance of contextual factors in deciding between one type and another. However, I want to show here that the lexico-grammatical patterns of realization of the sociosemantics of quoting and reporting relations must be taken into account when relating the forms of quoting and reporting discourse to their higher-order meanings and functions in the social semiotic system. In this section I will therefore examine Halliday's account of the lexico-grammar of quoting and reporting relations at the ranks of clause and clause complex.

In Halliday's (1985) account, quoting and reporting relations are not simply formal variants but differ in meaning and function. These differences derive from the general semantic distinction between parataxis and hypotaxis. The organization of the clause complex is said to have two dimensions: (1) taxis, which is the system of interdependency between clauses, that is, the resources through which clauses are connected as clause complexes, and (2) the logico-semantic system of expansion and projection (see Halliday, 1985: 192–96). Taxis comprises two kinds of interdependency. Parataxis links elements of equal status. Both the initiating and the continuing element are free; that is, each could stand separately as an independent, functioning whole. Paratactic relations are logically symmetrical and transitive. Hypotaxis is the binding of elements of unequal status. The dominant element is free and independent; the dependent element is not. Hypotactic relations are logically nonsymmetrical and nontransitive. Logico-semantic relations between clauses in the clause complex take two main forms. Thus, in *expansion* the secondary clause expands the primary clause by (1) elaborating it, (2) extending it, or (3) enhancing it. In *projection* the secondary clause is projected through the primary clause as (1) a locution or (2) an idea. A locution is a construction of wording—a lexico-grammatical construct. An idea is a construction of meaning—a semantic construct (see Halliday, 1985: 233).

A further distinction made by Halliday, which is important for our discussion, is embedding (Halliday, 1985: 219–28). Parataxis and hypotaxis are relations between clauses. Embedding is a form of "rank shift" whereby a clause or group (cf. phrase) functions as a constituent within the structure of a group that is itself a constituent of a clause.

Halliday (1985: 227–28) defines the logico-semantic relation of projection as a "relationship whereby a clause comes to function not as a direct representation of (non-linguistic) experience but as a representation of a (linguistic) representation." Three main kinds of projection are proposed, which Halliday (1985: 228) presents through the following examples:

"Caesar was ambitious," says Brutus (paratactic)
Brutus says that Caesar was ambitious (hypotactic)
Brutus' assertion that Caesar was ambitious (embedded)

The first type of projection here is quoting (direct speech). The projecting clause contains a verbal process of saying, and the projected clause encodes that which is said as a wording. The second type is reporting (indirect speech). The projecting clause contains a verbal process of saying, but the projected clause is a meaning, not a wording. The distinction Halliday makes between wordings and meanings will be developed in particular ways later in this chapter. The third type is an embedded locution. This type is still a form of projection, but the projecting element is the noun *Brutus' assertion,* which functions as Thing in the nominal group. In this case, *Brutus' assertion* is a verbal process noun, which is the name of a locution. The clause that it projects functions to define it, just as a defining relative clause defines the noun that is expanded by it. In quoting, the unmarked projecting element is a verbal process. The projected element is projected as a wording. In reporting, the unmarked projecting element is a mental process. The projected element is projected as a meaning. Something that is projected as a meaning is still a phenomenon of language—what Halliday (1985: 229) calls a "metaphenomenon"—but it is projected at a different level, that is, at the semantic rather than the lexico-grammatical level. When something is projected as a meaning, it has already been "processed" by the linguistic system, but only once, not twice as in the case of a wording (Halliday, 1985: 230). When the "same" phenomenon is encoded by a verbal process, it is the meaning that has been recoded to become a wording. A wording is said by Halliday to lie not at one but two removes from the experience. When something is projected as a meaning, it is not the exact words that are encoded, because there are no words. There is no observed event as a prior point of reference in the external world. The difference between wordings and meanings can be illustrated by the following examples:

(*a*) John said: "I will interview her tomorrow."
(*b*) John thought that he would interview her the next day.

In *a,* the deictic orientation in the projected clause is that of the Sayer,[1] John, and not the first-person Speaker of the entire utterance. John is the point of reference for the deixis, which thus preserves in the quoting relation the form of the original lexico-grammatical event: *I, tomorrow.* In *b,* the deictic orientation in the projected clause is that of the Speaker of the projecting one. Hypotactic projection retains the deictic orientation of the projecting clause, which is that of the Speaker.

It is also possible to report a saying by encoding it as a meaning. And it is also possible to quote a thought by encoding it as a wording. The principle is that the hypotactic projection of verbal events is not true to the wording. These principles are summarized by Halliday (1985: 233) as follows:

paratactic projection:	quote
hypotactic projection:	report
what is projected verbally:	locution
what is projected mentally:	idea

Halliday (1985: 233) then presents the differences between quoting and reporting relations, as in Table 2.1. This table shows how these differences in meaning and function derive from the general semantic distinction between parataxis and hypotaxis.

In quoting, the projected element has an independent status. It is therefore more immediate and lifelike. This effect is enhanced by the deictic orientation. Reporting presents the projected element as dependent. The projected element still makes a choice of mood, but in a form that does not allow it to function as a move in a speech exchange. The notion of free indirect discourse is introduced

Table 2.1. Four Types of Projection Complex

Type of projecting process	Taxis	Quote paratactic 1 2	Report hypotactic α β
Locution verbal	''	Wording 1 ''2 She said, "I can"	Wording represented as meaning α ''β She said she could
Idea mental	'	Meaning represented as wording 1 '2 She thought, "I can"	Meaning α 'β

by Halliday (1985: 238), where he points out that a reported proposition typically is realized by a set of lexico-grammatical features generally referred to as indirect speech. The deictic orientation is shifted away from reference to the speech situation. Personal pronouns shift from first and second person to third; demonstratives from near (here-and-now) to remote. Free indirect discourse is said to have features of both direct and indirect speech. The structure of free indirect discourse is paratactic. The projected clause has the form of an independent clause and so retains the mood of the "quoted" form. However, it is a report rather than a quote. This entails that time and person reference are shifted in the manner described above. Free indirect discourse may also be projected both mentally and verbally.

I noted above that locutions and ideas can be embedded. They can be rankshifted to function as Qualifiers within a nominal group, as in the example provided above. Halliday (1985: 243) goes on to explain that a *Fact* is a form of projection that does not include mental or verbal processes, but is provided in a "pregiven" form. In the example *That Caesar was dead was obvious to all,* the projected element is *That Caesar was dead,* and yet there is no mental or verbal process doing the projecting. It is said to have the status of a Fact. A Fact can function either as a Qualifier to a "fact" noun or as a nominalization in its own right. In both cases it is embedded. A Fact is always projected, but there is no participant who is doing the projecting. There is no Sayer or Senser who is acting as the projector. Halliday then proceeds to examine the typical environments in which a Fact is projected. Facts are projected impersonally. They may be projected either by a relational process of, say, the "being" type, as in *it is the case that,* or by an impersonal mental or process verb, as in *it seems (to be the case that)*. Halliday (1985: 243–48) discusses these types in some detail. However, I shall not pursue this matter any further. The central point I wish to make

Table 2.2. Summary of Principal Types of Projection (from Halliday, 1985)

Type of process doing the projecting (quotes & reports only):		Rank: / Orientation: / Speech function	Clause complex: Quote — Taxis: Paratactic	Clause complex: Report — 1 2	Clause complex: Report — Hypotactic α β	Nominal group: Embedded ⟦ ⟧:	Nominal group: Fact — as Postmodifier	Nominal group: Fact — As Head
Locution ' ' (Projected wording)	Verbal	Proposition	' '1. 2 "It is so," he said	' '1. 2 It was so, he said	α ' 'β He said that it was so	' '⟦. his assertion that it was so	→ the saying that is so	→ (it is said) that it is so
		Proposal	' '1! 2 "Do so!" he told them	' '1! 2 They should do so, he told them	α ' 'β! He told them to do so	' '⟦! his order to them to do so	→ the stipulation to do so	→ (it is stipulated) to do so
Idea ' (Projected meaning)	Mental	Proposition	'1. 2 "it is so," she knew	'1. 2 It was so, she knew	α 'β. She knew that it was so	'⟦ her knowledge that it was so	→ the fact that it is so	→ that it is so
		Proposal	'1! 2 "Do so!", she said to herself	'1! 2 She would do so, she decided	α 'β! She decided that she would do so	'⟦! her decision to do so	→ the need to do so	→ to do so
			"direct "	"free indirect"	"indirect"	"indirect qualifying"	"impersonal qualifying"	"impersonal"

→ = same as on left

is that a Fact is a meaning and not a wording. However, it is a meaning that is not projected from the presumed consciousness of some participant, nor is it sent from any specific Source that is explicitly realized in the lexico-grammar. It simply functions as a participant in some other process, typically a relational process. Halliday (1985: 246–47) further expands the projection types already given in Table 2.1 as Table 2.2.

Table 2.2 can be summarized in the following way. Quotes, reports, and facts are categories of the language and not of the real world. There is no implication that a fact has the status of a truth-value. Anything that can be meant in language can have the status of a fact. Ideas and locutions are distinguished from other elements in the language by virtue of the fact that their referents are linguistic phenomena. According to Halliday, an idea encodes a semantic phenomenon, while a locution encodes a lexico-grammatical one. The semantic phenomenon is said to be closer to the "real world" of nonlinguistic, phenomenal experience. A locution has been processed twice over: first it is encoded semantically and then recoded lexico-grammatically as a wording. This means that it is now presumed to be an exact replica of the phenomenon to which it is said to "refer"; that is, it is a quote. An idea has been processed only once, as a meaning. A fact is a kind of idea, one that is so fully semanticized that it is no longer explicitly projected.

In this section I have followed very closely Halliday's own functional grammar account of quoting and reporting relations in language. I have included very little commentary of my own in doing so in order to prepare the basis for a textual analysis of quoting and reporting relations in the next section.

Quoting and Reporting Relations in *Ada*: A Textual Analysis

Throughout the following analysis lexico-grammatical criteria will be used as much as possible to segment the various analytical units at the levels of the clause and clause complex. The analysis will focus on the logico-semantic relations of expansion and projection in order to describe the various kinds of quoting and reporting relations that occur in the textual excerpt to be analyzed from Nabokov's *Ada*. The text has been subdivided into clause complexes, which are labeled with arabic numerals. Each clause complex is further subdivided into its clause level constituents, which are identified by a lowercase letter. The textual excerpt to be analyzed is from chapter 1, section 31 of the novel:

1 She was on bad terms with memory.
2a She thought
2b the servants would be up soon *now,*
2c and then one could have something hot.
3 The fridge was all fudge, really.
4 'Why suddenly sad?'

5a Yes, she was sad,
5b she replied,
5c she was in dreadful trouble,
5d her quandary might drive her insane
5e if she did not know
5f that her heart was pure.
6 She could explain it best by a parable.
7a She was like the girl in a film
7b he would see soon,
7c who is in the hands of a triple tragedy
7d which she must conceal
7e lest she lose her only true love, the head of the sorrow, the point of the pain. (Nabokov, 1969: 192)

Clause 1 is free indirect discourse, although there are no explicit lexico-grammatical features at clause level that necessarily lead to this conclusion. Clause 1 is an independent clause that is not projected through any explicit reporting clause. However, the absence in the lexico-grammar of an explicit projecting clause does not mean that clause 1 cannot function as free indirect discourse. My argument for this is mainly semantic and contextual. I argued above for the need to avoid reductive, formalistic accounts of free indirect discourse. Halliday's functional grammar account analyzed quoting and reporting relations in terms of functional semantic criteria. Now, the great value of Volosinov's (1973) account of these relations becomes apparent here. Lexico-grammatical functions must always be interpreted semantically in relation to some higher-order social semiotic. Semantically, it is possible to constitute an interpretative environment for clause 1 that meets all the criteria for it to be free indirect discourse. At the semantic level the principal criterion is that the projecting and projected contexts intersect. This is what Volosinov is referring to when he says that free indirect discourse is "half narration and half reported speech" (1973: 134). Although there is no explicit realization of a reporting clause in the lexico-grammar, it is possible to infer a reporting (i.e., narrating) context at the semantic level. In clause 1 the discursive positions of Ada and the narrator intersect. The situation we have in clause 1 has been precisely formulated by Volosinov in the following way:

> One might enclose the whole narrative in quotation marks as narration by a "narrator," though no such narrator is denoted, either thematically or compositionally. However, the situation within the narrative is such that almost every epithet, or definition, or value judgement might also be enclosed in quotation marks as originating in the mind of one or another character. (Volosinov, 1973: 135)

This inferred narrating (reporting) context constitutes a reconstructed semantic environment through which clause 1 is projected as free indirect discourse. This semantic environment provides a functional context for the interpretation of clause 1. In this context 1 meets all the functional semantic criteria specified by Halliday for its interpretation as free indirect discourse. It has an independent, paratactic structure and does not therefore assimilate the mood element to the reporting context. It retains the mood of the reported context. However, time and person reference are shifted to those of the reporting context. This demonstrates very clearly Halliday's (1985: 238 n.) point that free indirect discourse is a "projection 'space' rather than a single invariant pattern."

Bronzwaer (1970: 50) has also argued against the idea that free indirect discourse is a "rigid linguistic category" (see above). Free indirect discourse is a semantically indeterminate category "in which *two* intonations, *two* points of view, *two* speech acts converge and clash" (Volosinov, 1973: 135). This is very different from Banfield's (1978b: 425) claim that the center of consciousness is the *unique* referent of the mental or verbal process verb of a given clause in free indirect discourse. The semantic indeterminacy I refer to here means that free indirect discourse is a linguistic category that is simultaneously contextualized in a plurality of often opposing and conflicting contextual domains. However, far from being the "anomalous" category to which Halliday (1985: 240) refers, free indirect discourse functions to foreground the potential that all semiotic acts have to index a plurality of overlapping and contradictory semantic registers and contextual domains. It is a concrete demonstration of the general principle of the plurifunctional nature of all semiotic acts, whereby these have the potential to instantiate the system of social heteroglossia through which the conflict of social discourses is realized in the patterns of use of the meaning potential of the social semiotic system. Free indirect discourse is a development of the systemic meaning potential of quoting and reporting relations (see Halliday's notion of "semogenesis," which I referred to above). Thus, free indirect discourse foregrounds the fact that form-meaning relations are not inherently stable or simply given. Rather, they covary in relation to higher-order contextual relations in and through which the dialectic of conflicting social discourses is enacted. This argument will be further developed in later chapters. I shall show in chapters 5 and 6 that intersections of conflicting social discourses and their realizations in particular textual productions are always made in relation to still wider intertextual formations in the systems of social heteroglossia of a given social semiotic system.

The logico-semantic relationship between 2a and 2b is itself ambiguous. Clause 2a is a reporting locution, which functions to project 2b as a meaning through the mental process verb *thought*. This implies a hypotactic reporting relation between the two clauses. However, 2b contains the deictic element *soon now* in which the temporal deixis of the reported context is retained. It resists the shift, which is typical in reporting, to the the deictic orientation of the reporting context. In this regard, it resembles a quote, which maintains the deictic orientation of the Sayer in the quoted element. However, 2b is not a quote. According to Bronzwaer (1975), the deictics of proximity, for example, *this, here, now,* signal free indirect discourse when collocated with the preterite. Bronzwaer claims that "empathetic involvement" between narrator and character is heightened by the use of free indirect discourse. Indeed, Bronzwaer argues that this heightened emotional involvement between narrator and character is a defining characteristic of free indirect discourse. In this connection, I shall have more to say about the anthropomorphism of lexico-grammatical class items in chapter 3. The use of *now* in 2b retains the deictic orientation of the reported context. In this regard, 2b more closely resembles free indirect discourse. If 2b is free indirect discourse, then it is paratactically projected by 2a. If 2b is read as being paratactically projected by 2a, then the tendency is to impose the intonation pattern of quoting. If, on the other hand, it is seen as hypotactically projected, then the intonation imposed is that of reporting (see Halliday, 1985: 240). These indeterminacies point to the fact that the logico-semantic relations between 2a and 2b can be interpreted both as hypotactic projection (reporting) and as paratactic projection (quoting). This is a good example of the fact that in practice no clear-cut distinction can be made between the various kinds of quoting and reporting relations on the basis of formal criteria alone. The transition from one classification to another is best described as "fuzzy." The two interpretations here of the relations between 2a and 2b are really two alternative contextualizations of the same formal item. In both cases, the intersection of projecting and projected contexts occurs. In the hypotactic reading, the deictic orientation is that of the Speaker. The occurrence of *now* is a local departure from the foregrounded norm, which indexes the deictic orientation of the Senser (i.e., *she*) rather than that of the narrator. In the paratactic reading, the reporting and reported contexts can be seen to intersect in a more dynamic way.

The occurrence of the projecting clause 2a is an explicit lexico-grammatical realization of the narrating (reporting) context referred to above. The lexico-semantic cohesive link between *memory* in 1 and *thought* in 2a enables a weak covariate[2] tie to be construed between the reported context of 1 and the reporting context of 2a. This tie establishes a covariate thematic relation between the functionally differentiated semantic roles of the character in 1 and the narrator in 2a. The thematic relation between the two is strengthened in three ways. First, *memory* and *thought* can be coclassified by virtue of the fact that both belong to the same lexico-semantic set. Second, in the intertextual thematic formations[3] to which *memory* and *thought* regularly belong, it is typical that this semantic relation be construed between them. Third, according to the generic conventions of narrative discourse, it is typical that covariate thematic relations be made between the functionally differentiated role relations of narrator and character in the projecting and projected contexts. The second and third reasons here help to strengthen the weak tie already implicit in the lexico-semantic taxonomic relations that inhere between *memory* and *thought*. The lexico-semantic tie that is thus construed between 1 and 2a strengthens a further kind of thematic relation between the two clauses. This relation is of the multivariate ideational-grammatical kind (see Lemke, 1983b). Lemke shows that the interpretation of the functional semantics of process-participant relations in the individual clause, for example, Actor-Process-Goal, becomes, in some intertextual set, a *typical* assignment of these relations or taxonomically related ones. This relates to the concept of abstract typical formations of intertextual relations, which we shall explore in chapters 5 and 6. Clause 1 has the ideational-grammatical pattern Carrier-Relational Process : Attributive. The noun *memory* is assimilated to the semantics of Attribute : Circumstance : Manner. It is an attribute of the Carrier *she*. Clause 2a is of the semantic pattern Senser-Mental Process : Cognition. The semantics of this pattern is typical of a narrator's (or Speaker's) projection of some phenomenon (see Halliday, 1985: chapter 5, for an account of the semantics of process-participant relations in the English clause). It follows the typical pattern for reporting (narrating) clauses, which are deictically oriented to the speech situation of the Speaker rather than the Sayer or Senser. The assignment of the ideational-grammatical relation Senser-Mental Process is therefore typical in a large class of texts, intertextually defined, in relation to which this clause can have the meaning it does. In clause 1 the Relational Process-Attribute pattern atypically (incongruently) realizes a mental process noun *memory* as the functional semantic role of Circumstantial Attribute. It does not follow the typical pattern for reporting (mental process) verbs, which are deictically oriented to the speech situation of the Speaker. Clause 1 is an independent, paratactic structure, as we have noted above, which is projected as free indirect discourse. Its mood element is oriented to the reported context of the Senser. The atypical assignment of a mental process to the Relational : Attributive pattern is semantically oriented to the Senser of the mental process noun *memory*. In Halliday's terms, the congruent realization would go something like, "She remembered badly," which follows the typical pattern for reporting clauses oriented to the deictic situation of the Speaker.

Now, the ideational-grammatical relations of 1 and 2a, thus tied thematically, instantiate a conflict among differing social discourses. Clause 1 assimilates the mental process noun *memory* of Ada's consciousness to the reported context by virtue of the ideational-grammatical pattern Carrier-Relational Process-Circumstantial Attribute. The intertextual thematic formation, which I shall gloss here as MEMORY-HUMAN CONSCIOUSNESS,[4] is the superordinate item, which is hyponymously related to the lexico-semantic relation between *memory* and *thought*. The abstract thematic formation item is here disjoined from mental process verbs of cognition and perception, which typically encode these relations in the semantics of process-participant relations at clause rank. The mental process noun *memory* has a typical grammatical-semantic relation to a Senser. In Ada's discourse the process of cognition is disjoined from the lexico-grammatical agent of cognition (i.e., the Senser in a mental process clause). In 2a the thematic formation of MEMORY-HUMAN CONSCIOUSNESS is encoded by the typical Senser-Mental Process pattern in the reporting context. The different patterns of use of this thematic formation instantiate a conflict between the differing discursive positions of the narrator and Ada. This shows that the semantic functions of ideational-grammatical relations in free indirect discourse are themselves relatively indeterminate and may be contextualized in a plurality of overlapping and contradictory semantic and contextual domains. The fact that 2a is an explicit lexico-grammatical realization of the narrating (projecting) context provides a contextual clue that the entire passage we are examining here is free indirect discourse. It specifies that the entire passage is projected from this particular semantic context. In Volosinov's terms, we can simultaneously read the passage as both "narration by narrator" and "in the mind of one or another character" (see above). Clause 2a is a local multivariate feature of the text that globally contextualizes the entire passage as free indirect discourse by indexing the relevant semantic environment. The interplay, which I explored above, between multivariate (lexico-grammatical) and covariate (thematic) ties between 1 and 2a provides the semantic environment that makes this global contextualization possible. There are many features in the preceding textual environment that strengthen this analysis. At this stage I want to make clear my basic assumption that the entire passage is free indirect discourse.

Clauses 2b and 2c are ideas (meanings) that are projected mentally through 2a. Clause 2c is an expansion of 2b. It is a paratactic extension of this clause. It simply adds a new element to what is projected through 2a. The paratactic extension strengthens my claim that both 2b and 2c are paratactically independent of 2a and so are free indirect discourse. In both clauses, time and person reference are shifted to the reporting context of 2a. However, the ideational grammatical relations and the mood are oriented to the reported context. Clause 3 is an independent paratactic construction like 1. The word *fudge* is from a semantic register that is more characteristic of the young Ada rather than the narrator in the reporting context. It is an example of a register-type that is semantically oriented to the reported context of the character. The use of *really* is one of those orthographic markers of direct (quoted) speech that frequently occur in free indirect discourse. It is more typical of a spoken register. All this adds up to the conclusion that 3 is the projection of a locution as a meaning rather than a wording. Clause 4 is a quote from Van's speech. The immediately preceding paragraph makes this clear. It is therefore a locution projected as a wording, although no projecting clause is explicitly realized in the lexico-grammar. It is also possible to contextualize 4 as a quote that is embedded within the free indirect discourse of Ada. In either case, it is a paratactic, independent clause that retains the mood—here the interrogative—of the reported context. In one reading it is projected as a report in free indirect discourse, whereby time and person reference are shifted to the reporting context; in another reading it is projected as a quote in which the deictic orientation of the Sayer is retained. The ambiguity (plurifunctionality) is strengthened because no explicit deictic reference is in fact provided in 4. This ambiguity is functional in this semantic context in a number of ways. The interrogative mood in 4 enacts a dialogic relation between the narrator-Van discourse and character-Ada discourse. The absence of overt deixis and of any explicit ideational-grammatical relations as well as the ambiguity described above mean that these deictic and semantic orientations in 4 cannot easily be assimilated to either the projecting or projected contexts, as was the case in 1 and 2a. The interrogative mood of 4 enacts a fully dialogic relationship with 5a. This notion of dialogism may be clarified by referring directly to the work of Bakhtin, from whom it is derived:

> Both of these judgements must be embodied in order for a dialogical relationship between them or toward them to arise. Thus, as thesis and antithesis, these two judgements can be united in a single utterance of a single subject, an utterance which expresses that subject's unified dialectical position on a given position. In that case no dialogical relationships arise. *But if the two judgements are divided between two different utterances of two different subjects, then dialogical relationships arise between them.* (Bakhtin, 1973: 152; emphasis added)

This is a crucial observation of Bakhtin's. Free indirect discourse is the site of a plurality of discursive positioned-practices and their textual voicings, which intersect within the same bounded utterance. A dialectical relation is enacted between the discursive positions that are so intersected. However, all forms of quoting and reporting relations entail various strategies and degrees of closure of the contextual relations between the projecting and projected contexts. This argument will be further developed in chapter 3. This dialectic can be said to occur between the idealized extremes of a cline between "monologic" contextual closure and "dialogic" openness. Bakhtin's formulation follows the Hegelian dialectic of thesis-antithesis-synthesis, and so it retains a decontextualizing opposition-identity relation, whereby the dialogic relationship is predetermined by the synthesis of the two preceding terms in the dialectic. The synthesis thus functions as a final cause that expresses the "reality" toward which the two subjects are striving. In this view, we have a relativistic conception of discursive subjects and objects. Each has its independent existence until it comes together in the dialogic relationship so as to strive toward a new common knowledge whose attainment is represented by the synthesis. In spite of this differential reductionism, Bakhtin is, however, working toward an alternative to the Hegelian unilinear causality in the form of a dynamic open system view of the social semiotic. In this epistemology an open-ended hierarchy of contextualizing relations discursively produces and punctuates (see Wilden, 1981) discursive subjects and objects rather than assuming that these exist independently of the social semiotic relations and processes that produce them. In the dynamic open system view, it is the work performed by social agents in and through their patterned meanings and transactions that constitutes these contextual relations. It is these relations that precisely punctuate the differences between discursive subjects and objects and social meaning making practices in a given context.

The dialogic relationship between 4 and 5a repunctuates the ongoing patterns of interaction among discursive positioned-practices in this passage. The dialogic relationship actively interrogates the global ideological patterning of the text as Other by repunctuating the patterned meanings and transactions that constitute this global patterning. However, it is a *local* repunctuation that is functional in building in counterfunctional meanings and practices so as to maintain the dialectic of self-regulation and self-interference at all (con)textual levels. Clause 5a is free indirect discourse. It is a paratactic projection of Ada's response to Van's speech and so is a locution projected as a meaning. Tense and person reference are shifted to the deictic orientation of the reporting context, but the occurrence of *Yes* is more typical of the semantic register of spoken dialogue and so can be taken to index the Sayer in the reported context. Clause 5b is the projecting clause for 5a, and like 2a it is an explicit lexico-grammatical realization of the narrating (projecting) context. These two clauses are functionally related in the sense that they encode semantic functions that are typical of the reporting context: 2a encodes the pattern Senser-Mental Process : Cognition; 5b encodes the pattern Sayer-Verbal Process. This similarity at the ideational-grammatical level means that a covariate tie can be construed between them. This tie has an intertextual basis insofar as narrators are typically Speakers who project Sayers and Sensers in the narrative. This helps to contextualize the passage as free indirect discourse.

Clauses 5c and 5d are independent, paratactic projections of locutions as meanings. Clause 5e is hypotactically dependent on 5d. It is an expansion of 5d, which projects it as a secondary clause of enhancement. It qualifies 5d as a circumstance of condition. Clause 5e also projects 5f as a meaning through the mental process verb *know*. Clause 5f is hypotactically projected through 5e. The clause complex 5 demonstrates the way that hypotactic and paratactic structures combine in the same clause complex. The conjunction *if* in 5e realizes both the hypotactic dependency and the circumstantial relationship of Condition. These hypotactic dependency relations occur within the global context of free indirect discourse, which is paratactic. The hypotactic relation between 5d, 5e, and 5f breaks with the paratactic reporting relation of free indirect discourse. Now, the logico-semantic relations of expansion and projection constitute the material linguistic practices that enact these relations among discursive positioned-practices and their textual voicings at the level of the clause and clause complex. This point has been made by Colin MacCabe in the following way:

> We can describe the non-restrictive relative in terms of a discourse turning back on itself and constantly providing a series of equivalences for the terms it is using. The non-restrictive relative produces evidence of an alternative which could say the same thing only differently and it is this possibility of an alternative or a set of alternatives, which constitutes the effect of sense and subjectivity and their necessary certainty. (MacCabe, 1979: 293)

The logico-semantic relations of the clause complex do not simply reproduce a given set of logical structures between clauses. Rather, the general character of the logical structures—either paratactic or hypotactic—in natural language means that these relations of interdependency between clauses provide a potential for adducing relevant intertextual formations. This "logic" is neither given nor natural. Rather, it is construable only on the basis of the specific relations of interdependency between clauses and the ways in which these are meaningful in the specific intertextual formations that are adduced. Thus, the logic of the relations of interdependency between clauses is not an intrinsic feature of the "tactic" relations involved. The logico-semantics of expansion and projection articulate the logical relations between clauses on the basis of wider intertextual formations (see Lemke, 1988a). Now, MacCabe's formulation differs from this insofar as it seems to leave intact the notion of a unified subject able to "say the same thing only differently." We are left with a unified subject of a plurality of social discourses. MacCabe's discussion is confined to the nonrestrictive (i.e., nondefining) relative clause. Nevertheless, it indicates the ways in which the logico-semantic relations of expansion and projection constitute relations of "sense and subjectivity" between clauses in a text. The relative indeterminacy of these logical structures is foregrounded in free indirect discourse, where the clash of a plurality of semantic and axiological positions is articulated.

Bronzwaer's anthropomorphic claim that free indirect discourse involves heightened empathetic involvement between narrator and character has quite a different implication. It serves to reproduce the Theological notion of the sovereign individual, who recognizes him/herself as a subject through his or her practices. It preserves the Imaginary symmetry of a presumed correspondence between the "utterer" and the "producer" of the meaning of a given utterance (see Chilton, 1983). The Hegelian idealism in Bakhtin's formulation retains a similarly Theological notion of the subject, with, however, the important difference that Bakhtin's anthropomorphism is mitigated by his attempt to construct a new discourse of the dynamic relations between material social meaning making practices in texts. Bakhtin's anthropomorphism retains a residual humanism of the individual as the unique author of acts of meaning. This is not so much a criticism of Bakhtin's struggle to construct an alternative to the humanism of the individual speaking subject. Rather, it is a good example of the ways in which the social discourse of the individual can even perfuse the language of a theory that attempts to resist and provide alternatives to it.

This brings us back to the problem of the articulation of self and other in language with which we began this chapter. The tendency in all the formulations of the intersubjective basis of self/other relations and transactions is the failure adequately to distinguish levels of power, responsibility, and context in the analysis of these relations. The presumed symmetry in the relations between, say, "utterer" and "producer" of social meanings engenders this confusion of levels of logical typing in all the accounts I have discussed here. This epistemological confusion or mistyping of levels of communication and metacommunication generates relations of paradox and contradiction that ramify in largely implicit ways both through social meaning making practices and our analytical representations of these (see Bateson, 1973d; Wilden, 1980: 390; Thibault, 1984). The concept of the text as a formal, necessarily coherent "unity" is just such a mistyping of the levels of context involved. For example, Banfield's representationalism projects an Imaginary unified SELF (= center of consciousness) onto formal syntactic structures *as if* these are relations at the same order of logical typing. This error is not individual but systemic in character. The epistemological confusion that it generates arises through the failure adequately to account for the hierarchical and dialectical nature of the relations between levels of communication and metacommunication. I shall examine these questions more fully in chapters 3 and 4.

I shall now use the remainder of the textual analysis in order to problematize still further the Imaginary projection of formal "unity" and "coherence" onto shifting fields of textual relations and practices. Clause 4 is a quote that interrogates the global dominance of free indirect discourse. As a quote, the deictic orientation of the Sayer is dominant. Here, this "I" is constituted in relation to the "other" of Ada's discourse. It enacts a dialogic interrogation of this discourse. Ada is *sad* 5a and *in dreadful trouble* 5c, and these items belong to a thematic formation PROHIBITION OF INCEST that functions to maintain a social norm of INTERDICTION. Clause 5a, which is free indirect discourse, recontextualizes 4 so that the "I" of the Sayer in 4 is no longer dominant. Clause 5a is a dialogic response to 4 and continues to maintain the relationship between self and other that had been formulated in 4. Clause 5b constitutes Van as narrator-I in a further dialogic relationship with the reader as "you." It is an explicit projecting clause in which the narrator-I's formulation of "reality" is dominant. Clauses 5c and 5d maintain the reality that was projected by 5a. This reality is the PROHIBITION OF INCEST that operates as a higher-order contextual Other in relation to Van and Ada. However, 5e qualifies 5d as a conditional in the way I described above. It recontextualizes the discursive reality of 5c and 5d by formulating an alternative discursive reality. Clause 5e is a projecting clause that constitutes the reader as "other" in relation to the narrator-I. Clause 5f is then projected by 5e as a meaning. In the local context of its projecting clause, it is a hypotactic report. More globally, it is subsumed by the global contextualization of the passage as free indirect discourse. As an indirect report at the local level of the clause, it is deictically oriented to the narrator-I. These two clauses function to position Ada in relation to an alternative social discourse to the globally dominant norm of INTERDICTION. However, this is not a fully articulated alternative to the dominant discourse of the Other. Clauses 5e and 5f are hypotactically dependent on the dominant discourse. Clause 5e is projected through 5d as hypotactic extension. This relation of hypotactic dependency is not able fully to articulate an alternative to the dominant discursive reality. Clauses 6 and 7a are free indirect discourse. Both are paratactic, independent clauses that maintain the dominant mode here. Clause 6 functions to frame the *parable* that begins in 7a. Clause 7b is a defining relative clause, which is embedded in the nominal group whose Head is the noun *film* in 7a. This defining relative clause further specifies the Head of the nominal group in which it is embedded. The process of embedding actually merges Van's discourse in 7b with Ada's discourse in 7a by rank-shifting 7b to function as a qualifier in the nominal group. The effect is to diminish the status of 7b as the formulation of an independent discursive reality. Here one discursive reality is subordinated to another. The defining relative is therefore "the site of two discourses intersecting and being homogenized by the action of the relative" (MacCabe, 1979: 293). On the other hand, clause 7c is a nondefining relative that functions as an elaboration of *girl* in 7a. This relation of equivalence has the further consequence that both *She* and *the girl* are inserted into the discursive reality formulated in 7c. Another implication arises from the fact that 7b is embedded in 7a. This process of embedding, along with the fact that Van is the spectator of a film here, functions to bind Van into the same discursive reality as in 7a. The relations of local thematic equivalence between *she, girl,* and *he* here further imply that all three voices are implicated in the discursive reality formulated in 7c. Clause 7d is another defining relative clause that is embedded in the nominal group that has as its Head *tragedy* in 7c. Clause 7d indexes the dominant global Other of the social norms and interdictions that impose a modulation of necessity *must* on the subject. Clause 7e is a hypotactic elaboration of consequence. It specifies the consequences if this constraint is violated. The local thematically equivalent relations I mentioned above generate a confusion of levels in the text. These relations of local equivalence assume that *She, the girl,* and *he* in 7a and 7b are all on the same level of logical typing. However, the relations of consequence specified in 7e clearly formulate the difference rather than the similarity between the Van and Ada discursive realities, although 7e still maintains the equivalence relation between Ada and *the girl in the film*. Silverman and Torode (1980: 310) show how this interplay of sameness and difference enacts the dialectic of appearance and reality in and through which discursive positioned-practices and their textual voicings are continually formulated and reformulated in and through the materiality of textual practice.

Quoting and Reporting Relations as Self-Other Dyad Transactions

Volosinov's (1973: 130–32) distinction between the "referent-analyzing modification" and the "texture-analyzing modification" recognizes that the various transforms or recontextualizations involved in direct and indirect quoting and reporting relations nevertheless enable us to postulate a sameness of experiential or propositional content. The "texture-analyzing function" may be formulated in systemic-functional terms as the textual metafunction. Volosinov defines the "texture-analyzing functions" as follows:

> It incorporates into indirect discourse words and locutions that characterize the subjective and stylistic physiognomy of the message viewed as expression. These words and locutions are incorporated in such a way that their specificity, their subjectivity, their typicality are distinctly felt. (Volosinov, 1973: 131)

Thus, the "message viewed as expression" can be defined in terms of the textual metafunction, which is, in Halliday's terms, the "enabling" function of language. The textual metafunction enables the experiential and interpersonal metafunctions to mean in units larger than the single clause, that is, as texts. This enabling function entails here that we look at quoting and reporting relations not only in terms of what is said (experiential meaning) but also in terms of both what is going on (interpersonal meaning) and *how* meaning choices from these relate to the (con)text in which they occur (textual meaning). In order to do this, we shall refer once again to Table 2.1, which is reproduced from Halliday (1985: 239). The complexity of these phenomena requires some simplification or idealization of the actual situation. Therefore, I shall start with the simplifying assumption that the two outer extremities of wordings and meanings in Table 2.1 represent the outer points on the language-as-action versus language-as-reflection cline (see Halliday, 1978: 71, 121). The two extremities of this cline are respectively concerned with wordings as the *reconstruction* of a social process and meanings as *commenting* on a social process (Martin, 1984: 36). Wordings are concerned with the reconstruction of a speech exchange through the logico-semantic resources of projection. Whether or not this presumes the reconstruction of some actually occurring speech exchange is not relevant here. A wording – that is, a quote – is typed by the meaning system as being formally identical to some actually occurring utterance-token to which it refers. It is therefore seen as experientially and interpersonally closer to the "original" utterance-token. Meanings, on the other hand, entail the experientialization of the interpersonal dimension (Martin, 1984:

45). In this sense it does not so much reconstruct what someone said, thought, felt, and so forth, as experientially comment on this.

The cline from wordings to meanings can be discussed in relation to both experiential and interpersonal distance. The present discussion will make use of the four distinctions in Table 2.1 to illustrate the implications of these for both experiential and interpersonal distance. The cline from wordings to meanings in Table 2.1 enables different dyad-types to be identified in which the relations between the projecting and projected contexts are defined and realized. Thus, the contextualization of the relations between projecting and projected contexts along the experiential and interpersonal dimensions has consequences for textual meaning. This is so both at the level of the clause complex as well as the level "above," that is, the level of discourse. So, the question of experiential and interpersonal distance necessarily entails specific choices in textual meaning and organization, as well. The different types of clause-complexing relations are central here. The relations between projecting and projected contexts can be thought of as different dyad-types that encode different types of self-other dialogic relationships. The contextual dynamics of these dyad-types and their transforms will be explored more fully in chapters 3 and 4. These different dyad-types presuppose different metarules of contextualization, depending on which dyad-type is in operation. The experiential and interpersonal meanings in both projecting and projected contexts are recontextualized at the level of the dyad in ways that can redefine the possible relations between the two contexts. This can occur along both the experiential and interpersonal dimensions, as we shall see below. Quoting and reporting dyad-types, unlike conversational structure, do not participate in the deictic here-and-now of conversational exchange. Quoting and reporting relations "reconstruct" exchange structures through the logico-semantic resources of projection. Along the experiential distance scale, the wording-meaning cline shows that quotes, as the unmarked projection of a verbal process (i.e. wordings), are most dependent on the notion of an "original" utterance-token that is reconstructed in the projected context. Now, the presumed relation of formal "identity" between the projected clause and some original discourse event is more accurately defined as one of homology rather than analogy. This relation of homology presupposes some relations of both similarity and difference between the "original" and the projected events. It does not start, as Banfield does, with an a posteriori assumption that, for instance, free indirect discourse represents the unique act of consciousness of some SELF. Banfield's assumption demonstrates the analogical method, whereby the correspondence between the lexico-grammatical form of, say, free indirect discourse and some center of consciousness is assumed already to exist. The analogy is then discovered a posteriori through the postulating of objective correlations between lexico-grammatical form and a prior act of consciousness. This ideology of reference or representation is rejected here. This ideology assumes that the discursive processes through which quoting and reporting relations are constituted are reducible to the analysis of formal linguistic entities taken as the formal representation of these same processes. On the other hand, the homological view starts from the dialectical premise that quoting and reporting relations do not derive from criteria of immediate external similarity between two events. The relations of homology and the ways in which these covary in the various transforms of quoting and reporting relations are derived from some factor that is common to their processes of production. Thus, we assume that the conditions of production of these forms are what unites them. The dualistic thinking of Banfield's analogical representationalism disjoins the linguistic act from its conditions of production through the a posteriori and contingent superimposition of an originary act of consciousness on lexico-grammatical form. The homological view is concerned with the ways in which quoting and reporting relations can be analyzed as a means through which discourse participants reconstitute in their discursive practices the dynamics of insider and outsider perspectives (see chapters 3 and 4). Quoting and reporting relations are then homologous in various ways and to varying extents to either text-as-record or text-as-product of some sociodiscursive practice. Text-as-record has some recognizable relation of homology (cf. identity) to the discursive practices of which it is a record. Text-as-product, on the other hand, is not homologous in this way to its conditions of production but to its conditions of use (see Lemke, 1984b: 79 for this last point and the distinctions used here).

Halliday (1985: 233–34) points out the limitations of the traditional grammarian's view that reporting relations are fully reversible. As Halliday shows, this may be so lexico-grammatically, but it is not necessarily the case semantically. The limits of the homology depend then on the limits to reversibility and on the asymmetry between the projecting and projected contexts. The cline from wording to meaning with respect to the experiential and interpersonal dimensions of meaning can therefore help us to formalize the kinds of homologies that are entailed in Table 2.1. Martin (1984: 45) points out that projection involves the experientialization of the interpersonal dimension of discourse meaning. I will start then with the oversimplifying assumption that the various transforms of quoting and reporting discourse nevertheless maintain the experiential or propositional meaning of the projected clause as a constant (see Silverstein, 1979: 212). This assumption will, however, be modified below. I shall now examine more closely the implications for both experiential and interpersonal meaning of the four types of quoting and reporting relations given in Table 2.1. Halliday (1985: 239) further refines these in terms of six types, which form the basis of my discussion. These six types have been numbered in the following discussion according to their left-to-right placing in our proposed cline. The purpose of this discussion is to relate these to their indexical functions as defined by Silverstein (1979). Silverstein makes a distinction between indexically *presupposing* and indexically *creative* uses of linguistic tokens. To quote Silverstein:

> Where the participants understand the copresence of some indexed feature of the context independently of the occurrence of the indexical feature of language—even though there is such an indexical relationship—we might say that the participants' understanding of speech-form to context *presupposes* the existence-in-context of the indexed feature. Contrastively, where the participants understand the copresence of some indexed aspect of the context only by the occurrence of the indexical feature of language, we might say that the participants' indexical understanding of speech-form in context *creates* the existence-in-context of the indexed feature. (Silverstein, 1979: 206–7)

The six distinctions, which I have developed on the basis of Halliday's (1985: 239) account, are as follows:

1. The projected (quoted) clause retains the deictic standpoint of the Sayer rather than that of the Speaker. Along the interpersonal dimension, the mood element is also that of the Sayer. A wording indexically presupposes a homological relation of identity to some discourse event.

2. In free indirect discourse—that is, a wording encoded as a meaning with the exception of intonation—the deictic standpoint of the projected clause is that of the Speaker. Contrastively, the mood element in this clause is that of the Sayer. Free indirect discourse indexically presupposes the "recoverability" of some actual discourse event rather than a relation of formal identity. Here, the discourse event is understood to be homologous to the projected clause both semantically and lexico-grammatically. Semantically, the deictic standpoint of the projected clause is that of the Speaker in the projecting context. However, the mood element at the lexico-grammatical level is that of the Sayer, as is the intonation contour. These two latter features, combined with the independent, paratactic nature of the projected clause, indexically presuppose a wording, that is, a quoted lexico-grammatical token, which can be derived from the projected clause and independently attributed to the Sayer. From this perspective, the deixis presupposes the "facticity" of the speech event that is so recovered. The issue is whether the projected speech event was uttered or not. Thus, the projected wording presupposes at the lexico-grammatical level a homology of similarity (rather than identity) to the recoverable form. At the semantic level, deixis and time reference are fully reversible, permitting the restoration of the deictic standpoint of the Sayer.

3. Reported speech is a wording encoded as a meaning, where both the deictic standpoint and the mood element in the projected clause are that of the Speaker. The projected clause is a meaning, which is semanticized to the extent that no independent quoted form is presupposed at the lexico-grammatical level. In other words, no independently observable or verifiable speech event is presupposed that is in turn taken to be homologically similar to the projected clause at the lexico-grammatical level. At this level it is possible to reverse the projected

clause. However, the semantics of reported speech do not presuppose that a Sayer actually uttered the reported clause. What is indexically presupposed is, rather, the modal stance of the Speaker in asserting the experiential meaning in the projected clause. Here, the projected clause is textualized rather than considered to be "referring to" some independent speech event (Halliday, 1985: 234). The homological reconstruction of the speech event is limited to the Speaker's textualization of the process. The projected clause is treated as a text – that is, a unit of meaning – produced by the Speaker rather than the Sayer. What is presupposed is the arguability of the experiential content rather than the facticity of some independently occurring language token. The emphasis is therefore on the modal stance of the Speaker in relation to the experiential meaning of the reported clause. The hypotactic, dependent status of this clause emphasizes the limits of the homology. The asymmetry between the projecting and projected contexts emphasizes the fact that reported speech entails the experientialization of interpersonal meaning. The exchange structure of the mood element in the projected clause is recontextualized in terms of the experiential context of the projecting clause.

4. Quoted thought encodes a meaning as a wording. Both the deictic standpoint and the mood element in the projected clause are that of the Senser. The projected clause is a meaning whose quoted lexico-grammatical form is presumed to be formally identical to the "thought-act" of the Senser. Now, its lexico-grammatical status as a wording indexically creates the existence-in-context of the presumed thought-act of the Senser. Semantically, the projected clause is a meaning because it does not correspond to any presupposed discourse event as its point of reference. The projected clause is not taken to be homologously related to some prior discourse event of which it is a record but to its conditions of use as a product. It is homologous to those processes whereby wordings are used to utter one's thoughts.

5. Free indirect discourse can also function as a meaning in which the intonation is encoded as a wording. The deictic standpoint in the projected clause is that of the Speaker of the projecting clause. The mood element in the projected clause is that of the Senser. The projected clause is a meaning that indexically creates the existence-in-context of the quasi-independent thought-act of the Senser. However, the imposition of the intonation of a wording indexically presupposes the projecting context of the Speaker, in which context the projected clause is uttered. Thus, this indexically presupposing/creative form paratactically projects a meaning, which presupposes at the lexico-grammatical level a homological relation of similarity to those processes and situation-types in which wordings are used to utter the thoughts of the Senser. At the semantic level, it is a textual product, assumed to be homologous to those processes whereby texts are used by Speakers to comment on propositions.

6. This is a reported thought, or a meaning. The deictic standpoint and the mood element in the projected clause are that of the Speaker. The projected clause is a meaning that indexically creates the existence-in-context of the Speaker's comment on (rather than reconstruction of) some discourse process. The projected clause is a fully semanticized metaphenomenon (Halliday, 1985: 229), which is homologous to those discourse processes and situation-types in which meanings are used modally as metalinguistic commentary. Thus, reported thought is homologous to the use of textual products modally to comment on experiential meanings. Here, the interpersonal meaning of the projected clause is most fully experientialized by the projecting clause.

In conclusion, the idealized cline from wordings to meanings, which we have used as the basis of the above analysis, provides some guidelines for the formalization of the kinds of homologies that are involved in the six types examined here. Wordings are formally homologous to the interpersonal here-and-now of conversational exchange, which is not the same as saying that they are identical to the exchange structure of dialogue. The interpersonal semantics of the projected clause in a wording is homologous to the contextual dynamics of conversational exchange structure through which language directly structures social action. In terms of our homology, wordings function to reconstruct discourse events such that the homological relation to the indexically presupposed discourse event entails minimal interpersonal distance from this event. The projected clause is typed by the meaning system as being in a relation of formal identity with some discourse event. A wording is then formally homologous to text-as-record as the reconstruction of some discourse process. Therefore, it takes a dynamic view of these discourse processes. At the other end of our proposed cline, meanings are homologous to the experiential textualization of linguistic tokens, taken to be contextually independent of the interpersonal here-and-now in which language is constitutive of social action. Interpersonal meaning is experientialized to the extent that language functions as a modal commentary on some discourse event. Meanings are homologous to the uses of textual products as metalinguistic commentary and generalization. Interpersonally, they are maximally distant from the here-and-now of conversation exchange, regardless of the experiential dimension's nearness to or farness from the social action. Meanings take a synoptic view of social process by virtue of the experientialization of interpersonal meaning. Here, the experiential meaning of the projected clause is formulated as a textual product, without regard to the conditions and processes that constitute it as a mode of social action and interaction.

Notes

1. Items such as Sayer, Senser, Actor, Process, Goal, and the like, which begin with a capital letter, are functional semantic labels. Class items (e.g., nominal group and verbal group) simply classify but do not represent relations between items in the grammar. Functional semantic labels describe

the part that a given class item plays in relation to other parts in some larger multivariate structural whole, for example, the clause. Functional semantic labels refer to the value an item has in some abstract grammatical relation on the syntagmatic axis. Thus *John knows* consists of two class items—*John,* classified as a nominal group, and *knows,* classified as a verbal group. However, these class labels say nothing about the grammatical relations between these items, which are functionally related in the more abstract structure Senser-Process. Thus class items realize functional semantic relations in syntagmatic sequences (Halliday, 1981: 29).

2. The concepts of covariate and multivariate relations are fully explained in chapter 5 (see also Halliday, 1981; Lemke, 1985b).

3. The notion of intertextual thematic formation is developed in chapters 5 and 6.

4. Abstract or superordinate intertextual thematic formations are glossed by the use of capital letters as here.

Chapter 3
Contextual Dynamics and the Recursive Analysis of Insider and Outsider Relations in Quoting and Reporting Speech

Halliday's account of the principal types of projection, which we examined in the previous chapter, provides an excellent survey of the various types of quoting and reporting relations and their various transforms. However, this account remains an idealized description because it does not explain how these lexico-grammatical forms are immanent in discursive practice. Halliday's semantically oriented functional grammar is useful for providing one of the important connections in my attempt in this chapter to relate an idealized functional lexico-grammatical description to its patterns of use in discourse. This must always be done against a background of idealized categories and relations as types. It is already apparent from the textual analysis in chapter 2 that textual patterns of use of these forms bring out distinctions and complexities that cannot be accounted for by limiting the discussion to idealized types. Now, both these perspectives must interpenetrate one another during the analytical process. This is an important dialectical principle that is, I think, insufficiently recognized in the humanities and social sciences. The idealized lexico-grammatical types provided by Halliday's account are important because they provide a framework for the investigation of these categories. This account enters into a dialectical relationship with the analysis of actually occurring instances in discourse. The dialectical relationship between this investigative framework and the analysis of textual patterns of use of these forms enacts the dialectical research method. The analysis of actual patterns of use is not proposed in order to "prove" the validity of the idealized categories. Rather, the relationship between the two constitutes the dialectic of theory and analytical practice, whereby theory has as its goal the producing of specific analytical practices.

The idealized background categories provide certain a priori classifications, which are then modified in the analytical phase. Throughout this second phase further distinctions and classifications are made that are not given in the idealized, a priori classifications. The latter help to formulate the background assumptions of the analysis. In the final stage of the analysis, when the conclusions are presented, these are largely determined by the developed analytic categories, but with reference to a background of idealized categories, which can be used to corroborate actual conclusions of the analysis. This dialectic has the advantage of enabling the analyst to distance him- or herself from the possibility of a predetermined analysis, because the text under investigation in chapter 2 is initially classified according to the idealized background categories and relations. If the analysis per se dominates, then one risks confirming a pregiven hypothesis. Furthermore, in the concluding stage it enables the analyst to distance him- or herself from the set of idealized categories and relations given at the beginning. This avoids merely reproducing these in the form of a scientific theory. The concluding stage of this process will be further developed in chapter 4 in connection with a formalism for the analytical representation of the contextual dynamics involved in quoting and reporting relations.

The Dialectical Interpenetration of Social Discourses in Quoting and Reporting Speech: Contextual Boundaries and Relations

In chapter 2 I discussed the problematic of the ontology of representation in Banfield's account of quoting and reporting relations. This ontology cannot adequately account for the dialectical nature of the mutually interpenetrating relations between the projecting and projected contexts. Volosinov (1973: 136–37) recognizes the importance of the fact that these relations are about the kind and degree of the interpenetration between one discursive positioned-practice, axiological orientation, and the textual voicings of these, and another. However, the tendency to anthropomorphism in many accounts—for example, Bronzwaer (1975) and Banfield (1973, 1978a, b)—perpetuates an ontology of representation in which the relations between subjects in the process of meaning exchange are seen as symmetrical. Quoting and reporting relations are not a mirror of social forms of dialogue. Rather, these relations actively constitute the dialectic of conflicting social discourses in textual practice. In this chapter and the following one I propose to explore how, within the bounded lexico-grammatical structure of a single utterance (cf. clause complex), quoting and reporting relations enact a dialectic of conflicting semantic and axiological orientations and discursive positioned-practices. In chapter 2 I pointed out that work is always performed by social agents in defining the boundaries between levels or between some subsystem-subsystem relations in the contextualization hierarchies of the social semiotic system. The ontology of representation is unable to recognize that the punctuation of the lexico-grammatical and semantic boundaries between the various forms of projecting and projected contexts is a dialectical operation involving both communication and metacommunication about the system of relations itself. The Imaginary symmetry that the ontology of representation projects onto these relations is unable to explain how the punctuation of these boundaries is not limited to the lower systemic levels of, say, lexico-grammatical form per se. It also occurs at the higher levels of semantic and contextual organization, as the quotation below from Volosinov penetratingly shows. This quotation is a useful starting point for developing the notion that quoting and reporting relations are, to use the words of Gregory Bateson (1973b: 377), a form of metacommunicative "mapping, translation or transformation." They involve processes of re-contextualization in which the concern is not with the reflection or representation of given discursive events, but with metacommunicative information about the dialectic of insider and outsider relations and practices and the joint or hybrid contexts these enact in the social semiotic system. Volosinov has formulated this question as follows:

> How, in fact, is another speaker's speech received? What is the mode of existence of another's utterance in the actual, inner-speech consciousness of the recipient? How is it manipulated there, and what process of orientation will the subsequent speech of the recipient himself have undergone in regard to it?
>
> What we have in the forms of reported speech is precisely an objective account of this reception. Once we have learned to decipher it, this document provides us with information, not about accidental and mercurial subjective psychological processes in the "soul" of the recipient, but about steadfast social tendencies in an active reception of other speakers' speech, tendencies that have crystallized into language forms. The mechanism of this process is located, not in the individual soul, but in society. It is the function of society to select and to make grammatical (adapt to the grammatical structure of its language) just those factors in the active and evaluative reception of utterances that are socially vital and constant and, hence, that are grounded in the economic existence of the particular community of speakers.
>
> There are, of course, essential differences between the active reception of another's speech and its transmission in a bounded context. These differences should not be overlooked. Any type of transmission—the codified variety in particular—pursues special aims, appropriate to a story, legal proceedings, a scholarly polemic, or the like. Furthermore, transmission takes into account a third person—the person to whom the reported utterances are being transmitted. This provision for

> a third person is especially important in that it strengthens the impact of organized social forces on speech reception. When we engage in a live dialogue with someone, in the very act of dealing with the speech received from our partner, we usually omit those words to which we are answering. We repeat them only in special and exceptional circumstances, when we want to check the correctness of our understanding, or trip our partner up with his words, or the like. All these specific factors, which may affect transmission, must be taken into account. But the essence of the matter is not changed thereby. The circumstances under which transmission occurs and the aims it pursues merely contribute to the implementation of what is already lodged in the tendencies of active reception by one's inner speech consciousness. And these tendencies, for their part, can only develop within the framework of the forms used to report speech in a given language. (Volosinov, 1973: 117)

The important distinction, which I discussed in the previous chapter, between text-as-record and text-as-product is relevant here. Text-as-record is a record of some discourse event – it may be a transcription of that discourse. Text-as-record is typed by the meaning system as being in a relation of homology to the discourse processes that produced it. It can be a textual record of those processes. More usually, however, a text is the product of some sociodiscursive practice(s). A text-as-product is homologous to the social functions and processes in and through which it is used in social practice. As Lemke (1984b: 79) points out, a product is used, whereas a record is read. The crucial point, according to Lemke, is the kinds, not the extent, of the homologies that are involved.

The long quotation from Volosinov cited above is concerned in the main with the relations of quoting and reporting speech and their contextualizations, which are homologous to text-as-record and text-as-product. Thus, the lexicogrammatical forms of quoting and reporting speech are homologous to the discourse processes in and through which they are used and/or produced, in the sense that these forms are the textual records and/or products of what Volosinov has called "steadfast social tendencies in an active reception of other speakers' speech." These relations of homology suggest that quoting and reporting relations and their various transforms are the prototype of metasemiotic acts and the site of much information about insider and outsider relations and categories, which is implicit in the kinds of homologies and the contextual dynamics involved. The dynamic and dialectical interrelations between the projecting and projected contexts and their various transforms thus provide a semiotic prototype for modeling the relations between theorist/analyst ("outsider") and participant ("insider") categories in the social semiotic system. These interrelations do not necessarily privilege either the outsider or the insider perspectives. Volosinov characterizes the joint contextualization dynamics of this process in the following way:

> The true object of that inquiry ought to be precisely the dynamic interrelationship of these two factors, the speech being reported (the other person's speech) and the speech doing the reporting (the author's speech). After all, the two actually do exist, function, and take shape only in their interrelation, and not on their own, the one apart from the other. The reported speech and the reporting context are but the terms of a dynamic interrelationship. This dynamism reflects the dynamism of social interorientation in verbal ideological communication between people (within, of course, the vital and steadfast tendencies of that communication). (Volosinov, 1973: 117)

The projecting and projected contexts do not function as if they are two separate and unrelated utterances that are simply brought together to describe the properties of the situation. This reminds us of Bourdieu's (1977: 81) strictures against the "occasionalist illusion," which I discussed in the previous chapter. The meaning relations of the projecting context are contextualized by their relations with the projected context and vice versa. The dynamic interaction between the two produces a joint system of meaning relations—an "interrelation," as Volosinov calls it, or a new "hybrid" context in Bakhtin (1981: 358–59)—that is different from either of the two sets of relations considered separately. The dyad transactions between the projecting and projected contexts are, in turn, contextualized by this new joint or hybrid system at a higher order of contextualization. The interrelations between the projecting and projected contexts are dialectically integrated into this new joint or hybrid contextualization. The advantage of this view is that the ideological and axiological positioning of the "outsider" theorist/analyst in the projecting context is not seen as uniquely contextualized by the meaning making practices of either the projecting or projected contexts in isolation from each other. Rather, it is contextualized in and through the dynamic interrelations of the new joint or hybrid context. This perspective provides us with much more than the possibility of a mere typology of the dynamic interrelations between projecting and projected contexts. It can provide us with important metasemiotic insights concerning the structuring of the relations between insider and outsider relations and categories in a given social semiotic system or some part of it. We shall explore below how this concerns the structuring and the punctuation of the contextual relations and boundaries between some theorist-system and some system of insider relations. The joint or hybrid contextualization that is enacted provides us with a metasemiotic prototype or model for a social semiotic praxis, whose goal is to include its own meaning making practices within the contextual domains within which it is made, used, and articulated. We shall further explore these issues in chapter 4, where I attempt to represent the joint or hybrid contextualization dynamics of these relations using the metaredundancy formalism first proposed by Bateson (e.g., 1973c).

Quoting and Reporting Relations as the Bounded Transmission of the Speech of the Other

The cline from wordings through to meanings, as we have already seen, can be related to the distinction between text-as-record and text-as-product. Wordings tend to be more iconic than meanings in that the quoting relation minimizes the experiential distance between its ideational-grammatical semantics and the indexically presupposed discourse event that is quoted. Meanings are less iconic in the sense that they are grammatically less "congruent" with some presumed discourse event. Experientially, they are grammatically more metaphorical, tending therefore toward increased experiential distance or abstraction (Martin, 1986: 241). Thus, the increased inconicity in wordings corresponds to a more dynamic modeling of the presupposed discourse event. The iconic relation in quoting relations does not mean there is a literal correspondence or isomorphism between the projected clause and a given discourse event. Rather, the iconic relation constitutes the set of conditions whereby the presupposed event can be reconstructed in the quoting context. In this sense, wordings can be related to the notion of text-as-record. Just as textual records are typed by the meaning system as being in a homological relation of identity to the original discourse processes of which they are a record, so are wordings typed as being in a homological relation of identity to some presupposed discourse event. Wordings take a dynamic rather than synoptic view of the presupposed event, which is concerned with the reconstruction of the processes that gave rise to the event. On the other hand, the increased tendency to grammatical metaphor in the encoding of meanings corresponds to a more synoptic modeling of the indexically created discourse event. (See Bourdieu, 1977; Lemke, 1984b: 74 for the distinction between synoptic and dynamic modes of analysis.) The tendency to experientialize interpersonal meaning is a form of grammatical metaphor (Halliday, 1985: chapter 10) in which the semantics of the clause is less iconic and hence more abstract. Meanings therefore are relatable to the notion of text-as-product. The indexically creative (rather than presupposing) function of meanings suggests that these are not concerned with the reenactment of some original discourse event. Rather, meanings are homologously related to the social practices and functions of their use-in-context. Meanings are a synoptic modeling of these practices and functions, which comment on rather than reconstruct sociodiscursive practices. This is also suggested by the fact that meanings are more hypothetical and modalized than wordings. Wordings indexically presuppose some original event, whereas meanings are treated as text in their own right (Halliday, 1985: 234).

These observations will serve to clarify Volosinov's characterization of quoting and reporting relations as the "transmission in a bounded context" of another's speech. Quoting and reporting relations are the selecting and making grammatical of "just those factors in the active and evaluative reception of utterances that are socially vital and constant and, hence, that are grounded in the economic existence of the particular community of speakers" (Volosinov, 1973: 117). Thus, the bounded transmission in lexico-grammatical form of another's speech is a metacommunication about the practices of some insider/outsider relations in the joint supersystem[1] of both insiders and outsiders. Quoting and reporting relations so conceived can be considered as a kind of microethnography of the meaning making practices of one's own culture or some part of it, where different situationally specific uses of these relations index the sociodiscursive positions of insiders and outsiders in different ways. If quoting and reporting relations are, as I suggested earlier, the metasemiotic prototype of much information about insider and outsider relations and categories, then the full relevance of the text-as-record and text-as-product homologies comes into view. The "double-voicedness" of the utterance, which is so central in the writings of Bakhtin and Volosinov, suggests that the bounded transmission of the speech of some other is a metalinguistic strategy by means of which the "alien word" of the other may be articulated or disarticulated in relation to the meaning making practices of some "self." Now, the examples in Tables 2.1 and 2.2 are, of course, no more than a typology of types. Nevertheless, they provide us, as I argued above, with a first, idealized notion of the kinds of relations and processes involved. Quoting and reporting relations, viewed as a microethnography of the meaning making practices of insider/outsider relations in one's own culture, are then a form of social semiotic praxis that views the practices of our own social semiotic system or some part of it through its own practices. These are metalinguistic strategies for the bounded articulation/disarticulation of the "alien" meaning making practices of the other, which reverses the traditional ethnographical problematic of the distance between the theorist/analyst (outsider) and participant (insider) relations and categories in the study of the alien meaning making practices of some other culture or social group. These metalinguistic strategies demonstrate that the presumed distance between the two sets of categories also occurs within the meaning making practices of one's *own* culture. The relations between the meaning making practices of self and other in the bounded lexico-grammatical context of quoting and reporting relations are the dialectical resolution of some insider/outsider relations in our own social semiotic praxis. Thus, these metalinguistic resources and their specific deployments ensure that we are both participants in (insiders) and observers of (outsiders) self/other dyadic transactions.

Hammersley and Atkinson (1983) propose two principal strategies for the interpretation of these two perspectives in ethnographic work: (1) "Everyone is a participant-observer, acquiring knowledge about the social world in the course of participation in it"; and (2) "Accounts are also important, though, for what they tell us about those who produce them. We can use the accounts given by people as evidence of the perspectives of particular groups or categories of actor to which they belong" (Hammersley and Atkinson, 1983: 105–6). The first formulation presumes that a shared participant-observer perspective can be constructed that allows the theorist/analyst to account for experience in ways that are recognized as meaningful by the participants. The second formulation presumes that the differences between observer and participant (cf. "alien") perspectives enable the recognition of alternative systems of meaning making practices, while remaining open to the risk of interpreting these practices ethnocentrically in terms of the sociodiscursive practices of some theorist-community. Now, both of these formulations reduce the problem to one of knowledge or perspective, as if these cognitive operations were divorced from the situationally specific meaning making practices of both observers and participants. Bourdieu acutely comments on this problem as follows:

> The arguments that have developed as much among anthropologists (ethnoscience) as among sociologists (ethnomethodology) around classifications and classificatory systems have one thing in common: they forget that these instruments of cognition fulfil as such functions other than those of pure cognition. Practice always implies a cognitive operation, a practical operation of construction which sets to work, by reference to practical functions, systems of classification (taxonomies) which organize perception and structure practice. Produced by the practice of successive generations, in conditions of existence of a determinate type, these schemes of perception, appreciation, and action, which are acquired through practice and applied in their practical state without acceding to explicit representation, function as practical operators *through which the objective structures of which they are the product tend to reproduce themselves in practices*. (Bourdieu, 1977: 97; emphasis added)

The two perspectives referred to by Hammersley and Atkinson presume either the essentially shared or the essentially alien nature of the cognitive operations and classificatory systems of insiders, but without demonstrating how these are the products of the practices of either insiders or outsiders or both in some new hybrid context. The distinction between text-as-record and text-as-product is again relevant here. Quoting and reporting relations are the textual records and/or products in and through which situationally specific metalinguistic accounts of social meaning making practices are produced. More precisely, they are, as we have seen, the bounded lexico-grammatical forms through which specific metasemiotic practices are enacted and realized. The further step is to inquire into the practices to which these forms are homologously related as textual records and/or products. We need to examine how these bounded lexico-grammatical forms function as microlevel social act-types (dyad-types), which are themselves contextualized by some restriction of the meaning potential of the contextual domains in which they operate. The cline between wordings and meanings once again suggests useful analytical distinctions. Meanings, in connection with the first of the distinctions made by Hammersley and Atkinson, relate to those metalinguistic accounting practices that project categories of the observer/theorist onto participants. Wordings, in connection with the second distinction, relate to metalinguistic practices of construal of the meanings of others. Once again, it should be emphasized that these are idealizations positioned at the two extremities of a simple cline.

These activities occur through the logico-semantic relations of projection at the level of the clause complex, whereby the projected clause is instated as a locution or an idea by the projecting clause (Halliday, 1985: 196). The typical assumptions made about the semantics of the projecting verbs in their clauses foreground specific tendencies in the reception of the speech of some other. These tendencies have important consequences for our argument. Here, we shall need to relate the logico-semantic relation of projection in Halliday's functional account to Silverstein's (1979: 200–201) formulation of the Whorfian "principle of referential projection." According to Silverstein this means that

> . . . we recognize the disjunction between the linguist's elaborate categorical analysis of language and the mechanisms of secondary rationalization put to the service of practical rationality. . . . [I]t is as though people quasi-consciously rationalize about situations based on "all the analogical and suggestive value of the patterns" (Whorf, [1941] 1956a: 147) of their language; that is, they objectify on the basis of analogies to certain pervasive surface-segmentable linguistic patterns, and act accordingly. This secondary rationalization of the linguistic system is, however, understood by the native speaker as a direct denotative relationship between surface forms and "reality out there." (Silverstein, 1979: 202)

At a later stage in the same paper, Silverstein goes on to explore some of the ways in which the meanings of projecting verbs are objectified in quoting and reporting relations (see Silverstein, 1979: 211–13). For instance, Silverstein characterizes the verbal process *say* in quoted speech as follows: "We might say with Whorf that the verb *say* is a lexical form, one of the selective cryptotypes of which is 'engage in language-specific speech activity with the resulting utterance signal ________.' Austin objectifies this meaning-category by declaring any so-describable action a 'phatic act.' Its resulting abstraction he calls a 'pheme,' that type which is reproduced framed in the utterance-token describing what went on" (1979: 212). Silverstein then contrasts this with the use of *say* in reporting speech or indirect quotation. Silverstein observes, "This use of *say* framing constructions would lead us to observe, with Whorf, that *say* is a lexical form, one of the selective cryptotypic categories of which is 'engage in referring-and-predicating linguistic activity with the resulting propositional content ________.' Austin objectifies this meaning category by declaring any so-describable action a 'rhetic act.'

Its resulting abstraction he calls a 'rheme,' that which is the specific propositional value characterized in the framed report construction" (1979: 212).

But what are the consequences of this line of reasoning, which Silverstein draws our attention to? The lexical form *say,* which is labeled as belonging to the grammatical class "verb," is then linked to its typical uses-in-context. Thus, in the two context-types of "direct" and "indirect" quotation, the verb *say* is observed to redound with the two meanings glossed by Silverstein above such that the propositional content, as Silverstein observes, is held to be constant. The next step is to objectify these meanings as types of social action with the labels "phatic" and "rhetic" that were deployed by Austin. The resulting objectification of these categories, which are taken to refer to classes of "phatic" and "rhetic" acts, means that the definitions of classes of social acts are taken to be the definitions of classes of metalinguistic terms, in this case verbs (see Halliday, 1983: 5). The terms are then said to have predictive power; that is, "phatic acts" (a situational category) are taken to be redundant with direct quotation (a linguistic category), and so on. As Silverstein shows, this gives rise to a folk-theory of "locution" versus "illocution" through the native speaker's objectification of his or her own metalinguistic glosses (cf. "phatic" and "rhetic" as illocutions) of lexico-grammatical forms (cf. verbs as locutions). Thus, the folk-theoretical distinction in our rhetorical tradition between direct and indirect quotation helps to maintain the distinction between the social act of *saying* (illocution) and what is referred to (locution) by assuming that what is referred to (the propositional content) is held constant even as the social action performed differs. The folk-theory upholds the ideologically functional disjunction between "meaning as reference" and "discourse as social action" through the objectification of the metalinguistic terminology as a typology of uses of these grammatical forms as particular speech acts. Such a theory certainly accords with the language user's sense that this distinction is made and makes sense in terms of their everyday uses of language. But what is the relevance of these metagrammatical rationalizations to social semiotic theory and practice? The problem arises when these metagrammatical rationalizations or folk-theoretical accounts ramify throughout our own theoretical and analytical practices as linguists and semioticians as if these were an adequate theoretical and explanatory framework (see also Reddy, 1979). Notions like "phatic" and "rhetic" acts are at too high a level of abstraction to be descriptively adequate, yet they are objectified so that scientific description itself embraces the folk-ideology of reference that is held by language users. Furthermore, the analytical classifications proposed by Austin (1962) constitute a typology of social acts as types. This is also true of the taxonomy of quoting and reporting relations that we have considered in Tables 2.1 and 2.2. With such typologies the analyst "wins the *privilege of totalization*" (Bourdieu, 1977: 106) that his or her theoretical practices make possible, but this "synoptic apprehension," as Bourdieu puts it, of sociodiscursive practices may well transform practice and its products in ways that ensure that the theorist cannot or does not ask how particular ideological formations are functional in a given social semiotic system or some part of it. The typology leads to the "theoretical neutralization" (Bourdieu, 1977: 106) of the ways in which, say, the distinction between locutions and illocutions may well exclude questions concerning the social semiotic functions of this very distinction in the maintenance of the most fundamental ideological axioms and assumptions in our own social semiotic system.

For example, Banfield's analysis of the center of consciousness in free indirect discourse begins with the distinction between the SELF or center of consciousness and the expressive (propositional) content that is attributable to the center of consciousness of a given expression (E). Thus, her analogical representationalism begins by making a distinction between structurally defined units or constituents (i.e., a nonembeddable, independent clause, containing some E) and criteria of meaning attribution (i.e., the center of consciousness). But what is not considered is the functional status of the criteria of meaning attribution presupposed by the theory. She does not demonstrate how the concept of a center of consciousness is produced in and through specific social semiotic relations and processes. Nor is the concept of *expression* (E) defined in anything other than purely formal structural, constituentlike terms. No functional semantic criteria for these constituents are specified. Banfield derives the notion of a center of consciousness, which is central to her criteria of meaning attribution, from two principal sources: (1) the practices of a humanistic, romantic ideology in literary criticism, and (2) the Cartesian autoconstitutive subject of transformational-generative linguistics. Both of these accounts presume an authoritative authorial/speaking presence (the autoconstitutive subject) and a unified, homogeneous linguistic norm (competence) that is shared by all speakers of a given language. Therefore, the notion of a center of consciousness is incapable of producing analyses that might reveal relevant heteroglossic differences, which are functional in articulating the plural, conflicting relations among voices in a given text. Banfield imposes a unifying principle of constituent structure, which is, however, unable to explain the plurifunctional nature of these semiotic forms in relation to different contextual domains and social practices. In Banfield's case, the "theoretical neutralization" of this plurifunctionality comes about through the projection of the ideology of reference onto a stable notion of constituent structure, which contains some expression or propositional content per se. In this way, the ideological notion of a fixed, stable center of consciousness or SELF, which is referred to and predicated by the expressive content of some E, is maintained.

A critical social semiotic theory and practice must go beyond such normative typologies and folk-rationalizations in order to explain how quoting and reporting relations function in specific domains of social practice in the social semiotic system. This requires that we go beyond the language user's sense that language use is functionally effective in the local attainment of aims, goals, and purposes in order to develop a functionalism of the uses and distribution of semiotic forms in their social contexts-of-use (see Silverstein, 1979: 206). Functional explanations of the second kind are concerned to show how criteria of meaning attribution may covary with higher-order contextual relations and processes. Such higher-order contextual relations are absent in Banfield's account in the sense that the higher-order contextual control of, say, the ideology of reference remains merely implicit in her analytical practice, that is, not itself a subject of metatheoretical discussion and evaluation. The functional criteria I have in mind are not interested in structural units defined as artifacts "impeccable as they are unreal" (Bourdieu, 1977: 108), divorced from specific social practices and their functions. We shall need to inquire into *which* quoting and reporting relations occur and *when*, in other words, in which contexts. These are defined, as we shall see below, in terms of (1) the relations between the projecting and projected contexts; (2) the relevant dyad-type in the transaction; (3) the thematic formations in operation; (4) shifts in deictic perspective of, say, Speaker, Sayer, and Source; (5) the heteroglossic relations of alignment, opposition, and conflict among textual voices; and (6) semantic register and social situation-type. Therefore, the transforms (recontextualizations) of the relations between the projecting and projected contexts in a given utterance can be analyzed in terms of changes in the whole system of contextualizing relations involved so that higher-order social semiotic relations and processes can be related to their textual patterns of realization.

As I suggested earlier, quoting and reporting relations are metalinguistic practices through which outsider relations and categories of the theorist/observer may be projected onto the meaning making practices of some other (wordings), or insider categories of participants may be construed by an outsider (meanings). The suggestion that quoting and reporting relations are a kind of prototypical microethnography of self-other dyad relations and transactions in our social semiotic system or some part of it has to do with these processes of projection and construal. However, the folk-theoretical distinction between locutions and illocutions in Austin's theory of speech acts and its correlative of a center of consciousness, which is "referred to," is likely to resist this alternative formulation. The ideology of reference here presumes that we all share the notion of a center of consciousness that can be referred to *as if* it preexisted linguistic and discursive practice. Thus, the referential projection can lead us to overstate the commonality or sharedness of our own and others' meaning making practices in a given social formation. We take for granted the shared assumption of an authentic prediscursive self that is expressed by language but ultimately referrable to as a prediscursive essence in the "really Real." This means that it is more difficult within, say, our own social semiotic system to break with the notion that there are functional differences and disjunctions between the meaning making practices of self and other in the social semiotic system or some part of it. In other words, we presume a commonality of meaning and experience, when in fact there are insulations between categories. This further entails that the realizations of these categories are themselves specialized to specific social practices (Bernstein, 1982: 313). More precisely, we can say in connection with our present line of argument that there are insulations between outsider and insider categories, which specialize to a particular voice the meanings and categories of both outsiders and insiders within the social semiotic. In our own social semiotic system it is therefore too easy to project the commonsense explanations and folk-theoretical rationalizations of some self onto the meanings and practices of some other, especially when these folk-theoretical rationalizations of linguistic practice are functional in maintaining the overall stability and hegemony of the dominant axioms and presuppositions of our culture. Potential differences, their insulations, and the disarticulation/rearticulation of these are thus neutralized and naturalized by their "synoptic apprehension" in and through a totalizing and objectifying ideology of reference.

Bakhtin's (1981) conception of social heteroglossia provides us with a very different way of talking about these relations. Social heteroglossia refers to the systematic and functional relations of opposition, conflict, alignment, and cooptation among the plurality of social meaning making practices (cf. positioned-practices) and their textual voicings in a given social semiotic system or some part of it. The heteroglossic relations among this plurality of differentially related positioned-practices work to foreground some possible intersections of social meaning making practices rather than others from the systemic meaning potential of the social semiotic. *Which* relations get foregrounded in textual productions and *when* (i.e., in which contexts) depends on the relations among specific positioned-practices, their textual voices, and the internal criteria of differentiation that are specialized to a given voice and its realizations. In terms of the dynamics of insider/outsider relations, these specializations entail that the specialized meanings and practices of a given voice constitute the means through which the meanings and practices of some other are construed. This systematically blinds us to the divergences among the meaning making practices of different groups within the *same* social formation. There are, as we shall see, different principles of classification and framing (Bernstein, 1982) of the relations between insider and outsider categories and practices. These differentially constructed and articulated principles of classification and framing can work, for instance, to maintain a strong insulation of the relations between different positioned-practices and their textual voicings in the discursive situation. This may take the form of divergent deictic standpoints and presuppositions, where the ideology of reference presumes a commonality or sharedness of perspective. Now, Bakhtin's notion of social heteroglossia suggests a quite different explanation. The gaps, insulations (Bernstein, 1982), and disjunctions (Foucault, 1971; Lemke, 1985a, b) enact a dialectic of system-stabilizing and system-changing functions. Therefore, positioned-practices and the textual voices that are specialized to them should not be reduced to the individual social agent, though they are enacted by them.

Positioned-practices are complex intersections of social meaning making practices, whose forms voice or articulate particular specializations and functional subdivisions within a given social semiotic system or some part of it. In broad terms, positioned-practices are functional intersections and complex unities comprised from the plural and stratified nature of the semantic registers of different social classes, age groups, gender classifications, professional jargons, subcultures, and so on, in a given social formation (see Bakhtin, 1981: 289). The concept of social heteroglossia does not presume a unified and given social totality in which positioned-practices and their voicings can be reduced to a necessary and inherent social logic. Nor does it presume a unitary, autoconstitutive subject in possession of its own consciousness. Instead, the shifting, contradictory nature of these relations is functional in the dynamic metastability of the patterned relations and transactions in and through which the social semiotic system is both maintained and changed. Bakhtin has used the concept of hybridization to conceptualize the social semiotic processes through which semantic registers and discourse genres are intersected and combined in both typical and atypical ways in the textual voicing of particular alignments and oppositions of positioned-practices:

> What is a hybridization? It is a mixture of two social languages within the limits of a single utterance, an encounter, within the arena of an utterance, between two different linguistic consciousnesses, separated from one another by an epoch, by social differentiation or by some other factor.
>
> Such mixing of two languages within the boundaries of a single utterance is, in the novel, an artistic device (or more accurately, a system of devices) that is deliberate. But unintentional, unconscious hybridization is one of the most important modes in the historical life and evolution of all languages. We may even say that language and languages change historically primarily by means of hybridization, by means of a mixing of various "languages" co-existing within the boundaries of a single dialect, a single national language, a single branch, a single group of different branches or different groups of such branches, in the historical as well as paleontological past of languages—but the crucible for this mixing always remains the utterance.
>
> The artistic image of a language must by its very nature be a linguistic hybrid (an intentional hybrid): it is obligatory for two linguistic consciousnesses to be present, the one being represented and the other doing the representing, with each belonging to a different system of language. Indeed, if there is not a second representing consciousness, if there is no second representing language-intention, then what results is not an *image* [*obraz*] of language but merely a *sample* [*obrazec*] of some other person's language, whether authenticated or fabricated.
>
> The image of a language conceived as an intentional hybrid is first of

> all a *conscious* hybrid (as distinct from a historical, organic, obscure language hybrid); an intentional hybrid is precisely the perception of one language by another language, its illumination by another linguistic consciousness. An image of language may be structured only from the point of view of another language, which is taken as the norm. (Bakhtin, 1981: 358–59)

Bakhtin's formulation here continues to speak the discourses of humanism and anthropomorphism in his efforts to construct an alternative discourse about our social meaning making practices. For example, Bakhtin refers to the presence of "two linguistic consciousnesses," which he says are "represented" in the same utterance. In the conceptual framework of social semiotic theory, hybridization is better understood as being analogous to the linguistic processes of creolization whereby different languages or, more restrictedly, different semantic registers intersect and combine to create an "interlanguage," which has properties different from either of the two languages taken separately (Ellis, 1984). As we shall see, the interrelation of the two (or more) semantic potentials in the new hybrid utterance is resolved at still higher orders of contextualization. This is so in the sense that the hybrid form is not a merely passive reflection of the new situation. Rather, as Volosinov puts it, "*the difference between situations determines the different meanings* of the same verbal expression. Therefore the verbal expression—the utterance—does not only passively reflect the situation. It is its *resolution,* [it] becomes its *valuational summing up* and, at the same time, the necessary condition for its further ideological *development*" (Volosinov, 1980: 113; emphasis in original). The resolution at higher orders of contextualization of this dialectic can skew or bias the hybrid semantic potential that is created in ways that may variously allow one or the other voice to dominate. A dominant "monologic" resolution articulates the meaning making practices of all other voices to a single dominant situational principle in such a way that the differences between competing voices may not be recognized.

Quoting and reporting relations, as we have seen in terms of our "microethnography" of insider/outsider relations, are strategies of articulation, rearticulation, disarticulation, and co-optation of the often contradictory and conflictual dialectic between the two perspectives. Quoting and reporting relations are a metalinguistic strategy or praxis that is deployed to "get above the fray" (Lemke, 1985a) of the conflicting voices in the form of some higher-order contextual resolution. This metasemiotic perspective constitutes an outsider's recontextualization of these relations in ways that articulate, rearticulate, disarticulate, or co-opt the relations between the two perspectives. The clause complex relations between the projecting and projected clauses constitute a dyad structure, which is a microlevel social action sequence, functionally interpreted. Therefore, we are concerned with the dialogic characteristics of the dyad as a form of meaning exchange. The func-

Figure 3.1. Dyad-type; context of reception

tional interpretation of the dyad as a microlevel social action sequence takes place along two principal dimensions, which distinction gets blurred in Volosinov's (1973: 122) account of the "actively responsive reception" of the meanings of the other. First, we shall refer, along with Volosinov, to the "bounded transmission" at the level of the clause complex of the "received speech" (Volosinov, 1973: 123) of the other. Thus, the projecting clause constitutes the context of reception of the Sayer/Senser, and the projected clause constitutes the received speech of the other. Second, we shall refer to the situational context of transmission of this bounded lexico-grammatical form whereby we refer to the Speaker's (not the Sayer's) uttering of this bounded form to some addressee in a given context of utterance. This second level constitutes the situational resolution or valuation referred to by Volosinov (see above). At the level of the bounded lexico-grammatical form, the dyad can be schematized as shown in Figure 3.1.

At the level of the context of utterance of this form, the relation in Figure 3.1 is resolved in a context of transmission between an addresser and an addressee (Figure 3.2).

These simplifying diagrams are not intended to represent the reality of the communication process. They are proposed in order to distinguish analytically the two levels of dyadic exchange that are involved in quoting and reporting speech. Volosinov's repeated reference to the "speaker" (e.g., 1973: 123) does not adequately clarify the functional semantic distinction between Speaker and Sayer/Senser. These are functional semantic labelings of grammatical class items (see Halliday, 1985: 30–32), which are necessary distinctions at the level of the dyad as social act-type. Nevertheless, the anthropomorphism that these functional semantic labels entail should not result in projecting the ideology of reference so that we assume that these functional labels refer to real human agents. The functional labels designate the relationally defined semiotic *valeur* of these terms in the overall action sequence. The anthropomorphism of these labels should not obscure the ways in which the projecting and projected contexts articulate specific discursive positioned-practices as textual voices.

The additional complexities entailed by the arguments I have introduced here require that we examine more closely Silverstein's (1979: 212) claim that the propositional content stays the same in transforming from direct to indirect

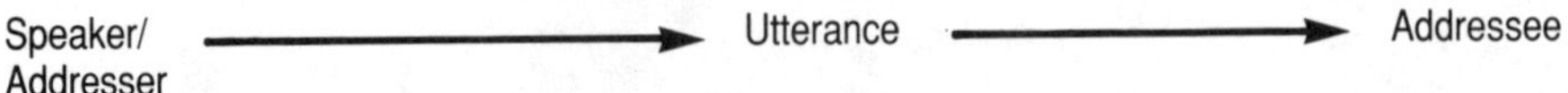

Figure 3.2. Dyad-type; context of transmission as situational resolution

speech. This presumes that this content is construable or made meaningful in the same way in spite of systematic and functional differences in the meaning making practices of, say, insiders and outsiders. It assumes that self and other construe the same content in the same way, as if propositional content or experiential meaning can be so easily separated from the other functional components of the situation. The notion of a given, invariable content is assumed, yet it seems more useful to examine, say, the differential indexing of experiential meaning in relation to the various perspectives involved. This claim also presupposes the reversibility of these transforms, when in fact we have already remarked that semantic reversibility is not necessarily entailed by lexico-grammatical reversibility. Before we consider the deictic relativity that is involved in these transformations, I shall briefly consider the question of autorecursion in theorist-analyst representations of the praxis of insider/outsider relations. Lemke (1984b: 72) points out that "a theory of sociosemiotic systems cannot avoid self-reference." Instead, self-reference must take place between the system of contextualizing relations (the metasystem) and the system of actions and transactions (the supersystem) in which meanings are always enacted and materially embodied. Thus, as Lemke (1984b: 73) shows, it is praxis that "connects supersystem and metasystem, and must include itself in its own domain." Lemke has formulated the problem of praxis as representation as follows:

> An open-ended contextualization hierarchy (cf. the infinite regress of contexts of contexts of . . .) is not representable in a closed formalism. Again we need to recall that this open-endedness in the metasystem is only possible because each level of the metasystem hierarchy expresses a relationship in the hierarchy of supersystem transactions. So it is only a formalization of some ensemble of supersystem transactions that can hope in turn to represent a SSS [social semiotic system]. These supersystem transactions can only be the praxis of the theorist, of which the theory is a (partial) formalization, but which *as praxis* is the fullest possible representation of the SSS. (Lemke, 1984b: 73)

What are the consequences of self-reference or autorecursion for a social semiotic theory concerned with the praxis of its own representations of insider/outsider relations in quoting and reporting speech? Let us return to the question of Banfield's analogical representationalism. As we noted above, Banfield postulates a posteriori an analogy or isomorphism between propositional content and some center of consciousness or SELF. This is parallel to the attributing of "inner" mental states and intentions to the other in, say, spoken dialogue. The problem arises in part because Banfield applies the same metarules of contextualization to both spoken dialogue and free indirect discourse. One set of rules is used to mispunctuate the levels of relations involved without apparently noticing the internal inconsistencies that this representational fallacy generates. But suppose that we shift the emphasis to quoting and reporting relations as praxis rather than as the representation or reflection of a unitary center of consciousness? This brings us back to the dialectical duality of the metasystem-supersystem relations discussed by Lemke. The open-endedness of these relations entails the autorecursion referred to above. But this does not mean, properly formulated, that a given relation is defined in terms of itself. Rather, the dialectical and hierarchical nature of metasystem-supersystem relations produces, at the various levels of the hierarchy, sets of contextual interdependencies between the metasystem and the supersystem that covary with relations on higher or lower levels. The recursive ordering of the hierarchy of contextual levels involved in this open-ended representation of the praxis of the theorist has been commented on by van den Daele in the following way:

> Dialectical logic is hierarchical in form and recursive in application. The content of the initial triad, self, object, and coordination, is reflected at successive levels to yield a pyramidal expansion of the structure of self, object, and coordination. This process is neither cyclic nor linear, but "spiralic, meaning that it returns to the same element on a new level" (Kosok, 1972, p. 274). Since content and orientation are interdependent, reflective orientation is preserved but with a successive enrichment of internal structure.
>
> If successive reflections are designated by order and if each reflection generates an additional level of reflective abstraction, then the first-order reflection differentiates the primitive structure or network of subjective, objective and coordinative experience. The second-order reflection operates on these structures to establish an expanded set of interdependencies, and so on for each level. Successive reflection increases both the breadth and the depth, or scope and generality, of interpretative distinctions.
>
> The union of a mode of orientation, subjective, objective, or coordinative, with a level of reflection, first order, second order . . . , yields an indefinite recursive set of stages. Since development is spiralic, each successive level of interpretation reintroduces rationales organized around the primary orientations. The problem of the self, the world, and the relation of the self to the world are reconsidered at each new level of interpretation. (van den Daele, 1975: 135–36)

Lemke's emphasis on praxis should make it clear that the abstract and general principles involved in the hierarchical and dialectical analysis of contextual relations should not be understood as referring to a necessary or pregiven hierarchy of formal relations. These relations are nonteleological and are conditional on the praxis of some theorist-community and its hybridizations with a given sub-ensemble of meaning making practices in some social semiotic system. The analytical formalism does not therefore suppose either the universalization of its formal categories or a closed formalism that is unable to account for contradictions in the system of relations.

In connection with the dyad-types proposed above, we can now formulate the principle of the relativity of deictic relations in the metalinguistic quoting and reporting of insider/outsider relations and categories. The principle of autorecursion allows us to build the following perspectives into our theoretical representation of the sets of relations involved at each level:

1. The meanings and practices of the other (i.e., the Sayee) in the projected clause;
2. The Sayer/Senser's perspective on the other in the projecting clause;
3. The Speaker's perspective on the Sayer/Senser's perspective on these meanings and practices;
4. The Sayer/Senser/other's perspective on the Speaker's perspective on the Sayer/Senser's meanings and practices;
5. The Addressee's perspective on the Speaker's perspective on the meanings and practices of the Sayer/Senser;
6. The Speaker's perspective on the Addressee's perspective of the meanings and practices of the Sayer/Senser;
7. The Speaker's perspective on the Addressee;
8. The Addressee's perspective on the Speaker.

The nesting of these levels, which is entailed by the recursion, may be diagrammatically represented as shown in Figure 3.3.

Figure 3.3 is, of course, a reification of these relations as praxis. It also suggests a symmetry at each level of the self/other dyad transactions that does not necessarily exist in discursive practice. The broken lines represent merely implicit transactions whose logic is recoverable from the operation of successively higher orders of contextualization in the hierarchy. This is based on the notion of "the restitution of continuity in the subject's motivations" (Lacan, [1956] 1968: 20). Lacan's discussion of the "transindividual" nature of the unconscious can be reconstituted in the conceptual framework of social semiotic theory in order to "reestablish the continuity," as Lacan puts it, of the dyad transactions potentially implicated at each level in the contextual hierarchy. Now, I am not proposing a psychoanalytic reading of quoting and reporting relations. Nevertheless, the frequently implicit nature of insider/outsider transactions in quoting and reporting speech seems to be an example of what Lacan has referred to in quite another context as "resonance in the communicating networks of discourse" (see Lacan

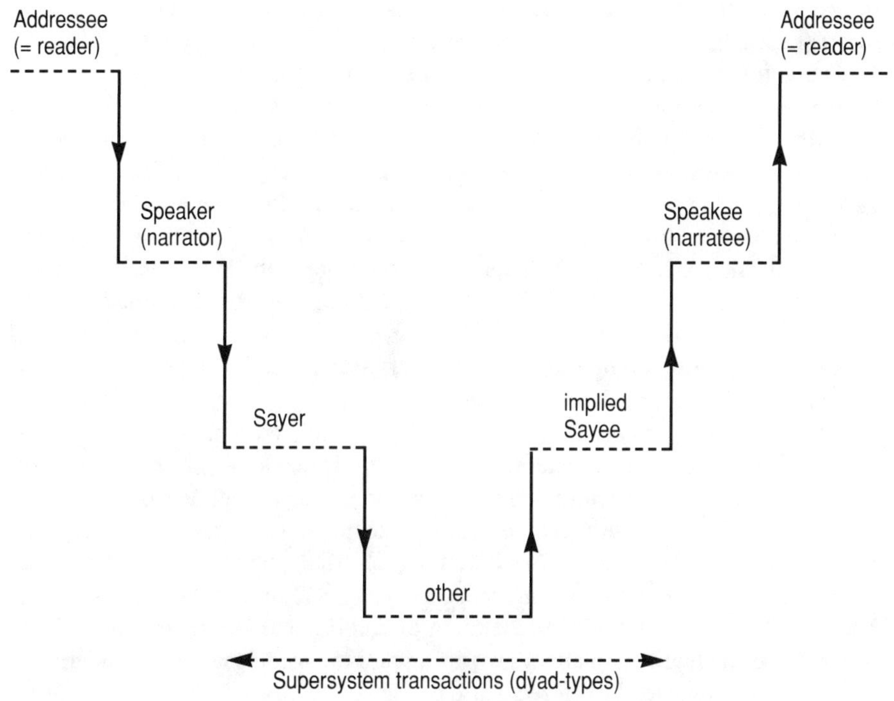

Sayer = projecting clause; other = projected clause; implied Sayee = other's view of Sayer; Speakee = view of narratee

Figure 3.3. Nesting of levels entailed by autorecursion

[1956] 1968: 27). In the present context, I take this to be relevant to the ways in which the supersystem contexts at all levels in the hierarchy dialectically integrate self into a relationship with some other, defined as a contextual relation, which may be implicit or explicit. Further, Lacan shows that this dyad is not reducible to a simple binary relation. Nor should it be reduced to a teleological necessity as in Hegelian dialectics (see chapter 2). The autorecursive nature of these relations means that we cannot adequately talk about insider/outsider or self/other relations in terms of a simple dyad per se. The regression of contexts means that the propositional content or experiential meaning in, say, the projected clause is not subject to the certainties of a simple, two-way exchange between two monads. The notion of "resonance" and the parallel notion of "reverberation" (*riverberazione*) in di Giovanni (1984) additionally suggest how a presumably stable, pregiven content is, in reality, subject to the relativization of this content to the plurality of contextual interdependencies that the open-ended, recursive, and hierarchical nature of these relations entails. Banfield's analogic representationalism, on the other hand, reduces to the monologic and hence normative logic of a contextually presupposed "referentiality," structurally isolable.

The autorecursion of the contextual hierarchy demonstrates that "self" and "other" are not simply constituents of an already given situation. The regression of levels of contextualization generates a resonating network of probabilities, which are always open to further regression in the orders of relations involved. However, for the purposes of a given analysis, and with practical limits on our ability to construct further orders of relations, the regression can always be closed off. This means, as in Figure 3.3, that the relevant contextual relations can be formalized to a given level of analysis. Thus, the metalinguistic resolution of some insider/outsider relation in quoting and reporting speech is similar to the map/territory relation proposed by Bateson (1973d: 153). Metalinguistic rules of contextualization at higher levels in the contextual hierarchy specify *which* insider and outsider categories and relations, and *how* they are related at any given level. The map/territory relation is a metasemiotic one that follows the same general principle of autorecursion such that the map, in the words of van den Daele (1975), "increases both the breadth and the depth, or scope and generality, of interpretative distinctions." The situational resolution of the dialectic of insider and outsider relations in quoting and reporting speech is just such an autorecursive mapping operation. This means that the resolution of conflict and contradiction at higher orders of contextualization always works toward the foreclosure of the relativization process. However, this foreclosure can never be absolute, monologic, or totally determinate because the resonance or reverberation in the contextual relations involved always entails the potential for the restructuring of the system of relations. A simplified illustration is given below of the deictic relativity, and hence the resonance, that the hybridization of the projecting and projected contexts in free indirect discourse involves. This example is restricted to an analysis of the two levels proposed in Figures 3.1 and 3.2. The following example is taken from the textual extract that was analyzed in chapter 2: *he was sad*, *she said*. The two levels of analysis are as follows:

1. **Context of Reception.** The projecting clause indexically presupposes the deictic standpoint of the Sayer. In the projected clause (1) the mood element indexically creates the relativized other in the context of received speech, and (2) the experiential meaning indexically presupposes the standpoint of the Sayer.
2. **Context of Bounded Transmission.** This indexically presupposes the univocal social context of reception of the Speaker.

The contextual relativity at the first order, along with its situational resolution at the second order, does not constitute a simple two-way dyad, but a resonating network of relations in which its resulting metalinguistic resolution is always incomplete. It is, to borrow the Freudian terminology, a "compromise solution" in which the hybrid combination of common and discrete components at the first level renders incomplete their transformation and displacement at the level above. The metalinguistic resolution or compromise, which the hybrid combination produces, is always problematic. Hybridization, as Bakhtin shows, is a powerful metaphor for showing how formal linguistic models are not adequate as models of social meaning making. Free indirect discourse is not reducible to a dyadic event structure at the first level of analysis. It is, rather, enacted in and through a plurality of social meaning making practices, which it simultaneously affirms and seems to deny on the level of manifest formal structure and continuity. However, free indirect discourse is a transform (recontextualization) of quoting speech in which the dialogic interplay of sameness and difference involves the displacement of conflicting social discourses onto their higher-order metalinguistic resolution or "summing up," which is always embedded in some social praxis. The two levels of analysis I have proposed above may serve as the basis of a praxis-oriented conception of insider and outsider relations and categories in quoting and reporting speech. These are the prototypes for a model of a social semiotic praxis in which social actions (1) are about something, that is, they indexically presuppose and/or entail some object of reference; (2) are doing something to someone by someone in the sense that they dialogically implicate some self and some other; (3) are always constituted in and through wider formations of (inter)textual meaning relations that resonate both synchronically and diachronically in a constant dialectic between semiotic forms and their uses in patterned social meaning making; and (4) have metasemiotic strategies and resources for the higher-order punctuation or framing of semiotic forms in ways that control the organization of (1) through (3) above. In the following chapter, I shall attempt to formalize the dynamics of quoting and reporting speech in terms of an open-ended hierarchy of contextualizing relations that illustrates the autorecursive and dialectical character of these. This will lead to further clarification and exploration of the four points I have outlined here.

Note

1. The analysis prioritizes the supersystem level of, say, A-B transactions over the level of subsystems A and B (Lemke, 1984a: 31).

Chapter 4
Redundancy, Coding, and Punctuation in the Contextual Dynamics of Quoting and Reporting Speech

A Metaredundancy Formalism for the Representation of the Contextual Dynamics of Quoting and Reporting Speech: Hybridization as Social Semiotic Praxis

We have considered in previous chapters the notion of the clause as the microlevel realization of a social act-type. The clause, functionally interpreted, is a mode of social action, which presupposes and/or entails a plurality of indexical values in its multiple contexts-of-use. This characterizes the dialogic nature of the utterance as a mode of social action and transaction. Volosinov, as we have seen in chapter 3, has described the lexico-grammatical forms of quoting and reporting speech as "an objective account"[1] of "the active reception of another's speech and its transmission in a bounded context" (1973: 117). Volosinov's description suggests how we require a metasemiotic awareness of these forms as modes of social action and transaction. Furthermore, it suggests how semiotic forms, as the realization of social actions, are to varying degrees the "objective" externalization of some metasemiotic consciousness, which is implicated in linguistic practice. The dialectical and recursive ordering of successive levels of contextualization, which we shall examine in some detail in this chapter, entails an exploration of the extent to which such metasemiotic reflections on each level in the contextual hierarchy are able to apprehend their indexical entailments and/or presuppositions as well as the extent to which these functionally covary with the forms used. This means that our ability as analysts to abstract the generally implicit rationale of insider and outsider relations and categories from the folk-ideological rationalizations of these in actual use depends on the extent to which we are able to generate what van den Daele (1975: 136) calls additional "levels of reflective abstraction" in our own metasemiotic awareness of these forms as the realization of social actions.

I shall now develop a formalism for the representation of the structural, dialectical, and recursive dimensions of the contextualizing relations in quoting and reporting speech. The analysis is structural because it is concerned with the patterned relations among "entities" rather than the entities per se. These patterned relations comprise a context for the construing of meaning in our social meaning making practices. The central premise of structuralism is that meaning is not reducible to "things" or "entities," but is enacted in and through patterned relationships. However, we need to go still further and explore the relations of relations of relations . . . and so forth in a recursively ordered hierarchy of contextualizing relations, which is potentially, if not necessarily in practice, an infinite regress (see Bateson, 1973d; Wilden, 1980: 329; Lemke, 1984a, b). The analysis is dialectical because we shall be concerned with the fact that quoting and reporting relations involve a plurality of social meaning making practices that enact conflicting and contradictory relations within the bounded lexico-grammatical context of quoting and reporting speech. We shall be concerned with the various strategies of punctuation in and through which these conflicting relations are resolved at some higher level in the hierarchy of contextual relations. The starting point for this analysis is that contextualizing relations are redundancy relations to increasingly higher orders in a recursively ordered hierarchy of contextualizing relations. The concept of redundancy is derived from the work of Bateson (e.g., 1973c) and Lemke (1984a, b) and will be developed in specific ways here. It is a concept that I shall use at various stages throughout this book. Bateson (1973c: 103–4) proposes a "metaslash" formalism, which he uses to formalize the redundancy relations between, for example, two entities a and b. The redundancy relation between a and b is formally represented as a/b, which means that "a is redundant with b." Bateson explains the concept of redundancy in the following way:

> "Meaning" may be regarded as an approximate synonym of pattern, redundancy, information and "restraint," within a paradigm of the following sort:
>
> Any aggregate of events or objects (e.g., a sequence of phonemes, a painting, or a frog, or a culture) shall be said to contain "redundancy" or "pattern" if the aggregate can be divided in any way by a "slash mark," such that an observer perceiving only what is on one side of the slash mark can *guess*, with better than random success, what is on the other side of the slash mark. We may say that what is on one side of the slash contains *information* or has *meaning* about what is on the other side. Or, in engineer's language, the aggregate contains "redundancy." Or, again, from the point of view of a cybernetic observer, the

> information available on one side of the slash will restrain (i.e. reduce the probability of) wrong guessing. (Bateson, 1973c: 103–4)

Bateson shows that a is redundant with b in the sense that the information contained in, say, a allows us to predict some or all of the information contained in b. This process is never entirely reversible, for the redundancy relations at any given level in the contextual hierarchy always covary with other levels of relations in a still wider system of contextual relations, whose conflicting, dialectical character means there is never any perfect or symmetrical match between levels. We can express this still more precisely by saying that the redundancy relations between a and b are not about the relations between two separate entities but about the probability of their copatterning in some still higher-order relation(s)[2] with which they covary. The structure of a/b relations is a copatterning of meaningful relations, which are themselves defined, interpreted, or typed by their copatterning with relations at still higher orders. The copatterning of the relata a and b to form the meaningful relation a/b means that the requisite diversity of a and b as separate "entities" is greater than the diversity of the structure a/b. Redundancy entails constraints on the kinds of patterned relations that can occur between some a and some b. These constraints are not represented in the structure a/b per se, for this amounts to what both Bateson and Lemke refer to as a first-order redundancy relation. The structure or patterned relation a/b is in turn redundant with some higher-order contextual relation c. The recognition or construal of the patterned a/b relations requires some still higher-order contextual relation c. The relation between a/b and c is a second-order redundancy relation, which is written a/b//c. This reads "c is redundant with the redundancy of a and b" (Lemke, 1984a: 36). The higher-order redundancy relation c constrains (contextualizes) the *types* of patterned relations that are regularly and typically construed in the lower-order relation a/b. It seems likely that the redundancy relations between a/b and c require that c represent the basic types of patterned relations in a/b, though certainly not all of the possible diversity of a/b relations. If a/b enacts certain types of regular and systematically coded relations, then c must contain corresponding relations with which the lower-order relations are redundant. The use of the slash as a metaredundancy marker is a formalism for representing the hierarchical nature of the orders of relations involved. Each order of relations specifies, as van den Daele (1975: 136) puts it, "an expanded set of interdependencies" at each of the levels involved (see chapter 3). The application of this formalism in the analysis that follows will show that it is often necessary to use third- and still higher-order metaredundancy relations in order to generate the various levels of abstraction that the analysis presumes.

Lemke (1984a: 36–37) proposes a "repertory" of readings in connection with this formalism. These can be summarized as follows: (1) the structure of a/b relations is related in the context c; (2) the relation a/b is of the type c; (3) the relation a/b is formed by rule c. The first and third readings are most relevant for our analysis. The implications of c as a relation at a higher order of logical typing than the patterned a/b relation is important for the multilevel contextual approach to social meaning making I am developing here. As a provisional assumption, I shall say that the a/b transactions, at the level of first focus, have the structure of a dyad in some context c. The level of first focus refers to what a given analysis defines as the "entities" for the purposes of that analysis. In principle, these, too, can be further analyzed as relations (see van den Daele, 1975: 136; Lemke, 1984a: 35). In the present analysis, the "entities" will be taken to be the projecting and projected clauses. These are, for the purposes of the present analysis, the "primitive structures" (van den Daele, 1975: 136) or the observed phenomena at the level of first focus. Thus, the entities or primitive structures are restricted to clause rank constituents in the present analysis. The different types of quoting and reporting relations will be thought of as different kinds of dyad structures, which can be seen as different kinds of relations between the projecting and projected contexts (see chapter 3) at the level of first focus. The projecting and projected clauses at this level combine as parts in relation to a larger whole, which enacts their *supersystem* contextualization structure. This then is the dyad-type at the next order of contextualization in the hierarchy. The dyad dialectically and structurally integrates (resolves) conflicting relations at the level below into some higher-order contextual relation (see Lemke, 1984a: 39). The structure of the dyad represents the horizontal contextualization of the dyad transactions that take place between the projecting and projected contexts. There is also, as Lemke shows, a *metasystem* contextual hierarchy in which the "entities" at the level of first focus are paradigmatically contrasted with alternative sets of choices. The metasystem is thus represented vertically. These two dimensions of contextualization are dialectically interdependent on each other.

The general aim of the analysis will be to relate the a/b dyad relations of the projecting and projected contexts to successively higher orders of contextualizing relations. The dialectical relations between one level and the next in the contextualization hierarchy constrain the possible meaning relations that can occur in the dialectical duality of supersystem and metasystem contextualization at any given level. As a first attempt at presenting these relations, I shall refer to the first example given in Halliday's summary of the principal types of projection (see Table 2.2). This is an example of a direct quote: *"It is so," he said.* In this preliminary analysis, I shall build up the various levels of the hierarchy one step at a time in order to explain the relations at each level. Halliday's summary is an idealized typology, and so it will not be possible to supply full contextual information at each level. Instead, I shall concentrate on the types of relations that are involved at each level.

At the level of first focus we have a structure a_i/b_j, where a_i is a projected clause (received speech) : wording : deictic orientation : Sayer, and b_j is a projecting clause (context of reception) : locution : verbal process : deictic orientation : Speaker. At the next level, the dyad a/b is in turn redundant with E′, that is, a/b//E′, where E′ specifies the logico-semantic relations at the level of the clause complex. In this example, E′ specifies a logico-semantic relation of parataxis, which links two independent clauses. A further level specifies that a/b//E′ is redundant with d, where d is a particular dyad-type, which has the form a/b relations at E′. In this example, the dyad structure can be glossed as direct quote. This models the dyad relation in the following way: the Sayer of a in the context of the received speech is projected through the third person perspective of b; b refers to the third person perspective of *he* as outsider in the context of reception; b projects a as insider perspective through the outsider perspective of b. The structure so far defined is contextualized at a still higher order by some metalinguistic rule of indexicality, namely, INDEX, which specifies the indexical relations between the message and some referent relation in the context of transmission. At this level, we are concerned with the redundancy relations between what Bateson (1973e: 390) calls "message *plus* external phenomena." This indexes the existence-in-context of a specific kind of homological relation between the bounded form as metalinguistic resolution of the dynamics of some insider and outsider perspectives and the social processes and/or products that they metalinguistically reconstruct and/or comment on. In the present account these relations do not involve any referential notion of representation or reflection. Instead, Bernstein's (1982: 318) notion of *referential relations* will be borrowed and adapted as a way of talking about the kinds of meanings that are indexed and the type and degree of the punctuation between categories in quoting and reporting speech. The various quoting and reporting relations (as messages) are typed at this level as having an indexical/homological correspondence with some set of referential relations in their contexts-of-use. This message-referential relation correspondence is not typed in the metasystem as one of formal identity with some previously occurring utterance-token. This relation can be glossed as follows: the first-person Speaker in the projecting context b, at time of speaking t_{sp}, quotes the Sayer in a at time of saying t_r in the projected context, where b refers to a's specific situation from the deictic standpoint of a as insider rather than interpreting it in relation to outsider (b) categories. The analysis so far may be formalized as a/b//E′///d////INDEX . . . The next level specifies the set of semantic register-types (i.e., R) that are interrelated in the new joint or hybrid context. Here we have the plurality of sociosemantic orientations that voice specific positioned-practices in the social semiotic system. These converge and conflict in the bounded context of the quoting relation. Thus, a/b//E′///d////INDEX/////R_1, R_2 . . .

At the next order of relations in the metaredundancy contextualization hierarchy we can specify the particular configurations of social semiotic coding orientations that are in operation. To clarify this concept, here is one of Bernstein's more recent statements on the concept of code:

> The general definition of codes which has been used since Bernstein 1977 and developed in Bernstein 1981 emphasises the relation between meanings, realisations and context. *Thus a code is a regulative principle, tacitly acquired, which selects and integrates relevant meanings, forms of realisations and evoking contexts.* It follows from this definition that the unit for the analysis of codes is not an abstracted utterance or a single context, but relationships *between* contexts. Code is a regulator of the relationships *between* contexts and through that relationship a regulator of the relationships *within* contexts. What counts as a context depends not on relationships *within,* but on *relationships between,* contexts. The latter relationships, *between*, create boundary markers whereby specific contexts are distinguished by their specialised meanings and realisations. Thus if code is the regulator of the relationships between contexts and, through that, the regulator of the relationships within contexts, then code must generate principles for distinguishing between contexts (classification) and principles, for the creation and production of the specialised relationships within a context (framing). (Bernstein, 1986b: 13–14; emphasis in original)

Bernstein is right to draw attention to the inadequacy of abstracted utterances for the analysis of social semiotic coding orientations. Certainly, this stricture applies to the example I am analyzing here. This is no more than an abstracted type of utterance. However, the purpose of the present analysis is to specify in the metaredundancy formalism just what the orders of relations look like at successive levels in the contextual hierarchy. There is no suggestion that coding orientations can be analyzed on the basis of strictly local criteria, such as the single clause or clause complex. We shall further develop the notion of coding orientation in relation to globally foregrounded copatternings of meaning relations in chapters 6 through 8. If the codes differentially distribute both the sociosemantic potential of different register-types and the access of social agents to these, then we can say, using Bernstein's terminology, that the coding orientations differentially classify and frame insider and outsider relations and categories both within and between contexts. The differential distribution of the sociosemantic potential within and between contexts means that the positioned-practices and their voicings, which are specialized to the particular relations within and between contexts, construct specific heteroglossic relations of alignment, opposition, conflict, and co-optation among voices in the systems of heteroglossia of a given social formation (see chapter 2). The voices that are specialized to a particular configuration of insider and outsider relations in a given context are therefore positioned in relation to the systems of social heteroglossia of the social formation. The coding orientations at the level above organize the strategic deployments of heteroglossic relations and their realizations in particular contexts. The potential for different coding orientations to specify *which* sociodiscursive positioned-practices are voiced in *which* semantic registers in relation to their classification and framing principles is organized at the next order of relations in the meta-redundancy contextualization hierarchy. Thus, a/b//E′///d////INDEX/////R_1, R_2//////C_1, C_2.

Volosinov (1973: 120) describes one form of reported speech as "pictorial," and the use of this visual analogue supplies us with an important clue concerning the iconic or functionally motivated character of the message-referential relations in quoting and reporting speech. Volosinov showed that quoting and reporting relations involve the "transmission in a bounded context" of another's speech. This bounded context is defined as we have seen by the logico-semantic relations in operation at the lexico-grammatical level of the clause complex. This logico-semantic organization is iconic in its realization of the referential relations involved. Bateson (1973c: 106) points out that linguistic structure is "digital or verbal at one level and iconic at another." It is digital at the lexico-grammatical level but iconic at the semantic level in the sense that the relations between the lexico-grammar and the semantics are functionally motivated and therefore nonarbitrary (Halliday, 1978: 44–45). The kind and degree of iconicity involved depend on the punctuation of message-referent relations in some context. At this level, the organization of the logico-semantic relations in quoting and reporting speech is nonarbitrary in relation to the referential relations that they index on account of the contextual redundancies involved. Logico-semantic relations organize the bounded context of the projecting and projected relations in such a way that they index a set of instructions for the construction of a specific referential relation to which a given message is homologously related in terms of the text-as-record or text-as-product relation. The bounded lexico-grammatical form is not in a relation of identity with some real-world entity. Rather, these instructions type the specific referential relations that can be constructed in the system of contextualizing relations (the metasystem) and in relation to which a given instance of quoting or reporting speech is said to be, to varying degrees, iconic.[3] I am not of course using *iconic* in the naive sense to mean that there is a visual likeness between semiotic acts and real-world phenomena. Volosinov's use of the term *pictorial* is, I think, a suggestive metaphor for talking about these relations insofar as it suggests the usefulness of the notion of iconicity for the present analysis. Volosinov (1973: 117) calls attention to the important differences "between the active reception of another's speech and its transmission in a bounded context." Quoting and reporting relations involve an iconic transformation of the self/other relations of spoken dialogue. On one level, they are an iconic metacommunication *about* this relationship. In spoken dialogue the subject-predicate frame is centered on the I-you relation. The subject is always either addresser or addressee, that is, self or other in the speech exchange.

More speculatively, I want to suggest that quoting and reporting relations and their various transforms are a form of iconic transformation of I-you transactions. This iconic transformation constitutes a form of metacommunicative "naming" of these as linguistic "entities" in the "external" environment of I-you transactions. To adapt somewhat metaphorically Halliday's notion of transitivity in the semantics of the clause, we can say that quoting and reporting relations are analogous to circumstantial relations in the ideational-grammatical relations of Participant-Process-Circumstance. This iconic transformation entails a shift of the subject-predicate frame from Process-Participant (I-you transactions) to Circumstances (third person). It is then possible to infer or reconstruct from quoting and reporting relations some relation of homology, though not analogy or identity, to "the active reception of another's speech" in ways that articulate and inform the deeply implicit structures through which we perceive the relations between self and other in the social semiotic system. This does not necessarily mean that there is full semantic reversibility, for there are always limits on the kinds and the degree of the homologies that are enacted. Nor does this mean that the repressed ghost of extralinguistic "reality" has returned to haunt the analysis in the form of a referential phantom. Rather, these relations are, as Bateson (1973a: 286) would put it, a closed circuit of a transform of differences. The differences at any given level in the hierarchy of contextualizing relations are relationally semiotic. They constitute a system of semiotic values in the Saussurean sense. This is systemic precisely because the differences on a given level of relations are transformed by their relations to value-producing distinctions on other levels in a dialectically and hierarchically integrated system of matter, energy, and information exchanges. To quote Bateson: "A bit of information is definable as a difference which makes a difference. Such a difference, as it travels and undergoes successive transformation in a circuit, is an elementary idea" (1973a: 286). The "bit of information" that constitutes, say, the difference between the projecting and projected clauses at the level of first focus in our analysis is relationally semiotic not just on its own level, but in relation to value-producing differences at all levels in the hierarchy. This bit of information is contextualized as meaningful in some social semiotic system of relations in and through the successive transformations (recontextualizations) it undergoes. This occurs on account of its dialectical and structural integration into the whole "circuit" of relations, formally represented by the metaredundancy contextualization hierarchy. This bit of information on, say, the lexico-grammatical level has a meaning potential that is contextualized as a more determinate and functional meaning by the successive transformations it undergoes at all levels. However, the open-ended regress of these relations also means that this meaning potential can never be totally exhausted or fixed as a single, determinate, or monologic meaning. There is always the potential for new contextualizing relations by virtue of the constant dialectic of supersystem-metasystem relations. I shall explore some further implications of Saussure's concept of semiotic *valeur* for a neomaterialist social semiotic theory in chapter 8 (see also Thibault, 1986e).

Quoting and reporting relations are a form of displacement (*Verschiebung*) of I-you transactions onto some metacommunication about these transactions. Insofar as quoting and reporting relations are a reconstruction of and/or commentary on I-you relations and transactions, they embody some notion of transcribing, translating, and transmitting of these relations. They are a form of displacement of these transactions in some "bounded context of transmission" in ways that foreground the otherwise implicit nature of the insider and outsider relations and categories that are entailed. Quoting and reporting speech stand in a metonymic relation with I-you transactions. There are functional elements of quoting and reporting speech that partially resemble the patterns of organization to be found in spoken dialogue, though with the loss of some contextual features and the nonreversible transformation of others.

I shall complete the present section with a formal analysis of the contextualizing relations in two instances of free indirect discourse. The first is from Halliday's summary of projection types (see Table 2.1). It reads: *It was so, he said.* The formal analysis of the metaredundancy contextualization hierarchy is as follows:

a:Sayer/b:Speaker//E′///d////INDEX/////R_1,R_2//////C_1,C_2.

Thus, a is the projected context, which functions as a wording; b is the projecting context, which functions as a locution : verbal; E′ is the logico-semantic relation of parataxis that links the two independent clauses; d is the dyad structure : report : free indirect discourse, which means that the Sayer of a is projected through the third-person perspective of b. Here b designates the third-person perspective of *he* as outsider in the context of reception, and b projects the insider perspective of a, which is deictically oriented to the outsider (Speaker) perspective of b. However, the mood form of a's perspective is retained. There is therefore an interpenetration of the a and b perspectives. INDEX here designates the first-person Speaker in the projecting context of b at time of speaking t_{sp}. The Speaker projects the Sayer in a at t_{sp} in the reporting context, that is, at the time of coding. The deictic orientations of a and b converge in a new hybrid context.

In the preceding analysis the higher orders are more generalized as types because these examples are taken from a decontextualized typology. However, our next example comprises clauses 5a and 5b from the textual analysis of *Ada* in chapter 2. This example reads: *Yes, she was sad, she replied.* The formal analysis now follows:

a:Sayer/b:Speaker//E′///d////INDEX/////R_1,R_2//////C_1,C_2.

Now, a is the projected context, which functions as a wording; b is the projecting context, which functions as a locution : verbal. E′ is the logico-semantic relation of parataxis that links the two independent clauses, and d is the dyad structure : report : free indirect discourse. The details of the analysis for the remaining levels until R are the same as for the previous example. The remainder of the analysis is, however, specific to the meanings defined in the textual analysis in chapter 2. Level R designates the semantic registers in use. R_1 is the register of social prescriptions, more delicately matrimonial and familial relations. R_2 is the register of interdictions, more delicately the prohibition of incest, the locus of the Law. The next order of relations, C, designates the coding orientations. C_1 can be defined as dominant, positional meanings and interactional practices; fixed narrator and character positions that classify and control narrative agents, positions, and practices; and strong framing. C_2 can be defined as relativity of meanings and interactional practices; no fixed, monologic narrator and character positions; and weak framing.

Punctuation, Discursive Closure, and Epistemological Discontinuity in Quoting and Reporting Speech

I shall now develop further my argument that quoting and reporting relations are a displaced form of I-you transaction. Once again Halliday's summary of projection types is a useful starting point for developing the sociopolitical implications of quoting and reporting speech. These entail various strategies for the production of specific knowledge-power relations in connection with the joint or hybrid contextualization dynamics of the meaning making practices of insiders and outsiders. The social semiotic codes function to classify and frame the relations between meanings, their realizations, and the contexts in which these occur (see Bernstein, 1982, 1986b). The different forms of realization of the various types of quoting and reporting speech are strategies of punctuation that regulate the production of specific positioned-practices and their voices *within* the bounded lexico-grammatical context of quoting and reporting speech. Let us now consider Halliday's typology of quoting and reporting speech in relation to the distinction that Pêcheux makes

> . . . between the two articulated figures of the *ideological subject,* in the form on the one hand of the *identification-unification of the subject with himself* (the "I see what I see" of the "empirical guarantee") and on the other of the *identification of the subject with the universal,* through the support of the other as reflected discourse, providing the "speculative guarantee" ("everyone knows that . . . ", "it is clear that . . . ", etc.), which introduces the idea of the *speculative simulation of scientific knowledge by ideology*. (Pêcheux, 1982: 91; emphasis in original)

The distinction Pêcheux makes here represents the beginnings of a recognition of the different strategies of punctuation and, hence, the different forms of realiza-

Table 4.1. Movement form Concrete Individual Subject to Universal Subject (adapted from Pêcheux, 1982)

	1 Origin	2 Discrepancy	3 Generalization	4 Universalization
Logico-grammatical reference categories	I	you/I	he, x/I	any subject (everyone, anyone whatsoever)
	see present here	say past elsewhere/ here	say past elsewhere/ here	think always everywhere
Basic form of the utterance	(I say that) I see this	you have told me that. . .	I have been told that. . . it has been observed that. . .	it is true that. . .

tion that classify and frame positioned-practices and their voicings in quoting and reporting speech. I shall not examine all of the possibilities presented in Halliday's account (see Table 2.2). The discussion will be limited to the cline from Quote to Fact in the declarative mood, and only verbal processes will be accounted for in the projecting context. This can be glossed as the cline from direct to impersonal forms. Pêcheux discusses the distinction he makes in connection with Table 4.1.

Pêcheux (1982: 87) points out that the cline from *origin* to *universalization* in Table 4.1 is based on the opposition between "situational" and "permanent" property relations. He adds that the continuity underlying this opposition depends

> . . . on the process of *identification* ("If I were where you/he/x are/is, I would see and think what you/he/x see(s) and think(s)"), adding that the imaginary of the identification radically masks any epistemological discontinuity. (Pêcheux, 1982: 87)

We can relate this same opposition to the cline from direct to impersonal forms, which is proposed in Halliday's schema of types of projection (see Table 2.2). These refer to the "identification unification of the subject with himself" and the "identification of the subject with the universal," which I cited earlier. This process of identification can have the consequence of masking epistemological discontinuities, as Pêcheux puts it, between the projecting and projected contexts.

It is this relationship of discontinuity that we shall now examine. In the following discussion, the Speaker is defined in functional semantic terms as the Agent of the utterance in the context of transmission; the Sayer is the Agent of the verbal process in the projecting clause.

The first type proposed in Halliday's schema is a direct quote, for example, *"It is so," he said*. The paratactic relations between the projecting and projected contexts, combined with the fact that the deictic orientation of the Sayer in the projected clause is retained, entail an insulation of strong classification (Bernstein, 1982: 315) between the two contexts. This lexico-grammatical punctuation of the relations between the two contexts presupposes a specific kind of epistemological relation. There is strong insulation in the projected clause between the Speaker and the Sayer, namely, the one who is quoted. This is an instance of Pêcheux's "identification-unification of the subject with himself." This relation can be glossed as "I quote what I hear," where the subject (the Speaker) acts as empirical guarantor of the other (the Sayer) as object.

Halliday's second type is free indirect report (free indirect discourse), for example, *It was so, he said*. The paratactic relation between the projecting and projected clauses remains, but the deictic orientation shifts to the projecting context, although the projected clause retains its own independent mood structure. The shift in deictic orientation and the semantic indeterminacy, which is a feature of free indirect discourse, mean that the principle of strong insulation has weakened to the extent that the two contexts interpenetrate. Free indirect discourse thus foregrounds those strategies that challenge the strong classification of the projecting and projected contexts in quoted speech. The discontinuity that strong insulation entails is problematized by the dialectic between the tendency to unify the Sayer with the Speaker and for the Speaker to mediate the Sayer. This relation can be glossed as "I report what I identify with."

The third type is indirect report, for example, *He said that it was so*. The dependent, hypotactic relation between the projecting and projected contexts, combined with the fact that the deictic orientation of the projected context is shifted to that of the projecting context, further weakens and declassifies the punctuation of the boundaries between the two contexts. The hypotactic subordination of the projected clause to the projecting clause tends further to weaken the insulation between the two. The effect is to increase the identification of the Speaker with the Sayer.

The fourth type is an embedded indirect qualifier, for example, *his assertion that it was so*. The projecting element is *his assertion*, which functions as the Head in a nominal group. The projected element is a defining relative clause, which is embedded in the nominal group. The personal pronoun *his* presumes that the nature and identity of the reality indexed are not sufficiently well known and so requires further identification by indicating a particular relationship between the Speaker and information contained in the context-of-utterance. The embedded relative extends the situation of this reality by reference to a second reality, which is projected through it. The Head noun *assertion* functions as a particular property that is specified by a particular relationship to the Speaker. This property is further qualified by a particular situation, which is projected by it. The subject is no longer the empirical guarantor of the situation. Rather, the situation is a contingent qualifying element of an "entity" or property whose identity or relation to the Speaker requires further semantic specification in this particular projecting environment. The Speaker is identified by the situation.

The fifth type is the impersonal qualifying nominal group, for example, *the saying that it is so*. This is what Halliday (1985: 243–48) refers to as a "fact." The projecting context here is a nominal group with a verbal process noun as Head. The projected clause is embedded as a qualifier of the Head of the nominal group, namely, *saying*. The projecting clause is an impersonal verbal process. Here the identity of the Speaker is not specified. Instead, the focus has shifted to the identity of the Head of the nominal group. The definite article *the* in this context indicates that a situational qualifier of the Head is required, which will answer the question *what?* The projected element is a situational qualifier of the projecting element, which does not specify any specific projecting subject. This greatly increases the tendency to identification of the Speaker with the Sayer. The discourse of the Sayer is an embedded situational qualifier in the discourse of the Speaker, itself now a nominalized property or "thing."

The sixth type is an impersonal, which functions directly as Head in the nominal group, for example, *(it is said) that it is so*. This is a type of Fact where there is no verbal or mental process that projects it. It is a projection, but there is no Sayer doing the projecting. It has the semantic status of a Fact. In this case, the insulation between the projecting and projected contexts is completely dissolved. The projected element functions as a nominalization on its own. The identification of the Speaker with the Sayer is now complete on account of the absence of any lexico-grammatical insulations that punctuate the boundaries between the two and, therefore, between situation and property. The tendency of the subject to identify with the universal or the impersonal is here completed (Pêcheux, 1982: 91). The position of the Sayer becomes the empirical support for the position of the implied Speaker (as subject).

The increasing tendency I have described here to weaken and finally dissolve the lexico-grammatical boundaries between the projecting and projected contexts should not obscure the fact that these lexico-grammatical transformations mask fundamental semantic and epistemological differences between the two contexts. This presumed epistemological continuity may conceal the dialectical struggle between opposing semantic and discursive positions in the projecting and projected contexts. This epistemological discontinuity and its punctuation may be displaced from the formal, lexico-grammatical level to more implicit, higher-order relations. This does not mean that the discontinuity has simply disappeared.

In the next section I shall examine some of the strategies of closure that articulate the epistemological relations of continuity and discontinuity between the two contexts.

Strategies of Closure and the Articulation of the Social Dialectic

Bakhtin's (1981) concept of social heteroglossia provides us with a framework for talking about the ways in which positioned-practices and their textual voicings in the social semiotic system are always constructed in and through their relations with other positioned-practices and voices in the systems of social heteroglossia of a given social formation. This does not mean that these sociodiscursive voices are on equal terms with each other. It is important not to interpret Bakhtin's concept to mean that different voices reflect different subjective "worldviews," with the implication this formulation has of an already given referential relation. The concept of worldview implies a total way of looking at some world. It retains the same subjectivist-empiricist epistemology that I critiqued in chapter 2. According to this view, events, structures, entities, and so on, in the "external" world are "represented" or "reflected" in a totalizing, essentialist "worldview." A given worldview is then taken to be a unified set of concepts, which are the possession of a given speaker or social group. It misses the point that it is the dialectical interpenetration of social meaning making practices that produces and articulates shifting, metastable formations of knowledge and belief. These are enacted in and through the dialectical interplay of homogeneity-heterogeneity and center and periphery by the stratified and discontinuous meaning making practices that make, maintain, and change the social semiotic system. Bakhtin's concept of social heteroglossia, which is central to the present study, shares some important and suggestive links with Antonio Gramsci's writings on the centrality of language in cultural and political life. These links will be explored more fully in chapters 7 and 8. Gramsci has posed the question of language and worldview in ways that are most relevant to the present argument:

> If philosophy is taken as a conception of the world and philosophical activity no longer conceived only as an "individual" elaboration of systematically coherent concepts but moreover and especially as a cultural struggle to transform the popular "mentality" and diffuse the philosophical innovations that show themselves to be "historically true" to the extent to which they will become concretely, that is, historically and socially, universal, the question of language and "technically" of languages must be placed in the foreground. . . . It appears that one can say that "language" is essentially a collective noun, which does not presuppose a "single" thing either in time or in space. Language also means culture and philosophy (even if at the level of common sense) and for this reason the "language" fact is in reality a multiplicity of

> more or less organically coherent and coordinated facts: in the extreme it can be said that every speaking being has his own personal language, that is, his own way of thinking and feeling. "Culture," in its various degrees, unifies a greater or lesser quantity of individuals in numerous strata, more or less in expressive contact, which are understood among them to different degrees. It is these historical-social differences and distinctions that are reflected in everyday language and that produce these "obstacles" and "causes of error" that the pragmatists have discussed. (Gramsci, 1977c: 30–31; my translation)

The central problem in all of the intersubjective and subjective-empiricist accounts of the relations between the subject and language (as object) is their allegiance to an epistemological formulation of the knowledge-being couplet (see chapter 2). Social reality is assumed to be representable as a totalizing worldview. Bakhtin's concept of social heteroglossia provides us with a way of breaking with the presumed intersubjective unity of the knowing subject and the object of knowledge, for example, language. Bakhtin's concept shows that there is no necessary and unified point of reference for social meaning making practices, just as there is no given, determinate worldview that is simply mirrored or reflected in, say, language. Social meaning making practices and the discursive subject positions these enact depend upon specific social and historical conditions, but these conditions do not add up to a total worldview, or even a set of opposing worldviews. The concept of worldview suggests that these are already fully articulated and fully given. The notion of the social semiotic as a systemic resource or "meaning potential" (Halliday, 1978) demonstrates the inadequacy of this conception, which is founded on the knowing subject/object of knowledge distinction. Alternatively, I have spoken of positioned-practices that are made, remade, and changed in and through contextually specific uses of this meaning potential. These positioned-practices and the social contexts with which they are redundant cannot be distinguished in the same way as the knowing subject/object of knowledge split. The social meaning making practices that are specialized to a particular context-type and to their textual voicings do not exhaust social practice. They are relatable to specific sociohistorical conditions and specific ideological effects, but the effectivity of these does not amount to a single, homogeneous, or totalizing worldview. They have no referential center and no determinate unifunctional pattern of effects, although there are always social constraints on meaning making practices that shape their form and functioning. In chapters 6, 7, and 8 we shall return to this important principle in relation to Bernstein's social semiotic coding orientations. Social heteroglossia emphasizes the dispersed, discontinuous character of meaning making practices and the social formations in which they are articulated. The relations of alignment, conflict, opposition, and struggle among social meaning making practices enact the dialectic of stability and change, hegemony and struggle in the social semiotic system or some part of it.

This dialectic manifests itself in the constant processes of articulation, disarticulation, and rearticulation of social meaning making practices in and through the joint or hybrid contextualizations these entail. Our study of quoting and reporting speech exemplifies these processes at the microlevel. They have provided a theoretical basis for our assumption of a dyadic structure rather than some individual "center of consciousness." The dyad is always resolved at successively higher orders in a contextualization hierarchy. The semogenic processes that hybridization brings about suggest this possibility. The conflict and struggle between positioned-practices at the level of the dyad may exceed certain parameters so that their global resolution at higher orders does not bring about a return to the previous global stability of the processes involved. What we have seen is that quoting and reporting relations are not fixed or stable forms but, as Halliday has written, a "projection space" in which higher-order changes to these relations take on systemic characteristics of their own. For instance, the functional relations and properties of free indirect discourse become supraordinate to, rather than merely deviant from, the seemingly anomalous combinations of its constituent elements from quoting and reporting speech. The entire systemic potential of quoting and reporting relations is therefore changed to a structurally and functionally more complex set of organizational principles that realign the probabilities of the system.

Gramsci's notions of struggle and hegemony may be rearticulated in the social semiotic conceptual framework in relation to the concept of social heteroglossia. This can help us to develop a clearer understanding of the strategies of closure and domination that are enacted in and through quoting and reporting speech and their various transforms. According to Gramsci, the dialectic between class struggle and class hegemony produces a hegemonic class or social grouping when that class or grouping succeeds in articulating to its own ideological position the consent of other classes and social forces to create a broad alliance of social forces. In the words of Chantal Mouffe (1979: 193–94), it is "a struggle between two hegemonic principles; it does not consist of the confrontation of two already elaborated, closed world-views." In the conceptual language of social semiotic theory, we can say that this involves a constant process of struggle among opposing positioned-practices and their textual voicings. This is a struggle by social agents for the articulation, disarticulation, and rearticulation of the differentially and unevenly distributed material and semiotic resources of the social semiotic system to opposing hegemonic principles. This involves, as Mouffe further points out, a process of "disarticulation-rearticulation" of these ideological elements in the struggle to "appropriate" them. However, the concept of appropriation in Mouffe's account requires critical examination. This concept postulates some notion of an object to be appropriated to a particular way of knowing or a particular worldview. The concept of appropriation maintains an allegiance to the subject/object dichotomy that I discussed in chapter 2. This posits sociodiscursive practice in terms of a subject with a necessary form of knowledge relation to some object. This then requires a reality or worldview appropriate to that relation. In the conceptual framework of social semiotics, the concept of social heteroglossia resists the idea that one discursive positioned-practice appropriates another. The relation between the projecting and projected contexts cannot be adequately talked about in terms of the one appropriating the other. The relation between the two contexts is, as the concept of hybridization shows, more adequately talked about in terms of the *articulation, disarticulation,* and *rearticulation* of positioned-practices and their textual voicings. We shall now consider how these involve various strategies of contextual closure in the different kinds of projection that may be deployed.

In direct quotes the relation between the projecting and projected contexts is a fully articulated one. The discursive positions of both contexts are fully articulated competitors or voices. The Speaker of the projecting context and the Sayer of the projected context are not, however, given in advance. Rather, they are enacted in and through the specific meaning making practices that bring these two contexts together in this way rather than some other. It is this bringing together that determines the relations of power and knowledge that operate between the two discursive positions. This does not mean that this relation between the two fully articulated positions is equal or on the same level. The projecting context is a metacommunication that frames the projected context at some metalevel of communication (Thibault, 1984: 107–11). The hegemonic strategy is to get above the alien discourse by embedding it in the metadiscourse of the projecting context. The alien discourse is not reformulated at the lexico-grammatical level and so is fully articulated at that level. It is framed in a semantic and lexico-grammatical context of projection that gives it a relatively full semantic weighting on its own level. Nevertheless, the strategy is to get above the alien discourse at some higher metalevel of framing.

Free indirect discourse involves the direct rearticulation of both discursive positions in relation to one another. Elements of both the projecting and projected contexts are recontextualized in relation to each other. The projecting context articulates to itself some elements of the projected context, and the projected context articulates to itself some elements of the projecting context. Free indirect discourse foregrounds at the local level of the clause complex the dialectic of discursive struggle and hegemony between positioned-practices and their voicings. It foregrounds the ways in which conflict and contradiction enact a constant movement and relativization among the various positions. Hegemony is not simply understood to be the domination of one position by another. Free indirect discourse suggests to social semiotic theory how, even at the microlevel, hegemony is actively contested in and through social meaning making practices by the dialectical movement referred to here. Hegemony is not an irreversible domination of one discourse by another. In free indirect discourse we see most clearly the processes of disarticulation-rearticulation of positioned-practices whereby two discursive positions engage in a struggle for the articulation of the alien discourse, each to its own ideological and axiological position.

Indirect reports involve the rearticulation of the alien discourse in terms of the reporting context. The deictic orientation of the Sayer or Senser is rearticulated in terms of the deictic orientation of the Speaker in the reporting context. In indirect reports, the hegemonic struggle is to recontextualize the reported context in terms of the reporting context. The "relative weight" (Mouffe, 1979: 192) of these relations has been shifted to the reporting context. The reporting context constitutes the hegemonic principle through which the reported context is articulated. The metalevel of power and ideological domination has recontextualized the alien discourse within its own domain. This enacts a form of relative contextual closure.

The indirect qualifying relation rearticulates the alien discourse in terms of the nominal group Head, which functions as the projecting element. The alien discourse is articulated as a situational qualifying element of the dominant position. The nominal group structure includes the alien discourse within its own lexico-grammatical structure. It no longer functions as a separate clause, but is rank-shifted to nominal group structure. The structure of the nominal group itself constitutes a form of contextual foreclosure of the relations between the two contexts. However, the Head element is a projecting element that maintains therefore a relative distinction in the lexico-grammar between the two levels.

Impersonal qualifiers further the process of foreclosure. There is no specification of a Sayer who does the projecting. This closure at the lexico-grammatical level of the relations between the two contexts reduces the very real differences between them. It is a form of lexico-grammatical foreclosure of these relations that mistypes the relations between the projecting and projected contexts as being on the same level in the lexico-grammar. It is a mistyping of these relations because they are restricted to the here-and-now of formal lexico-grammatical realizations. Further, the impersonal nature of the projecting element does not specify the different levels of power and responsibility that are always entailed in the relations between the projecting and projected contexts. Foreclosure involves a reduction in difference, and this confuses the relations of values and responsibilities between levels in the system of relations.

The impersonal form entails the complete foreclosure of lexico-grammatical options. There is no articulation at this level of some alien discourse, for there is a complete fusion of both discursive positions. The alien discourse is totally rearticulated to the hegemonic principle in the projecting context at the lexico-grammatical level. The metalevel of power and responsibility is, however, not so much absent but displaced to some more implicit level of contextualization. The grammatical foreclosure of options restricts the context to "its own" (i.e., the lexico-grammatical) level. There is always some metalevel of power and responsibility within the system of contextual relations, but this fusion closes off the dialectic of discursive positioned-practices on the lexico-grammatical level.

Figure 4.1 brings together the various components of our analysis, which have so far remained separated. The systems of social heteroglossia are instantiated in the dialectic of ideological struggle and hegemony in and through the articulation of social meaning making practices. The relations of alignment, conflict, opposition, and co-optation among discursive positioned-practices are regulated by the higher-order social semiotic codes. These regulate both the forms and the relations of production and distribution of material and semiotic resources. Specific configurations of these resources enact the social situation-types and the differential access of agents to these in a given social formation. It is at the level of actual social situations that social meaning making practices are made, remade, maintained, contested, and changed. At this level the articulation of the various strategies of struggle and hegemony takes place. This always entails, as we have seen, specific strategies of closure in the relations between one discursive position and another. The sociosemantic voicings of these relations in texts do not therefore correspond to fixed meanings that are already given in textual and linguistic forms. Meanings and social practices are always articulated in and through specific, though shifting and discontinuous, sociohistorical formations with which they covary.

Figure 4.1 does not assign the categories of ideology and power to any single level or position. The reconstitution of Gramsci's conception of hegemony in connection with Bakhtin's notion of social heteroglossia can help us to construct a social semiotic theory that recognizes that power, domination, and ideology are immanent in the system of relations at all levels. These issues are central in chapters 7 and 8.

In chapter 1 I suggested that the clause is a microlevel social act-type, functionally interpreted. Social semiotics is concerned above all with the meaning making practices of a given social formation; it has no need of reified psychological notions such as center of consciousness or the individual per se. At the clause complex level, we can begin to analyze the heteroglossic practices through which positioned-practices and their textual voicings are constructed through pluralities of intersecting social meaning making practices. The functional semantic interpretation of these clause complexes has provided the basis for the analysis of the particular forms of articulation these microlevel social acts take. The joint or hybrid contextualization dynamics that they enact serve to emphasize two main factors. First, the discursive subject/social agent is a heteroglossic construction from intersecting social meaning making practices (see chapter 8). These must be analyzed in terms of the social activity-structures that are enacted by the subject/agent in particular sociodiscursive formations. Second, hybridization, even at the microlevel we have so far considered, shows that social relations qua heteroglossic practices occur in dynamic interaction. The a/b dyad relations we con-

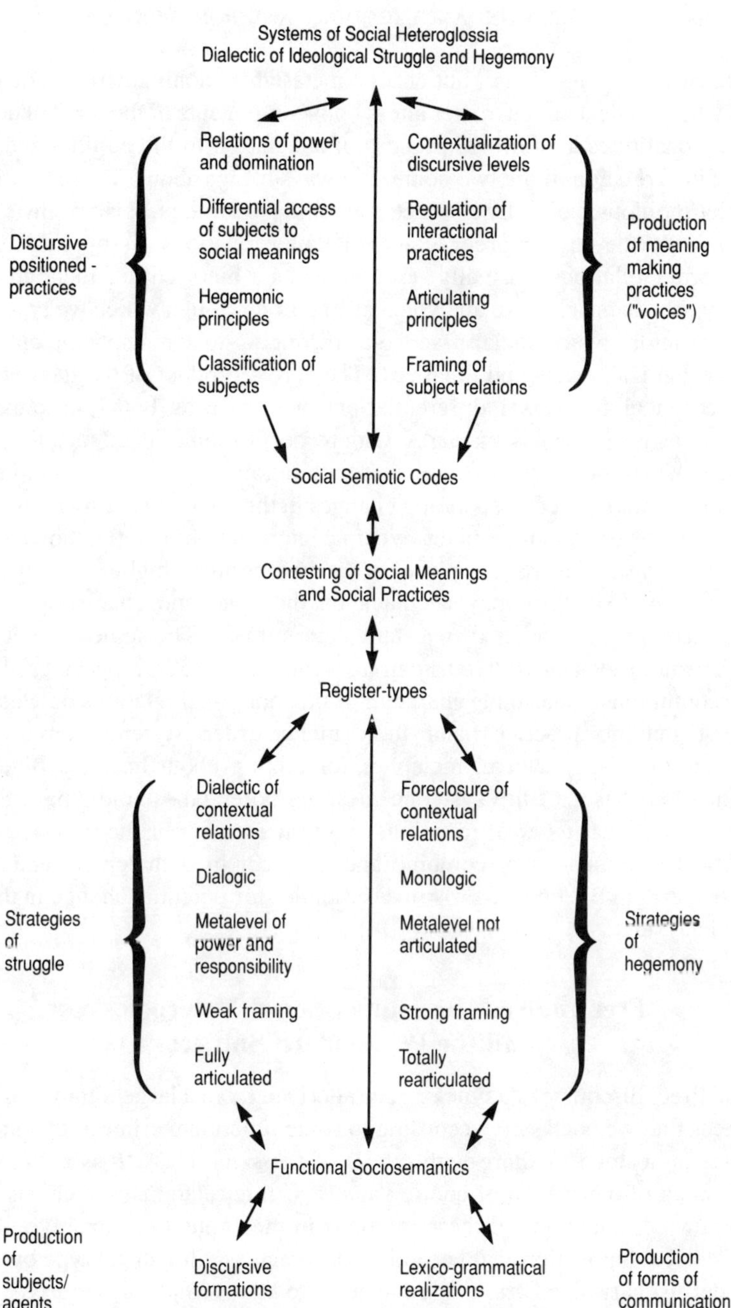

Figure 4.1. Outline of discursive relations in social semiotic system

sidered earlier are not static, but enact a metastable, nonfinalistic set of transactions, whose dialectical character alters both components of the dyad. The hybrid context constitutes a continual process of adaptation to the conflict and change that the interrelation of the two contexts always brings about. These relations are never harmonious, perfectly symmetrical, or in perfect equilibrium. Instead, they covary with the higher-order contextualizing relations in operation. These higher-order relations, formally represented as a hierarchy of metaredundancy relations, are themselves an analytical abstraction through which we type or classify a particular act or social practice as belonging to some specific class of socially recognizable acts and practices. They are a product of the theoretical and folk-theoretical functional differentiations we make as both participants and analysts—as insiders and outsiders—with respect to some social meaning making practice(s). To the extent that these are alterations in the dyad relations themselves, there must be corresponding changes in the contextualizing relations with which they covary. Changes in the dynamic interrelations and functional differentiations we construe at, say, the level of the dyad result in higher-order functional changes, which in turn may act back on the dyad and change it. This is a probabilistic process rather than a static determinism. The subject/agent, who is a participant in social activity-structures, is thus changed in ways that account for the discontinuous, metastable character of the functional relations between social meaning making practices and their higher-order systemic environments. Hybridization is a powerful metaphor for talking about how the diverse and plurifunctional uses of the systemic meaning potential—paradigmatically classified as functional *types* of meanings and practices in our theoretical and folk-theoretical accounts—may combine and intersect in both typical and atypical ways that are, in Bakhtin's words, the "crucible" for potential change in the social semiotic system.

Free Indirect Discourse, Social Heteroglossia, and the Postmodern Subject

Free indirect discourse is a type or class, derived from a large number of specific instances that we coclassify according to some functional criteria, that any given instance is deemed to share with others of the same class. It is a "semogenic" realignment of the system of quoting and reporting relations, which has brought about new combinations of these relations in the context of narrative fiction. It is a historical innovation that became widespread as a linguistic type by the time of modernist narrative fiction. We can begin to ask in what ways this type is functional in the wider sociodiscursive formations in which it is used. Volosinov (1973: 44), in connection with the work of the linguist Bally, suggests that free indirect discourse manifests a recent linguistic tendency toward parataxis rather than hypotaxis. I do not wish to make any claims about the language as a whole. However, this suggestion provides an important clue concerning the emphasis on this linguistic form in much modernist and postmodernist narrative fiction. To ask how and why this form is functional in modernist and postmodernist narrative requires that we avoid the hypostatization of lexico-grammatical form per se, as well as the nondialectical tendency to reify systemic meaning potential as the sole determinant of textual meanings. We are interested then in the ways in which the social agent/discursive subject can act on and change this systemic meaning potential. This requires a fully dialectical account of the relations between code, social situation, and text. It is a dialectic that must also be placed within the still wider framework of the sociohistorical formations in which social actions occur. This will be further developed in various ways in subsequent chapters.

Gramsci's conception of hegemony, reconstituted within the conceptual framework of social semiotics, can provide a way of linking together theoretically Halliday's notions of "social situation – semantic register – text," Bakhtin's notions of "dialogicity – social heteroglossia – voice," and Bernstein's notions of "code – textual message – subject." In this concluding section of the present chapter, I shall put forward some general and programmatic proposals suggesting that such a theoretical reworking can be useful in the development of a neomaterialist social semiotic theory. These proposals will be discussed here in relation to free indirect discourse. Gramsci's conception of hegemony is based on the premise that a hegemonic system of ideas and values and the social and political leadership of the hegemonic group are founded on two principles–"domination" and "intellectual and moral leadership." This is worth keeping in mind, for a social semiotic account of hegemony in discursive and textual practice must not be reduced to certain properties or effects of systems of signification. Gramsci's conception serves to remind us of the weakness of a semiotics based on the presumed ideological character of the formal properties of sign-tokens and sign-systems per se. Ideology is not a category that can simply be read off from the formal properties of systems of signification. This is not to say that the latter are not perfused with ideological values and significance. The problem arises when the formal and structural properties of sign-tokens and sign-systems are disjoined from social practice. The linking of the theoretical positions cited above is a starting point for building an alternative account of the ways in which social meanings are always made, remade, contested, and changed in the context of social struggle and change. The linguistic and textual strategies for the articulation of potentially hegemonic relations between one discursive positioned-practice and another in quoting and reporting speech were explored earlier. At the local level of the clause complex this is always a potential, functionally interpreted. The text we analyzed in chapter 2 shows how the foregrounding of free indirect discourse is linked to a multilevel context of articulated sociodiscursive practices within which a particular postmodernist form of decentered subjectivity is hegemonic.

The paratactic, independent relations between the projecting and projected contexts in free indirect discourse realize, at the lexico-grammatical level, a relative indeterminacy of ideological and axiological positions through the dialogic interplay of textual voices. The textual analysis in chapter 2 has already demonstrated how this involves the dialectical interplay of narrator-Van discourse and character-Ada discourse. Free indirect discourse is also functional in the binding in of the reader to the relations among the plurality of discursive positioned-practices constituted in and through the text. In free indirect discourse this dialectic is concerned with the struggle to establish a given discursive position as hegemonic. Free indirect discourse is then a linguistic attempt to resolve this dialectical struggle between discursive positioned-practices. In the present context, I shall suggest that it is a linguistic strategy for containing the contradictory, decentered subject of postmodernist textual practice. The hegemonic struggle for the binding in of the reader, which in the reflectionist epistemology of Banfield and Bronzwaer becomes an Imaginary, specular identification with some referentially projected and anthropomorphic self or center of consciousness, interestingly parallels Gramsci's development of the concept of *fascino-prestigio* (attraction-prestige), which he derived from the work of his teacher in linguistics, Bartoli, at the University of Turin (see Lo Piparo, 1979: 103–8). This concept was developed by Gramsci in his attempt to theorize the social and historical processes through which a conquering nation attains hegemony over the language and culture of a conquered nation:

> That which happens to the dialects of a nation that slowly assimilate their literary forms and lose their particular characteristics will probably occur to the literary languages in comparison with a language that overcomes them. But this could be one of the present languages, for example, the language of the first country that establishes socialism, which for this reason would become *simpatico*, would seem beautiful, because with it our civilization is expressed and affirmed in a part of the world, because in it will be written books no longer of criticism, but of descriptions of experiences seen, because novels and poems will be written in it, which vibrate with the newly established life, of the sacrifices for consolidating it, of the hopes that everywhere the same situation will be realized. (Gramsci, 1972: 178; my translation)

Gramsci illustrates the social and historical processes through which the social and linguistic practices of dominated social and cultural groups may be assimilated to the practices of some dominant group. Alternatively, these practices may come to define or typify in some way the "language that overcomes them" as well as the users of this language. Gramsci shows that this always involves a struggle between conflicting practices, values, and forms of consciousness for the establishment of a hegemonic realignment and rearticulation of these. Gramsci's discussion here takes place in terms of macrolevel concepts such as "nation." Hegemony is attained when the dominated enter into an Imaginary identification with the values and practices of the dominant. Gramsci defines this as a form of *fascino* (attraction) with these. Now, a social semiotic theory of hegemony cannot be based on purely local criteria at, say, clause level in the lexico-grammar. The construction and articulation of a particular copatterning of meaning relations that is hegemonic must be formulated in terms of more global criteria in some text or intertextual formation. It is not possible to argue for a hegemonic copatterning of meaning relations on the basis of the single, isolated clause or clause complex. These lexico-grammatical forms encode strictly local meaning relations. It is necessary to account for the ways in which local units are distributed and foregrounded as global copatternings of meaning relations. The local meaning relations constitute the semiotic resources through which global relations are assembled and enacted. The principles through which these linkages are constituted will be taken up in chapters 5 and 6 in connection with the concept of intertextuality. However, this foregrounded global copatterning of meaning relations does not in itself lead to the articulation of some hegemonic principle. Gramsci's development of the concept of *fascino-prestigio* suggests that social semiotic theory must also theorize the processes whereby one social group succeeds in imposing on some other group a particular set of social meaning making practices that reproduces and serves the ideological interests and values of the first group in ways that are legitimated or naturalized as a kind of ideological second nature (Sohn-Rethel, 1978). This would be the successful imposing of a hegemonic formation of values and social practices by one group onto some other(s). The particular means that are used to achieve this will not be discussed here. However, Gramsci's formulation above suggests that the concepts of hybridization and creolization are also relevant at the macrolevels of social semiotic organization (see chapters 7 and 8). The processes of imposing and of *fa accettare col fascino* (causing to be accepted with attraction) a hegemonic system can only be successful if the dominated collude with and/or identify with the dominant social meaning making practices in ways of which they are not likely to be fully conscious. This requires the investments of social agents in specific, overdetermined intersections of meanings and practices, fixing or binding agents to some sociodiscursive positioned-practices rather than others in regular and systematic ways (also see Hollway, 1984; Threadgold, 1988).

However, the local and global perspectives on this process need to be kept in focus at the same time. At the local level of the clause complex, we have seen how the linguistic forms of quoting and reporting speech potentially enact the dialectical struggle between discursive positioned-practices. The global foregrounding of free indirect discourse in modernist and postmodernist narrative articulates an ideology of *homo linguisticus,* whereby language itself becomes the sole site of revolutionary activity. Social praxis and, hence, social action are reduced to the contextual closure of a so-called open play of signifiers (e.g., Derrida and Kristeva). It is a contextual closure in which exchange-value dominates as the epistemological guarantor of a foreclosed interplay of a system of differences circulating in a reified social context of meanings-as-commodities. Meanings are therefore abstracted from social practice as linguistic products rather than as modes of social action. Thus, social relations and practices are assimilated to the postmodernist and poststructuralist "will to power" over the text. Social practices are mistyped in terms of an exchange-value that disjoins these from their social relations of production according to the logic of what Habermas has referred to as a "technical-cognitive interest." The decentered subject's victory over the text is characterized by Habermas as follows:

> The ego, which is formed in coming to grips with the forces of outer nature, is the product of successful self-assertion, the result of the accomplishments of instrumental reason, and in two respects. It is the subject that irresistibly charges ahead in the process of enlightenment, that subjugates nature, develops the forces of production, disenchants the surrounding world; but at the same time it is the subject that learns to master itself, that represses its own nature, that advances self-objectification within itself and thereby becomes increasingly opaque to itself. Victories over outer nature are paid for with defeats of inner nature. This dialectic of rationalization is to be explained by the structure of a reason that is instrumentalized for the purpose of self-preservation, which is posed as an absolute end. We can see in the history of subjectivity how this instrumental reason marks every advance that it brings about with the stamp of irrationality. (Habermas, 1984: 380)

The technical procedures that produce this technical-cognitive knowledge take place within the presumed intersubjective horizon of a decentered subject/text-as-object relation. This is always recontained within the foreclosed supersystem transactions of the community of poststructuralist practitioners. Certainly, it is a view that recognizes the productivity of social meaning making, but in a way that restricts this understanding to a metasystem view of the interplay of a system of differences. This restriction effectively disconnects the metasystem and supersystem views within this particular domain of practice. In simpler terms, we can say that the very important contribution that poststructuralism has made to our understanding of the plural and productive nature of social meaning making has occurred at the expense of a socially and politically situated praxis that is not confined to the text per se as the site of political praxis in the circumscribed domain of poststructuralist practitioners.

The semantic indeterminacy of free indirect discourse and its global foregrounding in *Ada* can be related to the postmodernist preoccupation with linguistic innovation. The preoccupation with the microlevel of linguistic innovation localizes power in a plurality of differentially defined subsystems. Conflict and struggle are articulated in a differentialist rather than dialectical mode at the level of this fragmentation of social relations and practices. It is a tendency toward an atomistic and nominalistic conception of relations of power and domination in social practice. In this sense, it is both nondialectical and antimaterialist. Habermas (1985) is one of the few contemporary thinkers to recognize the reactionary and neoconservative character of postmodernism. Postmodernism's preoccupation with performativity, a decentered subject, and the reification of linguistic practice through the notion of a permanent state of linguistic innovation, defined in terms of an ontology of difference, helps us to recall Volosinov's (1973: 159) concern with what he calls "an alarming instability and uncertainty of the word." Volosinov's concern to revive the word that "takes responsibility for what it says," Habermas's strategy for the reconstruction of a rational critical practice, and Gramsci's conception of political praxis are necessary starting points for articulating a social semiotic praxis that can begin to give voice to an alternative to the antidialectical and differentialist negation of historical identity and social identity that are the hallmarks of the postmodernist decentered subject and of the current historical phase of consumer capitalism (see Preve, 1984: 73–79). These are urgent themes, which I shall address more fully and directly in chapters 7 and 8.

Notes

1. "Objective" here refers to the material social, rather than individual, basis of meaning making.

2. The locative abstraction in the concept of higher or lower orders of relations does not designate any physical or spatial set of relations. It refers to the analytical reconstruction or approximation of the different levels of abstraction in the relevant system of relations. The relations on a given level of analysis are said to be of the same order of logical typing with respect to the relations on other levels (see Bateson, 1973d).

3. Iconicity does not entail a representational likeness to some object, event, or the like, in the "real world," to which it refers. It is a functional meaning relation, which constitutes the conditions of production of a homological relation of likeness or identity to some object or event.

Part III
Intertextuality

At any given moment of its historical existence, language is heteroglot from top to bottom: it represents the co-existence of socio-ideological contradictions between the present and the past, between different socio-ideological groups in the present, between tendencies, schools, circles and so forth, all given a bodily form. These "languages" of heteroglossia intersect each other in a variety of ways, forming new socially typifying "languages."

Mikhail Bakhtin (1981: 291)

The current preoccupation is with discourse analysis, or "text linguistics;" and it is sometimes assumed that this can be carried on without grammar—or even that it is somehow an alternative to grammar. But this is an illusion. A discourse analysis that is not based on grammar is not an analysis at all, but simply a running commentary on a text: either an appeal has to be made to some set of nonlinguistic conventions, or to some linguistic features that are trivial enough to be accessible without a grammar, like the number of words per sentence (and even the objectivity of these is often illusory); or else the exercise remains a private one in which one explanation is as good or as bad as another.

A text is a semantic unit, not a grammatical one. But meanings are realized through wordings; and without a theory of wordings—that is, a grammar—there is no way of making explicit one's interpretation of the meaning of a text. Thus the present interest in discourse analysis is in fact providing a context within which grammar has a central place.

It is also pointing the way to the kind of grammar that is required. In order to provide insights into the meaning and effectiveness of a text, a discourse grammar needs to be functional and semantic in its orientation, with the grammatical categories explained as the realization of semantic patterns. Otherwise it will face inwards rather than outwards, characterizing the text in explicit formal terms but providing no basis on which to relate it to the non-linguistic universe of its situational and cultural environment.

Michael Halliday (1985: xvi-xvii)

Chapter 5
Text, Discourse, and Intertextuality

Text and Discourse

The distinction between text and discourse cannot be adequately demonstrated with reference to the level of the formal lexico-grammatical realization of textual meanings, disjoined from social practice. In the conceptual framework of social semiotics, language is not a formal, rule-bound system but a resource for making, realizing, and enacting context-dependent social meanings. Patterns of social action and interaction are related to each other in regular, limited ways according to the demands of specific social situations. Language is then a resource for getting things done by enacting both the social activity-structures and the thematic formations that work to define and maintain a particular social formation or some part of it. The dual perspective that I am proposing here—language and social practice—relates to the distinction between text and discourse that I am introducing. In systemic-functional linguistics, text is seen as the realization of some higher-order social semiotic (Halliday, 1978: 130). Halliday defines text in semantic rather than formal terms as "language in operation." It is a semantic unit, which is realized by patterned lexico-grammatical selections at the level of its formal organization. Halliday draws on the Hjelmslevian concept of realization to define this principle: "A text is to the semantic system what a clause is to the lexico-grammatical system and a syllable to the phonological system" (1978: 135). Text, defined semantically, is, in turn, the realization of some higher-order social semiotic. Hjelmslev's concept of realization is itself somewhat ambiguous. It is, grammatically speaking, a process noun that can designate both an active, ongoing process and the completion of a process (see also Martin, 1985a). The text/discourse distinction will be resolved as follows. Text is a record or a product of the social semiotic processes in and through which it is made and used. It is both the realization of some social semiotic process or processes as well as existing in a relation of homology to these (see chapter 3). Text is the realization of (typically) a plurality of social discourses. Discourse is defined as fully contextualized social action and interaction. It refers to the social practices in and through which textual meanings are made. Social discourses are patterned, limited ways of meaning and ways of doing that function both to regulate and deregulate human social activity and the social formation itself. The higher-order social semiotic is itself constructed and maintained by the relations between the various social discourses in a given sociodiscursive formation. The concept of realization does not entail any isomorphic or one-to-one fit between text and discourse. A particular text is, generally speaking, the material site of a plurality of heteroglossically related social discourses and their voicings. Specific texts, therefore, both instantiate and realize the heteroglossic relations of alliance, conflict, opposition, and co-optation among discursive positioned-practices in the social formation.

The concepts of dialogicity and heteroglossia in the writings of Bakhtin and Volosinov help to restore to textual practice the material interplay of ideological and axiological positions in discourse. The text/discourse distinction, I would argue, is at least implicit in the work of Bakhtin and Volosinov. Their notion of the multiaccented "word," defined as a unit of social action (or utterance) rather than a formal linguistic token per se, indexes a plurality of overlapping contextual domains and ideological and axiological positions, which are "voiced" in the word. The concept of the word in Bakhtin and Volosinov runs parallel to the concept of text that I defined earlier. The interplay of voices in the word can be aligned with the present account of the distinction between text and discourse. The insights of Bakhtin and Volosinov help to clarify the notion of text as a socially made product in which lived, often antagonistic relations between social discourses are enacted. The text is a social site, which is overdetermined by a plurality of social discourses, each with their own specificity, which are articulated in and through specific social meaning making practices. Here is Bakhtin on the heteroglossic nature of social meaning making in the novel:

> The stylistic uniqueness of the novel as a genre consists precisely in the combination of these subordinated, yet still relatively autonomous, entities (even at times comprised of differerent languages) into the higher unity of the work as a whole: the style of a novel is to be found in the combination of its styles; the language of a novel is the system of its "languages." Each separate element of a novel's language is determined first of all by one such subordinated stylistic unity into which it enters directly—be it the stylistically individualized speech of a character, the down-to-earth voice of a narrator in *skaz,* a letter or whatever. The lin-

> guistic and stylistic profile of a given element (lexical, semantic, syntactic) is shaped by that subordinated unity to which it is most immediately proximate. At the same time this element, together with its most immediate unity, figures into the style of the whole, itself supports the accent of the whole and participates in the process whereby the unified meaning of the whole is structured and revealed.
>
> The novel can be defined as a diversity of social speech types (sometimes even diversity of languages) and a diversity of individual voices, artistically organized. The internal stratification of any single national language into social dialects, characteristic group behaviour, professional jargons, generic languages, languages of generations and age groups, tendentious languages, languages of the authorities, of various circles and of passing fashions that serve the specific sociopolitical purposes of that day, even of the hour (each day has its own slogan, its own vocabulary, its own emphases)—this internal stratification present in every language at any given moment of its historical existence is the indispensable prerequisite for the novel as a genre. The novel orchestrates all its themes, the totality of the world of objects and ideas depicted and expressed in it, by means of the social diversity of speech types (*raznorecie*) and by the differing individual voices that flourish under such conditions. Authorial speech, the speeches of narrators, inserted genres, the speech of characters are merely those fundamental compositional unities with whose help heteroglossia (*raznorecie*) can enter the novel; each of them permits a multiplicity of social voices and a wide variety of their links and interrelationships (always more or less dialogized). These distinctive links and interrelationships between utterances and languages, this movement of the theme through different languages and speech types, its dispersion into the rivulets and droplets of social heteroglossia, its dialogization—this is the basic distinguishing feature of the stylistics of the novel. (Bakhtin, 1981: 262–63)

The concepts of heteroglossia and dialogicity suggest ways in which the problematic of ideological conflict and struggle in discursive practice can be a starting point for a critical study of the ways in which texts and social discourses work to maintain and change the social semiotic system. This would be different from a model based on the notion of cultural reproduction. For instance, Foucault, in his earlier writings, has written of a normative and coercive "body of anonymous, historical rules" (Foucault, 1974: 117) that is responsible for the reproduction of the social order. Silverman and Torode (1980: 332–37) argue in their critique of Foucault's earlier structuralist position that this conception does not have anything to say about the ability of social agents to intervene in and transform social practice. Foucault's position remains incomplete in the absence of any notion of text as the site of possible interventions and conflicting social discourses. Texts and the relations among voices in textual practice are constantly recontextualized in and through the dialogic interactions between social discourses. Texts are never complete except, perhaps, in a formal or structural sense. There is always the potential for intervention and change in the patterned meaning making practices that enact them. The writings of Bakhtin and Volosinov suggest a materialist and dialectical account of discursive and textual practice in which the semantic selections in texts are viewed not only in terms of their determining social contexts but also in terms of material textual practice. Material textual practices may therefore be situated not only in relation to a politics of intervention, but also in relation to a political and social theory concerning the nature, limits, and the critical potential of such acts of intervention.

Text, Discourse, and the System of Disjunctions

The emphasis here on material textual practices points to the gaps, limits, and contradictions that occur in texts, viewed as the site of a plurality of conflicting social discourses. Lemke (1983a; 1985b) has formulated the concept of the system of disjunctions that ramifies throughout the social semiotic system and systematically connects and disconnects social discourses and contextual domains in ways that ensure that there is not an equal probability of a given discourse-type, contextual domain, or semantic register being related to all others. The system of disjunctions operates both locally at, say, the level of the individual text and globally across entire intertextual formations right up to the entire social semiotic system. The system of disjunctions imposes limits on the kinds of meanings and practices typically enacted by social agents. It ensures that certain regular, systematic connections and patterned relations are typically made between different social discourses, while other potential patterns and relations are typically not made, or not recognized when they are. This ensures the overall metastability of the social semiotic system as a dynamic, open, goal-seeking system. Yet, it is important not to reduce this concept to yet another structural-functionalist account of the contradictions of the system. Such a reduction can be avoided by an analysis that relates these to the differential access of social agents to the material and semiotic resources of the social semiotic system. This further entails the differential and conflicting power-knowledge interests and relations that are articulated by specific heteroglossic relations among discursive positioned-practices and their textual voicings. This general perspective is important for correcting the tendency in much of sociolinguistics to conceptualize a one-to-one fit between text and context. In systemic-functional linguistics, for instance, the contextual variables of field, tenor, and mode are often seen as determinants of the linguistic features selected in texts at the level "below." The top-down emphasis on these variables as determinants of the semantic selections in texts tends to reify the social context of situation in such a way that it is made out to reproduce itself independent of specific textual productions. A too normative, top-down model of the text-context relation cannot adequately conceptualize the text as the site of a plurality of overlapping and contradictory social discourses and semantic registers. I have argued elsewhere (Thibault, 1986f: 103) that the Hjelmslevian concept of realization does not entail a simple, one-way determination from the top down, from the social situation to the text. It is, rather, a productive, two-way dialectic in which texts enact, create, and produce their contexts of situation as much as they are determined by them. Texts cannot be reduced to the necessary properties of an a priori social situation. This would imply that texts are no more than the mere appearances of an underlying (social) reality that they "represent" or "refer to." Both the systems of social heteroglossia and the plurifunctional character of textual meanings emphasize the overdetermined nature of all social meaning making. Its overdetermined nature means that the meaning potential of the social semiotic system is never reducible to a single, determinate, or unifunctional textual meaning. This does not preclude the fact that there are regular and systematic meaning making orientations that work to fix and articulate the social formation in specific, historically contingent ways. These cannot, however, be reduced to some explanatory cause in terms of, for instance, determination in the last instance by social class. I have discussed this problematic in greater detail elsewhere (Thibault, 1986d: 63).

The concept of overdetermination enables us to link functional explanations of language with a materialist one (see Pateman, 1981: 8). This does not presume that a given formal feature in the lexico-grammar empirically correlates with or reflects, say, a particular social class. What is needed is a functional explanation based on the distribution and copatterning of meaning relations in their contexts of situation. These are then linked to determinate material social practices in the wider social formation. This requires that we look at the discursive situation as a social process and at the part played by language in it, rather than reifying language in the way accounts based on structural-functionalist sociological premises do (see Thibault, 1986c: 32). The work of Bakhtin and Volosinov helps us better to understand that textual and discursive practices are also social practices. Texts and social occasions of discourse are always constituted and overdetermined in relation to some still wider social formation. A particular text is constituted by the determinations arising from potentially all the processes and relations that enact a given social formation. Structural-functionalist accounts of language are reductionist when they argue, from a normative, consensus-oriented model of the social order, that a given formal feature in the lexico-grammar is uniquely determined by or is the effect of some aspect of the social structure. The concept of overdetermination is also important for the way in which it connects texts to specific social practices as well as to their determinate material relations of production. Texts, as the work of Bakhtin and Volosinov demonstrates, are not reducible to static determinations of, say, particular class values and interests.

Critical theories of textual intervention account for the ways in which specific domains of social practice either are enacted in and through their textual productions or else constitute the gaps, disjunctions, the missing registers, or the "yet-to-be-voiced" (Bernstein, 1982) in texts and intertextual formations. An important dimension of such a textual politics is a reading strategy that can reconstitute the intertextual formations and the social meaning making practices that are instantiated in particular textual productions. Such a reading strategy enables us analytically to reconstruct and approximate the kinds of relationships texts have with other texts, the heteroglossic relations that are articulated in and through these intertextual formations, and their particular intersections and voicings in a given textual production.

Critical Intertextual Analysis

A critical intertextual analysis is a means of challenging the autonomous, object-like status of texts. It is more than merely positioning the text in its context of situation. This would tend to fix or naturalize the text in terms of an already given social situation. Such a naturalizing function suggests a seamless, unproblematic relation between a text and its context, masking the gaps, disjunctions, incoherencies, and potential sites of intervention in texts and still wider intertextual formations. Critical analysis aims to relate the text to the social meaning making practices in and through which texts and their meanings are made, used, intervened in, and changed. Texts are not autonomous objects among other spontaneously arising objects. Instead, they are instantiations of the intertextual relations and processes out of which they are made. The dominant ideology functions to naturalize these processes by reifying these processes as textual objects and products. The system of disjunctions works to disjoin texts from the intertextual formations in and through which they are produced and are meaningful.

The patterned relations between texts and social meaning making practices are constructed and construed by social agents in and through the meaning making resources of the social semiotic system. This emphasis on the active, constructive role of social agents helps to refocus attention on the productive labor whereby social meanings are made. Textual meanings are not simply given *in* texts, but are made and transformed (recontextualized) out of specific intertextual co-patternings of meaning relations and their context-dependent uses in determinate social and historical situations. Textual meanings are enacted by human labor, which transforms social meaning making practices into reified textual commodities. Eco (1976: 151–56, 276) similarly points out, with the concept of "rhetorical labor," the importance of the work performed in the production and maintenance of social meanings. Some conceptual limitations of the production paradigm for social semiotic theory will be discussed in chapters 7 and 8.

In the following section I shall analyze a number of intertextual relations between Nabokov's *Ada* and *Lolita* in order to show that much more is involved than a mere mirroring of one text in the other. Intertextuality is not adequately defined as the mediation between *Lolita* as the anterior text and *Ada* as the final product of this process. The patterned meaning relations that we can construe between the two texts are assembled through processes of syntagmatic juxtaposition and transformation in relation to still wider and more abstract intertextual formations. At this stage, our analysis will attempt to reconstruct and approximate the recombinations and transformations in and through the specific meaning relations that are constituted between the two texts. This is not limited to a simple citing of or alluding to other texts as antecedent sources.

Intertextual Relations in *Ada:* A Preliminary Analysis

In this section, I propose to analyze a number of intertextual relations in an excerpt from *Ada* (chapter 1, section 13, pp. 77–88). The analysis will show how it is possible to reconstruct at least four sets of intertextual relations. This is not a simple matter of selection from a paradigmatic system of possible choices, although this is certainly one way of talking about a typology of intertextual systems. It is also a dialectical process of transformation and recoding. This first preliminary stage of the analysis will involve a retracing from the textual extract as finished product to the diachronic reconstruction of the intertextual relations that are coded in the text. The analytical reconstruction proposed here is best grasped in terms of Foucault's (1974) "archaeological" analysis. Foucault has specified four principles that are fundamental to this mode of analysis:

> 1. Archaeology tries to define not the thoughts, representations, images, themes, preoccupations that are concealed or revealed in discourses; but those discourses themselves, those discourses as practices obeying certain rules. It does not treat discourse as *document,* as a sign of something else, as an element that ought to be transparent, but whose unfortunate opacity must often be pierced if one is to reach at last the depth of the essential in the place in which it is held in reserve; it is concerned with discourse in its own volume, as a *monument*. It is not an interpretative discipline: it does not seek another, better-hidden discourse. It refuses to be "allegorical."
>
> 2. Archaeology does not seek to rediscover the continuous, insensible transition that relates discourses, on a gentle slope, to what precedes them, surrounds them, or follows them. It does not await for the moment when, on the basis of what they were not yet, they became what they are; nor the moment when, the solidity of their figure crumbling away, they will gradually lose their identity. On the contrary, its problem is to define discourses in their specificity; to show in what way the

set of rules that they put into operation is irreducible to any other; to follow them the whole length of their exterior ridges, in order to underline them the better. It does not proceed, in slow progression, from the confused field of opinion to the uniqueness of the system or the definitive stability of science; it is not a "doxology"; but a differential analysis of the modalities of discourse.

3. Archaeology is not ordered in accordance with the sovereign figure of the *oeuvres;* it does not try to grasp the moment in which the *oeuvre* emerges on the anonymous horizon. It does not wish to rediscover the enigmatic point at which the individual and the social are inverted into one another. It is neither a psychology, nor a sociology, nor more generally an anthropology of creation. The *oeuvre* is not for archaeology a relevant division, even if it is a matter of replacing it in its total context or in the network of causalities that support it. It defines types of rules for discursive practices that run through individual *oeuvres,* sometimes govern them entirely, and dominate them to such an extent that nothing eludes them; but which sometimes, too, govern only part of it. The authority of the creative subject, as the *raison d'être* of an *oeuvre* and the principle of its unity, is quite alien to us.

4. Lastly, archaeology does not try to restore what has been thought, wished, aimed at, experienced, desired by men in the very moment at which they expressed it in discourse; it does not set out to recapture that elusive nucleus in which the author and the *oeuvre* exchange identities; in which thought still remains nearest to oneself, in the as yet unaltered form of the same, and in which language (*langage*) has not yet been deployed in the spatial, successive dispersion of discourse. In other words, it does not try to repeat what has been said by reaching it in its very identity. It does not claim to efface itself in the ambiguous modesty of a reading that would bring back, in all its purity, the distant, precarious, almost effaced light of the origin. It is nothing more than a rewriting: that is, in the preserved form of exteriority, a regulated transformation of what has already been written. It is not a return to the innermost secret of the origin; it is the systematic description of a discourse-object. (Foucault, 1974: 138–40)

Foucault is concerned with a dynamic, historical analysis that attempts to relate the regularities of discursive statements and the principles of the construction and transformation of discursive subjects and objects to specific discursive fields of action and practice. The emphasis on the specificity of discourses helps to call attention to the ways in which literary texts, by virtue of their own discursive and generic specificity, organize and articulate (inter)textual thematic relations and social activity-structures and their interrelations in ways that are specific to the discursive formations in and through which the literary norm itself is articulated. John Frow cautions against a certain view of the literary text, derived from Bakhtin, as the transformations of general, nonliterary discursive norms that "ignore the complexity of the enunciative shift involved in the elaboration of one generic structure by another (this enunciative shift in turn produces more complex forms of modality and more complex reality effects)" (Frow, 1986: 128). Thus, the organization and articulation of *both* literary and nonliterary norms and values in the literary text constitute a productive, overdetermined process that is, however, not bound or limited by the foregrounding of specific intertextual references in the text (Frow, 1986: 130). Foucault points out that these are subject to the rules of discursive practices, whereby systems of intertextual meaning relations are organized in regular, limited ways according to the rules that govern their relations of combination, disjunction, and their functionality in *that* discursive formation.[1] The rules that specify which operations and combinations apply, and how, indexically create and/or presuppose the "reality effects" referred to by Frow. The overdetermined, contradictory nature of (inter)textual meaning relations enact or produce, in the literary text, semiotically under- and overcoded (Eco, 1976: 129–42) reality effects. The passage from *Ada* that I shall shortly analyze thus indexes and foregrounds its connections with an overdetermined intertextual field of meaning relations. These meaning relations are organized both synchronically and diachronically,[2] relating social meaning making practices to each other in three principal ways: (1) those that are copresent within the same set of discursive practices and thematic formation relations, (2) relations between discursive practices and thematic relations in different social discourse-types, and (3) diachronic relations to historically prior discursive practices and thematic relations.

The analysis will begin with the opening paragraph of the section referred to above:

> For the big picnic on Ada's twelfth birthday and Ida's fortysecond *jour de fête,* the child was permitted to wear her lolita (thus dubbed after the little Andalusian gypsy of that name in Osberg's novel and pronounced, incidentally, with a Spanish 't', not a thick English one), a rather long, but very airy and ample, black skirt, with red poppies or peonies, "deficient in botanical reality," as she grandly expressed it, not yet knowing that reality and natural science are synonymous in terms of this, and only this, dream. (Nabokov, 1969: 77)

The first of these synchronic reconstructions is the comparison of Ada with Lolita. This is also evident near the end of the episode under consideration. In the latter case, which we shall consider further on, Humbert is related to Van and Lolita to Ada. Our second synchronic reconstruction concerns the anagrammatic rewriting of the name of the Argentine writer Borges as *Osberg*. In the fictive world of *Ada*, Lolita is depicted as a character in a novel by Osberg. The comparison of Ada to Lolita also implies a diachronic reconstruction that links *Ada* to Prosper Mérimée's short story "Carmen." We shall also see in chapter 6 that Humbert Humbert compares Lolita to Carmen in Nabokov's novel *Lolita*. The comparison also implies the further link between Ada and Carmen. In the above passage, Ada's lolita skirt is linked with "the little Andalusian gypsy." And in Mérimée's story, Carmen is also referred to in the same way. This diachronic reconstruction implies a further one whereby the sexually ambiguous writings of Chateaubriand are invoked. Both Chateaubriand's *Atala* and *René* are referred to throughout *Ada*. These texts contain thematic implications of incest. Chateaubriand's *Les aventures du dernier Abencérage* is especially important for our analysis of intertextuality in the *Ada* episode. Ada is indirectly linked with Blanca de Bivar in this story by Chateaubriand. Blanca de Bivar is a Spanish seductress like Carmen. This story concerns her transgressions of dominant social interdictions when she develops a sexual relationship with a Moor:

> Blanca se trouva bientôt engagée dans une passion profonde par l'impossibilité même où elle crut être d'éprouver jamais cette passion. Aimer un Infidèle, un Maure, un inconnu, lui paraissait une chose si étrange, qu'elle ne prit aucune précaution contre le mal qui commençait à se glisser dans ses veines; mais aussitôt qu'elle reconnut les atteintes, elle accepta ce mal en véritable Espagnole. (Chateaubriand, [1826] 1962: 281)[3]

A further passage from the same work helps to show that Blanca de Bivar is constructed from the intersection of a number of different thematic systems. The INCEST thematic is invoked by virtue of her relations with her brother, her father, and even perhaps her now absent mother. The incest thematic articulates the violation of social prohibitions concerning sexual behavior. Blanca also invokes a thematic of SPONTANEOUS EROTICISM ("tout était séduction dans cette femme enchanteresse"). Third, she indexes a thematic of COURTLY BEHAVIOR ("l'élevation des sentiments de son coeur"):

> Blanca de Bivar, soeur unique de don Carlos, et beaucoup plus jeune que lui, était l'idole de son père: elle avait perdu sa mère, et elle entrait dans sa dixhuitième année, lorsque Aben-Hamet parut à Grenade. Tout était séduction dans cette femme enchanteresse; sa voix était ravissante, sa danse plus légère que le zéphyr: tantôt elle se plaisait à guider un char comme Armide, tantôt elle volait sur le dos du plus rapide coursier de l'Andalousie, comme ces Fées charmantes qui apparaissaient à Tristan et à Galaor dans les forêts. Athènes l'eût prise pour Aspasie, et Paris pour Diane de Poitiers qui commençait à briller à la cour. Mais avec les charmes d'une Française, elle avait les passions d'une Espagnole, et sa coquetterie naturelle n'ôtait rien à la sûreté, à la constance, à la force, à l'élevation des sentiments de son coeur. (Chateaubriand, [1826] 1962: 276–77)[4]

These two passages show that Blanca de Bivar is the intersection and voicing of a number of heteroglossically related thematic systems. The diachronic recon-

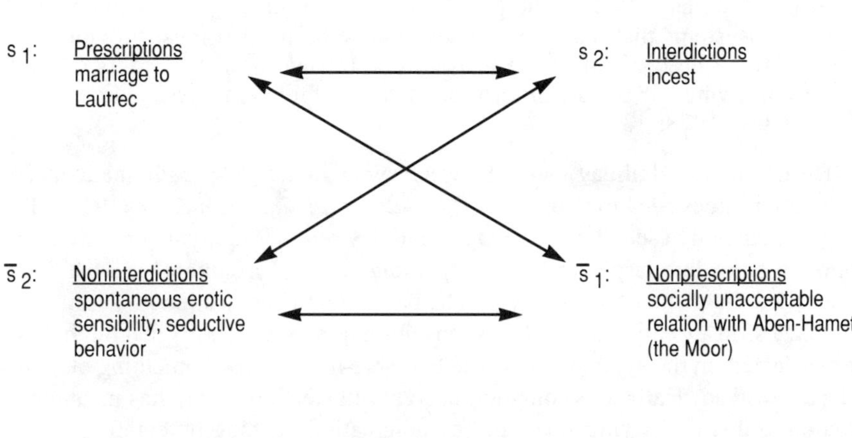

Figure 5.1. Homologization of sociosexual roles: Blanca de Bivar

struction of these does not imply a linear, evolutionary model of the text's history. Jameson (1981: 139) has proposed the suggestive metaphor of the X ray, by means of which we can analytically reconstruct a text's genealogy. Jameson speaks of selected "objective conditions" through which a text's synchronic existence contains its diachronic perspective, as well. The valorization of the text as a reified commodity separates the text from its social and historical conditions of production. The intersecting thematic relations in the above examples may be formalized with the help of the Greimasian semiotic square (Figure 5.1).

The use of this formalism does not in itself theoretically justify the derived semantic relations. The Greimasian elaboration of the structuralist principle of binary oppositions presents us with a relatively closed set of terms whose validity is not, in this form of analysis, sought outside the self-contained set of oppositions and permutations suggested by the square. The semiotic square remains an abstract formalism that does not relate semantic relations and their transformations to social practice. I am using the square here for strictly heuristic purposes.

Paradigmatic and Syntagmatic Relations and the Same/Different Dialectic

Halliday relates his concept of text as an "operational semantic unit" to the distinction between paradigmatic and syntagmatic relations in ways that are important for the concept of intertextuality:

> By "text," then, we understand a continuous process of semantic choice. Text is meaning and meaning is choice, an ongoing current of selections each in its paradigmatic environment of what might have been meant (but was not). It is the paradigmatic environment—the innumerable subsystems that make up the semantic system—that must provide the basis of description, if the text is to be related to higher orders of meaning, whether social, literary or of some other semiotic universe. (Halliday, 1978: 137)

The distinction Halliday makes between syntagmatic and paradigmatic meaning relations goes back to Saussure's *Cours de linguistique Générale* (1915). The "ongoing current of selections" to which Halliday refers is the syntagmatic combination of signs into larger units. The "paradigmatic environment" is what Saussure called the plane of *association*. The paradigmatic environment classifies or "associates" in absentia potential relationships among sets of units that might have been selected on the syntagmatic plane but were not because something else was selected instead. Halliday's "ongoing current of selections" only has meaning in relation to this underlying systemic (paradigmatic) meaning potential. The two planes relate elements according to differing principles, which entail different modes of analytical activity.

The syntagmatic plane entails the relation of "identifying something *with* something." The paradigmatic plane entails the relation of "identifying something *as* something." I have derived these two distinct but related kinds of identity relations from Joachim Israel's study concerning the laws of dialectical operations (see Israel, 1979: 101). The correct use of these two identity relations constitutes the "condition of identification" (Israel, 1979: 102). *Identifying with* involves relating, for example, social actions and linguistic tokens to their contexts-of-use. *Identifying as* involves the recognition of the appropriate syntagmatic units to be used in a given context. Fulfillment of the "conditions of identification" entails the interaction of these two axes. *Identifying with,* for our present purposes, is concerned with the "ongoing current of selections," namely, the syntagmatic plane. *Identifying as* is concerned with comparing an element with its past and future (i.e., absent) forms and relations (see Israel, 1979: 103–7). *Identifying with* is, on the other hand, concerned with the present form of the element. The introduction of the temporal dimension enables us to focus on paradigmatic relations as *valeur* producing through the same/different dialectic.

A given text is simultaneously contextualized along a number of different dimensions: (1) the syntagmatic relations among co-occurring units in some larger structural whole, (2) the paradigmatic systems of potential choices[5] that always constitute the environment within which a given meaning selection is made, and (3) the intertextual meaning relations in relation to which a given textual production is always construed as meaningful. These contextualizing relations are relationally semiotic and therefore always enact specific systems of *valeur* in the social semiotic system. They do not rely on any notion of some more objective "reality" lying "behind" these relations and that is simply referred to. If two texts are said to share some common intertextual meaning relation, then it is possible to assign them to some wider intertextual set. The two texts can, in some sense, be said to be the "same." There is an identity relation between them in the sense I defined above. At the same time, the two texts are also different. This is so for two main reasons. First, text users construe specific types of regular, systematic relations between some kinds of texts and not others. Second, text users may recognize some features as the same in two (or more) texts, while other features are not seen as potentially related or coclassified. Intertextuality therefore enacts a same/different dialectic, which is central to the relational character of semiotic *valeur*. Saussure has formulated the concept of *valeur* as follows:

> Values always involve:
> (1) something *dissimilar* which can be exchanged for the item whose value is under consideration, and
> (2) *similar* things which can be *compared* with the item whose value is under consideration.
> These two features are necessary for the existence of any value. To determine the value of a five-franc coin, for instance, what must be known is: (1) that the coin can be exchanged for a certain quantity of something different, e.g. bread, and (2) that its value can be compared with another value in the same system, e.g. that of a one-franc coin, or of a coin belonging to another system (e.g. a dollar). Similarly, a word can be substituted for something dissimilar: an idea. At the same time, it can be compared to something of like nature: another word. Its value is therefore not determined merely by that concept or meaning for which it is a token. It must also be assessed against comparable values, by contrast with other words. The content of a word is determined in the final analysis not by what it contains but by what exists outside it. As an element in a system, the word has not only a meaning but also—above all—a value. And that is something quite different. (Saussure, [1915] 1983: 113–14)

In terms of the analysis above, we can exchange the signifier *Ada* for the signified *spontaneous eroticism*. We can also compare the signifier *Ada* with the signifier *little Andalusian gypsy*. This sets up a same/different relation through a process of paradigmatic classification and reclassification (cf. association). It is clear that the establishment of the value "Ada : little Andalusian gypsy" at the level of the signifier leads to the setting up of a similarity in the signified. In this case, the construction of semiotic values presupposes the construction of a same/different dialectic at both the levels of signifier and signified.

How can two (or more) texts, which are related by virtue of a shared intertextual relation, be said to be the same? The relations of *identifying with* and *identify-*

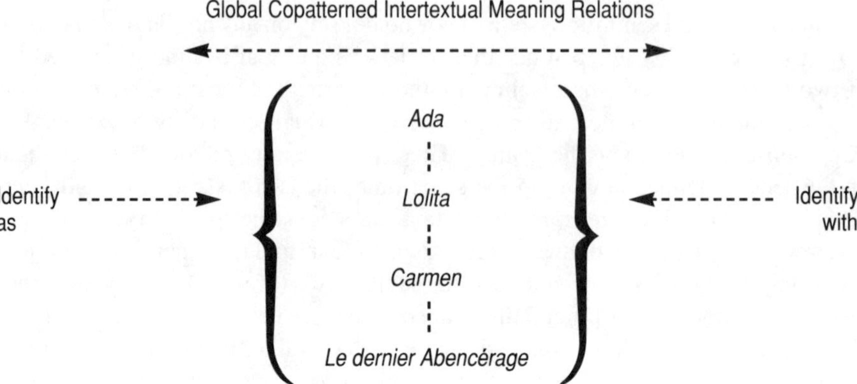

Figure 5.2. The operation of intertextual relations of identity

ing as are useful here. We can identify some type-feature of a given abstract intertextual formation "a" *as* a feature that texts X and Y have in common. This means that in some sense type-feature "a" is appropriately used or meaningful in the same way in both X and Y. This further entails that we can identify X with Y according to some wider contextualizing relation or principle. The earlier analysis showed that the following texts are related in some wider system of intertextual relations: *Ada* (Nabokov), *Lolita* (Nabokov), *Carmen* (Mérimée), and *Les aventures du dernier Abencérage* (Chateaubriand). Figure 5.2 is a schematization of these relations.

We cannot identify the four texts *with* each other if we have not also, according to some criterion, identified them *as* both different from each other and specific. Furthermore, we cannot identify them as different and specific if we have not identified them with text-specific patterns and meaning relations. It is important to bear in mind that both identifying operations are necessary and that they mutually presuppose and interact with each other. What do we identify? We identify an element with something according to its position in syntagmatic structure. We identify an element as something by paradigmatically comparing (associating) it with its past and future (i.e., absent) forms and relations in a structured system of alternatives. These operations can occur in both single texts and across wider intertextual sets, both synchronically and diachronically. A given syntagmatic unit can be compared and/or associated with other elements that precede it in the same text or in some historically prior text. The latter would refer to Jameson's "objective preconditions" or textual "genealogies" mentioned above. The point remains the same in both cases: syntagmatic relations (both near and far in time) enact and confirm specific semiotic values through their association with historically and textually prior forms. Alternatively, a given syntagmatic relation may lead us, on account of the paradigmatic *identifying as* relation in the signified, to anticipate some future value or relation. The dual perspective I have outlined here shows how specific semiotic values are always produced in and through shifting, contingent social and historical processes. The constant dialectic between semiotic forms and their synchronic and diachronic dimensions means that texts always have an intertextual history of other texts, meanings, and practices. This perspective is not possible if we confine our discussion of semiotic forms to the intrinsic, formal properties of texts per se. Alternatively, a critical intertextual analysis can deconstruct the text as reified commodity and reconstitute it within a genealogy of intertextual relations. I shall consider further aspects of semiotic *valeur* in chapter 8.

Covariate and Multivariate Relations

In chapter 4 I pointed out that global (inter)textual meaning relations are always assembled and enacted in and through local units, which are combined and copatterned to form larger-scale (inter)textual meaning relations. These occur on the basis of the interplay of multivariate and covariate syntagmatic relations at all levels—from the strictly local to the most global—across texts and even entire intertextual sets (Lemke, 1983b: 164). Multivariate syntagmatic relations are defined by the functional relations among a finite set of functionally differentiated parts, which make up some larger structural whole (Lemke, 1983b: 163). The parts that constitute this syntagmatic relation are functionally related to each other as a multivariate whole. This multivariate relation defines the functional relations of the parts to the whole. A multivariate structure is recognized as complete when all the functional role-slots in the structure are occupied by their constituent functional parts. For example, the functional semantic roles in the ideational-grammatical structure of a clause-type such as Actor-Process-Goal are the functionally related parts that comprise the clause-level multivariate whole, functionally interpreted as a microlevel social act-type.

Covariate relations work according to the principle that it is possible to construct or construe a meaningful relation between two or more texts, social activities, and so forth, on the basis of some still wider or higher-order contextual relation that both are recognized as sharing. Two texts so identified can be said to share a particular covariate tie-type on the basis of some common feature that links them together as belonging to the same class or type. Lemke (1985b) gives the example of a typology such that "if A and B are, at some level of the typology, both members of the same class (i.e. share a type feature *z*) then there is a z-relation between A and B and between them and any other member of the z-class." The occurrence of a sufficient number of members of the z-class in a text is said to constitute a cohesive chain relation among its tokens (members) by virtue of the common feature *z* that they all share. Covariate relations are not dependent on the functional relations of parts to some larger structural whole, nor do they constitute any necessary linear ordering in syntagmatic structure. They occur distributionally across texts and still wider intertextual sets and are not "locally compact" in the way multivariate relations are. Covariate relations enable connections to be made between features by virtue of shared cohesive or thematic ties between them. Two or more elements so tied are construed as sharing some meaning relation common to both, regardless of the fact that there may be no local, multivariate structural relation linking them. Covariate relations work on the basis of the potential for two or more items to be functionally coclassified as belonging to the same class on the basis of wider contextual and distributional principles.

These claims may now be linked with the preliminary intertextual analysis above. The multivariate relations among the items *Ada*, *lolita*, *little Andalusian gypsy*, and *Osberg's novel* are locally compact by virtue of the functional role relations they perform in the clause complex of which these units are constituent parts. The occurrence of these items within the same clause complex is a local strategy that foregrounds and indexes a more global system of relations to which these items are assignable. The local foregrounding of these units in this way indexes a more global, abstract intertextual formation to which these items belong, or to which they can be assigned according to specifiable criteria of coclassification. Figure 5.3 draws on the principles of thematic analysis developed by Lemke (1983b; also see Thibault, 1986d) in order to present diagrammatically the abstract (inter)textual relations that connect these items.

The unbroken horizontal line that connects the lexical items in the top row indicates the multivariate relations among these in the ideational-grammatical semantics of the clauses they belong to. The unbroken vertical lines connect these items to their principal thematic relation tie-types. The broken lines indicate the covariate ties that construct thematic links among the various items irrespective of the linear, syntagmatic structuring of the text. The covariate tie-types link textual features on the basis of some shared type-feature. For example, the (superordinate) type-feature glossed as INCEST in some abstract intertextual formation coclassifies or types the syntagmatic units *Ada*, *little Andalusian gypsy*, and *Osberg's novel* as belonging to some wider intertextual formation INCEST. A given syntagmatic combination may selectively foreground some thematic relations rather than others in ways that index specific abstract intertextual formations, which are relevant for the meaning of the text.

Cothematic and Coactional Intertextual Relations

Intertextuality is not adequately defined in terms of a positivistic recovery of antecedent source texts. Frow discusses this problem in connection with the distinction between "weak" and "strong" forms of intertextuality. This is proposed as a

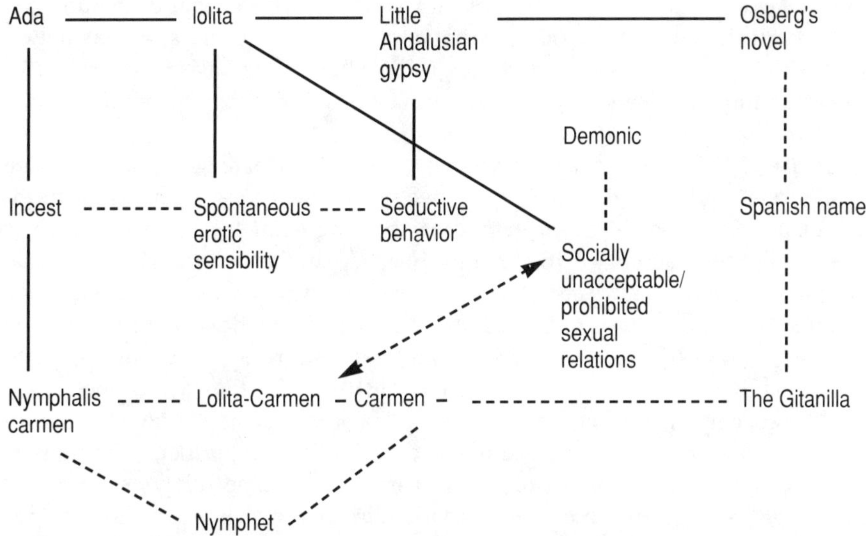

Figure 5.3. Common intertextual thematic formation relations linking *Ada*, *Lolita*, *Carmen*, and *Le dernier Abencérage* (general specification only)

way of distinguishing between "thematic allusion on the one hand and an explicit, extended, verbally and structurally close reference on the other" (Frow, 1986: 156). Intertextual meaning relations are not necessarily or simply constituted by shared meaning relations between, say, two or more specific texts. The problem is more adequately theorized, as Lemke (1983b) points out, in terms of the level of abstraction at which two or more texts are construed as belonging to the same intertextual set. Instead of a positivistic search for antecedent texts and explicit links between one text and another, we can talk about the ways in which specific textual productions can be construed as belonging to the same more abstract or higher-order class of meaning relations according to some functional criteria. The resulting abstract intertextual formations (Lemke, 1988a) constitute an analytical construct abstracted from many texts taken to share the same meaning relations according to some functional criteria of coclassification. These functional criteria, according to which texts are assigned to a given intertextual formation, are, in the words of Foucault, "characterized not by principles of construction but by a dispersion of fact, since for statements it is not a condition of possibility but a law of coexistence, and since statements are not interchangeable elements but groups characterized by their modality of existence" (Foucault, 1974: 116). We are thus concerned with the copatterned meaning relations in particular texts and how they contribute to the maintenance and development of the more abstract intertextual formations to which they belong as types or classes of meaning relations, whose "modality of existence" is articulated according to some functional criteria deployed by the users of those texts. These are shifting, discontinuous, and historically contingent sociodiscursive practices that coclassify texts not on the basis of intrinsic textual properties per se, but on the basis of the selective foregrounding of some kinds of meaning relations rather than others in connection with specific social practices.

Lemke (1985b) has further shown that the kinds of meaning relations that can be so foregrounded are definable along two main dimensions. Intertextual meaning relations, functionally interpreted, may be *coactional* or *cothematic*. Two or more texts are coactional if they regularly enact similar or the same functional roles in some multivariate social activity-structure type. Two or more texts may be *cothematic* on the basis of shared lexico-semantic and ideational-grammatical meaning relations from the lexico-grammatical resources of the language. (Inter)textual thematic meaning relations are construable on the basis of the typical patterns of combination and co-occurrence of lexico-semantic and ideational-grammatical items. These enact networks of thematic relations both within single texts and across entire intertextual sets. Thematic meaning relations are global copatternings and distributions of semantic relations, which are covariately tied on the basis of some wider contextual relation. Cothematic ties in texts share close affinities with the concept of textual cohesion (Halliday and Hasan, 1976; Hasan, 1980, 1984). Hasan's concepts of "cohesive chain" and "cohesive chain interaction" will be used later as a first step in the analytical reconstruction of cothematic meaning relations between *Ada* and *Lolita*. Textual cohesion is constituted by the covariate ties between textual features in ways that contribute to the thematic development of texts. Covariate thematic ties link and selectively foreground some kinds of lexico-semantic and ideational-grammatical relations rather than others and as such are part of the partial hierarchies of global meaning relations that contribute to the meaning(s) of a text. These relations are not confined to single texts. A given text may also share covariate thematic ties with other texts on the basis of some wider contextual principle. This means that cothematic relations occur distributionally not only in individual texts but across entire intertextual formations. A given covariate thematic tie in a single text is also potentially the realization of some more abstract cothematic relation, intertextually defined. Just as text-specific thematic relations do not enact isolated copatternings of items, so do intertextual cothematic relations enact relations of continuity and disjunction between wider intertextual formations.

The distinction made by Lemke thus provides us with two analytically separable dimensions of social meaning making for the analysis of (inter)textual meaning relations. This makes it possible, in the social semiotic framework, to deal with what Frow designates as "the functional integration of intertextual material" whereby specific texts transform or recontextualize their relations with other texts "in accordance with an internal textual logic" (Frow, 1986: 157). The intertextual transformation (recontextualization) of social meanings and values can only be adequately theorized in terms of a *social semiotics of action*. Social semiotics recognizes that, say, thematic meaning relations are enacted and used in and through specific social activity-structures with which they combine. We are not therefore concerned with a reified text-semantics, abstracted from the social activity-structures and practices that enact semantic meaning relations. Social activity-structures are multivariate syntagmatic combinations of functionally related constituents in and through which context-specific social actions are performed by social agents. They are also the means by which thematic (semantic) relations in texts are put into operation. In systemic-functional linguistics, these activity-structures have been analyzed at the textual level in terms of the staged schematic structure elements that comprise the global (macro) structure of the textual dimension of a given social activity-structure (see Hasan, 1978; Martin, 1985b, 1986). Similar work has also been undertaken in the tagmemic tradition on "discourse genre" (e.g., Longacre, 1974) and by Labov (1972) on conventional narratives of personal experience. For example, Labov (1972: 363) proposes the following macrostructural sequencing of functional constituents in the episodic structure of conventional narrative: ABSTRACT + ORIENTATION + COMPLICATING ACTION + EVALUATION + RESULT or RESOLUTION + CODA. These constituents and their combinations enact the partially determinate sequencing of a number of optional and obligatory functional units, which comprise the "generic structure" of the text.

The analysis of social actions and their realizations in multivariate social activity-structure sequences is an essential component for theorizing what is done to particular thematic meaning relations and their deployments in the processes of intertextual transformation referred to by Frow. Social semiotics is interested in the particular ways in which "the functional integration of intertextual material" entails specific social semiotic action productions. The analysis of these in terms of an idealized text-semantics or reified generic typologies abstracted from social practice is inadequate for showing how the operations referred to by Frow are forms of social action. This functional integration may bring about new or changed uses of thematic and actional meanings and new combinations of these. The distinction between cothematic and coactional intertextual relations also requires that the presumed unity of text and context be problematized. Lemke (1983a: 11–16) has split the traditionally unitary notion of context of situation in systemic-functional linguistics into two analytically separable dimensions, which are useful for this purpose. These are the *interactional context* and the *thematic context*. For example, in narrative discourse the participants enact both particular interactional strategies and action sequences (advancement of the plot, the activity of narrating) and thematic (semantic) relations in the text. The problematizing of the traditional text-context dichotomy requires that we reject the view that texts have a pregiven content or topic that is then simply encoded into a suitable lexico-grammatical form. Much of contemporary text linguistics, with its epistemological basis in the cognitive science paradigm, epitomizes this way of talking about textual meanings. (See Thibault, 1986c, for a critical discussion of this paradigm.) For instance, Beaugrande (1978: 8) proposes a model of textual coherence in which two general principles are important: (1) text users expect a continuity in the presented material, and (2) the occurrence of the first part of a given structure raises expectations that the structure will be completed. Beaugrande argues seemingly unproblematically that the raising of a "topic" leads to the expectation that the topic will be pursued and that the presentation of this topic will conform to already defined lexico-grammatical criteria in the text. Similarly, Eco (1980) claims that a topic is activated as a reading hypothesis, which indicates the appropriate contextual selections and therefore imposes a semantic coherence on our reading of a text. However, the concept of topic in these accounts continues to operate the folk-theoretical distinction between form and meaning-as-underlying-content.[6] Beaugrande puts it this way:

> WORDS or WORD GROUP UNITS are EXPRESSIONS: SURFACE MEANS for UNDERLYING concepts and relations. The use of expressions in communication ACTIVATES these concepts and relations, that is, enters their content into ACTIVE STORAGE in the mind. The transition between expressions and their content is an aspect of MAPPING. (Beaugrande, 1980: 66)

Elsewhere in the same study Beaugrande develops the notion of "conceptual connectivity," represented by relational networks of "expression" and the "underlying concepts and relations" that map onto these. These are represented diagrammatically as relational networks which are *formally* quite similar to the analysis of thematic relations first proposed in Lemke (1983b) and developed in Thibault (1986d). Nevertheless, there are very substantial differences in the epistemological claims of the two approaches. Beaugrande argues that the word has a pregiven content, which is represented in cognitive terms as "underlying concepts and relations." Thematic analysis assumes, on the other hand, that the meaning of a given formal item is built up from its context-dependent copatterned relations with other lexico-grammatical items, representable in thematic analysis as nonlinear relational networks (see Lemke, 1983b: 160–61). Thematic analysis rejects the idea that words and their combinations are the expression or representation of some pregiven, underlying content, which can be abstracted away from, or seen as somehow existing either "behind" or independently of (in our minds?) or even prior to, their copatterning in specific thematic and interactional domains. The analysis of both cothematic and coactional (inter)textual meaning relations is then critically important for a social semiotics that is endeavoring to break with the powerful folk-theoretical assumption that meanings "exist" independently of the copatterned relations and the social practices in and through which they are *made*.

Intertextual Analysis: *Ada* and *Lolita*

In this section I shall analyze the intertextual relations between an excerpt from *Lolita* (Nabokov, 1959: 60–61) and an excerpt from *Ada* (Nabokov, 1969: 83–84). The two excerpts share very close cothematic and coactional ties; this will be the basis of the analysis both in this chapter and in the following one. The two excerpts have been segmented into clause level constituents in Appendix 1.

Criteria of lexico-semantic coclassification are, as Hasan (1984: 201) shows, either *systematic* or *instantial*. Systematic cohesive relations exist in the linguistic system, whereas instantial ones are textually specific. Thematic relations are not then necessarily constituted on the basis of readily specifiable systematic relations. They can also be instantiated on the basis of a highly specific set of relations within a single text or a restricted number of texts. We shall return to this argument in the following chapter. In this connection, it is useful to mention some of the difficulties Hasan (1984: 202) refers to in her attempt to operationalize the concept of collocation. These difficulties may well highlight the need for a context-dependent intertextual analysis as the basis of all cohesive relations. In the present analysis, the two excerpts will be analyzed in terms of lexico-semantic cohesive chains and lexical chain interaction (Hasan, 1984). This analysis is presented in full in Appendix 2 and Appendix 3. These two appendixes display the distribution of the principal lexico-semantic chains and their patterns of interaction in the two textual excerpts. They help to illustrate the global patterning of these relations across the two excerpts. There is no attempt at this stage to specify the clause level ideational-grammatical resources that contribute to this patterning. These will be analyzed in the following chapter. Lexico-semantic cohesive chains can then be analyzed in terms of the kind and degree of the interaction between chains. Appendix 2 and Appendix 3 are organized into columns, with each column representing a specific cohesive chain or lexico-semantic macroset. The headings I have assigned to each column are no more than a shorthand superordinate gloss on the lexico-semantic relations in that chain. The analysis shows that covariate ties are construable between the two texts on the basis of shared lexico-semantic relations. However, this does not tell us how the two texts enact a shared system of intertextual relations. Lemke (1985b) argues that we need some further multivariate structural criteria for foregrounding the specific intertextual ties between two (or more) texts. In the *Ada* excerpt, the relationship with *Lolita* is indexed in clause 2d. Additionally, there is a covariate tie between *pine-smelling skirt* and the previous occurrence of the *lolita* skirt at the beginning of this episode. This covariate tie enables a "Lolita" frame to be adduced, which is construable as relevant to the meaning of the text. The more abstract thematic ties indicated in the analysis enable shared abstract intertextual relations to be construed. The concepts of dialogicity and social heteroglossia show how this involves the articulation of a plurality of semantic registers, thematic and actional meanings, and their textual voicings. These relations involve patterns of semantic conjunction and disjunction and "unresolved ambiguities" (Hasan, 1984: 109) rather than notions of semantic coherence, conceived in terms of pregiven and unified discourse topics.

The distinction between multivariate and covariate relations shows that meaning relations cannot be adequately talked about solely in relation to multivariate structural relations, based on the notion of constituency. As Hasan (1984: 183) points out: "Nonstructural relations are crucial to the creation of coherence not because structure is entirely irrelevant to it, but rather because structure is a uniformly integrative device; and as an integrative device, it does not go far enough in the explication of the notion." The lexical chain interaction analyses in Appendix 2 and Appendix 3 show that meaning relations are not confined to the multivariate structural relations at the level of the single clause. Nor are they, I would argue, confined to larger-scale multivariate structural relations such as textual macrostructure or textual generic structure. Lexico-semantic cohesion chain analysis shows that clauses both near and far from each other in a text may be covariately related as part of a still higher-order semantic macroset or semantic field. Thus lexico-semantic chain analysis demonstrates that the lexico-semantic items so grouped are related through some principle of coextension. They belong to some common semantic field, defined by functional criteria of coclassification from "above." In other words, they realize the same higher-order semantic relation. However, Hasan's notion of lexical chain interaction goes further and shows that the integration between different lexico-semantic chains "is a product of the cohesion between specific parts of individual messages" (Hasan, 1984: 187). The analysis of lexical chain interaction in Appendix 2 and Appendix 3 shows that only some chains are directly related to other chains through multivariate criteria in the sense that items in two distinct chains belong to the same clause. Thus lexico-semantic chain analysis and the analysis of the interaction between chains operate relations of both semantic conjunction and disjunction between the semantic macrosets constituted by the chains. This means that the probabilities of interaction among different semantic macrosets are differentially skewed in texts.

What is of further interest here are the ways in which these semantic patterns and the lexico-grammatical selections that realize them are coextensive with some still wider system of intertextual relations, a system shared and foregrounded by the copatterned formal and semantic relations in our two texts. Each clause, as I observed at the end of chapter 4, encodes strictly local meaning relations. However, the principles of lexico-semantic cohesion and chain interaction are utilized in order to show how clause level multivariate relations are deployed in order to construct global meaning systems both within individual texts and among the texts in some intertextual set. The global relations of semantic conjunction and disjunction result from skewing the distribution and modes of deployment of local clause bound relations in particular, contextually constrained ways. Thus a semantic disjunction is constructed globally between contrasting lexico-grammatical tendencies. (These will be discussed in some detail in chapter 6.) In other words, the semantic and structural integration between clauses in texts is not uniform, given, or unproblematically "coherent." There are stronger and weaker ties between different kinds of lexico-grammatical relations, which means that there is a stronger or weaker potential for semantic relations in one part of the text to be integrated with other parts of the same text or with some still wider intertextual set. Thus nontransitive material and nonmaterial processes tend to co-occur in the semantic environment of Van/Humbert, and transitive material processes tend to occur in the semantic environment of Ada/Lolita. These contrasting semantic patterns enact a thematic disjunction, which is functional, as we shall see in chapters 7 and 8, in the articulation and maintenance of specific ideologically functional power-knowledge relations. The detailed lexico-grammatical analysis on which this is based is undertaken in chapter 6 (see also Appendix 4). The analysis of lexico-semantic chains and their interaction in the two textual excerpts demonstrates through bottom-up distributional analysis the copatterning of lexico-semantic and ideational-grammatical relations. Chains and chain interaction show how foregrounded copatternings of these relations are "chunked" into higher-order patterns. The analysis has helped to determine which patterns are shared by both texts. The analysis as it stands so far shows that the two texts are cothematic on the basis of shared lexico-semantic macrosets and shared patterns of lexical chain interaction.

The two texts are also coactional in the sense that the activity-structure sequences that enact their thematic relations are of the same functional *type*. This does not mean that they are alike in every detail. Activity-structure sequences will be talked about here at the level of textual or generic schematic structure elements, their combination, and sequencing to form some larger multivariate functional whole, corresponding to the activity-structure that is construcd.[7] In systemic-functional linguistics, the concept of generic structure schemata has been developed in order to show how the lexico-grammatical resources and their combinations in texts are chunked into larger-scale pattern-schemas (or macrostructures), which typify a particular textual generic structure (see Hasan, 1978). Models of generic structure are analytical reconstructions and approximations based on the shared features of many texts that are coclassified as belonging to the same generic class of texts. The analytical criteria used are based on distributional principles, which are concerned with the typical ordering, sequencing, and recursive structuring of schematic structure elements. These enact the textual dimension of some social process or social activity-structure. They correspond to the distinctive functional stages that are recognized as salient by social agents in the performance and completion of a given social activity-structure type. Related work on the "eidochronic" sequences in Guatemalan folktales (Colby and

Colby, 1981) and on the rhetorical structure of Native American folktales (Hymes, 1981) is within the same tradition. Hymes (1981: 106–7) uses the conventional narrative generic sequence EXPOSITION + COMPLICATION + CLIMAX + DENOUEMENT. I shall use the same analytical schema in order to show that the two textual episodes are intertextually cothematic and coactional according to specifiable functional and distributional criteria. The textual generic structure and the thematic relations that map onto it are summarized in the following tabulation for both texts.

1. *Ada*

Clause No.	Schematic Structure	Thematic Sequence
1a–2f	Exposition	1. Transgression of social norm 2. Awareness of social norm
3–10	Complication	3. Inversion of social norm
11a–11h	Climax	4. Desire 5. Constraint 6. Constraint asserted 7. Desire deferred

Sample thematic tokens corresponding to each stage of the schematized thematic sequence are (1) "the children's first bodily contact"; (2) "both were embarrassed"; (3) "dreadful, brutal, dark"; (4) "the core of the longing"; (5) "he had to control"; (6) "the girl's governess saved the situation"; (7) "mournful dullness of unconsummated desire."

2. *Lolita*

Clause No.	Schematic Structure	Thematic Sequence
1	Exposition	1. Transgression
2a–6d	Complication	2. Inversion of social norm 3. Awareness of social norm
7a–17a	Climax	4. Desire 5. Constraint
18a–18z	Denouement	6. Constraint affirmed 7. Desire deferred

Sample thematic tokens corresponding to each stage of the schematized thematic sequence are: (1) "I felt the minute hairs . . . "; (2) "a mysterious change came over my senses"; (3) "tense, tortured surreptitiously labouring lap"; (4) "deep hot sweetness . . . ultimate convulsion"; (5) "controlled delight," "shadow of decency"; (6) "I crushed out . . . "; (7) "the longest ecstasy man or monster had ever known."

The preceding analysis of coactional intertextual relations helps us to focus on the functional integration of intertextual material in specific textual productions. At the level of social activity-structure we can begin to focus more clearly on the question of "who is doing what to whom with this text?" (Lemke, 1983b: 159). This does not mean that the text is reducible to a concrete context of situation or empirical setting. Rather, the intertextual framing and reframing that this functional integration entails is a discursive attempt to work through and articulate a resolution of specific social and historical contradictions (Jameson, 1981: 118). On the intradiagetic level,[8] Humbert's courtroom confession functions to relativize the power-knowledge relations of the confessional genre to a juridical discourse in which the confessional speech act has the dual function of both fulfilling a particular juridical purpose and cleansing the soul. The confessional discourse dually constitutes the speaker as both subject and object of these relations. The confessional genre enacts two principal types of speech functions: (1) self-examination and (2) the revealing of the "truth" of one's inner self through language. The dialogic relativization of this process to the courtroom in *Lolita* makes it coextensive with the domain of public morals and dominant sociosexual codes rather than a strictly private affair between, say, priest and penitent, as in the historically prior codification of the confessional genre in the discourse of religion. The dialogic relativization of this discourse to the juridical domain also involves a heteroglossic intersection with a parodied medical and psychological discourse of SEXUALITY. An overcoded, perverse sexuality is transferred from a legal discourse of SOCIAL TRANSGRESSIONS to its codification in the body itself. The heteroglossic intersection of these social discourses in the text points to the body itself as a productive site of specific truths and reality-effects in discourse. These discursive effects include: (1) the body as a site of medical and psychoanalytical intervention in the determination of specific truths through the in terpretation of codifiable symptoms; (2) sexuality as a causal explanation of "inner" human motives and "outer" behavior; (3) the belief that the confessional genre makes possible the revealing of the hidden truths of the speaker, which are then interpreted by the addressee; and (4) sexuality as regulated by a medical discourse that constructs specific interpretative practices based on concepts of the normal and the pathological rather than on the historically prior religious concepts of sin and transgression. Thus, the parodic intersection of the two genres in the *Lolita* excerpt is a discursive attempt to work through and resolve the contradictory relations between the juridical/social domains and that of the body as the site for the organization of (perverse or pathological) desires and pleasures.

Now, the episode from *Ada,* while sharing the same general action structure and many of the same thematic relations, reverses many of the presuppositions in the *Lolita* episode. The autobiographical mode, Ada's dialogic interruption in connection with the earlier Mascodagama episode, and, above all, the incest thematic displace the representationalism of the confessing I in *Lolita*, seen as the source and unity of certain knowledge-effects, and brings us to the limits of the a priori truths that are presumed by the representationism of both the juridical and medical discourses.

Dialogicity and Cothematic Relations

The concept of social heteroglossia (Bakhtin, 1981) shows that (inter)textual thematic relations may be subclassified in many different ways and contextualized in a plurality of different social discourse-types. The "internal stratification" of language into a plurality of semantic register-types, genres, social dialects, and their textual voicings means that a given utterance potentially indexes a multiplicity of overlapping and contradictory relations with other social discourses in the system of social heteroglossia of a given social formation. A given social discourse and its textual voicing are always strategically positioned in relation to other social discourses, which they constantly try to anticipate, respond to, silence, co-opt, dominate, and subvert. This is the essence of Bakhtin's concepts of dialogicity and social heteroglossia. The most basic way in which this works is by defining relations of "equivalence" and "contrast" (cf. alliance and opposition) both locally and globally between discursive positioned-practices and their voicings in some text or intertextual formation. Dialogicity functions on the basis of relations of relative sameness and difference between voices in the system of social heteroglossia. The system of social heteroglossia is thus constructed in and through partial hierarchies of (inter)textual cothematic and coactional relations, whose relations of sameness and difference may be selectively foregrounded by the meaning making practices in operation. In this way, meanings, actions, events, and even whole genres may be contingently related to each other by the local and global covariate foregrounding strategies in operation even when there may be no multivariate (structural) links between them. Dialogicity can involve (inter)textual recontextualizations of the "same" feature such that the samenesses and differences, the invariants and the transformations are selectively foregrounded (or backgrounded) through the dialogic interplay of cothematic and coactional meaning relations. Dialogicity is thus a way of linking social meanings and practices independently of their possible occurrences in any particular syntagmatic sequence. However, it must also be emphasized that (inter)textual relations do not operate independently of the social activity-structures by virtue of which they occur. The dialogic interplay of relative sameness and difference has been formulated by Bakhtin in the following way:

> Every concrete utterance of a speaking subject serves as a point where centrifugal as well as centripetal forces are brought to bear. The processes of centralization and decentralization, of unification and disunification, intersect in the utterance; the utterance not only answers the requirements of its own language as an individualized embodiment of a speech act, but it answers the requirements of heteroglossia as well; it is in fact an active participant in such speech diversity. And this active participation of every utterance in living heteroglossia determines the linguistic profile and style of the utterance to no less a degree than its inclusion in any normative-centralizing system of a unitary language. (Bakhtin, 1981: 272)

Dialogicity thus emphasizes the plurifunctionality of all social meaning making. A given utterance may index and voice a plurality of cothematic and coactional intertextual relations by virtue of its positioning in the system of social heteroglossia. It is never reducible to a monologic or centered speaking subject per se, but actively participates in social heteroglossia through its dialogic transactions with other positioned-practices and their textual voicings. These transactions function to foreground the many potential meanings and practices in relation to which a given voice may be articulated, disarticulated, and rearticulated. The plurifunctional nature of the "concrete utterance" suggests that meanings are always overdetermined in the system of social heteroglossia. This is so on account of the fact that a given utterance is contextualized, as we saw earlier in this chapter, along both structural and systemic dimensions. The utterance occurs structurally in a specifiable syntagmatic environment; yet, the indexing of a plurality of contextual domains depends on the paradigmatic (systemic) meaning potential of all the systems in which the utterance *can* have meaning. Dialogic discourse, as I have suggested elsewhere (Thibault, 1984: 104), involves the foregrounding of this potential for an utterance simultaneously to index a plurality of contextual domains. Potential relations of sameness and difference between texts are either foregrounded or backgrounded in and through the intertextual ties that are construable between them. These may be talked about in terms of a cline between strong and weak intertextual ties (Lemke, 1985b), which emphasizes that intertextual relations constitute a potential of shifting relations rather than, say, a fixed typology. Paradigmatic (systemic) relations are, as we saw earlier, concerned with relations of sameness and difference between the features they subclassify. These involve both the actional and thematic coclassifying of meaning relations, as we noted above. The syntagmatic dimension of contextualization is concerned with combinations of elements, not necessarily seen in terms of the same/different dialectic. We have already seen how the *Ada* excerpt deploys a multivariate lexico-grammatical strategy to index its links with *Lolita*. We can say that the two texts are construable as part of some larger syntagmatic whole. The construing of a syntagmatic link *between* the two texts also entails that paradigmatic relations of sameness (equivalence) and difference (contrast) are invoked at all levels "up" to the most global copatternings of meaning relations between the two texts. In the partial hierarchies of intertextual relations between them, these paradigmatic relations of sameness and difference are projected onto the syntagmatic links between the two texts. Simultaneously, the construal of a syntagmatic relation depends on some still wider system of thematic and actional equivalences and contrasts. This emphasizes the dynamic, partial, and contradictory nature of all meaning making. In other words, the construing of cothematic and coactional intertextual relations is a function of the polysemic and overdetermined nature of all social meaning making, which is never reducible to a single, determinate or monologic meaning in a univocal context-of-utterance.

Notes

1. I do not take the concept of rule here to refer to any normative, consensus-oriented, or ontological account of, say, linguistic rules, assumed to "underlie" linguistic forms and able causally to explain their social uses. Foucault's use of the term can be taken, in the social semiotic conceptual framework, as a gloss on the probabilistic, metastable, and systemic character of realization as a process of making meanings in contextually constrained ways.

2. Strictly speaking, social semiotics does not presume the Saussurean dichotomy of synchronic and diachronic states of the system. The emphasis on the metastable and dialectical character of system/process and realization means that a description of the metastable and dynamic character of the system also entails an analysis of both system-maintaining and system-changing relations and practices. The synchronic system so defined encodes "information about the possible histories and futures of the system" (Lemke, 1984a: 31).

3. "Blanca soon found herself deeply in love in a way she thought would have been quite impossible ever to experience. To love an Infidel, a Moor, a stranger—he seemed so strange that she took no precaution against the evil that began to creep into her veins, but as soon as she recognized these effects, she accepted this evil like a true Spaniard" (Chateaubriand, [1826] 1962: 281; my translation).

4. "Blanca de Bivar, only sister of Don Carlos and much younger than he, was the idol of her father: she had lost her mother, and she was entering into her eighteenth year when Aben-Hamet appeared at Grenada. All was seduction in this enchanting woman; her voice was ravishing, her dance lighter than the zephyr; sometimes she liked to drive a chariot like Armide, sometimes she would fly on the back of the fastest Andalusian charger like those charming fairies who appeared in the forests before Tristan and Galaor. Athena took her for Aspasia, and Paris for Diane of Poitiers who began to stand out at court. But with the charms of a French woman, she had the passion of a Spanish woman, and her natural coquetry took nothing away from the steadfastness, the constancy, the strength, and the loftiness of the feelings in her heart" (Chateaubriand, [1826] 1962: 276–77; my translation).

5. The metaphor of "choice" in Halliday has nothing to do with intentionality or teleological explanations of social meaning making, although it has frequently been read as if it did. This is also true of some systemic linguists. "Choice" refers to the probabilistic (rather than deterministic) nature of all social meaning making. It refers to the ways in which the semantic probabilities of the systemic meaning potential are skewed and reskewed according to the social situation-type (see Thibault, 1988:

607–8, 610). This does not mean that the social agent is simply or unproblematically a free chooser, nor does it mean that all choices (i.e., options in meaning) are predetermined. I would say that the deep semantics of a natural language—its cryptogrammar, in Whorf's terms—entails that some choices are relatively fixed, while others are dependent on the register- and genre-specific skewing of the semantic probabilities in a given text or social occasion of discourse. The probabilistic concept of choice allows for both the dynamic interaction of systemic choices and their social contexts in ways that can change both.

6. I am not suggesting that Eco and Beaugrande are using the notion of topic in exactly the same way, though I do argue that the use of this term in discourse and text analysis is inadequate. Eco (1980: 145) defines *topic* in pragmatic terms as "an abductive schema that helps the reader to decide which semantic properties have to be actualized, whereas isotopies are the actual textual verification of that tentative hypothesis." Thus Eco uses top-down "pragmatic" criteria that make no contact with the copatterning and distribution of lexico-grammatical forms or the systematicity of their internal functional organization. The notion of isotopy does not adequately fulfill these criteria because it is already a textual abstraction, which is based on the form of the content in Hjelmslev's terms. The concept of textual isotopy does not adequately relate the level of content to its realization in the lexico-grammar, thereby perpetuating a form/content dichotomy (see Eco, 1984: 189–201 for further discussion of this concept). Elsewhere in the same paper Eco relates this concept to the currently fashionable notion of frame, derived from cognitive psychological and artificial intelligence models of text-understanding. Frames, like topics, remain highly schematic, global notions that talk in highly reductive ways about textual content or isolated themes as if these were somehow independent of the co-patterned lexico-grammatical selections in and through which global meanings are made in texts. The assumption that meaning can be analyzed independently of the system/process and realization dialectics amounts to the imposition of ad hoc situational criteria. Topics have no meaning and could not occur except in and through the copatterned meaning selections in texts and the social practices that enact these. Both Eco and Beaugrande end up talking about a preconceived "entity" or "content," abstracted from these processes. However, Beaugrande has the linguist's advantage of lexico-grammatical criteria. Unfortunately, these get explained in terms of the cognitive discourse of "mind" rather than social meaning making practices. The discourse of mind is really no more than old wine in new skins, in that abstract propositional criteria for talking about meaning are relocated in a normative, asocial discourse of mind (see Thibault, 1986c, for a more detailed critique). Frames and pragmatic criteria all too frequently amount to a poor man's linguistics for those who lack any detailed framework for the description and analysis of the lexico-grammatical systems and patterns of realization of natural language. One asks what the status of text would be if the systematicity of semiotic forms (e.g., the lexico-grammar of a natural language) were simply removed.

7. This is not to say that this textual dimension corresponds to all dimensions of the social activity that is taking place. I am currently preparing another study in which I examine more fully the relations between genre, language, and social action.

8. The intradiagetic level refers to the level of events narrated in the primary narrative—the level of third-person characters and their actions, and so on (see Genette, 1972).

Chapter 6
Intertextuality, Social Heteroglossia, and Text Semantics

In the previous chapter I argued that the construing of a syntagmatic intertextual link between two (or more) texts occurs on the basis of the paradigmatic relations of equivalence and contrast that are activated. Dialogic relations of sameness and difference among social discourses, thematic relations, and activity-structure types are constructed against a background of intertextual meaning relations. The cohesive chain interaction analysis in chapter 5 shows that particular lexico-semantic relations are globally distributed and copatterned in specific and typical ways in both excerpts. We have also seen that more is at issue than the similar copatterning of lexico-semantic cohesive chains in the two texts. These are combined with similar multivariate activity-structure types in both episodes. The two texts thus share closely parallel cothematic and coactional intertextual relations. These relations are in turn realized by specific foregrounded copatternings of lexico-grammatical selections, which both constitute and are constituted by the higher-order thematic and actional semiotic systems that are in operation. These two types of semiotic are analytically, if not constitutively, separable in ways that help to show that not all possible combinations of thematic and actional meanings actually do co-occur. Instead, there is a probabilistic skewing of the tendencies for only *some* kinds of thematic relations typically to combine with only *some* social activity-structure types. To quote Lemke:

> This framework for the analysis of intertextuality does not presume that texts dictate to us their relationship, or that there *are* existing relationships objectively there to be found out. Relations of meaning are *made*

> in human communities, and made differently in different communities. Of all the possible meaning relations within and between texts and social events only some are foregrounded by the particular meaning-making practices of a community. (Lemke, 1985b: 286; emphasis in original)

The construction of intertextual meaning relations between *Lolita* and *Ada* in the present analysis occurs on the basis of the patterned prominence (or foregrounding) that may be construed within the (inter)textual patterns of use of the meaning making (e.g., lexico-grammatical and other) resources of the social semiotic system. Global cothematic and coactional relations can be constructed both within and between these different systems. The overall effect, as we shall see further on, is a consistency of semantic orientation(s) in the copatterned meaning relations that are selected from the systemic resources of "all the possible meaning relations" (Lemke, 1985b: 286) in the two texts. This foregrounded consistency of patterning across the different types of semiotic in the two texts is built up from the ways in which copatterned meaning selections enact a consistency of semantic orientation, which is contextually specific. We shall see below how relations of sameness and difference between these differentially copatterned meaning relations in the texts are made in and through still wider, more abstract intertextual formations. The differential distribution and skewing of the lexico-grammatical selections will be shown to realize two principal orientations to meaning or consistent semantic frames (Hasan, 1986; Thibault, 1986f: 134–37), corresponding to two heteroglossically related social discourse-types and the thematic relations these enact.

Halliday's (1982) discussion of patterned prominence in the lexico-grammatical selections and combinations to do with tense, modality, and modulation in J. B. Priestley's play *An Inspector Calls* demonstrates the importance of recognizing that a text is a product of the linguistic system. A text is both an instantiation of this systemic meaning potential and the realization of specific, context-dependent social meanings. This dual perspective enables us to ask why one set of linguistic selections was made rather than some other in a given text. This question may also be extended to the analysis of more global intertextual meaning relations. We can ask, why is it that the same kinds of foregrounded copatternings of meaning selections are realized in two or more texts, which are then coclassified as belonging to the same more abstract intertextual set according to some functional criterion? This local foregrounding in a given text or intertextual set takes place in relation to a more global system of possible paradigmatic choices and their combinations. This foregrounding is, however, only relevant or functional across the different types of semiotic that constitute the meaning making resources of a given social formation. Foregrounded copatternings of meaning relations do not simply occur per se, as a form of statistical prominence.

These are constructed in relation to wider cothematic and coactional meaning relations, their combinations and disjunctions, and the specific social meaning making practices in operation. Foregrounding is not then reducible to a psychologized aesthetics of artistic perception, as in the original Prague school formulation. Halliday's analysis of Priestley's play further shows how deautomatized copatternings of lexico-grammatical selections in modality, modulation, and primary tense realize and enact a higher-order semiotic concerned with social obligations and responsibilities, which is one of the principal themes of the play. At a still lower level of semiotic organization, these copatternings of lexico-grammatical selections are also the realization of the immediate context of situation of the participants in the dramatic situation of the text (see also Halliday, 1973: 121).

The analysis below is concerned with the copatterned meaning selections that enable globally foregrounded intertextual relations to be construed between *Lolita* and *Ada*. The differential semantic orientations that result give voice to distinct, though dialectically related, sets of discursive positioned-practices. The textual voicings of these through their distinctive semantic orientations systematically both foreground and background specific meaning relations and their potential combinations. The specific meaning relations that are involved voice a conflict of semantic and axiological positions between heteroglossically related discourse varieties in the two texts. Thus, the meaning(s) of a given text or intertextual set has/have no necessary or predetermined orientation to a fixed, monologic, or referential center, but is/are made in and through the text's participation in the dynamic processes of social heteroglossia. The analysis will show that there is a consistent and systematic copatterning of lexico-grammatical selections at all levels from word through to clause and clause complex. The global intertextual relations that can be construed between the two texts require us to inquire as to how the specific meaning relations that are selected constitute specific effects of knowledge and power arising from the articulated relations between heteroglossically related social discourses. We shall be concerned with the ways in which the differential skewing of the semantic selections across the two texts enact specific power-knowledge relations, which constrain in critical ways the kinds of meanings typically made available to different categories of discursive subjects (cf. positioned-practices). The differentially related semantic orientations in the two texts are the result of both selection and preselection at all levels of textual organization, both enabling and constraining the production and articulation of these semantic orientations and the discursive positioned-practices they give voice to. Table 6.1 presents in a highly schematic way the principal kinds of meaning selections according to their relative frequency of occurrence across the two textual excerpts. These will be analyzed in greater detail below.

A number of additional observations of a general kind need to be made. Grammatical metaphor is a prominent feature of both texts. Grammatical metaphor is the "uncoded" or "incongruent" use of ideational-grammatical and interpersonal-

Table 6.1. Lexico-Grammatical Selections in *Lolita* and *Ada* Excerpts (generalized options only)

Frequency	Lexico-grammatical selections in *Lolita* and *Ada* excerpts
High	1. Nominalization 2. Extensive pre- and postmodification of nominal group Head 3. Interpersonal lexical epithets in nominal group 4. Nonfinite elements in the verbal group 5. Nontransitive Actor + Process and Medium + Process clause types 6. Elaborate circumstantial elements containing nominalizations 7. Declarative mood 8. Van/Humbert—marked thematization of circumstantials and nominals 9. Ada/Lolita—unmarked thematization of subject pronouns 10. Van/Humbert—complex hypotactic interdependencies in clause complex 11. Ada/Lolita—mainly parataxis in clause complex 12. Incongruent (metaphorical) encoding of processes
Low	1. Mental and verbal process types in verbal group 2. Transitive material process types 3. Modality in verbal group 4. Modulation in verbal group 5. Imperative and interrogative mood

grammatical meaning relations to encode atypical form-meaning relations in the grammar (Halliday, 1978: 180; 1985: chapter 10). "Atypical" simply means text whose semantics are not highly coded or stabilized in the system. "Congruent" refers to text whose semantics are encoded by the most typical grammatical patternings with respect to some systemic or generic norm. What is of interest here is that the incongruent or metaphorical encoding of process types at clause rank is skewed in a very specific way in our two texts. Metaphorical (incongruent) modes of meaning most typically copattern with Van/Humbert as semantic Actor, whereas nonmetaphorical (congruent) modes of meaning typically copattern, with the lower overall occurrence of tokens that realize Ada/Lolita as semantic Actor. This is further evidence for an overall tension between two distinct, though heteroglossically related, semantic orientations.

A number of heteroglossically related thematic systems also contribute to the intertextual relations that can be construed. In the previous chapter, I showed that cothematic relations are partly based on relations of semantic conjunction and disjunction on the basis of the copatterning and distribution of lexico-semantic chains. We are therefore considering two main ways in which intertextual relations are constructed: (1) the global copatterning of lexico-grammatical selections in some intertextual set, and (2) the abstract intertextual formations to which a given text or occasion of social discourse is assignable on the basis of the higher-order metaredundancy contextualizing relations in operation. The occurrence of the same kinds of lexico-grammatical selections in two or more texts does not in itself mean that a given abstract intertextual relation can be construed. Instead, the copatterning of the same *types* of lexico-grammatical selections in two or more texts constitutes a productive potential for stronger or weaker intertextual ties to be adduced on the basis of the local and global covariate and multivariate foregrounding strategies in operation. *Which* ties get foregrounded by social agents depends on *which* social meaning making practices are in operation, and *when*, that is, in which context(s).

Intertextual relations between the two texts can also be construed at the level of context of situation on the basis of shared field, tenor, and mode values. Intertextual field relations can be construed on the basis of similar action structures in both episodes, similar fictive situations, and subject matter. Intertextual tenor relations can, obviously enough, be construed on the basis of the common authorship that links the two texts. However, an important difference in the interpersonal situations of the two excerpts is that *Lolita* is written in first-person I-narration, whereas the relevant excerpt from *Ada* is in the so-called omniscient mode (see below). Table 6.1 also shows that selections in mood, modality, and modulation are similar both in type and in overall frequency and distribution in both texts. Intertextual mode relations constitute covariate cohesive ties between the two texts on the basis of shared lexico-semantic relations (see chapter 5).

Text, Context, and the Semantic Metafunctions

In systemic-functional linguistics, the variables of field, tenor, and mode represent the context of situation of a text. Context of situation is defined semiotically rather than empirically as a configuration of field, tenor, and mode values that "determine" the semantics of the text at the level "below." These contextual variables are realized in the lexico-grammar of texts by selections in the three semantic metafunctions, corresponding to options in ideational, interpersonal, and textual meanings. In systemic-functional theory, perhaps the central claim is that the lexico-grammar of language at all ranks, from clause complex (sentence) through clause to group (phrase), word, and morpheme, are organized in terms of three basic types of options in meaning. These are the semantic metafunctions specified above, although the ideational metafunction is further subdivided into the experiential and logical subcomponents. The importance of Halliday's (1969, 1973, 1978, 1979, 1985) metafunctional hypothesis is that the semantic functions of language are not simply defined externally in relation to the uses to which language is put in a given context of situation. This step had already been taken in various ways by Bühler (1934), Malinowski (1923, 1935), Jakobson (1960), and J. R. Firth (1957, 1968) in the European tradition of contextually oriented studies of language and linguistic function. Austin's (1962) speech act theory in the English tradition of "ordinary language" philosophy has close affinities with these. In spite of individual differences in emphasis and terminology, these trends exemplify an externally defined, socially oriented view of linguistic functions in terms of language-as-use and language-as-action. Language and its uses are defined in terms of their pragmatic functions, where these are taken to refer to the contextually specific meaning of an utterance as if this occurred independently of the systematicity of lexico-grammatical and other semiotic forms, which I referred to in chapter 1. The resulting split between the semantics of these forms and their pragmatic meanings-in-context has meant that an ad hoc, situationally specific pragmatics of the individual utterance or text bears no principled relation to the systematicity of the semiotic forms in and through which context-dependent social meanings are made. Indeed, the disjunction between semantics and pragmatics relies on an epistemology that distinguishes a context-free formal semantics from the semantics of individual utterance-tokens (i.e., pragmatics). Pragmatics is thus an externally defined functional semantics of the utterance-token, which fails to understand the systematicity of the links between the formal organization of the lexico-grammar, its internal functional basis, and the meanings of these forms in context.

Halliday's metafunctional hypothesis goes a significant stage further and demonstrates that the distinction between semantics and pragmatics is unnecessary in a linguistic theory such as the systemic-functional one, which can link in a principled way the systematic and plurifunctional nature of semiotic forms with their multiple contextual meanings. Halliday shows that the *internal* organization of the lexico-grammar has a functional basis, which corresponds to the organization and realization of the three semantics metafunctions. The metafunctions are the interface between the internal functional organization of the lexico-grammar and the contextual variables of field, tenor, and mode. The lexico-grammar at, say, clause rank is internally organized into three different kinds of structure that are simultaneously mapped onto the syntagm of the clause in a polyphonic, plurifunctional fashion. No single type of structure or mode of meaning is given priority, for all are considered equally important in the meaning and function of the clause. At clause rank and below these correspond to options in transitivity, mood, and theme. The metafunctions are the interface between the contextual

Table 6.2. Types of Meaning Options, Their Contextual Determinations, and the Types of Grammatical Structures by Which Realized

Context of Situation Variable	Semantic Metafunction Component	Type of Grammatical Realization	Clause Rank Meaning Option
Field (social activity)	Ideational: (a) experiential	Constituent (particle-like); Segmental	Transitivity
Tenor (social relations)	Interpersonal	Prosodic (fieldlike)	Mood
Mode (symbolic channel)	Textual;	Culminative;	Theme
	ideational: (b) logical	Recursive	Logical

variables of field, tenor, and mode and specific selections in the lexico-grammar. They attempt to specify which contextual variables redound with which formal features in the lexico-grammar. This is not, however, a one-to-one or biunique connection but a many-to-many one. Nevertheless, the process is not random, and the concept of semantic register-type is an attempt to generalize and interpret in functional terms the nonrandom and probabilistic skewings of semantic selections in the three metafunctions according to social situation-type and discourse genre. This two-way interface between field, tenor, and mode values and the internal functional organization of the lexico-grammar via the semantic metafunctions may be schematized in Table 6.2, which I have adapted from Halliday (1978: 188–89).

The fact that this interface is not a simple one-to-one relation between, say, clause and social situation helps to reemphasize the productive dialectic that the realization of textual meanings involves. It is not a top-down determinism from social situation to text. In systemic-functional linguistics, language is viewed in terms of its plurifunctional, polyphonic, and multistratal organization as a resource through which the different modes of meaning are organized in texts. Systemic-functional linguistics is one of the very few current theories—two others are Kenneth Pike's (1967) tagmemic theory and Michael Silverstein's

(1979, 1985a) "systematic pragmatics"—that is able to grasp both in theory and practice the following fundamental observation on language by the biochemist Giorgio Prodi in his book *Le basi materiali della significazione:*

> Two characteristics coexist in language, and the scholar must bear these in mind: its openness toward the environment on which language is adjusted and the internal compatibility of the entire linguistic instrument, its theoretical-structured character. It appears ordinarily that these are opposed, and that accepting one, the other must be excluded. From this is born a structuralist study in which every element is opposed to others, where everything proceeds as a dialectical game inside the magical coherence of language. In this way, the things that are acted upon, the information that is exchanged, the world that is transformed by words, are like indeterminate shadows in the background. What then is the word used for? Only to speak of unimportant things. On the other hand, "structure" (simply seen as the finished composition of the various parts of the instrument) is the organized means through which we must pass in order to understand the openness of language, its possibilities of use, its capacity for connection and transformation. (Prodi, 1977: 238; my translation)

For instance, Chomsky's (1965) transformational-generative grammar and later developments of this prioritize the constituentlike or part-whole segmental structure of the clause and the referential or propositional meaning this realizes. Similarly, the case grammarians such as Chafe (1970) and Fillmore (1968, 1977) have concentrated on meaning of the referential or propositional kind, which they have frequently justified with direct recourse to real-world criteria. In this way, they effectively blur paradigmatic (systemic) functional semantic contrasts in the lexico-grammar (see Painter, 1984: 21–22; Thibault, 1986d: 84). Linguistic pragmatics and speech act theory rely on externally defined functional criteria (e.g., performativity); this reliance, in actual practice, amounts to the literalization of the metaphor of performativity of certain classes of speech acts. This metaphor is, as Silverstein (1979) shows, then "referentially projected" from the propositional content of these semiotic forms onto real-world phenomena *as if* this in itself constituted an adequate scientific explanation of the uses-in-context and distribution of these forms. All three approaches mentioned here have no contextual basis other than in an ad hoc fashion. Furthermore, they continue to prioritize just one or another of the various modes of meaning in ways that remain largely tied to the folk-theoretical formalism of the sentence, itself a product of the written language and the pedagogical grammars based on it.

At the level of context of situation, the two-way distinction that Lemke makes between social activity-structure and thematic meaning is able to subsume Halliday's tripartite one. In Halliday's schema, *field* covers both the social activity that is taking place, as well as the "subject matter" (Halliday, 1978: 110). *Tenor* refers to the social relations between discourse participants. *Mode* refers to the text-making resources through which coherent texts are made and functionally linked to their contexts of situation. Thus social activity-structure subsumes both the social activity dimension of field as well as tenor. The thematic context subsumes both the subject matter dimension of field and the mode values of textual and lexico-semantic cohesion, as well as cohesive harmony. We are now in a position to ask how the two "separate" texts are connected to their abstract intertextual formations through the coactional and cothematic meaning relations they share. In chapter 5 I showed how the *Ada* text indexes specific links with the *Lolita* text. We saw that specific covariate and multivariate links and the contextual relations they adduce are relevant to the intertextual meaning relations that can be construed. The indexical operations so performed contextualize the relations between the two texts in *situationally specific* ways. This criterion is crucial for the construction of social meanings. Peirce's (1974) distinction between sign-types and sign-tokens shows that meaning relations are constructed between classes of social acts (cf. sign-types) rather than between unique occurrences on the basis of some higher-order functional criteria of coclassification. Yet, in actual texts and social occasions of discourse these are indexed as *specific* to the situation in which they occur (cf. sign-tokens). Thus the indexical link to the *Lolita* text in *Ada* functions to specify the potential relevance of some coactional and cothematic context(s) and to coclassify or "type" the meaning relations construable between the two texts in particular ways. The distinction between types and tokens suggests that the ability to construct some meaning relation between two or more texts means that the meaning relations the texts may have had as separate texts are retyped or recontextualized by some new shared higher-order intertextual relation, which is different from the meaning relations of the two texts not considered to be so related. These meaning relations are constructed on the basis of functional criteria of similarity (equivalence) and difference (contrast), which are either foregrounded or backgrounded in and through the covariate and multivariate patterns of use of the lexico-grammatical resources of the linguistic system. In the following section we shall explore in some detail the global copatterning of the lexico-grammatical selections in and through which these intertextual meaning relations are instantiated and realized.

The Foregrounded Global Copatterning of Lexico-Grammatical Relations between the Two Texts

The detailed analysis on which the discussion in this section is based is located in Appendix 4. This analysis is organized in terms of lexico-grammatical selections from all three semantic metafunctions. Appendix 4 provides a detailed microanalysis of the lexico-grammatical selections that are systematically copatterned across the two texts. The two passages that are analyzed have been segmented into clause level constituents in Appendix 1.

The discussion in this section will attempt to generalize a semantic interpretation of the two major semantic orientations realized by the copatterned lexico-grammatical selections in the two texts. I shall propose a more generalized semantic interpretation of these patterns. However, these will be discussed only after some general observations on the lexico-grammatical selections made up and down the rank scale. The analysis in Appendix 4 reveals that the copatterning of lexico-grammatical selections tends to be organized into two major patterns. I shall henceforth refer to these as Van/Humbert discourse and Ada/Lolita discourse. These are no more than shorthand glosses to designate certain regular and systematic semantic tendencies that the lexico-grammatical patterning realizes. They refer to two distinct orientations to meaning rather than two absolutely clear-cut differences. The distinction is therefore a fuzzy one.

Van/Humbert discourse is typically characterized by the incongruent or metaphorical encoding of semantic meanings in the lexico-grammar. Ada/Lolita discourse is typically characterized by congruent or nonmetaphorical encodings of semantic meanings. The globally foregrounded and dominant Van/Humbert discourse realizes the semantics of INDETERMINACY. This is no more than a gloss on a least delicate semantic option, which can be further subclassified into more delicate systemic options (see below). The semantics of INDETERMINACY is realized in the ideational-grammatical semantics of the clause by a predominance of nontransitive material and behavioral process-types – relational, mental, and verbal processes. There is a correspondingly low incidence of transitive clauses of the type Actor + Process + Goal, which expresses the relation of *extension* of a process from one participant (i.e., the semantic Actor) to a second participant (i.e., the Goal) (Halliday, 1985: 145). Van/Humbert discourse also shows a strong tendency toward metaphorical encodings of verb processes as nominalizations. The ideational-grammatical semantics tend to be less iconic, with little sense of participants actively and causally interacting with each other. Actions, events, and processes tend to be backgrounded in favor of abstractions. The predominance of the declarative mood and the low incidence of both modality and modulation in the verbal group reinforce this tendency. This tendency in the interpersonal-grammatical semantics is congruent with the overall drift away from an interactive, cause-and-effect mode to a noninteractive one, concerned with elaborate and complex abstractions and states of being, feeling, or perceiving. As we shall see, the semantics of Van/Humbert discourse, taken as an overall pattern, indexes a more monologic contextual orientation. A consideration of selections at group level bears out the same overall tendency. Nominalizations are strongly foregrounded and this indexes the orientation away from processes to objects, entities, and participants. Processes get experientialized as Things.

There is an implied contrast between abstractions and Things on the one hand and processes, whereby the former are foregrounded, on the other.

This contrastive backgrounding of processes is an icon of the indeterminate nature of the relations between participants and processes. For instance, the foregrounding of nominalized verb processes entails a lack of presupposed contextual information concerning the precise relations between processes and participants. The emphasis is on the ambiguous and indeterminate encoding of these as abstract nominalizations. The metaphorical encoding of verb processes as nominalizations also allows these processes-as-things to accept extensive pre- and postmodification of the Head in the nominal group. There is also a higher proportion of interpersonal lexical epithets in these nominal groups, which is consistent with the low incidence of modality and modulation in the verbal group.

The verbal group in Van/Humbert discourse exhibits a relatively high incidence of tokens with nonfinite elements. The category of finiteness, as Halliday (1985: 183) points out, relates the verb process to the deictic here-and-now of the speech situation. The relatively high incidence of nonfinite elements further suggests the indeterminate nature of the relation between the speech event and the speech situation. These nonfinite elements either have no primary tense or no modality, which means there is no clear deictic orientation to a specifiable context-of-utterance. The deictic indeterminacy of the speech event further suggests the problematic nature of the relations between processes and participants in Van/Humbert discourse.

The analysis in Appendix 4 also shows a high use of circumstantial elements, many of which are marked Themes in the clauses in which they occur. Once again, the overall semantic drift is toward attributes, qualities, and spatio-temporal relations rather than actions, events, and processes. Van/Humbert discourse also demonstrates a preference for complex hypotactic relations of interdependency in the clause complexing semantics of this discourse. Thus, the relations of qualification and elaboration that are entailed by relations of dependency between clauses of unequal status show that Van/Humbert discourse tends toward a complex relativizing (e.g., qualifying, elaborating, etc.) of the logico-semantic relations between clauses. The intricate logical distinctions that hypotaxis entails here help to foreground the shifting, indeterminate, and qualified nature of these relations.

The globally less dominant Ada/Lolita discourse shows a different copatterning of lexico-grammatical selections that realizes a different semantic orientation. I shall refer to this as the semantics of DETERMINACY. As before, this is a least delicate option, which can be further subclassified (see below). Lexico-grammatical selections realizing Ada/Lolita discourse are also less frequent overall than the dominant Van/Humbert discourse. Ada/Lolita discourse is characterized by a higher proportion of congruent or nonmetaphorical realizations of nontransitive material process-types, few metaphorical encodings of process-participant relations, unmarked thematization of subject pronouns, and a higher incidence of paratactic clause complex relations. Paratactic relations are logically symmetrical and transitive. Both of the linked elements are of equal status, and each could stand as an independent clause (Halliday, 1985: 198). This feature of Ada/Lolita discourse marks a contrastive pattern to the extensive hypotactic elaboration, and so on, of Van/Humbert discourse. The predominance of parataxis in Ada/Lolita discourse, along with the overall tendency toward both congruent and unmarked encodings of semantic options in the lexico-grammar, suggests a tendency toward determinate participant-process relations rather than Things and abstractions. The paratactic, additive "and" relation in the clause-complexing semantics and the use of material Actor + Process type clauses exemplifies a conventional narrative genre based on a sequential cause-and-effect structuring of narrative events. All of these lexico-grammatical selections copattern to enact a consistent semantic orientation that I have glossed as DETERMINACY.

The foregoing discussion and the detailed microanalysis in Appendix 4 show that the lexico-grammatical selections in the two texts copattern according to two consistent semantic orientations. These can be represented systemically as a "choice" between the semantics of INDETERMINACY and DETERMINACY. The system network in Figure 6.1 further subclassifies these two options into more delicate paradigmatic sets of options on the basis of the above discussion.

These two consistent semantic orientations across the two texts are realized by contrasting tendencies in the copatterning of lexico-grammatical selections. The analysis in Appendix 4 shows that there is a high degree of internal consistency of the copatterning within each of the two orientations. Thus these consistent semantic orientations frame an entire complex of diverse lexico-grammatical features in terms of a specific functional orientation. We are thus concerned with the dialectical relations between semiotic forms and their functions rather than with either forms or functions in isolation. These consistent semantic orientations or frames thus index and give voice to specific positioned-practices in the social formation. The functional contrasts between the two orientations may also be considered in terms of the marked/unmarked contrast. The foregrounded and globally dominant Van/Humbert discourse is unmarked in terms of its functional contrasts with Ada/Lolita discourse in this intertextual set. However, the grammatical complexity and elaboration of Van/Humbert discourse and the tendency toward grammatical metaphor suggest that it is the marked tendency in some still wider set of functional contrasts at, say, the levels of semantic register-type and discourse genre. Now, these two contrasting orientations do not coincide with the levels of either register or genre, for they can occur within the same text, register, or genre. Instead, I have said that they articulate or voice heteroglossically related discursive positioned-practices, which are dialogically related to each other both within and across the two texts we have analyzed. These contrasting semantic orientations are iconically related to the heteroglossic relations of alliance, oppo-

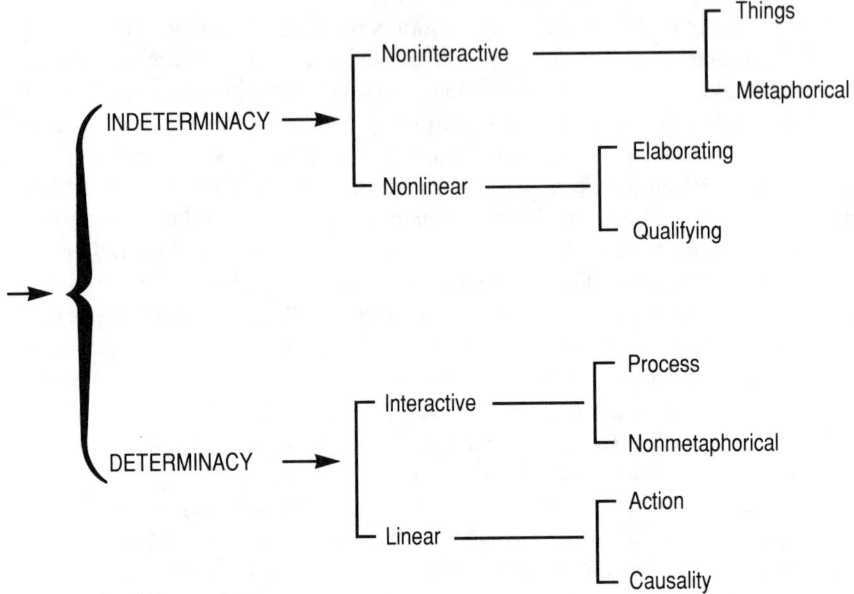

Figure 6.1. Intertextual semantic options in *Lolita* and *Ada* (general and partial description only)

sition, conflict, and co-optation among their social discourses in the system of social heteroglossia. The principal differences between these two heteroglossically related semantic orientations are summarized in Table 6.3.

Social Heteroglossia and the Text/Context Opposition: Rethinking the Distinction

The contextual variables of field, tenor, and mode are generally assumed to be above or external to the semantics of the text in the form of a one-way, top-down determinism, leading from the social situation to the text. The locative metaphor in the preposition *above* is itself literalized and referentially projected so as to set up a reifying opposition between text and the social context of situation. This opposition is, in its epistemological consequences, remarkably like the oppositions thought/language, reality/language, truth/meaning, deep structure/surface structure. This does not mean, however, that all of the epistemological implications of these various oppositions are identical. The opposition between text and context takes the context to be the condition for actual expressions of language (i.e., text). This maintains a phenomenology of the subject's experience of language in which the linguistic system is put in a relation of potentiality to the subject. In

Table 6.3. Relevant Differences between Van/Humbert and Ada/Lolita Discourses (general specification only; not motivated by formal criteria)

Relevant Feature	Van/Humbert Discourse	Ada/Lolita Discourse
Context	Self-contextualizing	Context-dependent
Meaning orientation	Global, abstract, transcendental	Local, concrete, mundane
Grammatical encoding	Incongruent, metaphorical	Congruent, nonmetaphorical
Power	+ power	- power

this way of thinking, the contextual variables of field, tenor, and mode are related to a hermeneutic practice that presupposes the unity of the social Real, of which language is said to be an expression or representation (see chapter 2). This hermeneutic practice works to interpret or rewrite language (text) into the categories of the social Real through the categories of field, tenor, and mode. This has the additional effect of both presupposing and representing the subject as a unified and centered participant in a continuous, unified, and stable social Real. A phenomenology of self and other is presupposed whereby the determinant conditions of the social situation are opposed to the experiential realm of language (see chapter 2). Now, this does not mean that we abandon the categories of field, tenor, and mode. The text/context dichotomy can be rethought along the lines I discussed earlier so that the lexico-grammatical selections in texts and the metafunctional semantics they realize are themselves determinate features of the discursive situation. This has its own social and historical specificity and is not subject to the epistemological guarantor of a unified social Real. The selection of a given lexico-grammatical form is not the expression or representation of a given social context of situation, which is located on some other level. A text can be the site of a plurality of heteroglossically related social discourses that are always constituted within a determinate configuration of discursive and prediscursive relations and practices and intertextual formations (see chapter 5).

I argued in chapter 1 that the Hjelmslevian concept of realization is better understood as a productive dialectic between semiotic forms and functions and texts and contexts rather than a static, one-way determinism (see also Thibault, 1986f: 102–3). Halliday comes very close to such a formulation in his discussion of deautomatized patterns of language in J. B. Priestley's *An Inspector Calls*. Halliday explains the concept of deautomatization, which is derived from Mukarovsky (1977), in the following way:

> The term "de-automatization," though cumbersome, is more apt than "foregrounding," since what is in question is not simply prominence but rather the partial freeing of the lower level systems from the control of the semantics so that they become domains of choice in their own right. In terms of systemic theory the de-automatization of the grammar means that grammatical choices are not simply determined from above: there is selection as well as pre-selection. Hence the wording becomes a quasi-independent semiotic mode through which the meanings of the work can be projected. (Halliday, 1982: 136)

Halliday's distinction here between "selection" and "pre-selection" suggests that texts are not simply determined in a top-down fashion by an external social situation. Nor are selections at the phonological and lexico-grammatical strata simply determined or preselected by a higher-order semantics or social semiotic. Texts and the patterned meaning making selections in them on all strata are productive and constitutive of their contexts as much as they are produced or constituted by them. This suggests that the text/context opposition needs to be reconsidered. Halliday's discussion is perhaps too closely tied to an aesthetic ideology of the literary text. What is needed is a social semiotic account of the productivity of all forms of social meaning making and the ways in which they both enable and constrain (cf. select and preselect) specific orientations to meaning, social discourses and power-knowledge relations. In an earlier paper, I discussed the concept of deautomatization, suggesting that dialogic discourse foregrounds the dialogic process itself (Thibault, 1984: 102–4). The deautomatization of the seemingly inevitable, frozen, automatic, and referential relations between textual meanings and their related sociodiscursive practices through the processes of dialogic interruption can be a political strategy for the transformation of social meaning making practices rather than for their hermeneutic interpretation in terms of a pregiven and unified social Real. A critical social semiotics can interrupt, reformulate, and displace the relations between discursive positioned-practices and their textual voicings. Such a strategy can destabilize the seeming givenness and coherence of these relations, thus disarticulating their "automatic" relations with the referentially projected really Real "out there."

Foucault's (1974) concepts of *discursive formation* and *discursive practice* are relevant to the task of rethinking the text/context distinction. Foucault constructs a conceptual and methodological framework that endeavors to move beyond the notion of the internal structuring of social practices, which are then expressed in a suitable linguistic form. Foucault defines a discursive formation as a systematic ordering of "statements" (cf. meaning relations) and discursive practices that cannot be translated back into a set of pregiven social or mental categories existing in some other ontological domain. A text does not stand in an essentially metonymical relation to the higher-order categories of field, tenor, and mode. Instead, the patterned meaning making selections at all levels of (con)textual organization are articulated in a complex, overdetermined field of discursive and prediscursive relations in and through which they have their specific functions and meaning-effects. Here is Foucault on the concept of "statement":

> The field of statements is not described as a "translation" of operations or processes that take place elsewhere (in men's thoughts, in their consciousness or unconscious, in the sphere of transcendental constitutions); but that it is accepted, in its empirical modesty, as the locus of particular events, regularities, relationships, modifications and systematic transformations; in short, that it is treated not as the result or trace of something else, but as a practical domain that is autonomous (although dependent), and which can be described at its own level (although it must be articulated on something other than itself). (Foucault, 1974: 121–22)

A discursive formation is a typical codification of a given ensemble of socio-discursive practices and social meanings, which are recognized according to some functional criteria as having a regular and systematic basis in the social formation. In terms of social semiotic theory, it is an analytical approximation of the specific kinds of social activity-structure types, thematic meaning relations, and their interrelations that enact a particular discursive formation and the forms of knowledge and belief and truth effects these entail. A discursive formation is a partial hierarchy of overdetermined, yet discontinuous, discursive and material relations. Foucault's concept does not presume that meanings, forms of knowledge and belief, and specific "truths" pre-exist discursive practice and hence their production and articulation in a given discursive formation. These do not exist in some ontologically distinct domain and are then encoded in a suitable semiotic form. Nor can specific social meanings, forms of knowledge, and the like simply be "read off" from these forms. Rather, they are produced, articulated, and transformed in and through shifting, discontinuous, and metastable intertextual formations of discursive practices and meaning relations. The production of these is dependent on the iteration and transformation of the limited ways of saying and doing that are made possible in a particular discursive formation. These meaning-effects are instantiated in and through the (inter)textual resources of the discursive formation. Discursive formations are thus definable as regular, systematic orderings of intertextual meaning relations and the practices that maintain them. Thus Foucault's mode of archaeological analysis emphasizes the ways in which meanings are not objectively "there" and waiting to be discovered. The concept of discursive formation is an analytical abstraction at a very high order of analysis that attempts to correlate on the basis of some functional criteria the systemic regularities of specific, historically contingent ensembles of sociodiscursive meanings, practices, and the subjects and objects these produce.

Bakhtin's concept of social heteroglossia can be rearticulated in relation to these Foucauldian concepts in the social semiotic conceptual framework. The concept of social heteroglossia serves to show that language articulates "a multitude of concrete worlds, a multitude of bounded verbal-ideological social belief systems" (Bakhtin, 1981: 288). What Bakhtin enables us to add to Foucault's conceptions of discursive formation and discursive practice is a clearer view of these as internally "stratified and differentiated" (Bakhtin, 1981: 289). Foucault shows that the meanings, forms of knowledge and belief, and truth-effects in particular discursive formations are made and remade in regular and limited ways by specific functional configurations of cothematic and coactional (inter)textual meanings and practices. The concept of social heteroglossia adds to this perspective by showing how these are always articulated in and through complex and shifting intersections and disjunctions of heteroglossically related social discourses, which are not reducible to a single, normative codification:

> What is important to us here is the intentional dimensions, that is, the denotative and expressive dimensions of the "shared" language's stratification. It is in fact not the neutral linguistic components of language being stratified and differentiated, but rather a situation in which the intentional possibilities of language are being expropriated: these possibilities are realized in specific directions, filled with specific content, they are made concrete, particular, and are permeated with concrete value judgments; they knit together with specific objects and with the belief systems of certain genres of expression and points of view peculiar to particular professions. Within these points of view, that is, for the speakers of the language themselves, these generic languages and professional jargons are directly intentional—they denote and express directly and fully, and are capable of expressing themselves with mediation; but outside, that is, for those not participating in the given purview, these languages may be treated as objects, typifactions, as local color. For such outsiders, the intentions permeating these languages become *things*, limited in their meaning and expression; they attract to, or excise from, such language a particular word—making it difficult for the word to be utilized in a directly intentional way, without any qualifications. (Bakhtin, 1981: 289)

Both Foucault and Bakhtin demonstrate the critical importance of deconstructing normative and essentialist views of language as unified and homogeneous. Abstract intertextual formations are constructed in and through partial hierarchies of cothematic and coactional meaning relations and semantic register-types from the paradigmatic systems of meaning making resources in the social semiotic system or some part of it. Yet, these remain typifactions or abstractions on the basis of some global criteria of coclassification. In a given intertextual set, however, there are always specific and stratified uses and forms of articulation of these resources, which index and voice specific social relations and positioned-practices. These are always in some articulated relation to other positioned-practices in the system of social heteroglossia. Thus, semantic registers, discourse genres, social dialects, and thematic and actional meanings are involved in a constant dialectic of articulation, disarticulation, and rearticulation in relation to each other. Social heteroglossia is enacted in and through the clashes, oppositions, struggles, conflicts, alliances, and hybridizations between socially differentiated and stratified orientations to meaning in texts and social occasions of discourse.

Intertextual Semantic Frames and the Regulation of Social Practice

The perspectives of Bakhtin and Foucault show that context-dependent social actions and meanings are always bounded or framed by specific knowledge-power relations that regulate and deregulate the practices of social agents. We are not therefore talking about a mere differential plurality of positioned-practices and textual voices in the social semiotic system. The system of social heteroglossia is regulated and controlled by higher-order classification and framing principles through which the social semiotic codes differentially distribute the material and semiotic resources of the social formation and the access of social agents to these (Bernstein, 1982, 1986a, b). This question will be explored in a preliminary way in the following section and in some detail in chapters 7 and 8. The analysis of the intertextual meaning relations that relate Ada/Lolita discourse and Van/Humbert discourse show that particular texts and social actions are always bound or framed by, to borrow Urwin's (1984: 283) term, some "discursive frame of reference," which regulates the social activity. Urwin illustrates her argument in connection with the discursive frames that bound and sanction child-rearing practices:

> Consider, for example, "table setting" or "nappy changing." Neither of these are discourses as such; they are social practices. But there may well be a good deal prescribed or written about them, in books on etiquette or child-care, for example. Here, the coherence between the

> actions regulating the social practices of table setting or nappy changing and the production of discourses about these practices depends on their being regulated through the same regime of truth, in accordance with the same law. That is, they are produced through power-knowledge relations. (Urwin, 1984: 282)

Thus the concept of discursive frame of reference is linked to the notions of intertextual formation and intertextual frame whereby specialized forms of knowledge and belief, truth-effects, social relations, and identities similarly regulate social actions and practices. Now, the formal representation of semantic frames in discourse has been extensively developed on the basis of research into artificial intelligence models of text processing and text understanding. This work is largely based on Minsky's (1975) model of frame-system analysis and developments of it. These include the work of Schank and Abelson (1977), Charniak (1977), and Beaugrande (1980) in the cognitive science paradigm and the somewhat different orientations in the work of Downes (1978) and Colby and Colby (1981). All of these approaches assume that organized sets of semantic propositions and schemas are globally organized in a frame-structure and are somehow correlated with the structure of particular texts or social activity-structures. The first three of the above approaches very much exemplify a normative view of semantic representations and prioritize stereotypical "data structures" (Minsky, 1975) and routine stretches of social behavior (Schank and Abelson, 1977) in a psychological discourse concerned with internal mental representations. I have elsewhere critiqued the discourse of mind that typifies this epistemology and I shall not repeat those arguments now (see Thibault, 1986c). The normative psychologistic basis of this research presumes a culturally nonspecific other with whom the individual is assumed to interact. In discursive practice there can be no such thing as a nonspecific other, for all discourse and all interactants in discourse are situationally and socially specific.

Downes exemplifies a further trend that seeks to correlate the meaning of texts with the sets of truth-conditions that underlie a given semantic proposition. Downes's interesting discussion of belief systems in the discourse of McCarthyism maintains the philosophical distinction between belief and truth, as if these are measurable against an empirically verifiable set of truth-conditional semantic entailments. This derives from the positivist's commitment to a normative definition of truth in terms of either the internal semantic coherence of logical statements or their presumed empirical correspondence to conditions, events, states of affairs, and so forth, in the real world "out there." However, Downes also analyzes the pragmatic dimension of language use as institutionally bounded and sanctioned social action. Nevertheless, the allegiance of linguistic pragmatics to a normative, positivistic notion of truth and social action is not able to show how truth and social actions are differentially constructed and accessed through conflicting discursive and social relations. Truth is restricted to logical criteria based on semantic entailments and relations of inference, taken to be normatively and empirically matched with the real world.

Alternatively, the proposals of Bakhtin and Foucault suggest that the concept of frame can be used to schematize and formalize the heteroglossic interplay of intertextual formations in terms of the intertextual frames that are indexed by specific textual productions. Frames are an analysts's schematic reconstruction of these meaning relations; they are an attempt to construct a formal model of them. Colby and Colby (1981: 112) usefully point out that these relations need not be restricted to the kinds of relations allowable in formal logic. All sorts of linguistic relations, social actions, contextual features, and chunks of discourse are potentially usable in a given frame. The frame is an analytical strategy for schematizing these relations in a more formal and global way. They may also involve complex embeddings of meaning relations as well as more complex networks of macroframes. Intertextual discursive frames control and limit the kinds of meanings that can be made in a given social practice. However, the overall metastability of the partial hierarchies of meaning relations and social practices in a given text all the way up to an entire discursive formation means that these relations may change. Changes in the relations between social practices and their intertextual discursive frames entail, as we shall see below, changes in the classification and framing principles in and through which social practices are coded and regulated in the social semiotic system.

The heteroglossic relations between Ada/Lolita discourse and Van/Humbert discourse are articulated in and through particular intertextual discursive frames. These frames dialectically interpenetrate social practice, making redundant the distinction between outer observable behavior and inner consciousness in the cognitive paradigm. Volosinov (1973) showed that inner consciousness and subjective view are themselves specific, overdetermined components of the social formation (see chapters 2, 3, and 4). Thus "inner speech" is a specific context-dependent appropriation of the resources of the social semiotic system. The dialectical interpenetration of social practice and intertextual discursive frames means that there is no need in the conceptual framework of social semiotics of the disjunction between "inner" mental representations and "outer" behavior. It is the metafunctional organization of the semantics in a functionally organized lexico-grammar that is the locus of this interpenetration:

> So language, while it represents reality *referentially,* through its words and structures, also represents reality *metaphorically* through its own internal and external form. (1) The functional organization of the semantics symbolizes the structure of human interaction (the semiotics of social contexts . . .). (2) Dialectal and "diatypic" (register) variation symbolize respectively the structure of society and the structure of human knowledge.

> But as language becomes a metaphor of reality, so by the same process reality becomes a metaphor of language. Since reality is a social construct, it can be constructed only through an exchange of meanings. (Halliday, 1978: 191)

What is important for our discussion of intertextual discursive frames is that the thematic meaning relations these enact are not built up on the basis of stable semantic categories and fixed, literal correspondences between forms and meaning (Thibault, 1986e). Thematic meaning relations – (inter)textual semantic relations – are always heteroglossically situated and framed in a plurality of contradictory ways. Bakhtin has put it like this:

> [The speaker's] orientation toward the listener is an orientation toward a specific conceptual horizon, toward the specific world of the listener; it introduces new elements into his discourse; it is in this way, after all, that various different points of view, conceptual horizons, systems for providing expressive accents, various social "languages" come to interact with one another. The speaker strives to get a reading on his word, on his own conceptual system that determines this word, within the alien conceptual system of the understanding receiver; he enters into dialogical relationships with certain aspects of this system. The speaker breaks through the alien conceptual horizon of the listener, constructs his own utterance on alien territory, against his, the listener's, apperceptive background. (Bakhtin, 1981: 282)

The emphasis Bakhtin gives to the specific and dialogical nature of meaning relations means that (inter)textual meaning relations depend on the shifting orientations of the word (cf. utterance) in specific social and historical determinations. The semantics of the text or utterance, heteroglossically defined, are not adequately formulated in terms of stable lexical taxonomies, semantic fields, componential sets, or "prototypical" categories (Rosch, 1977). All of these attempts to characterize semantic meanings in terms of some more basic or underlying features remain merely formal, decontextualized accounts. They attempt to generalize about the semantics of natural language on the basis of a restrictive experimental or positivistic methodology and epistemology divorced from both the social practices in and through which meanings are made and the covariate and multivariate strategies and modes of deployment of specific combinations of thematic and actional meaning relations. These accounts tend to be limited to isolated lexical items separate from both the grammatical relations in which they are encoded and their copatterned selections and distributions in the specific texts and intertextual sets where meanings are made.[1] Thus Bakhtin's emphasis on the "orientation toward a specific conceptual horizon" agrees with the argument I have made here. Lemke (1983b: 160) further shows that "words do not have definite meanings of their own; rather, the meaning of a word is only approximately invariant in relation to its semantic valences to (usually a small set of) other words *in a specific set of texts*" (emphasis in original). Thus the meanings of formal lexico-grammatical features are always construed in and through their patterned combinations with other items in a specific text or intertextual set rather than as isolable formal items per se.

The main purpose of the present section is to show how intertextual discursive frames can be used to systematize the "conceptual systems" to which Bakhtin refers on the basis of their analytical reconstruction as global semantic tendencies, which are, however, derived in the present analysis from the actually occurring lexico-grammatical selections in the two texts. Frames thus organize these selections into salient higher-order patterns, which are an attempt to characterize in more general terms the conceptual systems that their heteroglossically related semantics index. Figure 6.2 displays six such frames, which can be characterized as follows: (1) narration of self, (2) power relations, (3) consumer culture, (4) voyeurism, (5) interdiction, and (6) solipsism. Each of these frames consists of a number of slots or micropropositions that are organized into a conceptual system. They are analytical approximations of (inter)textual semantic macrostructures, heteroglossically related. The analysis here is a purely synoptic representation. There is no suggestion that these represent dynamic discursive processes.

The absence of dynamic criteria here is also related to the lack of any syntagmatic criteria of combination at this level of analysis. These abstract conceptual systems entail principles of classification and coclassification of (inter)textual semantic features into a higher-order pattern. Furthermore, the dialogic nature of these relations means that a particular semantic feature "in" a given frame can index relations with other frames in a complex network of interrelations between frames. Figure 6.3 attempts to characterize the dialogic interplay of (inter)textual semantic frames in our example.

The concepts of dialogicity and social heteroglossia show that (inter)textual semantic meanings are not mere data, referentially describable, as formal semantic models tend to assume. Semantic meanings are made in and through articulated copatternings of meaning selections in specific texts and intertextual sets. These are not simple givens. The shifts and transformations in the local and global relations of equivalence and contrast in (inter)textual formations change the semantic meanings themselves. Semantic models based on isolable formal features come up against the problem of the articulated nature of the copatterned (inter)textual relations—covariate and multivariate—in and through which the meanings an item has are construed. The concept of text-semantics needs to be reformulated in terms of the copatterning and distribution of specific thematic and actional meaning relations and the lexico-grammatical selections that realize them. The concept of heteroglossia is therefore a way of analyzing the articulated semantic orientations that voice specific social practices and strategic alignments of them. They enact metastable conditions of functional stability and change by

1.

NARRATION OF SELF

Monologic consciousness as narrating agent

Confession

Sexual life history

Hidden sexual impulses revealed

Singular, self-originating consciousness revealed

Continuous, unified life History

2.

POWER RELATIONS

Narrating agent as subject of narrated statements

Interiorization of consciousness

Increased regularization of sexuality through confessional mode

Sexuality as site of discursive intervention

Sexuality as site of "truth" in medical and legal discourse

Juridical coding of sexuality

Confessional as the conditions for the production of "truth" as the effect of specific power-knowledge relations

3.

CONSUMER CULTURE

Individual as commodity on display

Ethic of self-realization

Self-conscious cultivation of style

Secularized body on display

Self-conscious narcissism

Cult of personality, appearance, bodily presentation

Cult of performing self, social actor

4.

VOYEURISM

Male gaze structures scene

Female positioned in relation to male look

5.

INTERDICTION

Social taboo

Incest

Child sexuality

Interrogation of discursive limits of discourse on sexuality, the erotic

6.

SOLIPSISM

Imaginary oppositions

Splitting of self/society

Imaginary identification: narrative Doubles

Figure 6.2. Intertextually derived frame structures in Van/Humbert and Ada/Lolita discourses

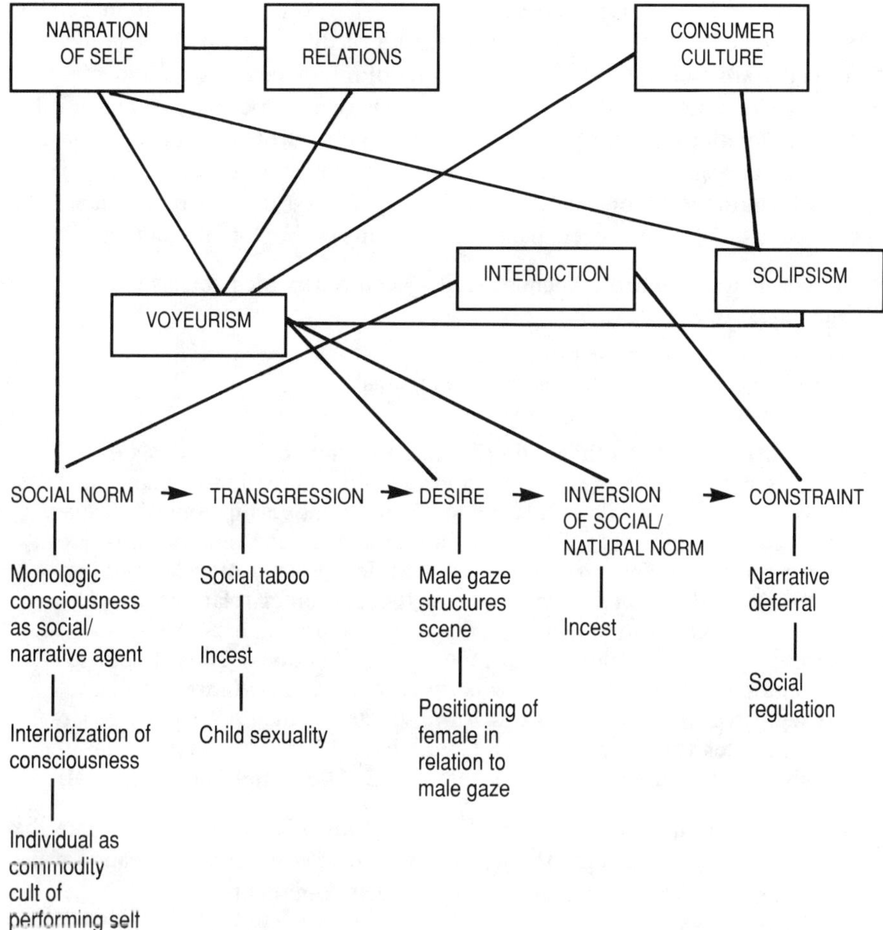

Figure 6.3. Dialogic interplay of intertextual frames and thematic macrosequences

virtue of the local and global relations of equivalence and contrast between meaning selections in texts and intertextual sets, which instantiate higher-order social semiotic relations and practices.

Coding Orientations, Social Heteroglossia, and Text Semantics

Eco (1980) claims that the actualization of a discourse "topic" allows for the appropriate contextual selections by virtue of the codes that correlate an expression plane with its content plane as a particular semantic interpretation. This semantic interpretation, Eco claims, is determined by the coherence relations at all levels of textual organization. Eco's (1980, 1984: 171–72) notion of correlational codes is related to the Hjelmslevian concept of realization discussed above. The correlational codes are used to hypothesize how rules of inference and semantic interpretation arise (see Eco, 1984: 173–79), but in a way that does not account for the contextual relations involved or the social forms of control of the distribution and differential access of social agents to them. The concept of code to be used here derives from the work of Basil Bernstein, which I first introduced in chapter 1. One of Bernstein's more recent papers defines this concept in the following way:

> A code is a regulative principle, tacitly acquired, which selects and integrates:
>
> (a) relevant meanings meanings
> (b) forms of their realization realizations
> (c) evoking contexts contexts
>
> (1) It follows from this definition that the unit for the analysis of codes is not an abstract utterance nor a single context but relationships between contexts. Code is a regulator of the relationships *between* contexts and, through that relationship, a regulator of the relationships *within* contexts. What counts as a context depends not on relationships *within,* but *relationships between* contexts. The latter relationships, *between,* create boundary markers whereby specific contexts are distinguished by their specialized meanings and realizations. Thus if code is the regulator of the relationships *between* contexts, *and* through that, the regulator of the relationships *within* contexts, then code must generate principles for the *creation and production* of the specialized relationships within a context. (Bernstein, 1982: 306; emphasis in original)

Bakhtin's notion of social heteroglossia had already begun to articulate the question of "specialized relationships within a context" within an account of the system of social heteroglossia in a given speech community:

> Language—like the living concrete environment in which the consciousness of the verbal artist lives—is never unitary. It is unitary only as an abstract grammatical system of normative forms, taken in isolation from the concrete, ideological conceptualizations that fill it, and in isolation from the uninterrupted process of historical becoming that is characteristic of all living language. *Actual social life and historical becoming create within an abstract unitary national language, a multitude of concrete worlds, a multitude of bounded verbal-ideological and social belief systems;* within these various systems (identical in the abstract) are elements of a language filled with various semantic and axiological content and each with its own different sound. (Bakhtin, 1981: 288; emphasis added)

The concept of boundedness suggests Bernstein's notion of "specialized relationships." A code is a contextual restriction among all the possible social meanings and their realizations in a metaredundancy hierarchy of context-types. The social semiotic system comprises numerous potentially interacting subsystems that contextualize in regular and systematic ways the redundancies of social practices with their intertextual discursive frames. Code thus regulates and distributes power-knowledge relations and their access in the social semiotic system. It regulates the relative semiotic freedom available to social agents and their positionings as discursive subjects in texts and social occasions of discourse. Power-knowledge relations are immanent in social meaning making practices. They are therefore immanent in the *recognition rules* and the *realization rules* of the social semiotic or some part of it. They correspond to the forms of intelligibility of the social formation. These questions will be developed in greater detail in chapters 7 and 8.

The above proposals suggest a rather more complex set of operations than merely attaching some frame to a particular discourse "topic" (cf. Beaugrande, 1980: 169). The regulatory functions of the codes index specific power-knowledge relations in discourse by (1) constraining the type and the form of the meaning relations that are made in a given social situation-type; (2) specifying their forms of realization; (3) specifying the operational procedures—the strategies and tactics—that are enacted; and (4) specifying the interactional practices, by whom, and for whom.

The differences between Van/Humbert discourse and Ada/Lolita discourse, which we explored earlier, articulate an asymmetry in the power-knowledge relations between the two discourses. Bernstein's concepts of classification and framing principles, through which these relations are regulated, are relevant to our attempt to relate the differential semantic orientations in the two texts to the social meaning making practices in and through which the former are articulated. This will be a major theme throughout chapters 7 and 8. The comments I shall make now are very much of a preliminary nature. Here is Bernstein on the concept of framing:

> *Framing* stands in the same relation to *principle of communication,* as *classification* stands in relation to the *principles of the relation between categories*. In the same way as the relations between categories can be governed by strong or weak classification, so principles of communication can be governed by strong or weak framing. From this point of view, it does not make sense to talk about strong or weak principles of communication. Principles of communication are to varying degrees acquired, explored, resisted, challenged, and their vicissitudes are particular to a principle. *Control* is always present, *whatever the principle*. What varies is the *form* the control takes. The *form* of control is described here in terms of its framing. (Bernstein, 1982: 325; emphasis in original)

In the textual excerpts we examined earlier, Humbert's lexico-grammatically explicit first-person narration constitutes strong framing. The I-narrator explicitly regulates the interactional situation. Van's narration is in the so-called omniscient mode whereby the speaking presence of the narrator-I is backgrounded and not made explicit in the lexico-grammar. Van's role as narrator is relatively weakly framed because of the dialogic challenge of Ada. Ada's dialogic interruption in this excerpt constitutes a local challenge to the global dominance of narrator-Van in the interactional situation of the novel. The strong framing of monologic omniscient narration is challenged by a dialogic interruption of narrator-Van as the single, univocal authority in the text. Dialogicity can therefore foreground potential points of resistance in dominant meaning making practices. This does not mean that the power-knowledge relations of narrator-Van have been globally reframed. Humbert's first-person narration is strongly classified because the narrating agent is sharply distinguished from other agents in the interactional situation. Ada's dialogic interruption means that the principles of classification are weaker in the *Ada* text. The monologic narrator is a generic norm that legitimates this univocal claim to power and authority in the interactional situation by linking specific (inter)textual discursive frames to socially specific practices of telling and receiving stories.

The copatterned lexico-grammatical selections that realize Van/Humbert discourse give voice to a more abstract, more global set of interactional practices and thematic meanings. Van/Humbert discourse is more self-contextualizing or less tied to a specific, concrete interactional situation. By contrast, Ada/Lolita discourse is embedded within Van/Humbert discourse and is therefore more contextually tied to it. Ada/Lolita discourse tends to more local meanings and interactional practices and may be said to be dominated by Van/Humbert discourse. There is then a systematic, though articulated, gap or disjunction between the interactional practices and the thematic meaning relations of the two discourses. The differential skewing of the meaning selections in the two semantic orientations is not therefore confined to the lexico-grammatical selections. Skewing also occurs in the copatterning of interactional practices and thematic meanings in the two discourses. This concretely demonstrates the point made at the beginning of this chapter that not all possible combinations of thematic and actional meanings actually do occur. Nevertheless, principles of classification and framing help to show that monologic and dialogic are not textual givens. They have been seen to correspond to generically specific classification and framing principles and the intertextual discursive frames these enact in particular combinations of interactional and thematic contexts.

Note

1. This point hinges on the theoretical assumption that "lexis can be defined as 'most delicate grammar' " (Halliday, 1976a: 69). The internal functional organization of the lexico-grammar means that functional relations are also the property of lexical items. Thus the study of lexis and the ways in which it is encoded in grammatical relations cannot be separated from the study of grammar, hence the term lexico-grammar (see also Halliday, 1976b: 77; Silverstein, 1980: 20–21; Hasan, 1987b).

Part IV
Subjects, Codes, and Discursive Practice

It is necessary to understand man as a series of active relationships (a process) in which, if individuality has the greatest importance, it is not, however, the only element to consider. The humanity that is reflected in every individual is composed of diverse elements: (1) the individual; (2) other men; (3) nature. But the second and third elements are not as simple as might appear. The individual does not enter into relationships with other men by way of juxtaposition, but organically, that is, insofar as he enters to be part of organisms from the most simple to the most complex. Thus man does not simply enter into a relationship with nature because of the fact of being himself nature, but actively, by means of work and technique. Further, these relationships are not mechanical. They are active and conscious; that is, they correspond to a greater or lesser degree of intelligence that the individual man has of them. Therefore it can be said that everyone changes himself, modifies himself, insofar as he changes and modifies the entire complex of relationships of which he is the center of the knot. In this sense the real philosopher is and cannot be other than the politician, that is, the active man who modifies the environment, [where] the environment is understood as the whole of the relationships into which every individual man enters and takes part. If one's own individuality is the whole of these relationships, to become a personality means to acquire awareness of these relationships, to modify one's own personality means to modify the whole of these relationships. But these relationships, as has been said, are not simple. While some of these are necessary, others [are] voluntary. Moreover, to be more or less deeply conscious of them (that is, to know more or less the means by which they can be modified) already modifies them. The same necessary relationships insofar as they are known in their necessity, change in appearance and importance. Knowledge is power, in this sense. But the problem is also complex from another perspective: it is not enough to know the whole of the relationships insofar as they exist in a given moment in a given system, but it is important to know them genetically, in their means of formation, because every individual is the synthesis not only of existing relationships but also of the history of these relationships, that is, the recapitulation of all the past.

Antonio Gramsci (1977d: 33–34; my translation)

For a theory of communicative action only those analytic theories of meaning are instructive that start from the structure of linguistic expressions rather than from speakers' intentions. And the theory will have to keep in view the problem of how the actions of several actors are linked to one another by means of the mechanism of reaching understanding, that is, how they can be interlaced in social spaces and historical times.

Jürgen Habermas ([1981] 1984: 275)

The consequences of specific speech forms or codes will transform the environs into a matrix of particular meanings which becomes part of psychic reality through acts of speech. As a person learns to subordinate his behaviour to a linguistic code, which is the expression of a role, different orders of relation are made available to him. The complex of meanings which a role-system transmits reverberates developmentally in an individual to inform his general conduct. On this argument it is the linguistic transformation of the role which is the major bearer of meanings: it is through specific linguistic codes that relevance is created, experience given a particular form, and social identity constrained.

Basil Bernstein (1971: 125)

Chapter 7
Social Meaning Making, Textual Politics, and Power

The Problematic of Ideology

In this chapter I attempt to develop a critical neomaterialist social semiotic account of ideology and discursive practice. My starting point in this discussion is Gramsci's formulation of the practical and epistemological difficulties that have beset this problematic concept:

> An element of error in the consideration of the value of ideologies appears to me to be owed to the fact (a fact that is, however, not casual) that the name *ideology* is given both to the necessary superstructure of a determinate structure and to the arbitary lucubrations of determinate individuals. The inferior meaning of the word has become extensive, and this has modified and altered the substance of the theoretical analysis of the concept of ideology. The process of this error can be easily reconstructed: (1) ideology is identified as distinct from structure, and it is asserted that ideologies do not change structure but vice versa; (2) it is asserted that a certain political solution is "ideological," namely, is insufficient to change the structure, as long as it [the political solution] believes it is able to change it [the structure], it is affirmed to be useless, stupid, and so on; (3) one proceeds to assert that every ideology is "pure" appearance, useless, stupid, and so on.
>
> It is necessary then to distinguish between organically historical ideologies that are namely necessary to a certain structure and arbitrary, rationalistic, "chosen" ideologies. Insofar as they are historically necessary, they have a validity that is a "psychological" validity, they "or-

> ganize" the human masses, form the terrain on which men move, acquire consciousness of their position, struggle, and so forth. Insofar as they are "arbitrary," they create no more than individual "movements," polemics, and the like; (not even these are completely useless because they are like the error that is opposed to truth and [that] alters it. (Gramsci, 1977e: 58–59; my translation)

The implications of Gramsci's analysis for our exploration of the concept of ideology are fourfold. First, social meaning making practices enact regular, systematic, and limited patterns of action and meaning within socially and historically constructed discursive formations. Second, the discursive subject/social agent relation does not designate a self-originating, pregiven center of consciousness; nor is it reducible to the mere structural "effects" of discursive practices as functional supports of the system that they "reproduce." Third, Gramsci's conception of struggle articulates the uneven distribution of the material and semiotic resources in the social semiotic system and the differential access of social agents to these. Fourth, ideology refers to a system of local and global determinants that constantly articulate, disarticulate, and rearticulate these relations of struggle to opposing hegemonic principles and the copatternings of discursive and prediscursive (material) relations that are specialized to them.

These initial proposals are intended as a break with representational accounts of ideology as "false consciousness." In this section, I shall examine this notion and its potential relevance for the alternative proposals that I have summarized above. Frow (1986: 55–58) argues that the concept of false consciousness is founded on a static set of oppositions such as truth/falsity rather than a dynamic interplay of social meaning making practices. False consciousness is conceived of as the articulation of "falsity," whose "truth" can only be known from a position external to or above the ideological. This implies a static opposition between self and other in which the other is a representative of the subject-of-mastery or the scientific subject-who-is-supposed-to-know. This position of mastery is articulated from an external position of both epistemological and political authority, whereby the hierarchically organized and articulated conflict between self and the alienating, subjecting other are reduced to a static, symmetrical, and Imaginary opposition (Wilden, 1981). Further, the relation between the representation and that which is represented is itself founded on an Imaginary unity of the two levels. False consciousness is founded on just such an epistemological unity in which the gap between false representations and truth is reunited in the teleology of the final state when the gap between the two is closed. Derrida's (1974, 1978) deconstruction of the "metaphysics of presence" in representationalism has shown how this metaphysic presupposes the identity of a representation with its represented, which is, however, paradoxically absent. The presumed identity between the representation and the absent represented is constituted through the interplay of sameness and difference, which Derrida has called *différance*. Thus, the discursive or semiotic character of the relations between representation and represented, relations that remain unstated within the problematic of representationism, can become the terms of their deconstruction as articulated and overdetermined discursive relations and practices. False consciousness is here rejected as a useful concept for a social semiotic theory of ideology. Nevertheless, Marx himself also argued, especially in his writings from 1845 onward, that social agents enter into *productive* social and political relations and practices. The issue here is not whether individuals and social groups are placed in a relation of truth or falsity to the empirically defined social Real. The point is that it is social and discursive practices that productively maintain and change the social formation.

Marx made a careful analytical distinction between two different modes of social consciouness. The first is "spontaneous" and is linked to "productive" labor. The second is "intellectual" and is linked to so-called nonproductive labor. Neither were presumed to exist empirically in a necessary relation of truth or falsity to the empirical social Real. This conceptual distinction refers to the social division of labor in specific social and historical formations. Spontaneous, practical consciousness is linked to the active production of wealth. The second category designates intellectual, "unproductive" labor, which is based on the interpretation of social reality. It is the realm of abstract social consciousness. Bernstein's (1971, 1977, 1982, 1986a, b) distinction between restricted and elaborated coding orientations can be related to Marx's distinction. This does not mean that the two sets of distinctions are identical, but I think they can be usefully related to each other in anticipation of my attempt below to reconstitute Bernstein's theory of coding orientations in the conceptual framework of social semiotics. The forms of social consciousness and practices associated with spontaneous or practical consciousness can be transformed by determinate social and historical practices in the superstructure. The spontaneous thoughts and practices of, say, a dominant social group may well be elaborated in a systematic way in the superstructure. The spontaneous thoughts and practices of a dominated social group may not be so elaborated. The specificity of practices in the superstructure means that some practices and concepts are elaborated while others are not. The elaboration in this way of a given practice in the superstructure means that the forms of social consciousness and the social relations so produced are so abstracted from their material base that they serve merely to reproduce and legitimate the forms of social consciousness of their producers and no other group. It is in this sense that Marx intends the term "unproductive." These processes do not occur spontaneously on the basis of individual decisions, desires, and the like (see the quotation from Gramsci above). They occur as a result of determinate social and historical relations and practices. Now, the distinctions made by Marx and Bernstein do not refer to individual forms of consciousness. They designate specific, differentially defined forms of the social division of labor and social meaning making, which Bernstein has characterized as particular coding orientations. These are not, I would argue, reducible to forms of class consciousness. I shall develop this point at a later stage. Nor is there any necessary or intrinsic way in which one coding orientation or form of social consciousness is "truer" or superior to another. Such judgments are themselves contingent on socially and historically determinate, but shifting, axiological standpoints. The elaborated coding orientation is related to its material base in a less direct, more abstract way. It is the coding principles themselves rather than the material base that determine and articulate the products of this mode of social consciousness and its forms of labor. Marx's distinction between spontaneous and intellectual labor, like Bernstein's, is related to different forms of social consciousness (subjectivity), which are articulated in and through specific forms of the social division of labor. Ideology is then definable as specific configurations of the forms of social consciousness, the social division of labor, and social meaning making practices. In terms of the social semiotic conceptual framework of this book, the distinctions made by both Marx and Bernstein relate to the ways in which the uneven distribution of and the differential access of social agents to the material and meaning making resources of the social semiotic system produce and articulate particular, heteroglossically positioned, discursive positioned-practices (subject positions). The juxtaposition and comparison here of Marx's concepts of forms of social consciousness and their unequal distribution in the social formation and Bernstein's theory of coding orientations suggest, in a preliminary way, that a materialist theory of social and discursive practice holds out the best possibility of constructing useful links between the concept of ideology and social meaning making practices in ways that can show that "subjectivity" is socially and discursively constructed. However, both the conceptions of Marx and Bernstein retain an allegiance to the essentialist and unifying logic of social class, which is seen as the a priori epistemological guarantor of both Marx's forms of social consciousness and Bernstein's coding orientations. These are conceptualized in terms of the base/superstructure distinction in relation to which representations of forms of social consciousness are said to be articulated and thought. In the conceptual framework of the present study, social class is not assumed to be the a priori functional basis of either forms of social consciousness or the coding orientations. These are not reducible to an essentialist unity whereby two (or more) fully articulated principles stand in an already fully defined relation to each other. Both Marx and Bernstein rely on functional criteria whereby social agents are the structural supports of particular forms of social consciousness and/or coding orientations. These are seen as essentialist and unified totalities, which are driven by a causal and finalistic teleology of the needs of the social totality to which the various forms of social consciousness, their interrelationships, and their social agents conform in order to reproduce the social totality. In the conceptual framework of the present study, we are concerned with the constant processes of articulation, disarticulation, and rearticulation of social meaning making practices and their intersections and disjunctions without presuming a single unitary causal logic. Nevertheless, Bernstein's theory of coding orientations is of considerable importance to this project, and I shall later propose how this can be reconstituted within the social semiotic conceptual framework.

The opposition of "truth" to "falsity" suggests a further series of oppositions: deep structure/surface structure, reality/appearance, latent content/manifest content, thought/language. In each case, a particular kind of relation between knowledge and a knowing subject is presupposed. The concept of ideology as worldview is predicated upon this kind of opposition. This concept is founded on the assumption that ideology is a normative body of opinion or a system of ideas and beliefs, which are expressive of a given social totality. The worldview is the superstructural expression of the relations that social agents have to the material base in a given social group. It comprises the knowledge of a determinate social subject, seen as either the individual or the collectivity, who reflects this deep structural material base more or less truthfully in his or her social relations and practices. This presumes that ideologies originate in superstructual practices that may be differentially related to the material base. It relies on positivistic and representational criteria according to which worldview is a "true" or "false" reflection of the material base. In this way, the oppositions referred to above reduce ideology to the status of some epiphenomenal appearance, which works to distort or mystify the individual's or the social group's perception of the underlying "real" conditions of their social existence. Ideology becomes a surface misrepresentation of some more real underlying content, which presupposes a phenomenology of the subject's experience of these illusory surface forms and the underlying real base. The material base is therefore positioned in a relation of potential truth or falsity to an already given subject, who is, however, always external to it.

Functionalism and Materialism

The critical linguistics of Hodge and Kress (1979) is an important attempt to link the functional organization of linguistic structure to a materialist theory of the social structure. Critical linguistics attempts to theorize the constrained nature of the meaning choices available to social agents in specific social contexts and to link these to structures and patterns of interaction that encode relations of power and domination in the social structure. Critical linguistics is then motivated by a political program that seeks to ask questions of social relevance (Kress, 1987: 2). The critical linguistics of Hodge and Kress (1979) is, in part, based on Halliday's systemic-functional theory of language. However, Hodge and Kress tend to use specific areas of the lexico-grammar in texts and to relate these to the social structure in a more or less direct way.[1] For instance, Halliday's model of transitivity (i.e., process-participant-circumstance) relations in the grammar of the clause is used as a model of the systems of classification or the models of reality that shape the language user's perception of reality. Kress (personal communication) argues that there is a relation between psychological perception and linguistic structure, which in turn have socially learned values in their contexts of use. Hodge and Kress link this claim to the work of Benjamin Lee Whorf (1956). Whorf wrote of "our linguistically determined thought world" (1956a: 154), which suggests that the speakers of a given language are constrained by a limited number of linguistically determined models of reality. As this stands, it is likely to read as if it is hypostatized lexico-grammatical form that somehow directly determines our "thought world." Certainly, this is the simplistic and incorrect reading of Whorf that has predominated. However, Whorf (1956a: 138) maintained the distinction between the language habits of a given speech community ("cultural and behavioral norms") and lexico-grammatical form ("large-scale linguistic patterns") in ways that indicate that he was not talking about a simple one-way linguistic determinism whereby causality or agency is directly attributed to linguistic form per se (see, however, Pateman, 1981). Instead, Whorf argued that language users construct folk-theoretical rationalizations of automatized copatternings of linguistic features to selectively analogize these patterns to extralinguistic "reality." These automatized patterns are then, as Silverstein (1979) has shown, "objectified" and "referentially projected" onto extralinguistic reality *as if* these linguistic patterns correspond to that reality in a straightforwardly referential way. Now, these processes of objectification and referential projection do not imply a one-way determinism leading from the lexico-grammar to the "thought world" of speakers. Whorf understood that it is selected and foregrounded *patterns of cultural behavior* that lead the members of a given culture to act *as if* their habitual patterns of behavior correspond in a routine and straightforward way to selectively foregrounded copatternings of linguistic features. The selective analogizing of automatized linguistic copatternings to "reality out there" (i.e., objectification) and the consequent "referential projection" then have consequences for human action. To illustrate this, here is Whorf on the concept of time in Standard Average European languages and the referential projection of linguistically coded temporal categories that occurs:

> Still another behavioral effect is that the character of monotony and regularity possessed by our image of time as an evenly scaled limitless tape measure persuades us to behave as if that monotony were more true of events than it really is. That is, it helps to routinize us. We tend to select and favor whatever bears out this view, to "play up to" the routine aspects of existence. (Whorf, 1956a: 154)

Thus Whorf was suggesting a complex dialectic between routine, habitual patterns of behavior (social meaning making practices), foregrounded copatternings of lexico-grammatical forms, which Whorf refers to as "fashions of speaking" or particular "configurative rapports" (Whorf, 1956b: 80–81) of linguistic features, and the folk-theoretical rationalizations of the relations between linguistic forms and extralinguistic reality, which are routinely deployed by speakers to account for their own linguistic practice. Whorf (1956a: 152) himself wrote of our "common sense" ways of talking about these relations. These "fashions of speaking" or "configurative rapports" of lexico-grammatical features produce consistent semantic frames or orientations that cannot be reduced to isolated formal features of the lexico-grammar. The emphasis is on the consistency of copatterning of lexico-grammatical selections, which can only be adequately analyzed on the basis of texts and social occasions of discourse rather than of isolated, decontextualized sentences. This depends on the patterns of use and modes of deployment of the lexico-grammatical resources of the linguistic system:

> Concepts of "time" and "matter" are not given in substantially the same form of experience to all men but depend upon the nature of the language or the languages *through the use of which they have been developed*. They do not depend so much upon ANY ONE SYSTEM (e.g. tense, or nouns) within the grammar as upon *the ways of analyzing and reporting experience which have become fixed in the language as integrated "fashions of speaking"* and which cut across the typical grammatical classifications, so that such a "fashion" may include lexical, morphological, syntactic, and otherwise systemically diverse means coordinated in a certain frame of consistency. (Whorf, 1956a: 158; emphasis added)

Whorf, however, did not fully develop all of the links that I have outlined above. The weakest link, theoretically speaking, remains the one between the "fashions of speaking" and the social structure. In Hodge and Kress the attempt to reconstruct this link analytically is vitiated by their tendency to read off ideological categories in a more or less direct way from specific formal features in the lexico-grammar. There is little systematic concern with either the internal functional basis of paradigmatic (systemic) relations or with the foregrounded copatternings of lexico-grammatical selections from all three semantic metafunctions (see chapter 6). In this regard, it is worth noting that Whorf's own discussions are largely in terms of ideational-grammatical relations. There is in Whorf (1956) only one systematic discussion of interpersonal meanings and their encoding in the lexico-grammar (1956c). (See, however, Thibault, 1986f, for an attempt to relate the Whorfian hypothesis to copatterned selections from all three semantic metafunctions.) Hodge and Kress are then more concerned with specific lexico-grammatical features—for example, transitivity, modality, tense, and negation—and their relations to the social structure. Pateman (1981: 10), in his review article of Hodge and Kress (1979), asserts that theirs is an "equifunctional" account in which a one-to-one fit is postulated between some feature in the lexicogrammar and some feature in the social context. I fully share Pateman's commitment to link functional explanations of linguistic structure to the material social circumstances of language use. However, Pateman's "realist" criteria lead him to miscontrue in rather serious ways the theoretical claims of systemic-functional linguistics and its possible contribution to such a project. Pateman's realist perspective postulates that the goals of theory are the underlying causal relations that must constitute the explanatory basis of linguistic behavior. In order to do this, Pateman explicitly opposes a deterministic reading of Whorf to a functional explanation based on the communicative needs, goals, and purposes of language users (Pateman, 1981: 8). These are required, Pateman argues, in order to explain the causal link between society and language in which the direction of the fit is from the former to the latter. I argued in chapter 6 that this form of functional explanation, which is based on externally derived, ad hoc pragmatic criteria, is in fact a folk-theory of language use. It is a folk-theoretical rationalization of linguistic tokens and their context-dependent meanings, founded on the language user's perception that these forms are actually causally efficacious in fulfilling the local needs, goals, and purposes of language users (Silverstein, 1979: 206). Thus, "explanation" starts when its object and its purposes are already given by the folk-theoretical rationalizations of social agents. It is one thing to recognize the role these have in the agent's own accounting for his or her actions; it is quite another to presume these commonsense rationalizations as the basis for a "scientific" theory. What Pateman assumes to be a central component of functional explanations of language structure and language use is, in fact, a partial view as far as a semantically oriented functional grammar is concerned (e.g., Halliday, 1985). Pateman's counterproposals remain tied to the semantics-pragmatics disjunction in his discussion of individual utterance-tokens. Once again, the copatterned meaning selections in texts, their patterns of use, and the social activity-structures with which these combine are not accounted for in a systematic way. Pateman's (1981: 23) recourse to "extralinguistic apparatus" or pragmatic criteria for the explanation of social action remains closely tied to specific folk-theoretical rationalizations of language use in which context is thought of in terms of individual extralinguistic competences, intentions, and the like. Furthermore, Pateman (1981: 23) continues to operate the positivistic distinction between language and its "intended referents" without apparently realizing that this formulation continues to operate the folk-theoretical disjunction between the system of meanings and the extralinguistic, referentially real world "out there." Pateman's critique thus miscontrues and dichotomizes functionally based accounts of the internal patterning and distribution of linguistic forms in their contexts-of-use on the one hand and Whorf's subtle critique of the folk-theoretical rationalizations that operate the disjunctions referred to above, on the other. What goes unnoticed in Pateman's discussion is (1) that Whorf's theory of grammar is itself a functional semantic one based on the relations between overt surface segmentable "phenotypic" categories in the form of the lexico-grammar and their "reactances" with covert "cryptotypic" categories, which are the "deep" semantics of a language and (2) that Pateman's account itself operates the very folk-theoretical rationalizations that are the focus of Whorf's critique. Unfortunately, space does not permit a fuller discussion of Whorf's significance for social semiotic theory. Further discussion of Whorf that is relevant to my concerns is to be found in Halliday (1983), Hasan (1986), Martin (1988), Silverstein (1979), Thibault (1986f), and Threadgold (1987, 1989).

From the side of social theory, the causal or teleological model of functionalism in Pateman has its epistemological basis in structural-functionalist models of society (Durkheim, 1964; Parsons, 1964). Structural-functionalism postulates that social customs, relations, and institutions persist through time on the basis of their inherent or intrinsic functions, which work to maintain the social totality in a state of equilibrium. It is a consensus model of the social structure, conceptualized as an integrated set of interacting functional parts, which are directed toward a global condition of relative equilibrium or homeostasis. It is a normative conception of the social totality, which is unable to account for social conflict except in terms of deviance from the norm. Thus, change in this totality is always conceived of as some modification or adaptation of the functional relations of the system in order to achieve or restore its equilibrium. Structural-functionalist accounts of the social order follow the epistemology of classical thermodynamics—systems whose processes are reversible at or near a state of equilibrium—such that the random deviations from this norm are evened out and the overall long-term equilibrium of the system is maintained. The social order is maintained on the basis of the normatively defined functional goals, purposes, and needs—the control values—of the whole social system. In this way, the members of the social totality are taken to be the functional supports of the system, and its control values are taken as givens. Habermas ([1967] 1988: 87) shows that this "empirical context of actions regulated by social norms" corrects the bias toward "subjectively intended meanings." Further, the absence of historically substantive and value-interpretation criteria fails to grasp that social action is also *intentional* and *communicative* action among social agents.

Structural-functionalist models of society are therefore conservative and non-dialectical. It is a model of society that is unable adequately to theorize contradiction, conflict, and change. In part, this is so because it is unable to theorize the specificity of the conflicting relations that enact the constant metastable dialectic between system-maintaining and system-changing relations and practices. Durkheim's conception of the *conscience collective* closely resembles Saussure's concept of *langue,* in which systematicity and regularity in language are recognized to the exclusion of variability and change. In both conceptions, normative models of society and language are postulated along institutional lines such that there is a fixed and coercive agreement among the members as to the rules of conduct or the meanings of linguistic forms. It amounts to what Harris (1981: 153) has aptly named the "fixed-code fallacy." The root metaphor that frequently informs structural-functionalism is a sociobiological determinism, which derives from systems analysis of biological and physical systems as normative, self-regulating, and teleological closed-system cybernetic models. I am not necessarily opposed to the use of biological and physical models in the conceptualization of the social semiotic (see below). What concerns me is the inappropriate, illegitimate, and reductionist use of such metaphors in ways that epistemologically confuse or mistype the levels of relations involved (Wilden, 1980, 1981).

A central aim of the social semiotic conceptual framework is to theorize and rearticulate the relations among the functional systematicity and variability of semiotic forms; their copatterned uses, modes of deployment, and patterns of distribution in texts and intertextual sets; and determinate social and discursive practices. This requires that we look at the combined effects of all these relations as a social semiotic process rather than reifying, say, linguistic forms in the way that an empirical, correlational sociolinguistics, with its epistemological basis in structural-functionalist models of the social structure, does. These reifying models assume a functionalism of already given form-meaning relations per se, which are then correlated empirically with selected features of the social structure, such as social class, gender, ethnicity, and the like. These inevitably work to confirm pregiven, usually implicit structural-functionalist assumptions about the social structure as a whole. Thus both the linguistic and the social assumptions of this kind of theory entail an epistemological relation between form-meaning relations and the represented social Real. Structural-functionalist models of the social totality act as the epistemological guarantor of the correspondence between the two. Empirical sociolinguistic models of this relation articulate this correspondence in the following terms: (1) the assumption of a tautological relation between forms and meanings (cf. signifiers and signifieds); (2) a normative structural-functionalist model of the social structure, which takes the relation between microlevel linguistic form-meaning relations and the macrolevel organization of the social structure as a referential and empirical given rather than a constitutive and productive one; and (3) the a priori assumption that a particular sociolinguistic model can simply read off or discover social relations and categories, which are objectively there in formal, surface segmentable lexicogrammatical forms per se. This is a formalistic conception of linguistic functions, seen only from below, which ignores both the way in which particular linguistic theories construct specific knowledges about language and the two-way productive dialectic of linguistic forms and functions seen both from below and from above. The critical linguistics of Hodge and Kress (1979) is, I believe, an important, though theoretically and methodologically flawed, early attempt to articulate these relations and to challenge the normative social content and the empirical and correlational methodological basis of sociolinguistics. The important task for a social semiotic account of ideology, power, and domination is to develop a conceptual framework that is able to (1) relate ideological formations to the local and global foregrounded and backgrounded copatternings of thematic and actional meaning relations in texts and intertextual sets; (2) connect textual interpretations and practices to social practice; (3) show how choices in meaning are constrained at higher orders such as those of semantic register, social semiotic code, and discursive formation; (4) show how regular, limited patterns of social meaning and action enact the metastable conditions of possibility of the social semiotic system and its agents by virtue of a constant dialectic between system-changing and system-stabilizing relations and practices. In my view, the work of Hodge and Kress (1979) in the critical linguistics paradigm provides partial solutions to some of these questions, as well as important indications of the work that is yet to be done if this enterprise is to achieve the above goals.

Social Semiotic Codes and Neomaterialism

A neomaterialist social semiotic theory has no need of the ontological distinctions material/ideal, representation/represented, and signifier/signified. Discursive subject positions, social agents, social meaning making practices, semiotic forms and their functions, and the material physical and biological domains are interrelated in complex, hierarchically ordered, and overdetermined systems of matter, energy, and information exchanges and transformations (see Lemke, 1984a, b; Prodi, 1977; Wilden, 1981). Neomaterialist social semiotic theory does not grant a privileged epistemological status to the physical and biological "real" worlds. They are not taken to be more real or objective than the systems of social meaning making practices. The fundamental distinction, then, is between the *prediscursive* and the *discursive*. The use of the prefix *pre-* rather than *non-* is used to emphasize that prediscursive patterns in the material physical and biological domains always have the potential to be indexed and hence contextualized in some way by the social meaning making practices and functions in the discursive. Thus the indexing of objects, entities, states, actions, events, and so on, in the prediscursive means that these are contextualized in some metaredundancy hierarchy as part of the form-form relations in and through which social meanings are made. The discursive is no mere epiphenomenon of the prediscursive, because it is only through situationally specific contextualizing relations in the discursive that it is possible to know or define the prediscursive. Thus, the prediscursive is always dependent on the social meaning making practices (i.e., the discursive) that it both embodies materially and with which it intersects and copatterns. In other words, matter, energy, and information exchanges and transformations in the prediscursive materially realize the social semiotic but are not reducible to it (see Prodi, 1977: 151). Prodi points out that this reduction of one order of relations to the other loses sight of the way in which semiotic systems are defined in and through the logic of the matter, energy, and information exchanges that enact them. The history of these exchanges is what constitutes the system of relations. However, this does not mean that social meaning systems are reduced to the physical and biological systems in which they are materially embodied. Social semiotic systems are constituted on the basis of these, but the rules of transmission of natural and social semiotic codes as well as the functional basis of their organization are very different. The material exchanges of the prediscursive and the meaning exchanges and relations of the discursive are in a relationship of dialectical duality (Lemke, 1984b: 63). This dialectic can privilege either aspect at some metatheoretical level, whereby the insistence on "objective reality" privileges the materially "given" physical and biological domains, insofar as these are given to our senses just as much as formal semiotic and/or semantic idealisms privilege a reified set of meanings independent of either the prediscursive exchanges that materially embody them or the social meaning making practices through which they are made. The ontological dualisms referred to here are reconstituted in the neomaterialist social semiotic framework as a dialectical complementarity in which complex intersections and relations of homology between the two may be postulated.

The social semiotic is therefore conceptualized as the dialectical duality and/or complementarity of the prediscursive and the discursive. These relations are, however, never one-way or symmetrical except in the Imaginary mistyping of the levels of relations involved (Wilden, 1980, 1981). Instead, the two components of this dialectic comprise partial (not total) hierarchies of local and global relations in which actions, events, objects, and the physical and biological domains are made meaningful. The discursive has material effectivity because the relations between social actions, texts, and contexts are always immanent in the material exchanges and transactions that constitute the prediscursive. However, we need to be heedful of the ideological and ontological implications of the sociobiological models through which the epistemology of the recently emergent "ecumenical" semiotic paradigm has tended to sacrifice human social meaning making on the altar of the Great Computer, whose totalizing tendencies have disposed of the dialectic of historical memory and human identity at the same time that consumer capitalism proposes the new manipulatory program for the future:

> Taking into account all that is now understood about throughput dynamics in dissipative structure, we can appreciate human language as one more energy-information processor, along with trophic level, thermoregulation, play, dreaming, and art; all are self-serving and *not*

explicable through function. (Anderson, Deely, Krampen, et al., 1984: 21; emphasis in original)

Here is technocratic capitalism's semiotic "mind-swap" show, which is preparing us for market management's "soft" introduction to the clockwork horror show world of 1984. The epistemological confusion of levels here mistypes the ways in which dynamic, open systems of social semiotic relations and processes cannot be reduced to just "one more energy-information processor" without doing violence to the ways in which hierarchically organized systems of contextualizing relations constitute prediscursive/discursive relations and the potential for intervention and change in the range of human social possibilities that these can potentially make available. The reduction of social meaning making to the structurally stable informational forms that can store them mistypes the relations between these forms and their metastable conditions of social interaction and patterns of use. The implied analogy with biochemical forms of information storage, processing, and transmission (e.g., DNA) cannot account for the very different processes and rates of evolution in biological systems on the one hand and in social semiotic systems on the other. Social semiotic forms and functions are not reducible to the epistemological status of just one more energy-information processor without totally failing to account for patterns of stability and change in the social patterns of use and modes of deployment of them. This is not an argument against the general applicability of the epistemology of dynamic, open systems to both the biological and the social semiotic. It is, however, an argument against the constitutive reduction of the one to the other, as if the biological were a sort of procrustean bed against which everything is in the last analysis measurable. This can only be done by ignoring the conceptual differences between the two domains in the name of a totalizing enterprise whose own ideological assumptions and political commitments remain unstated.

All actions, events, objects, and entities, as well as matter-energy exchanges in the prediscursive, in order to be construed as socially meaningful, must be contextualized in situationallyspecific ways. The indexical resources of the social semiotic (the discursive) type actions, events, objects, and entities in the prediscursive by the discursive so that they are redundant with some set of social meaning relations. Actions, events, and so on, in the prediscursive can only be construed as meaningful in the specific contextualizing relations that are selected from the systemic meaning potential of the social semiotic. There is, of course, no unitary, one-way causal link between the prediscursive and the discursive. Instead, the dialectical duality of the two domains enacts a dynamic, open system of metastable conditions and processes. This conceptualization is *neomaterialist* because it recognizes the specific, real, and material social semiotic processes that operate both in and on prediscursive and discursive relations according to specific contextualizing relations. These in turn construct the distinction between the prediscursive and the discursive itself (Lemke, 1985a).

I have argued elsewhere in this study that the concept of social semiotic coding orientations is a way of analytically reconstructing the differential access of social agents to the material (prediscursive) and social semiotic (discursive) resources of a given social formation. Bernstein (1982) provides us with the important notion that social semiotic codes position social agents as discursive subjects in unequal and discontinuous ways in relation to these resources. This is responsible for the uneven distribution of power, the unequal social division of labor, and the forms of investment that social agents have in differential orientations to social meaning making. Frow (1986: 75) expresses an ambivalence in his assessment of Bernstein's earlier formulations of the concept of code (e.g., Bernstein, 1971, 1977), which seems to me typical of many linguistic appropriations of this concept. This ambivalence refers to whether the codes are internal to semantic register or whether they are a differential mode of access to register. However, this matter is put very clearly by Hasan:

> The code-correlating factors belong to a high-level of abstraction. The theory of code is not only the theory of a linguistic variety; it includes a theory of both verbal and non-verbal behaviour in the sense that it offers some hypothesis regarding the effect of certain social phenomena upon the community's living of life. Code is thus a much more global concept than register. (Hasan, 1973: 286)

Code, like register, though at a higher level, is an analytical concept, which is not reducible to semantic register or the consistent semantic orientations discussed in chapter 6. In the present study, code is used to show how social agents are socially and discursively positioned as subjects in relation to specific meaning orientations in and through the social and discursive practices of agents. Code is then a way of analytically reconstructing the subject's formation in specific configurations of prediscursive and discursive relations. Code is the organizing concept that relates particular patterned articulations of these "downward" to intertextual formations, the system of social heteroglossia, semantic register-types, and specific textual productions and their copatterned meaning selections. Hasan (1973: 287) shows that code is a concept that can relate the linguistic to the extralinguistic in the organization and articulation of social meaning making practices. This is important for relating the coding orientations to specific patterns of textual realization in ways that Bernstein does not do. Frow (1986: 75) points out that Bernstein's conception of elaborated and restricted coding orientations is essentially tied to the notion of class-based languages, with the consequence that the linguistic order is reified. It is not only language that is reified in Bernstein's account but also the notion of social class itself. Bernstein (1982: 311) argues that the social group that dominates and controls the social division of labor determines the extent to which the positioning of social agents gives access to specific coding orientations. Bernstein emphasizes the determining relation of social class with respect to coding orientation insofar as social classes are contesting the social division of labor. But I do not think that coding orientations simply express or are reducible to social class, nor are they uniquely determined by it. In order not to reify social class, it is necessary to demonstrate that the class character of a given social ideology is a function of the articulation of those configurations of prediscursive and discursive relations in a way that confers upon them a class character. The class character of an ideology is not something that is necessarily intrinsic to it but is, rather, conferred upon it by its coding orientation, or, in Gramscian terms, by its articulating principle. As I pointed out early in this chapter, coding orientations articulate particular forms of social consciousness. This occurs in and through the differential meaning orientations they articulate. Coding orientations thus articulate functional positions for discursive subjects, namely, positioned-practices. They construct and articulate functional orientations to specific ways of acting and meaning. At the same time, subjects are not mere structural effects, for the social agent can act and mean in ways that are not congruent with a given discursive subject position. Thus there is a dialectical tension between the social agent as "instrument" and the discursive subject as "function" (see chapter 8). These are always intersected in typical or atypical ways in the constitution of agents as subjects. This process contributes to the metastable dialectic of system-maintaining and system-changing relations and practices.

Bernstein's earlier theorization (e.g., 1971) of the relations between coding orientations and social agents tends to be a direct one in which a functionalist model of cultural reproduction, as Frow (1986: 75) points out, "causally equates socioeconomic position with the subject's position in discourse." Social class is functionally and causally linked to those social agents who are purported to be the structural supports of that class. I do not think the problem is entirely resolved in Bernstein's most recent work. The tendency to view social agents as empirically constitutive of particular coding orientations remains. Bernstein does not specify how coding orientations are always articulated in relation to each other. These relations are articulated by typical overdetermined configurations of the prediscursive and the discursive in ways that produce their typical sociodiscursive positionings. These always occur in contradictory and conflicting ways both within and between (inter)textual formations, the system of social heteroglossia, and particular textual productions. A social semiotic theory must construct ways of talking about these multilevel, discontinous, and differential positionings in ways that can reconstitute the productive dialectic between microlevel textual realizations and macrolevel relations in the social formation. These usually disjoined frameworks and analytical methodologies will need to be reconstituted within the same conceptual framework (Lemke, 1985a). I shall explore the problem of the macro-micro disjunction in the following chapter. In the present chapter, I shall suggest further some ways in which Gramsci's conception of hegemony provides a solution to the problem addressed here.

Bernstein's functionalist model of cultural reproduction is closely tied to the production paradigm. According to Habermas ([1985] 1987a: 80), this paradigm sees practice as "a process of production and appropriation, which proceeds in accordance with technical-utilitarian rules and signals the relevant level of exchange between nature and society." On the other hand, there are the processes of social interaction, regulated by differential norms and validity claims. Yet, this dichotomizing of the two domains does not allow us to inquire as to how the forces and relations of production regulate the differential access of social agents to the material and semiotic resources of the social semiotic system. Bernstein's theory of coding orientations, as I showed earlier in this chapter, points in this direction, and in ways that Habermas's problematic of rationalization does not. Bernstein's theory can be related to a number of distinctions made by earlier social theorists: Marx's distinction between productive and nonproductive labor, Weber's distinction between traditional and rational-bureaucratic forms of social organization, and Durkheim's distinction between mechanical and organic solidarity. All of these distinctions in their various ways designate two different forms of social organization under capitalism. Habermas's ([1981] 1984) distinction between communicative action and strategic action represents an attempt to work through Weber's problematic of modernization in terms of a theory of communicative rationality. Talcott Parsons's distinction between Particularistic and Universalistic forms of societal organization attempts to work through the same problematic in an explicitly evolutionary and implicitly teleological structural-functionalist framework, which has been penetratingly critiqued by Habermas ([1967] 1988). In the Weber-Habermas view, modernization involves the increasing penetration of social life and its norms by cognitive-instrumental rationality instead of norms and validity claims regulated by communicative action oriented to understanding. I have argued elsewhere (Thibault, 1989a, b) that cognitive-instrumental rationality rationalizes language form and function both at the level of our local folk-theoretical explanations as well as a good many more scientific ones, and in ways that have definite effects on socialization and pedagogic practices. But this amounts to the diagnosis of a pathology that ramifies throughout the *linguistic* practices of the modes of production of technocratic-industrial capitalism. Such a diagnosis still does not tell us how we can overcome the dichotomy between the production paradigm and the processes of social interaction. Bernstein's theory of coding orientations does move in this direction. This is so because his theory poses in a unitary framework the question of how the modes of production, the social division of labor, and the means of control of the relations of production both limit and control the access of agents to the differential forms of socialization. Further, the theory at least begins to pose the question of how these factors have shaped the structuring of the linguistic codes themselves.

The dominance of the production paradigm in Bernstein suggests that both domains are subsumed by the categories of labor and production. Thus, the reproduction thesis does not free itself from the tendency to conceive of the coding orientations as normative spheres of "external necessity," conceived in terms of production. Silverman and Torode (1980: 174) point out that Bernstein "is committed to transcendental universalism as the *telos* of the pursuit of meaning." The quest for transcendentalism is, to be sure, emancipatory in its intent. It is the elaborated code that makes available to subjects a "reflexive relation to the social order" (Bernstein, 1972: 164), and to the speech codes that control access to this. Bernstein thus envisages a distinction between external necessity and the social moment of self-reflexivity. But this is dominated by the production paradigm to the extent that Bernstein's earlier work (e.g., 1971, 1972) does not show how this reflexive moment is built into social meaning making. It is this that must also be acted on and changed if the members of a society are to reach understanding as to just what is meant by "access to the grounds of his own socialization" and how to change this (Habermas, [1985] 1987a: 82). Habermas argues that praxis philosophy, which is still tied to the production paradigm, is, accordingly, vitiated in this attempt by its failure fully to theorize the communicative relations – the social meaning making practices – in and through which autonomy, responsibility, and self-reflexivity are realized. But the opposition Habermas makes between the labor or production paradigm and norms of social interaction can also be questioned (Callinicos, 1989: 114–15). Bernstein's theory of coding orientations is, in part, a development of the Marxist insight that "the production of ideas, of conceptions, of consciousness, is at first directly interwoven with the material activity and the material intercourse of men, the language of real life" (Marx and Engels, [1846] 1969: 24–25). This does not presuppose a necessarily totalizing relationship between the two, though this may be an effect of the totalizing tendencies of specific forms of socioeconomic organization, such as technocratic late capitalism and positivistically driven conceptions of "scientific socialism," which govern in the name of the people of which they are the "expression." Indeed, Bernstein's theory of coding orientations represents a further working through of the implications of this Marxist insight, and in ways that suggest that the potential for its further theoretical development is far from exhausted (see chapter 8).

Bernstein's causal link between social class and the coding orientations retains, therefore, an allegiance to the base-superstructure distinction, which is rejected in social semiotic theory. As I said above, it is the overdetermined, articulated nature of the coding orientations that confers their class character. Bernstein's distinction between "elaborated" and "restricted" codes and Marx's distinction between "philosophical" and "practical" consciousness, as I suggested early in this chapter, can be usefully combined so as to suggest how this might be done. Let us start by saying that matter, energy, and information exchanges and transactions both within and between the prediscursive and the discursive dialectically interpenetrate and transform each other in specific ways. The resulting contextually specific patterns of interaction confer, through the work of social agents, a class or other (e.g., gender, ethnic) character on the coding orientations. These can be stable or unstable, dominating or dominated, and so on, according to the constant dialectic of articulation, disarticulation, and rearticulation that takes place between hegemonic and counterhegemonic social meaning making practices. Eco's (1976: 133–36) distinction between *overcoding* and *undercoding* is useful here. Eco's distinction is, incidentally, interestingly parallel to Halliday's (1978: 180) distinction between "congruent" or highly coded meaning relations and "incongruent" or not typically coded meaning relations. Overcoding refers to a relatively stabilized coding orientation, which is recognized as such on the basis of the regular and systematic redundancy relations between some expression plane and its content plane and the context(s) in which it is typically used. It is thus typed as a typical and regular correlation for the members of that culture. Undercoding refers to the reverse situation, where the redundancy relations are not highly coded and so are more open to the processes of interpretation and creative abduction. Eco points out that the two tendencies (not types) are frequently intertwined in a given textual production. Eco's distinction can be adapted in the present framework in order to illustrate the constant dialectic between social agents and discursive subject positions and the ways in which the social agent can enact atypical patterns of meaning and action that can contribute to the alteration of the larger ensemble of interacting subsystems to which these patterns belong. Threadgold (1986b: 113) similarly points out the relations between these concepts from Eco and Halliday and their relevance to variability and change in the social semiotic. Dynamic metastability is therefore functional both at the level where agents intersect with subjects and in the wider patterns of action and meaning these enact. The above proposals from Bernstein, Eco, and Marx can be reconstituted in this framework. I shall now propose two principal coding orientations on this basis. These do not amount to a simple, given binary opposition. They are two divergent sets of meaning making tendencies on a scale of potential and may intersect and interact in typical and atypical ways in the constitution of social agents as subjects. Any tendency to dichotomize these tendencies must do so in relation to the relevant higher-order systemic environment. Thus:

Coding Orientation A	**Coding Orientation B**
1. Elaborate, abstracted discursive transformations of prediscursive matter-energy exchanges	1. Discursive transformations of prediscursive matter-energy exchanges index material social situation

2. "Philosophical" consciousness; intellectual, unproductive labor	2. "Practical" consciousness; manual, productive labor
3. Dominant ideology	3. Alternative, counterhegemonic ideologies
4. Production, legitimation of forms of subjectivity and knowledge by dominant, alienating nonproducers	4. Production of nonalienating forms of subjectivity and knowledge
5. Production and control of meanings according to logic of commodity by a hierarchical organization of producing and consuming agents	5. Production of meanings in relation to individual social needs of users
6. Commodified consuming individual	6. Collective strategies for challenging and reclaiming production of social meanings
7. Self-affirmation through commodity consumption	7. Self-realization through control of productive labor
8. Overcoding; stable meaning making practices	8. Undercoding; change of meaning making practices
9. Social agents enact metadiscourse of control	9. Social agents resist, contest metadiscourse of control
10. Legitimation of discursive subject positions of dominant and dominated	10. Discursive subject positions changed through alternative practices
11. Congruence of agent/subject intersections in relation to dominant, hegemonic patterns and practices	11. Incongruence of agent/subject intersections in relation to counterhegemonic patterns and practices

Signification and Representation: Meaning and the Represented Real

The central problematic in our discussion of false consciousness at the beginning of this chapter concerned the epistemological relation between meaning and the represented real. Frow's (1986: 57–58) recognition of the material effectivity of semiotic systems, which at the same time avoids "postulating the autoeffectivity of discursive systems and reducing all signification to the single model of highly autonomous systems," is an attempt to break with this epistemological relation. Frow also argues that the signifieds of discourse are not tied to a pregiven, extra-discursive Real but that these are produced within specific systems of signification. Frow's rejection of any absolute ontological distinction between the material and the symbolic is in agreement with one of the central assumptions of the social semiotic conceptual framework. Nevertheless, the theoretical privileging of signification over representation continues to operate the ontological distinction between signifier and signified (cf. form and meaning), which is itself in need of deconstruction. However, this will not be undertaken on the basis of Derrida's critique of a purported "metaphysics of presence" in Saussure's distinction. I pointed out in chapter 1 that Derrida has systematically misread both Saussure and Hjelmslev on the sign and has incorrectly attributed to them an ontology of representation (Hasan, 1987a). More interesting, as Hasan also notes, is the way in which nominalizations like *sign, signifier,* and *signified* are, in Whorf's terms, "objectified" and "referentially projected" in ways that construct a folk-theoretical ontology of the dualism between signifier and signified. *Sign* is an experientially abstract nominalization, *signifier* is a nominalized agentive, and *signified* is an underived verbal noun. Thus the latter two are less abstract than *sign,* making it easier for the indexical relations they create and/or presuppose to become the basis for the objectification and referential projection of these grammatical categories. By analogy, these then form the basis for the more abstract nominalization *sign* to be objectified and projected as if it referred to a substantive and perceptible entity, just as the other two are more readily seen to do. Thus the lexical distinctions referred to here are analogically projected onto their presumed referents, indexically creating the distinction between form and meaning. We can get a better sense of this if we consider their grammatical reactances with the transitivity relations with which they occur in the clause.

Let us consider in this connection the ideational-grammatical semantics of the following clauses:

1. The red light signifies the meaning "stop."

Identified	Process	Identifier
Token		Value

2. The meaning "stop" is signified by the red light.

Identifier	Process	Identified
Value		Token

3. The red light is a signifier of the meaning "stop."

Identified	Process	Identifier
Token		Value

The ideational-grammatical semantics of these clauses are all of the type Relational : Intensive : Identifying (Halliday, 1985: 115). Relational processes of the identifying type encode the meaning "*a* serves to define the identity of *x*," where *a* and *x* "are two distinct entities, one that is to be identified, and another that identifies it" (Halliday, 1985: 115). The identifying relation is not one of class and member, for the Identified and the Identifier are of the same level of generality. Identifying processes relate different types of phenomena of different orders of abstraction (Martin, 1987). Examples include red/stop, wording/meaning, actor/role. Halliday also shows that identifying clauses conflate a further pair of semantic functions with those of Identified and Identifier. These are Token and Value. Thus in the identifying relation one element is also the Value (meaning, referent, function, status, role) and the other is the Token (sign, name, form, holder, occupant). Halliday explains the relation between these two independent (though related) sets of semantic variables with this example:

> If we are looking at a photograph and ask *Which is Tom?*, the answer is something like *Tom is the tall one*. In this case, Tom is being identified by his form; we are told how he is to be recognized. But if we are discussing the children in the family, and someone says *Tom is the clever one*, Tom is being identified by his function—in this instance, his standing or role in the group. Thus the relationship between "Tom" and "the tall one" is the reverse of that between "Tom" and "the clever one": in the former, "Tom" is the meaning and "the tall one" is the outward sign, while in the latter "the clever one" is the meaning and "Tom" is the outward sign. (Halliday, 1985: 115)

The Token-Value distinction constitutes a metasemantic reading of the Identified-Identifier relation. The two different orders of abstraction that the identifying process relates as a single proposition enact an indexical connection between Identified and Identifier (see Lee, 1985: 106). The further question, as the examples show, concerns whether the grammatical Subject is conflated with Token (active voice) or Value (passive voice) (Halliday, 1985: 116). The Subject indexes a relation with some entity to which is then predicated some quality or relation through the identifying process. The Token-Value relation is a metasemantic reading of this identifying proposition, which indexes the relationship between Identifed and Identifier. The metasemantic reading of this relation is then referentially projected onto the presumed referents of the Identified and Identifier. Thus the phenomena, things, or referents that these index at the semantic (not metasemantic) level are endowed with metasemantic (i.e., Token-Value) properties as if these correspond to real entities "out there." These metasemantic properties are objectified and projected on account of a dual—that is, metasemantic/semantic—movement. In our examples, the different orders of abstraction in the semantics of the identifying relation postulate a relation of *realization* between different orders of relations. The Tokens in our three examples are the *signifiers* that signify or realize the Values (the meanings or significances) that correspond to their *signifieds*. A metasemantic Token/Signifier-Value/Signified relation reads the Identified-Identifier relation such that their metasemantic construal as signifiers and signifieds gets referentially projected as properties of the entities to which Identified and Identifier refer.

A look at the grammatical reactances of these semantic functions supports my argument. Halliday (1985: 149) points out that the Token in identifying clauses is analogous to semantic Agent in material processes in the ergative (not transitive) semantics of their ideational-grammatical relations. The Agent in the ergative model is the external "causer" of a material process. This relation between Token and Agent is, in Whorf's terms, a covert or cryptotypic one in which the overt surface segmentable category Token in identifying clauses is a grammatical reactance that constitutes a cryptotype of agency. In the above examples, the Token *the red light* is a nominalization, which is the signifier of its Value. The Token is covertly assumed to take on the semantic property of agency through a process of metaphorical analogy between different classes of clauses. The movement that occurs goes something like this:

SEMANTIC	METASEMANTIC		CRYPTOTYPIC
IDENTIFIED	TOKEN	SIGNIFIER	AGENT
IDENTIFIER	VALUE	SIGNIFIED	MEDIUM

This movement means that the semantic relations of Subject-Predicate relations in the identifying clause relate entities in an indexical movement from Identifier to Identified (Lee, 1985: 106). Second, the metasemantic reading of these as Token-Value relations is projected onto the Identified-Identifier relation. Third, the selective objectifications of their cryptotype categories are referentially projected as properties of their nominal groups onto Token and Value such that words/signifiers are the agents or causers of meanings and meanings are the effects of words. This agrees with my initial observation that *signifier* is a nominalized agentive and *signified* is a derived verbal noun.

The interaction of overt copatterned surface segmentable forms with their reactances is then redundant with what Whorf (1956b: 81) referred to as "a deep persuasion of a principle behind phenomena." Whorf is referring to the covert semantic categories or cryptotypes, which cannot easily be glossed or lexicalized in ways that capture the deeply implicit character of their semantic relations, at least not without selectively foregrounding and/or backgrounding aspects of these. They refer, rather, to

> . . . the ideas of inanimation, of "substance," of abstract sex, of abstract personality, of force, of causation—not the overt concept (lexation) corresponding to the WORD causation but the covert idea, the "sensing," or, as it is often called (but wrongly, according to Jung), the "feeling" that there must be a principle of causation. Later this covert idea may be more or less duplicated in a word and a lexical concept invented by a philosopher: e.g., CAUSATION. (Whorf, 1956b: 81)

Thus the lexical concepts invented by philosophers to explain these semantic principles are, as we have seen, folk-theoretical rationalizations that selectively attend to automatized patterns of language use. These patterns are then reified as linguistic products and projected as if they correspond to reality "out there" rather than to specific and partial social meaning making practices. In other words, the philosopher's folk-rationalization of these practices creates in the signifier/signified dualism a conceptual hypostatization when it attributes to these a full-blown ontological status. This is at the expense of the conditions and patterns of use of these items, which includes the philosopher's own theoretical labor. Rossi-Landi has insightfully commented on the neopositivist turn that has dominated discussion of Whorf (see also Threadgold, 1987):

> The thesis of linguistic relativity, on the one hand, stands on the splitting of the language [*langue*] from the rest of language [*langage*], which leads it to ignore the self-extensive power of language itself; while on the other hand it mentalizes the use of the language, that is, it confuses, in bourgeois fashion, the use of the already existing linguistic capital with its production, and attributes, to the system of products, properties which by rights belong only to labor." (Rossi-Landi, 1973: 65)

The concepts of signifier and signified thus derive their semiotic *valeur* only in and through the use value and the exchange value they acquire in determinate hierarchies of contextualizing relations. The conceptual hypostatization of these items and the ontological status they are granted reduce the use value and exchange value of these *lexical* forms to reified "facts" about language.

My argument here proposes a radical problematizing of the *ontological* dualism signifier/signified. Further, the Saussurean concept of semiotic *valeur* and Whorf's subtle critique of the ideology of reference can be reconstituted within the social semiotic conceptual framework. This does not mean that Saussure's distinction is rejected altogether. Saussure understood the distinction to refer to "*a segment of sound which is, as distinct from what precedes and follows in the spoken sequence, the signal of a certain concept*" (Saussure, [1915] 1983: 102; emphasis in original). Thus the relation between sound unit (signifier) and concept (signified) is not, for Saussure, an ontological distinction but a relation whereby formal differences in "segments of sound" correlate with differences in the value of concepts. Saussure thus provides in a somewhat inchoate form the functional basis for relating lexico-grammatical forms to the meanings they realize. The Saussurean concept of *valeur,* which is the conceptual basis of this formulation, is articulated on the grounds that it is the differential relations among the units in the entire system of relations that constitute differences in sense. I would argue that *valeur* is the most radical concept in Saussure's theory but that its radical potential was not fully developed. Systems of signification are not constituted on the basis of a form/meaning dualism. Instead, I would argue that they are constituted on the basis of the relations of *forms to forms and their semiotic functions* in a metaredundancy hierarchy of contextualizing relations. Silverstein (1979: 206) points out that a generalized indexicality is a condition of all semiotic systems (see also Lemke, 1983a: 18). The indexical resources of language and other forms of semiotic are not confined to a restricted number of specialized linguistic devices. Discourse acts create their specific contexts of situation by virtue of occurring. Whatever is indexed in a given context of situation is constitutive of it. The indexical function of specific copatterned meaning relations may selectively type *which* specific features and *when* of the extralinguistic context of utterance are themselves indexically created and/or presupposed. The performing of an indexical operation in this extended sense means that objects, entities, events, and so on, in the prediscursive physical and biological domains that are so indexed are themselves constitutive of the value-producing relations at all levels that constitute a given utterance, right up to the entire social semiotic system or some part of it. This means, for example, that a given real-world object, which is indexed in a specific context of utterance, becomes one of the forms that are differentially related to all the other forms that constitute that context of situation. Semiotic forms do not stand in a simple relation of reference to real-world objects, and so on, but they selectively redound with them in both typical and context-specific ways such that there are both typical (cf. types) and specific (cf. tokens) copatternings and redundancy relations between the discursive and the prediscursive. In social semiotic theory, the ability of the material world to enter into form-form relations in this way shows that these are always relationally semiotic. There is no more essential or truer reality behind these relations, which are simply named or referred to. Instead, value-producing semiotic relations are not limited to the internal patterning of semiotic forms. They include the entire system of contextualizing relations that is involved. There is thus no ontological division between internal semiotic relations and the extrasemiotic in the conceptual framework of social semiotics. Meaning making always occurs at the intersection of the material, the social, and the discursive and the systems of value these enact.

The extended sense in which I have used both the Saussurean concept of *valeur* and the concept of indexicality recognizes what Frow (1986: 60) calls the "discontinuity" between the Real and the Symbolic. However, I would want to call into question the root metaphor of "language-as-game" through which Frow claims that systems of signification can be conceptualized as "particular kinds of game rather than as a reflection of the real" (Frow, 1986: 65). The idealized and reductively formalistic implications of this metaphor need to be called into question. It is, I think, important to heed Buckley's (1967: 121–22) strictures against the use of game theory in the analysis of social systems. Buckley points out that game theory can only be applied to the most basic interaction processes. It is an analytical formalism that defines the logical structures of games in situations whose parameters are clearly definable. Game theory assumes a relatively closed-system epistemology, which is not able to account for the metastable, open, dynamic and systemic nature of social semiotic relations. In Halliday's tristratal model of language, relations of value are elaborated on the basis of the differential relations among forms on each of the meaning making strata (i.e., phonology or graphology, lexico-grammar, and semantics) that constitute the linguistic system. Frow (1986: 69) argues that linguistic value is produced only within particular configurations of field, tenor, and mode values. Relations of value are thus produced *between* strata, including the level of context of situation. However, it is important not to minimize the full implications of Saussure's original formulation. Value is also produced, as Saussure showed, by the relations among the forms at the level of their *internal* organization. Frow recognizes the fundamental role of contextualizing relations in the production of value but does not fully acknowledge that Saussure's insight made possible the systematic analysis of the lexico-grammar and the meanings it can realize on the basis of their patterns of combination, their contextual distributions, and their semiotic functions. It should be clear that I am not assuming a formalistic conception of *valeur,* as structuralism tended to do. Value-producing relations are not reducible to internal rules of ordering and combination or to some formal logic, both of which exclude the systemic character of the exchange process and the metastable nature of form-form relations and their semiotic functions.

Saussure's methodological (not ontological) dichotomizing of "internal" (*langue* based) and "external" (*parole* based) linguistics, along with the fact that the theory of linguistic value is primarily *langue* based, mistakenly leads deconstructionists such as Jonathan Culler to assume that *difference* or the "trace" constitutes an entire ontology of the way the world is:

> The arbitrary nature of the sign and the system with no positive terms gives us the paradoxical notion of an "instituted trace," a structure of infinite referral in which there are only traces—traces prior to any entity of which they might be the trace. (Culler, 1983: 99)

Culler presumes that difference is founded on an ontological distinction between the internal organization of language as a system of differences and the "external" reality of social meaning making (cf. *parole*). The former would be projected onto the latter as a kind of secondary gesture. This fails to understand that the relations between language and the realities it talks about and construes are best seen, as Halliday (1987) argues, in terms of nonreferential "complementarities." These occur "between language and the things spoken about, between the constitutive understanding of the world and what is constituted in the world" (Habermas, [1985] 1987b: 319). On the other hand, the ontology of difference constitutes an a priori understanding of the world, cut off from the productivity of social meaning making practices.

Ideology is then immanent in the multilevel meaning relations and systems of value and the ways in which systems of value on a given level may constrain or operate on value-producing relations at other levels. The relations between levels in the metaredundancy contextual hierarchy are nonsymmetrical and dialectical. Value-producing relations are productive social semiotic relations in the sense that a determinate contextualization of the meaning potential of the social semiotic system or some part of it is both enabling and constraining in the articulation of what agents can do and can mean. However, changes at lower systemic levels do not necessarily lead to more global changes at higher levels, for these can always be resolved in ways that maintain the global metastability of the system. Ideological formations are constituted in and through the combined effect of all the processes and relations at all levels in a given social formation. The multilevel and systemic character of these relations therefore requires that we reject the epiphenomenalist conception of ideology as a more or less distorted reflection or representation of some more essential base. This also requires that we reject the corresponding reductionism of a one-way relation of cause-and-effect that leads from the base to the superstructure. Ideological formations are overdetermined and productive systems of social meaning making practices such that no single, determining, or antecedent cause can be localized on any given level.

Ideology and Register

The work of Bakhtin and Volosinov shows that ideological formations are constructed in and through the texts and social discourses of a given social group. Meanings are socially made in and through regular and limited patterns of action and interaction in particular discursive formations. In chapter 6 it was shown that copatterned lexico-grammatical selections can only have meaning in relation to higher-order intertextual formations. The traditional dichotomy between text and social situation, which informs most contemporary linguistics, postulates a formal model of grammar as an autonomous domain of authority in relation to which the practices of social agents are considered to be contingent, random, and subjective effects. As we saw earlier in the present chapter, this is the essence of the Saussurean dichotomy of *langue* and *parole*. The following passages by Volosinov represent a critique of this dichotomy:

> Signs also are particular, material things; and, as we have seen, any item of nature, technology, or consumption can become a sign, acquiring in the process a meaning that goes beyond its given particularity. A sign does not simply exist as a part of a reality—it reflects and refracts another reality. Therefore, it may distort that reality or be true to it, or it may perceive it from a special point of view, and so forth. Every sign is subject to the criteria of ideological evaluation (i.e. whether it is true, false, correct, fair, good, etc.). The domain of ideology coincides with the domain of signs. They equate with one another. Wherever a sign is present, ideology is present, too. *Everything ideological possesses semiotic value. . . .*
>
> *The actual reality of language-speech is not the abstract system of linguistic forms, nor the isolated monologic utterance, and not the psychophysiological act of its implementation, but the social event of verbal interaction implemented in an utterance or utterances.* (Volosinov, 1973: 10, 94; emphasis in original)

Volosinov's conception of ideology as a sign that "reflects or refracts another reality," while implying a critique of the abstractionism in Saussure's dichotomy, conceives of ideological production as a form of consciousness that is explainable in terms of its origin in social being, that is, in "another reality." A sign is for Volosinov located in the superstructure as a reflected or refracted expression of a specific socially and historically constructed economic base. Volosinov's formulation retains elements of a referential conception of language, which links signs to their referents in the social reality (see also Frow, 1986: 64–65).

The concept of semantic register in systemic-functional linguistics is a useful starting point for rethinking the problematic that Volosinov struggled to resolve. Halliday (1978: 111) defines register as "the configuration of semantic resources that the member of a culture typically associates with a situation-type." Register is a local restriction from the global meaning potential of the social semiotic to the *typical* configuration of semantic resources in a given social situation-type. It is a generic concept that specifies that the same kinds of semantic configurations from the three metafunctions are made in regular and typical ways in a given situation-type. This further implies that other possible semantic configurations are *not* typical of that situation-type. Register is an analytical approximation and abstraction that refers to classes of meaning relations, thereby maintaining the distinction between types and tokens. Register, seen as a semantic variety or type, is, as I pointed out in chapter 6, related to, though different from, the concept of voice, which I have adapted from Bakhtin and Volosinov. The textual voicings of the heteroglossic relations among sociodiscursive positioned-practices do not occur on the basis of abstract register-types. Voices articulate the *actual* intersections, hybridizations, and copatternings of semantic registers, generic structures, and thematic and actional meanings in a given textual production. A particular voice is not a pure category but can be the intersection of a plurality of semantic varieties. The concept of voice is a very suggestive metaphor for the conceptual framework of a neomaterialist social semiotic theory. It evokes the materiality and the physicality of the speaking voice at the same time that it designates a specific material intersection of meaning relations in a given text or intertextual set. This duality in the one concept is then a very precise metaphor for the dialectical interrelation of the prediscursive and the discursive in the processes of social meaning making. The concept of semantic register is a further development of the Prague School's concern with functional semantic variation in texts. Mukarovsky (1977) and others in the Prague School developed the concept of foregrounding as a way of talking about contrasting semantic patterns in texts. Patterns of semantic variation in texts are said to be foregrounded in relation to either local or global norms, which may be textual, intertextual, or generic, or may even comprise an entire language. The criteria for establishing patterns of semantic contrast and variation must be nontrivial and are therefore functionally motivated. Two or more texts that are coclassified as belonging to the same register are functionally related on the basis of the same kinds of foregrounded lexico-grammatical selections from all three semantic metafunctions. Register is said to be predictive of the types of lexico-grammatical selections that are made and their copatternings. However, for the concept of register to be useful for the analysis of ideological formations in discourse, it must also be seen to articulate particular ideological and axiological positions and the subjects who bear these in the system of social heteroglossia. We must reject a normative view of register, which is concerned merely to predict the probability of co-occurrence of lexico-grammatical selections. There is no necessary, empirical correlation between linguistic and social functions. Normative accounts of register tend to reduce the social situation to a set of abstract, pregiven determining factors. A social semiotic theory of ideology needs to be able to specify in a given social and historical formation just what are the limits to the articulation and operation of social ideologies in and through specific configurations of meaning relations. The concept of semantic register needs to be able to relate actual meaning relations to potential ones in the maintenance and change of the social semiotic. Thus Lemke (1985b: 277) argues that some kinds of meaning relations, semantic registers, social situation-types, and social activity-structures, and so forth, are regularly and systematically disjoined from others in the global organization and distribution of the partial hierarchies of meaning relations that enact the social semiotic. The resulting *system of disjunctions*, as Lemke defines it, operates a global system of limits that functions to stabilize not only what kinds of meanings and practices are regularly and typically made but also the connections and disconnections between them, which ensures that not all meanings and practices are related to each other with equal probability. Lemke proposes the notion of "missing registers" as a means of explaining the gaps and inconsistencies in the system of meaning relations. Missing registers thus correspond to kinds of meanings

> . . . that simply are not made, or at least not made with language, and here certainly would be a powerful stabilizing mechanism for a community's social order and, at the same time, a system of critical points of potential change should these meanings come to be made and recognized in a community where they formerly were not. (Lemke, 1985b: 277)

Lemke's notion of missing registers does not presuppose any necessary global consistency in the system of discursive practices; nor does it conceptualize any necessary continuity between a particular register-type and the global organization of the social semiotic system. The concept of missing register has more in common with Bernstein's (1982: 320) notion of "yet-to-be-voiced" meanings and practices. The system of disjunctions (cf. Bernstein's "insulations") means that atypical intersections of the material and the discursive and atypical intersections and hybridizations of social meaning making practices can and do occur. These allow for a reserve adaptive potential whereby some differences that did not previously make a difference in the partial hierarchies of meaning relations are now typed as socially meaningful. New intersections of previously disjoined meaning relations and social practices may give voice to new possibilities in the system of social meaning making practices. The constant articulation, disarticulation, and rearticulation of voices can alter their framing and classification principles and the insulations (cf. disjunctions) between categories and agents and so can recontextualize the relations both within and between voices and the sociodiscursive positioned-practices that they articulate.

The System of Disjunctions and the Foregrounded Copatterning of Meaning Relations

In chapter 6 I showed that two distinct semantic orientations are realized in and through the regular and systematic copatternings of two major tendencies in the lexico-grammar. I pointed out that the differential skewing of these meaning selections enacts both thematic and actional disjunctions between Van/Humbert discourse and Ada/Lolita discourse. Foregrounded patterns of semantic contrast are realized by global copatternings of lexico-grammatical selections rather than single, isolable formal features. However, foregrounding is not adequately describable in terms of a positivistically defined statistical norm, that is, independently of the relevant social meaning making practices in and through which specific patterns get foregrounded and/or backgrounded (see also Thibault, 1986f: 135). Patterns of semantic variation are functionally motivated in ways that may be more or less automatized or deautomatized in relation to some norm or social practice. Fully automatized patterns encode a fully unmarked or maximally redundant relation between semiotic forms, their functions, and their higher-order social semiotic. Thus the gaps, the inconsistencies, the points of resistance, and the disjunctions in their (inter)textual patterns of use are masked, go unnoticed, and are therefore least likely to be challenged. This process is not confined to any specific level but goes on at all levels of textual organization. This automatization or redundancy is a consequence not only of the patterned relations between the Van/Humbert and Ada/Lolita discourses but also of the higher-order contextualizing relations with which these in turn copattern. These relations can be formally described with the metaredundancy contextualization hierarchy that I introduced in chapter 4. The analysis that follows attempts to show how the relations between these two consistent semantic orientations may covary with differentially selected contextualizing relations, which I shall gloss as MONOLOGIC and DIALOGIC.

The Van/Humbert and Ada/Lolita discourses are to be taken as the level of first focus in the present analysis. The relations at this level are treated as the entities that are the primary focus of the analysis. The specific copatternings of lexico-grammatical selections will not be taken into account here since they are at a level below the present level of first focus. Thus Van/Humbert discourse (A_i) has a specific relation with Ada/Lolita discourse (B_j) such that not all possible combinations of A_i and B_j co-occur with equal probability. At the level of first focus, the redundancy relations between the two discourses is formalized as A_i/B_j; that is, A_i is redundant with B_j, and vice versa. However, the specific combinations of the A's and the B's are dependent on a still higher-order context. This is formally represented as a second-order redundancy relation $A_i/B_j//C_k$, where C_k represents a selection from the range of possible C contexts for the A/B relations. Further, the C_k contextualizing relation is, in turn, redundant with the redundancy between A_i and B_j. In some specific context, say C_1, there will be a specific set of combinations between the A's and the B's. In some different context, C_2, a different set of combinations will copattern. The Van/Humbert and Ada/Lolita discourses are contextualized by some higher-order contextualizing relation C_k, which is in turn constituted by the A/B relations and patterns at the level below. Bernstein, as we have already seen, argues that the codes are the regulator of the specialized relationships both within and between contexts. At the level of C_k in the present analysis, the regulatory principle of the code produces a differential orientation to the two consistent semantic orientations that I analyzed in chapter 6. The articulated differences between their lexico-grammatical patterns constitute what Bernstein (1982: 306) refers to as *realization rules*. The relations between these two orientations can be summarized as follows:

Meaning Orientation A	Meaning Orientation B
abstract	concrete
global	local
monologic	dialogic
self	other
male	female
dominant	dominated
subject	object
+power	−power
reflection	action

A monologic contextualization of the relations between these foregrounds the global dominance of Van/Humbert discourse, not only backgrounding Ada/Lolita discourse but also masking the disjunctions between the two. One effect of this is to establish an Imaginary relation of symmetry between the two semantic orientations. This Imaginary contextual relation is punctuated as a differential set of binary terms or opposites. Thus the alienating Other, itself a specific contextual relation or pattern, is represented as the other *as if* the A/B relations were symmetrically related on the same level. The dominant, monologic Other, which corresponds to a specific higher-order coding orientation or regulatory principle, mediates the relations between the Ada/Lolita and Van/Humbert discourses as an Imaginary single-level relation, which is fully automatized. A monologic contextualization entails the complete foreclosure of these relations by a globally dominant and univocal norm, which has completely rearticulated Ada/Lolita discourse to the dominant Van/Humbert discourse. Thus the formal lexico-grammatical differences between the two are local differences and perturbations that are overridden and remain subordinate to the monologic norm of a seemingly coherent and unified textual product.

In chapter 6 I argued that *monologic* and *dialogic* are contextualizing principles rather than formal properties of texts. A dialogic contextualization of the A/B relations foregrounds a different set of possible relations and their related sociodiscursive practices. These relations are no longer symmetrical and on the same level. There is therefore no Imaginary identity of the two discourses. The local differences between the two discourses constantly articulate, disarticulate, and rearticulate the asymmetrical relations of power between them. A dialogic contextualization foregrounds the contradictions, the gaps, and the disjunctions between Van/Humbert and Ada/Lolita discourse. These are not random deviations, which are reassimilated to a globally coherent norm. They constitute, instead, a microlevel set of conditions that have the potential globally to ramify across the system of relations in ways that are not reversible. Thus the entire system of relations may alter, foregrounding the antagonistic, contradictory nature of the relations between the two semantic orientations. A dialogic contextualization foregrounds (rather than backgrounds) the potential for "slippage" to occur between semiotic forms and their functions. This creates the potential for new meaning relations and patterns of interaction, which were not previously foregrounded in the relevant system of relations. New dialogic patterns of meaning and interaction and new connections between these can enact challenge and resistance to stable, dominant, and monologic norms. A dialogic recontextualization of the relations between Van/Humbert and Ada/Lolita discourse is an icon of the constant metastable dialectic between system-maintaining and system-changing relations and practices.

The power relations that the differential contextualizations of monologic and dialogic entail are not reducible to "a simple binary structuration of most genres, specifying a dominant (unmarked) position as that of a ruling-class adult male and a repressed position as that appropriate to members of dominated classes, females, or children" (Frow, 1986: 73). This tends to reduce these relations to that of a textual a priori. It tends to assume that relations of power are already represented in the structure of the discourse. Alternatively, Foucault (1978: 92) proposes that power is "the multiplicity of force relations immanent in the sphere in which they operate." Relations of force are enacted by the relations of conjunction and disjunction, the gaps and "missing registers" in and through which social meanings and practices are systematically connected and disconnected in nonrandom ways. Relations of force are articulating, disarticulating, and rearticulating relations that are never, as Foucault (1978: 93) points out, one-way in their effects. Instead, they are constituted out of the contradictory and antagonistic relations of struggle in which forces both act on others and are themselves acted upon. However, Foucault's formulation does not go far enough toward theorizing the effectivity of specific articulations of power relations. I would say that the effectivity of a given articulation of power depends on the capacity of the forces to articulate their own "inside" in relation to some "outside," which is not, however, to be understood in terms of the distinction between "interior" and "exterior." In chapters 3 and 4 we considered some dimensions of insider and outsider relations and their recursively analyzable hybrid contextualizing relations. As we saw in those chapters, what constitutes some inside and outside is immanent in the relevant hybrid or joint contextualizing relations. In a monologic contextualization, the relations of force between the two discursive positions are articulated in terms of a globally dominant metalevel Van/Humbert discourse, which is "above" the dominated Ada/Lolita discourse. We shall see in greater detail in the following section how the foregrounded copatterning of meaning selections in Van/Humbert discourse articulates to its own hegemonic principle the dominated Ada/Lolita discourse. These relations are not given "in" the text. They depend, as we have seen, on the higher-order contextualizing relations that we construct in and through our social meaning making praxis. The recursive analysis of these relations produces representations of theorist-text-social semiotic system hybrid relations and practices in which power relations are always immanent. The effectivity of textual power relations is, as Foucault says, "outside" insofar as this effectivity is maintained by recursively analyzable systems of social meaning making practices that are not, however, reducible to the text.

Hegemony and the System of Disjunctions

The system of disjunctions is a global system that ramifies across all aspects of the social semiotic system. The paradoxical consequence of this is a metastable dialectic of system-maintaining and system-changing relations and practices. To quote Lemke:

> If we describe the "gaps" in a meaning system, we will not find them random; we will find that they function to inhibit behaviors which might be socially destabilizing by not contextualizing meaning relations of certain sorts. This functional subsystem of the Meaning System, a system of absence, we will call its system of *disjunctions*. At the same time these disjunctions stabilize the Interaction System, there is a sort of "tension" across these gaps, an area, as it were, waiting to be filled in or crossed, and thus a dynamic potential for the very system changes they inhibit. The system of disjunctions must cover its own tracks if it is to be effective and persist; there must not *appear* to be gaps or limits or constraints on meaning. Thus the system of disjunctions must be a *global* subsystem, the ultimate paranoid fantasy, subtly distorting and distracting possible attention from itself throughout the entire Meaning System. (Lemke, 1983a: 31; emphasis in original)

The gaps or missing registers or the not-yet voiced are, as Foucault says:

> . . . based on the principle that *everything* is never said, in relation to what might have been stated in a natural language (*langue*), in relation to the unlimited combination of linguistic elements, statements (however numerous they may be) are always in deficit; on the basis of the grammar and of the wealth of vocabulary available at a given period, there are, in total, relatively few things that are said. (Foucault, 1974: 118–19; emphasis in original)

Thus the system of disjunctions is a system of constraints on what social agents can do and can mean. It provides us with a way of relating limited, regular microlevel patterns of interaction to patterns at higher or macrolevels of analysis without depending on a concept of power in terms of one-way or efficient causes. Thus the dichotomy dominant/dominated can be misleading if it is taken to refer to the power of a dominant personality, social grouping, or political party, as if these simply exerted some force or imposed from above their sovereignty on their subjects. Van/Humbert discourse is hegemonic because of the regular and systematic patterns of use of specific *globally* foregrounded lexico-grammatical selections in and through which monologic contextualizing relations and practices are enacted. Foregrounding cannot occur on the basis of single, isolated formal features. It is the cumulative sense of some global copatterning, in contrast with alternative, even absent, patterns, that articulates an automatized, monologic, and hegemonic pattern. Gramsci's conception of hegemony can help us more adequately to reconstitute the system of disjunctions in relation to questions of power and struggle in the social semiotic system. Gramsci defined hegemony and power as the ability of a given social group to articulate to its own hegemonic principle the interests and the social semiotic and material resources of other social groups. However, this is not a question of a one-way imposition of force or of already fully articulated worldviews in conflict with each other:

> One could study in actual fact the formation of a collective historical movement, analyzing it in all its molecular phases, which is not usually done because every treatment would become boring: instead we assume the currents of opinion already established around a group or a dominant personality. It is the problem that in modern times is expressed in terms of a party or a coalition of like parties: how to initiate the founding of a party, how to develop its organized force and social influence, and so on. It is a question of a molecular process, very detailed, of extreme analysis, extending everywhere, whose documentation is constituted by a boundless quantity of books, pamphlets, articles in journals and newspapers, conversations and oral debates *which are repeated an infinite number of times and which in their gigantic unity represent this work from which is born a collective will of a certain level of homogeneity*, of that certain level that is necessary and sufficient for determining a coordinated action that is simultaneous in time and in the geographical space in which the historical fact occurs. (Gramsci, 1977f: 101; my translation; emphasis added)

Hegemony and power are then consequences of the myriad investments and "molecular" processes, the sayings and doings of social agents in certain regular, limited ways that grow to articulate a given hegemonic principle in relation to other hegemonic principles in the social formation. Chantal Mouffe has explained Gramsci's conception of hegemony in a manner suggestive for social semiotic theory:

> The interests of these groups can either be articulated so as to neutralize them and hence to prevent the development of their own specific demands, or else they can be articulated in such a way as to promote their full development leading to the final resolution of the contradictions which they express. (Mouffe, 1979: 183)

A monologic contextualization of the relations between Van/Humbert and Ada/Lolita discourse means that the former succeeds in articulating the plurality of knowledge-power relations in the discursive situation to a single, normative, and unified locus of power and knowledge. Thus a monologic articulation enacts a global foreclosure whereby opposing positioned-practices and their textual voicings are disarticulated from their "own" position and rearticulated to the hegemonic principle. Alternatively, a dialogic contextualization can rearticulate this plurality of discursive positioned-practices and voices to destabilize monologic closure. Far from being a mere differentialist plurality and relativity of discursive positioned-practices, dialogicity entails the full articulation of one discourse in relation to others in ways that can, as Chantal Mouffe puts it, "promote its full development." A monologic contextualization works to neutralize this process through the collective rearticulation of all the separate voices to a single, univocal authority. In the patriarchal order of Van/Humbert narration, this works to transform difference into sameness and thus to rearticulate the gendered differences between the two discursive positions to the patterns of male domination. In the following chapter we shall further explore Gramsci's conception of hegemony as a system of articulated social meaning making practices in and through which social agents invest in and identify with specific, limited patterns of meaning and action in the social formation.

The use of the term *dialectical* throughout much of this discussion does not presuppose any notion of the negative dialectic, which is based on the negation and transcendence of the existing social order. The system of disjunctions, on the other hand, is maintained and changed through a constant dialectic of articulating, disarticulating, and rearticulating practices and relations. These are always available to critical analysis and transformation precisely because critical analysis is itself a potentially transforming social meaning making praxis. With the concepts I have elaborated in this chapter I have sought to rethink and develop the notions of ideology, power, and domination and to break with both the static representationism of false consciousness and normative, equilibrium models of the social totality. Thus, critical analysis of these is not fated to be subordinated to the ontology of, for instance, economism or social class as forms of determination in the last instance. Neomaterialist social semiotic theory has no need of the essentialist ontological dichotomies referred to earlier. The idealistic presuppositions of these are always constituted as if one of the poles of their dualisms lay outside our social meaning making practices. *Which* one does not in the final analysis really matter, for the dualism itself functions to conveniently position either analyst or object of the analysis *as if* they were above, outside, or external to the social meaning making practices that make them and in which they are immanent.

Note

1. This is not the current position of these authors, who have since rejected and/or reformulated critical aspects of their 1979 position. Kress (1987) is explicit about this. Kress's current position relates textual patternings to the higher-order semiotic of genre and discourse and to notions of reading and writing practices (Kress, 1985a, b). Unfortunately, space does not permit further discussion of their recent work.

Chapter 8
The Neomaterialist Social Semiotic Subject

The Problematic of the Subject

The problematic of the opposition between language and social situation was first introduced in chapter 6. The effect of this opposition is to represent the subject as a unified, self-evident category in relation to the "objectivity" of a continuous, unified, and stable social Real. This enacts the subject/object split that I discussed in chapter 2. This is not a necessary consequence of the relation between language and the social. Rather, it is a consequence of a specific strategy of punctuation, which proposes a disjunction between the individual and the social. It is a Lockean conception of the social contract through which this relation is articulated in homeostatic structural-functionalist models of society. Locke ([1690] 1965: 328) explains the social in terms of a "state of nature" in ways that resemble the static *langue/parole* opposition. Locke's conception of government amounts to a formal agreement among independent social agents about the nature of a social reality that is given in advance. Thus Locke says that men are "possessors of themselves," so the formal agreement made among them is a means of guaranteeing their own self-possession, as well as the possession of their private property. Analogously, the fixed-code concept works by guaranteeing the autonomy of the speaking subject as well as the individual's possession of the faculty of language. The opposition between language and the social therefore presumes the reduction of the ideological to some epiphenomenal appearance, which functions to alienate the subject from the "true," objective social Real. Ideology is in this conception, as we saw in the previous chapter, the mystifying or distorting function that mis-presents the subject's relation to this objective social Real. The social Real is therefore presumed to correspond to the "truth" in relation to which the subject may be positioned in an epistemological relation of truth or falsity. In this order of things, the subject is treated as an autonomous, stable, self-reflexive center of consciousness and authority. The "autoconstitution" of the subject depends on a necessarily empirical correlation between the subject's positioning and the social Real. The following quotation from Basil Bernstein, however, suggests an alternative formulation:

> Thus we now obtain the following causal chain. The features which create the speciality of the interactional practice (that is, the *form* of the social relationship) regulate orientation to meanings, and the latter generate through *selection* specific textual productions. From this perspective, the specific text is but a transformation of the specialized interaction practice; the text is the form of the social relationships made visible, palpable, material. (Bernstein, 1982: 307; emphasis in original)

The text is the means in and through which the social meaning making practices of social agents are "made visible." The text, according to Bernstein, is the means by which the "specialized interaction practice" is realized in a material form. Bernstein's formulation turns on a notion of the text as the visible product or record of social agents and the social meaning making practices to which they are specialized. I do not assume here that the metaphor of the visible, along with its correlative of the invisible, presumes any sort of empirical, unified social Real as the necessary center or source of textual meanings, or any dichotomy between "outward appearance" and the "internal essence of things," as in Marx's account of social relations.

In chapter 7 I argued that the subject is not the necessary starting point from which its ideological relations to the Real are constituted. Nor is it a stable self-identity that is internally constituted out of its own cognitive processes (see chapter 2). Nor do I accept the kind of ideological projection that informs Frow's (1986: 61) claim that a semiotic theory of the subject-in-process must "theorize the category of subject not as the origin of utterance but as its effect." Similarly, Silverman (1983) construes the problematic of the subject in terms of a field of discursive and textual determinations that produce and represent their forms of subjectivity. Silverman writes:

> In ordinary conversational situations, the speaking subject performs both of these actions; that subject automatically connects up the pronouns "I" and "you" with those mental images by means of which it recognizes both itself and the person to whom it speaks, and it identifies with the former of these. However, when a subject reads a novel or views a film it performs only one of those actions, that of identification. The representations within which we recognize ourselves are clearly

> manufactured elsewhere, at the point of the discourse's origin. In the case of cinema, that point of origin must be understood as both broadly cultural (i.e. as the symbolic field) and as specifically technological (i.e. as encompassing the camera, the tape-recorder, the lighting equipment, the editing room, the script, etc.). (Silverman, 1983: 197)

A subject-centered account such as Silverman's does not permit the rethinking of the category of subject except in terms of the text as the expression or manifestation of discursively and culturally determined subjectivities. The focus is on the subject as the effect of texts rather than on what social agents do in and through texts. This enacts the text/context dichotomy that I discussed in chapter 6. Thus the context (cf. Silverman's "symbolic" and "technological" fields) becomes an extrinsic field of determinations. Ian Hunter has made the following relevant observation:

> The concept of context as a field of determinations is inseparable from the concept of experience and of an experiencing subject who (consciously or unconsciously) carries these determinations. Language (or the text) thus remains the expressive vehicle for a "structurally determined" consciousness. Consequently, the specific actions of various discursive apparatuses in *producing* textual meaning are ignored in favour of a more generalised concept of expressive mediation. As a result the text becomes a singular and homogeneous site, in which the author's experience may be read off from the social context and vice-versa. (Hunter, 1982: 80)

Hunter's account is most explicitly directed at expressive realist and representational accounts of consciousness and its textual manifestations. However, the growing emphasis in much of semiotics on the production of the subject within systems of signification seems to me to be no more than a displacement of the same general problematic onto the concept of signification. The emphasis on the textual manifestation of subjectivity does not account for the discursive procedures and practices and their iterations, which make possible specific forms of textual readings and the subjectivities these manifest. Thus the social formation remains untheorized and recontained within the text as the sole site of specific subjectivities. Further, Silverman homogenizes the technological as a field of "real" determinations, which are then opposed to the textual representations of subjective "identifications." These are said to be produced in the Real and conceived of as the unified origin of their effects. The extraordinarily widespread contemporary emphasis on the subject continues to think of the problem in terms of textual expressions and representations, read as the effects of a textually experienced social structure. The text thus remains "inscribed" within the (decentered) consciousness of the author-reader or the social Real. Silverman's formulation shows that much of semiotics is still reeling from the effects of Benveniste's work on the indexical functions of the European pronoun system (see chapter 2). What is lacking here is any sense that indexicality is not restricted to the specialized linguistic devices (e.g., the personal pronouns) to which certain effects are attributed. Nor can these effects simply be read off from reified and isolated pronominal forms, to which we attribute mental images of addresser and addressee (see Silverman, 1983: 197). In this regard, the following passage from Hunter (1982) may be interestingly compared to the earlier one from Bernstein:

> Once we conceive of meaning not as something to be recovered from its origin in an author's experience but rather as the shifting result of the activation of certain rules and practices of reading, we begin to construct a quite different account of the social emergence of Literature. Instead of searching for points of origin in which social structure is experienced and expressed once and for all, by an authoring consciousness, we can look instead to the divergent historical and contemporary apparatuses in which literary objects and meanings receive their shifting determination. In this way we put into question that moral-pedagogical construction of literature as a collection of texts inscribed with the consciousness (or conscience) of an age or class. (Hunter, 1982: 82)

In this chapter I shall attempt to explore these issues further within the conceptual framework of this book. Before beginning that task, I shall consider some of the wider social and political implications of the notion of the subject as an effect of discursive practice.

The Subject as Effect of Discursive Practice

Let us first consider some of the implications of the ideological disjunctions that Friedrich Nietzsche identified in the philosophical practices of the late nineteenth century:

> One must, however, go still further and declare war, a pitiless war to the knife, even against the "atomistic needs" that still lead a dangerous afterlife in domains where no one suspects it, like the more famous "metaphysical needs": one must also above all finish off that other and more inauspicious atomism that Christianity has taught best and longest, the soul-atomism. Let it be permitted to signify with this word those beliefs that consider the soul as something indestructible, eternal, indivisible, as a monad, as an atom: these beliefs must be banished from science. It is, between ourselves, not completely necessary to throw out "the soul" in this way and to renounce one of the oldest and most venerable hypotheses: as happens to the rudeness of the naturalists, who can hardly touch on "the soul" without losing it. But the way is open for new affirmations and refinements of the soul-hypothesis: conceptions such as "mortal soul," "soul as subjective plurality," and "soul as social

> construction of desires and affects" want henceforth to have citizen's rights in science. In that the new psychologist is preparing an end to the superstition that has thrived until now with an almost tropical luxuriance around the soul-representation, he has certainly, so to speak, thrust himself into a new desert and a new mistrust—it may be that the older psychologists had it more comfortable and merrier: finally, however, he knows exactly that he too is condemned to invent—and, who knows? perhaps to discover. (Nietzsche, [1886] 1980: 26–27; my translation)

Nietzsche identifies in this passage a disjunction that is pivoted on what he refers to as the "soul-hypothesis" (*Seelen-Hypothese*). It is the disjunction between the belief in "the soul as something indestructible, eternal, indivisible, as a monad, as an atom" (*die Seele als Unvertilgbare, Ewiges, Untheilbares, als eine Monade, als ein Atom*) and conceptions such as "mortal soul," "soul as subjective plurality," and "soul as social construction of desires and affects" (*sterbliche Seele, Seele als "Subjekts-Vielheit,"* and *Seele als Gesellschaftbau der Triebe und Affekte*). Nietzsche refers to the "new psychologist" (*neue Psycholog*) who maintains that this new conception of the "soul-hypothesis" is philosophically and epistemologically different from the claim it seeks to replace. Nietzsche shows that the "new psychologist," like his predecessor, is however "condemned to invent." In other words, the "new psychologist" is also involved in social meaning making. Nietzsche's "deconstruction" of these premises produced a radical skepticism of notions like soul, truth, knowledge, and logic in Western culture. Nietzsche emphasizes in this passage that the "new psychologist," like his predecessor, is involved in a rhetorical project, a praxis, in and through which the central axioms and presuppositions of Western culture are constructed rather than simply given. More recently, Jacques Derrida has appropriated Nietzschean skepticism to a radical deconstruction of representationism and the "metaphysics of presence" this entails. Derrida has identified this as underlying the core ideology of the superior reality and truth of the referentially real world "out there." Derrida (1978: 289) has argued for a praxis of social meaning making in which both slippage and stability are accounted for in and through the play of praxis. This emphasis on the play of praxis has, I believe, led to the privileging of the superior reality of the decentered play of textual meanings in the contemporary discourses of deconstruction. It is as if many practitioners of deconstruction are slipping and sliding dizzyingly on the signifier of a highly ritualized academic game in which the meaning potential of certain classes of textual products is relativized in and through really quite specific reading procedures. Frow (1986: 2) has remarked on this tepid and sterile exercise in North American liberalism as "the rapid installation of deconstruction as a new and depressingly depoliticised orthodoxy." The point I would emphasize here is that social meaning making practices are never open or free in the way these practitioners apparently believe.

Michael Halliday's concept of meaning potential more subtly renders the idea that social meaning making is both enabling and constraining of social agents. This concept refers to what social agents typically can do and can mean in particular social situation-types. Chilton (1983) has drawn attention to the semantic ambiguity of the modulation *can* in this formulation. Chilton makes the distinction between what the social agent can mean (i.e., *is able to mean*) and what the agent can mean (i.e., *is permitted to mean*) and further poses the question: "Whose meaning is produced?" This leads to the important recognition that "the individual performer's utterance in certain situations is a constrained 'choice' of meanings from a potential produced or controlled at certain power points in social structure" (Chilton, 1983). For instance, the articulated relations between the Van/Humbert and Ada/Lolita discourses are not the result of a free, unconstrained play of discursive positions.[1] They are, rather, the combined effects of the articulating principles through which the two discourses enact a struggle between hegemonic principles. Thus the higher-order constraints on the access of social agents to the sociosemantic potential of social situations has been formulated in this study in terms of the concepts of social semiotic code and hegemony. The distinction I made in chapter 7 between monologic and dialogic contextualizing relations has nothing to do with a free or open play of textual meanings. It demonstrates that both selection and preselection operate at all levels of social meaning making in nonrandom and unevenly distributed ways.

The discourse of deconstruction thus operates a differentialist pluralism, which disjoins the localization of power in a plurality of microsystems of social meaning and interaction from the higher-order systemic constraints on social meaning making. Deconstruction posits an infinite relativity of social discourses, which are never related explicitly to their wider social functions or to the practices of the theorist-community that produces them. Both the discourse of the subject as an effect of discursive practice and the free play of textual praxis in deconstruction are differentialist and nondialectical formulations, which are unable to theorize the dialectic of system-maintaining and system-changing relations and practices in the social semiotic. Henriques and others (1984: 110–11) well argue that discourse determinism tends to displace the critique of a relativity of decentered truth-effects onto an epistemological domain that is, as they point out, always articulated in relation to "what the dominant discourse in any specific field asserts to be true and to correspond to reality" (Henriques et al., 1984: 111). Thus, opposing views are always required to justify their claims to rationality and intelligibility in the terms already preconstructed by the hegemonic discourse. The disjunction between discursive practice and the subject-as-discursive-effect is a differentialist one little different from the social-individual disjunction I discussed in chapter 7. The subject is articulated in terms of a permanent play of reified linguistic positions in which all possibilities are preconstructed by the hegemonic discourse of consumer capitalism. The subject is defined in terms of performativity oriented toward success and does not derive its social identity and historical memory in and through a constant metastable dialectic. Instead, it is defined only by its differences to others in ways that set in play a plurality of positions. It is a reified and nondialectical conception of the discursive subject/social agent relation, which is unable to explain the effects of unity and identity experienced by social agents (see below). It is an alienated notion of subjectivity, which has confused the use of a given system of (linguistic) relations with its production (Rossi-Landi, 1973: 65). It therefore collaborates perfectly with the ideology of the competitive consumer individual and the success-oriented instrumental rationalization of human action critiqued by Habermas (1984). The notion of the subject as an effect of discourse falls into the very theoretical trap to which Nietzsche draws attention. Thus this new "soul-hypothesis" remains a subject-centered account, which is unable adequately to theorize social and discursive practice. It is not so very different from structural-functionalist models of social role-functions, which are determined in advance by a normative social order. Thus it seems to me that both deconstruction and poststructuralist accounts of the subject have led to theoretical impasses whose terms remain tied to the dominant cultural axioms and presuppositions of Western culture.

The work of Michel Foucault, I believe, makes a central contribution toward the possibility of theorizing an alternative to this impasse. Foucault constructs a theoretical discourse that attempts to relate social power and its articulations in microlevel patterns of action and interaction to higher-order systems of social and discursive relations and practices, which Foucault calls *discursive formations* (see Foucault, 1974, 1978). Nevertheless, Foucault retains a nominalist conception of power, which is not without its own tendency to hypostatize and totalize the concept of power. Thus:

> Power is everywhere: not because it embraces everything, but because it comes from everywhere. . . . One should probably be a nominalist in this matter: power is not an institution, nor a structure, nor a possession. It is the name we give to a complex strategic situation in a particular society. (Foucault, 1978: 93)

However, the claim that power is everywhere does not specify any criteria for its articulation, namely, *which* practices, axiological criteria, normative contents, social agents, and *when*. Foucault's theorization of power as a diffuse, anonymous category may render it unable to theorize specific strategic situations. Foucault has constructed a conceptual and methodological framework that comes close to relating microlevel articulations of power to higher-order discursive formations. What is missing, however, is the link between specific textual productions, social activity-structures, and higher-order systemic regularities in the relevant system of relations. Foucault's later works begin to elaborate a conception of the subject that is constituted in and through its agonistic relations with its outside. Relations of force are constituted through the subject's encountering resistance to or constraints on its goal-seeking activities, whereby the subject's folding back in on itself means that the subject is a locus of resistance with respect to the forces that press in on it and contrast with it. The goal-seeking activities of social agents enact overdetermined relations of knowledge and power, which produce effects of both self-government and subjection:

> Nature had invested human beings with this necessary and redoubtable force, which was always on the point of overshooting the objective that was set for it. One understands why, in these conditions, sexual activity required a moral discrimination that was, as we have seen, more dynamic than morphological. If it was necessary, as Plato said, to bridle it with the three strongest restraints: fear, law, and true reason; if it was necessary, as Aristotle thought, for desire to obey the reason the way a child obeyed his tutor; if Aristippus himself advised that, while it was alright to "use" pleasures, one had to be careful not to be carried away by them—the reason was not that sexual activity was a vice, nor that it might deviate from a canonical model; it was because sexual activity was associated with a force, an *energeia,* that was itself liable to be excessive. In the Christian doctrine of the flesh, the excessive force of pleasure had its principle in the Fall and in the weakness that had marked human nature ever since. For classical Greek thought, this force was potentially excessive by nature, and the moral question was how to confront this force, how to control it and regulate its economy in a suitable way. (Foucault, [1984] 1986: 50)

Goal-seeking social semiotic activities are immanent in patterned social and discursive relations. These are not reducible to a subject-centered account per se. The neomaterialist social semiotic conceptual framework attempts to account for discursive subjects/social agents in terms of their constituting and constituted nature. It must account for the typical and atypical intersections and patternings of social meaning and practices in which social agents/discursive subjects are immanent. The criterion of immanence does not entail their passive insertion into the social but rather entails relations of both complicity and resistance, contributing to the metastable relations of force between the effects of self-government and the effects of subjection. The constant metastable dialectic that results has the potential to disarticulate and rearticulate these relations of force in ways that can deregulate both the totalizing hegemonic expansionism of desire and the constraints of self-government in order that the subject not lose itself in these same relations of force. It is through the subject's agonistic deregulation of these, as well as its regulation by them, that the constant metastable dialectic of social agent/discursive subject is enacted.

The Neomaterialist Social Semiotic Subject

Social agents are constituted as discursive subjects in and through the positions they regularly and typically occupy in the social activity-structures that are enacted in some social formation. Thus we are concerned with the social actions and interactional practices that are typical or characteristic of certain kinds of social subjects from one performance-specific occasion to another. The relevant question is *which* subject positions occur and *when* (i.e., in what positions) and with *what* wider social functions in a given multivariate social activity-structure type. The emphasis here on the typical does not entail a normative definition of functional roles as in structural-functionalism. The emphasis is on those features that are taken to be usual, most frequent, regular, or expected on the basis of some functional criterion of coclassification and distribution, which is abstracted from a large number of specific occasions. However, the specific performances of discursive positioned-practices by social agents in their social activity-structures enact contradictory and overdetermined relations and processes, which are not reducible to functional typifactions per se. If so, then we would be talking about fully automatized performances of social activity-structures. But performance-specific instances are not usually fully automatized on account of the overdetermined and indexical nature of the contextualizing relations involved. Lemke (1988b:8) points out how there are "features of a performance of a role in an activity structure that are noncriterial for the role may be made criterial for the semiotic embodiment of the role." Thus a given performance may intersect features of contrasting paradigmatic (systemic) relations that are not typical of that social activity-type but specific to a given enactment of it by some social agent. Further, the plurifunctional and overdetermined character of the redundancy relations involved means that a specific performance not only enacts many different systems simultaneously but may selectively foreground some features rather than others in a given performance. These are, as Lemke points out, "the 'little things' which become signs of the person as a unique individual." It is thus this dynamic relation between the typical and the specific that maintains the metastable dialectic referred to above. In this way, the individual social agent is given a metastable repertoire of both personal and social voices by virtue of the selective foregrounding and backgrounding of performance-specific uses in real time of the semiotic resources for assembling and enacting particular social activity-structures. The concept of voice is, of course, a textual one that simply captures in the present context the fact that a specific biological individual/social agent semiotically embodies and enacts shifting intersections and copatternings of social meaning making practices that voice the particular positioned-practices (cf. subject positions) and heteroglossic alignments of these in their contexts-of-use. The concept of voice is, of course, a textual concept (in the extended sense) that is not therefore reducible to the social agent/biological individual, which both operates and embodies typical and atypical intersections of social meanings and practices, taken as the textual indexes of particular social semiotic subjectivities and identities. Thus postmodernist and poststructuralist accounts, which have abstracted and privileged this textual dimension, do so in terms that reify language as an abstract set of forms (cf. signifiers) whose contextualization dynamics and internal systematicity do not get related to copatterned contextual uses and distributions of these, which are functional in the maintenance and/or change of social situations. For example, Silverman's semiotic/psychoanalytic account of subjectivity remains entirely subject-centered in the way I described earlier. Silverman's use of Benveniste's (1966) work on the personal deictics and the problem of intersubjectivity in language locates processes of subjective identification and recognition in the isolated, abstract forms of the personal deictics. It is always the subject who will somehow "fill them up conceptually" or "supply them with a signified" (Silverman, 1983: 197). Thus the relations between these forms and their "filling up" totally confuse the relation between abstract semiotic forms (as types) and their functions in specific contexts-of-use. It is as if there are indeterminate, free-floating forms just waiting to be "filled up." A psychoanalytic model of interpretation is then imposed on these abstract forms without any regard for their copatterned distributions and uses. The personal deictics are not simply filled up by speakers on the basis of abstract cognitive notions like identification and recognition. Their shifting and indeterminate nature must also be related to discourse-level, not merely clause-level, relations through which structures of information, presupposition, entailment, and implication are organized at levels above the single, isolated clause (see Halliday and Hasan, 1976).

The following programmatic statement by Foucault better formulates the starting point for a neomaterialist social semiotic account of the discursive subject/social agent:

> In the proposed analysis, instead of referring back to *the* synthesis of *the* unifying function of *a* subject, the various enunciative modalities manifest his dispersion. To the various statuses, the various sites, the various positions that he can occupy or be given when making a discourse. To the discontinuity of the planes from which he speaks. And if these planes are linked by a system of relations, this system is not established by the synthetic activity of a consciousness identical with itself, dumb and anterior to all speech, but by the specificity of a discursive practice. I shall abandon any attempt, therefore, to see discourse as a phenomenon of expression—the verbal translation of a previously established synthesis; instead, I shall look for a field of regularity for various positions of subjectivity. Thus conceived, discourse is not the majestically unfolding manifestation of a thinking, knowing, speaking subject, but, on the contrary, a totality, in which the dispersion of the subject and his discontinuity with himself may be determined. It is a

space of exteriority in which a network of distinct sites is deployed. I showed earlier that it was neither by "words" nor by "things" that the regulation of the objects proper to a discursive formation should be defined; similarly, it must now be recognized that it is neither by recourse to a transcendental subject nor by recourse to a psychological subjectivity that the regulation of its enunciation should be defined. (Foucault, 1974: 54–55)

The program outlined by Foucault for a theory of the subject situates the problem in relation to both typical and specific parameters of social and discursive practices in and through which subjectivities are made. This is conceptually quite close to the intersections and copatternings of social meaning making practices in my account. This framework enables us to construct a theoretical discourse that is not trapped in the "social-individual" disjunction, which has already been critiqued in the work of Henriques and others (1984), Lemke (1985a, 1988b), and Thibault (1986c). These new theoretical constructs are not reducible to the individual or to functional role-slots per se because the relevant level of theorization concerns the typical and atypical higher-order *formations* in which discursive subjects and objects are made. We shall see that these comprise both their actional and their thematic dimensions of meaning. A given formation is a specific subsystem of relations, which interacts with other subsystems in both typical and atypical ways in the social semiotic by virtue of the system of disjunctions (see chapter 7). Thus some kinds of subsystem-subsystem interactions occur more regularly and typically than others in the constant metastable dialectic of system-maintaining and system-changing relations and practices. Atypical subsystem-subsystem interactions may or may not have consequences that ramify throughout the system, thereby disturbing its typical patterns in ways that might destabilize them (see Lemke, 1984c, 1985a). Individual social agents participate in these larger ensembles of subsystem-subsystem transactions but are not analytically or constitutively reducible to them. A given typical formation is defined at a higher order of logical typing than the individual social agents who participate in them. We shall explore in the following section the relevance of this argument for articulating an alternative to the "macro/micro" disjunction in social analysis. Neomaterialist social semiotic theory recognizes that just as the individual social agent is not reducible to the biological organism, so a given typical formation is not reducible to the discursive subject positions immanent in these or to the social agents who enact them. The social agent/activity-structure relation entails different orders of logical typing, whereby the one is not reducible to the other without producing an Imaginary mistyping or mispunctuation of the levels of relations involved (see Wilden, 1980, 1981). The social semiotic conceptual framework endeavors to punctuate these in terms of Real rather than Imaginary relations. This recognizes that there can be no direct matter-energy and information flows across the different levels in a given hierarchy of relations (Lemke, 1985a). This means, as Lemke (1985a) shows, that individuals cannot change a given system of relations in any direct way, although they are immanent in these. It is, rather, the socially structured interactions between, say, subsystems (e.g., social activity-structure types) or typical formations that bring about systemic change. This point was also well understood by Antonio Gramsci, as the quotation at the beginning of Part IV testifies.

The question that needs to be posed at this point concerns the theoretical status of the individual in this framework. Henriques and others (1984) have also posed the question as to how we can go beyond the poststructuralist deconstruction of the unitary, rational, and centered subject and its nonconstituted character. They, too, argue, as I have also done above, that such a deconstruction is not adequate for a theory that attempts to account for both system stability and change within the same conceptual framework:

> Now in displacing the individual as a simple agent the post-structuralists achieved a massive and important step. However, we are left with a number of unresolved problems. First, in this view the subject is composed of, or exists as, a set of multiple and contradictory positionings or subjectivities. But how are such fragments held together? Are we to assume, as some applications of poststructuralism have implied, that the individual subject is simply the sum total of all positions in discourses since birth? If this is the case, what accounts for the continuity of the subject and the subjective experience of identity? What accounts for the predictability of people's actions, as they repeatedly position themselves within particular discourses? Can peoples' wishes and desires be encompassed in an account of discursive relations? (Henriques et al., 1984: 204)

As I argued in the previous chapter, the neomaterialist social semiotic framework does not ontologically privilege, on the one hand, the material prediscursive physical and biological domains or, on the other hand, the discursive domain of the social semiotic. Rather, it privileges the constitutive and dialectical duality of both. Thus the effects of "continuity" and "identity" that Henriques refers to may be accounted for in the following terms: (1) the biological individual is not only a component in these effects of unity, continuity, and identity but is itself socially constructed in and through specific foregrounded copatternings and intersections of the biological and the social semiotic in a given social formation; (2) the social agent's typical or atypical positionings in and enactments of social activity-structures articulate both the overdetermined, contextual nature of these and the differential strategies and principles of foregrounding that may selectively attend to some features rather than others in the construction of social and personal identity; (3) effects of "continuity" are construable on the basis of the selective foregrounding of certain meanings and practices in the social construction of a historically continuous individual social agent, presumed to be coextensive with the individual biological organism; (4) the opposition between inner mind or consciousness and outer behavior does not account for the ways in which "inner speech" (Volosinov, 1973) or so-called thought is a specialized part of a wider set of social meaning making practices; Volosinov argued that "inner speech" is a specific appropriation of these, such that thought, internal mental representations, and feelings are not autonomous inner domains separate from the same meaning potential in terms of which we speak about outer behavior (see also Lemke, 1988b); and (5) normative psychological discourses of the life history of the individual have preconstructed a set of naturalized stages through which the unitary individual passes. (See Sinnott, 1981, for a critical discussion of this and some proposals for the application of relativity theory to life-span developmental psychology.)

It is the structured and articulated social semiotic relations among positioned-practices in a given social formation, and the social relationships (disjunctions and conjunctions) among different typical formations, that define the individual. *Which* relations, and *when,* may foreground different social constructions of the "self" and their embodiment in biological individuals. These include self-as-formally-unified-consciousness, self as social agent, autobiographical self, moral self, corporeal self, and so on (see Harré, 1983; Lemke, 1988b).

The effects of continuity and unity we have identified here are socially constructed through the material, constitutive, and dialectical relations of the prediscursive and the discursive. I argued above that the poststructuralist deconstruction of the unitary individual is both idealist and differentialist rather than dialectical. This is so because the poststructuralists have privileged in their own metatheory the textual per se as the constitutive site of subject positions at the expense of its material embodiment in the physical and biological interaction systems of the social formation. It is differentialist because the emphasis on the "free" or "open" play of subject positions is not dialectically articulated in relation to still higher-order typical formations or subsystem-subsystem transactions. Poststructuralism has succeeded in disarticulating the unitary individual but has failed to rearticulate the theoretical pieces that remain to an alternative social praxis. Foucault's own discourse fails to rearticulate the theoretical pieces in ways that lead to an alternative to subject-centered reason. Habermas ([1985] 1987c: 274) makes the point that Foucault "abruptly reverses power's truth-dependency into the power-dependency of truth." But this reversal or negation merely enacts its most fundamental axioms from the other side. As Habermas observes, the aporias on which this reversal are based—"cognitive relationships regulated by the *truth* of judgements; and practical relationships regulated by the *success* of actions"—are the fundamental axioms of subject-centered reason. Not even the dissolution of the centered subject into nominalist and totalizing external formations can escape the fact that a conceptual hypostatization has taken place, in which the subject of instrumental and success-oriented action also defines the terms in which the relevant formations are theorized. Thus the poststructuralist critique of a strong classification of social and political subjects in favor of a weak classification, defined as a differential plurality of positions, results in what Costanzo Preve (1984) has rightly, I think, criticized as the antidialectical and antimaterialist products of the dominant technocratic culture of the Right in which social identity, historical memory, and political responsibility are negated in favor of a reified interplay of goal- or success-oriented linguistically defined subjectivities. One form this has taken, as Preve (1984: 70) shows, is the postmodern critique of, say, the strong classification of the Bourgeois and Proletarian subjects in classical Marxism (e.g., Marx and Engels, [1848] 1969), as if these categories correspond to a *topoi* of actual social identities, defined in terms of the epistemology of representation. Thus Preve argues:

> Dialectical materialism, in fact, not only sediments historical memory (in a temporally discontinuous *multiversum* and in a granular series of moments), but it also produces theoretical identity. As happens with memory, identity is also something discontinous and noncumulative. In fact, "strong identities" (Jacobin, Bolshevik, authoritarian, centered) do not exist to be undermined in the name of "weak identities" (federated, plural, dispersed, disseminated): this is an entirely abstract and empty antinomy, even if today it is fashionable under the name of "weak thought" and "critique of centered systems" (uniting together very different thinkers like Vattimo and Rovatti, Negri and Bodei); since identity is something processual and mutable, it is structurally a contradictory unity of continuity and discontinuity, and as such responds fully to dialectical logic. The polemic against identity, to be justified, must then apply only against "rigid" and neurotic conceptions of identity (and on this point, in fact, psychoanalytic criticism has achieved very interesting results, which are to be fully vindicated). (Preve, 1984: 69; my translation)

The categories of Bourgeois and Proletarian subjects do not correspond to pregiven social categories of particular classes of social agents, defined as "strong identities." Rather, they represent a theoretical and political strategy in a specific social and historical formation for attempting to think through the potential social consequences of their theoretical and practical disarticulation and their rearticulation in a counterhegemonic discourse of social change. Marx and Engels ([1848] 1969) argue that Bourgeois and Proletarian subjects are the site of contradictory social relations and practices. The Bourgeois subject is the subject of technical progress, the transformation of nature into culture, the unevenly distributed creation of social wealth, but also of the destruction and exploitation of the environment. The Proletarian subject is the subject of social oppression, but also of the potential for revolutionary social praxis. This is *not* an argument in favor of a return to a representationism of static social types. It is, however, an argument against the poststructuralist critique's failure to move very much beyond forms of radical skepticism that in themselves are unable to provide the conceptual and practical framework for an analysis of both the discursive and social functions of particular social meaning making practices. Radical skepticism has disarticulated core cultural axioms such as the meaning/reality disjunction but in terms that remain unable to rearticulate these to alternative practices. As such, these disjunctions and their most powerful presuppositions continue to operate even if from the standpoint of their (pessimistic) negation. Radical skepticism appears to assume a net result of no change at all.

The Macro/Micro Disjunction: Rearticulating the Links

Lemke (1985a) has commented on the disjunction between the macro- and the microlevels of social analysis. The central problem is that macro- and microrelations and forms of analysis are insufficiently articulated in relation to each other. However, the problem is not simply one of size in the sense of, say, individuals versus institutions. This is not to deny that such differences of scale do exist. What is important is an analytical strategy that does not assume a priori that the macro- and the microlevels are to be theorized on the basis of different analytical and epistemological criteria. It is necessary that the macro- and the microlevels are dialectically reconstituted within the same conceptual framework so that relations on any given level are articulated with regard to relations on any other level. Callon and Latour (1981: 280) point out, "*There are* of course macro-actors and micro-actors, but the difference between them is brought about by power relations and the constructions of networks that will *elude analysis* if we presume *a priori* that macro-actors are bigger than or superior to micro-actors" (emphasis in original). These "constructions of networks" that have eluded analysis share some affinities with the concept of typical formations, as we shall see below. Now, the metaredundancy contextualization hierarchy does not presume a priori differences of size because meta relations are dialectically related at all levels of analysis (see chapter 4). Nor are we concerned with some a priori distinction between the discursive and the Real whereby the problem becomes one of determining or verifying the existence of some irreducible determining economic base as in, for example, Althusserian reproduction theory. A third objection takes us back to the issues raised by Ian Hunter (1982), which I discussed early in this chapter. Hunter, like Foucault, focuses attention on the discursive practices and procedures that make possible certain kinds of discursive subjects and objects. Theories of cultural reproduction tend, on the other hand, to be more concerned with *what* is reproduced rather than with the discursive and social means through which a given discourse or a specialized meaning making practice enacts what Hunter calls "the divergent historical and contemporary apparatuses in which literary objects and meanings receive their shifting determination" (Hunter, 1982: 82). Bernstein's most recent work on pedagogic discourse has articulated a very similar problematic. Thus Bernstein comments on the predominant focus on "what is reproduced" in pedagogic discourse:

> It is as if the specialised discourse of education is only a voice through which others speak (class, gender, religion, race, region). It is as if pedagogic discourse is itself no more than a relay for power relations external to itself; a relay whose form has no consequences for what is relayed. (Bernstein, 1986a: 2–3)

This is a key statement that will be central to my attempt in this section to reformulate Bernstein's proposals in the social semiotic conceptual framework in ways that can rearticulate the macro/micro disjunction identified by Lemke. Now, I do not assume that "form" in the above passage refers to a formalistic conception of the text. Rather, it is concerned with the form of the discursive apparatuses through which particular practices and procedures of reading and their discursive subjects and objects are produced. This means that we are concerned to develop a model capable of explaining how a particular discursive apparatus produces the meanings and the texts that it does.

Bernstein's concept of the "pedagogic device" supplies us with some important components for the construction of just such a theoretical model. The pedagogic device is "a grammar for producing specialised messages, realisations, *a grammar which regulates what it processes*. A grammar which orders and positions and yet contains the potential of its own transformation" (Bernstein, 1986a: 16; emphasis in original). Bernstein's use of the word *grammar* here does not refer to formal linguistic grammars but to the rules of formation, to use Foucault's term, or the higher-order regulating principles through which the subjects and objects of a given discursive formation are assembled and articulated in discursive practice. However, the metaphor of grammar, seen as an ordering and positioning device or apparatus, reminds us again of one of the central arguments of this study. Texts are the products or records of social meaning making practices. In the final analysis, they are the fundamental data on which all our higher-order or macrolevel hypotheses about a given social formation are built. Thus the metaphor of a grammar reminds us that Bernstein's pedagogic device, specific discursive apparatuses, and discursive formations are always constructed on the basis of situationally specific occasions of social meaning making and their textual productions. The purpose then of rearticulating the macro/micro link between, say, higher-order discursive formations and the copatterned meaning selections in texts is not a straightforward translation from one to the other. Neither Bernstein nor Foucault, as I observed in chapter 7, makes contact with actual texts, just as, for example, correlational sociolinguistics, linguistic pragmatics, and most text linguistics at best get related to no more than a positivistically defined microinteractional setting. The analytical task then is to reconstitute the relations between analytical practice, macrolevel hypotheses about the social formation, and actual textual productions in a unified conceptual framework.

Bernstein's analysis shifts our immediate attention from *which* discursive subjects and objects are assembled and articulated to the question of the internal ordering of a given discursive formation. This is taken to be a function of its role in maintaining or potentially changing a given cultural order. Bernstein does not, however, make explicit the link between his pedagogic device and Foucault's concept of discursive formation. Foucault emphasizes the "rules of use" of statements in the enunciative field of a given discursive formation but without saying very much about the specific internal ordering principles of these (cf. Bernstein's "grammar"). Bernstein makes a three-way distinction between *distributive rules, recontextualizing rules,* and *rules of evaluation.* I suggest that these can be assimilated to a description of the grammar or internal ordering principles of a given discursive formation. Bernstein (1986a: 4) points out that these are hierarchically related insofar as distributive rules regulate recontextualizing rules, which in turn regulate the rules of evaluation. Following Bernstein's own procedure, I shall now attempt to describe each of these separately. However, my purpose is not simply to repeat Bernstein's account but to rearticulate it in terms of the social semiotic conceptual framework.

Distributive rules order and control "the specialisation and distribution of different orders of meaning" (Bernstein, 1986a: 5) through which different knowledge-power relations are constructed. This effects the differential distribution of specialized positioned-practices on the basis of the relations of force that articulate and distribute the power relations among the positioned-practices (actual and potential) in a given discursive formation. Thus the social division of labor that enacts the distinction between the producers (authors, creators) and reproducers (critics, readers) of literature is not arbitrary or natural but is constituted through the operation of a given enunciative field (cf. order of meaning relations or intertextual formation), which articulates a particular relation between these categories. The enunciative field thus enacts the distribution of social meanings and actions between the producers and reproducers to create the relations between, as Bernstein (1986a: 7) puts it, the "thinkable" and the "unthinkable." The distributive rules control and position the producers and reproducers of these categories by specializing different knowledge-power relations and validity claims to different positioned-practices. Here is Nabokov positioning himself as producer in an interview reprinted in *Strong Opinions*:

> Paradoxically, the only real, authentic worlds are, of course, those that seem unusual. When my fancies will have been sufficiently imitated, they, too, will enter the common domain of average reality, which will be false, too, but within a new context which we cannot yet guess. Average reality begins to rot and stink as soon as the act of individual creation ceases to animate a subjectively perceived texture. (Nabokov, 1973: 118)

Nabokov thus operates the voice of the "unthinkable" that transcends local space and time. The "unthinkable" is transformed into the "thinkable" by the reproducers who give voice to those rules and practices of reading and their forms of transmission, thus relating the "thinkable" to the "unthinkable" (Bernstein, 1986a: 7). Here are two examples of this process as voiced by two critics of *Ada:*

> In re-creating the scene of Lucette's fatal plunge, Van has to rely primarily on his imagination. As a narrator who refers to himself in the third person, he lapses into the first person at times of intense emotion, and he is unable to write this scene dispassionately. (Mason, 1974: 105)

And

> Van's position of priority amongst the characters in the novel is mainly due to the fact that he acts both as narrator and author of the "Family Chronicle." Our consideration of the way the characters are presented already showed that *Ada* might more aptly be described as Van's autobiography than as a family chronicle. At any rate this chronicle is written by the main performer in the incidents that are portrayed. (Grabes, 1977: 75)

These two texts articulate the view that the literary text has a "content,"—a "theme," "characters," and a "narrator" that can be named and described. This embodies a referential semantics of the meaning(s) "in" the text. These two critical texts foreground the narrating function of the novel, using terms that either designate the narrator as a specific identity or refer to the act of narrating. In chapter 2 we saw how Banfield, using more formal linguistic procedures, defined the narrator as the unique referent of the first-person pronoun cotemporal with the present tense on the level of Performative time, namely, the time of the narrative speech act as distinct from Narrative time, which is the fictive level of the characters. Banfield's account is a demonstration of what Silverstein (1980: 34) calls the "functional regimentation" of linguistic tokens, whereby the use of these tokens is rationalized by language users in terms of a folk-ideology of purposive, intentional social effects. The linguistic tokens that are taken to index the presence of the narrator enact a structure of what Silverstein (1980: 35) characterizes as "rigidly presupposing indexical forms" in which the presence and identity of the narrator is fixed and not open to negotiation. These indexicals are assumed to name an objectified and referentially projected "person." Banfield's formal linguistic account, as well as the two critics cited above, selectively attends to the indexical forms of the personal pronouns, serving to background not only other possible ways of talking about these but also the lexico-grammatical selections with which these are copatterned. To these forms they then attribute a full-blown referential status. In Whorf's terms, these indexical forms are the "outward marks" (Whorf, 1956b: 80) around which a semantically more covert "abstract personality" (Whorf, 1956b: 81) constitutes the "deep persuasion of a principle behind phenomena." Thus the abstracted lexical concept "narrator" in these critical accounts constitutes a selective automatization of the indexically presupposing pronominal forms in the novel, but without relating these to the copatterned meaning selections with which they occur in a consistent semantic frame or "configurative rapport." The two critical passages selectively foreground and automatize lexico-grammatical selections whose "configurative rapport" frames and constructs the "idea" or "sensing," as Whorf (1956b: 81) puts it, of a "personal identity" for Van as the "main performer" (Grabes, 1977: 75). Further, Banfield's linguistic account is confined to the sentence-internal relations of lexico-grammatical forms, thereby failing to address the matter of interclausal cohesive relations, which are always the basis of pronominal reference in discourse. The result is that the functional distinction in text-linguistics between *exophoric* (situational) reference and *endophoric* (textual) reference is lost. The former designates an item that is indexed as occurring in the context of situation of the text and the latter designates an item that is indexed as being identifiable in or recoverable from the surrounding co-text (see Halliday and Hasan, 1976: 32). Banfield's sentence-internal criteria cannot account for this distinction, with the consequence that the referents of the personal pronouns are construed as naming narrators or characters independently of either situational or textual criteria. This is also evident in the passages from Mason and Grabes in the confusion concerning the semantic distinction in the personal pronoun system between first-person "I" (i.e., speaker only) and third-person (i.e., other noncommunication) roles. Thus the indexical properties of exophoric and endophoric uses of the personal pronouns are totally bypassed in favor of a folk-ideology of direct reference or naming.

There can be no doubting the similarity of the implicit rules and procedures that these two readings articulate. What both readings demonstrate is the application of quite specific and restricted meaning making (reading) practices, which produce their textual meanings. Texts do not tell us how to read them, nor are meanings simply contained "in" texts, waiting for the reader to extract them during a purportedly asocial reading process. Textual meanings are made in and through specific socially and historically contingent meaning making practices, which enact specific systems of foregrounded meaning relations. Meaning making practices construct and index both local and global relations of equivalence, contrast, generality, and specificity in the partial hierarchies of thematic and actional resources in the social semiotic. The meaning relations so constructed are transmitted and disseminated in specific ways. In these two critical texts the following discursive rules or procedures operate:

1. The text is read as uttered by a narrator-I whose speaking voice corresponds to a centered locus of power and knowledge in the narrative.
2. The narrator-I refers to or portrays a represented reality.
3. The narrator and the characters represent specific moral and psychological essences and character traits.
4. The textual world is the unique artistic vision of its author, here transmitted by the reproducers of this discourse.
5. The narrative constitutes the unfolding of an autobiographical subject whose confessional practices enact the self-discovery of a person taken to be historically continuous with authorial subjectivity and experience.

Thus we have emphasized the productive dialectic between foregrounded copatternings of meaning relations and the meaning making practices in operation. Textual meanings are made and construed in and through copatterned meaning selections by what Hunter (1982: 88) calls "a dispersed field of practices whose iteration and articulation to a wider field of pedagogic, legal, and economic ensembles determines the shifting object: Literature." These practices are not extrinsic to the context but constitute part of the productive dialectic in and through which (inter)textual meanings are made. We can now begin to see more clearly that "monologic" and "dialogic," as I proposed in chapter 7, are not formal, intrinsic properties of texts. They are relatable to the meaning making practices whose iterations and transformations determine how social agents make textual meanings. The discursive "rules" I have schematized above can be glossed as monologic reading practices, whose particular rules of distribution regulate the differential specialization of power-knowledge in terms of (*a*) the author's subjectivity as the origin of the represented experiences (i.e., the "unthinkable"), which are taken to be continuous with the monologic narrator-I, and (*b*) the institutional reproducers or transmitters of the meaning making practices and pedagogical discourses through which specific, limited procedures of reading and the agents who perform them are positioned and regulated. These monologic practices articulate this presumed continuity, ensuring that the self-confession of the narrator-I is coterminous with the fixing of the reader's self-awareness of his or her own self-originating consciousness, whose "autoconstitution" guarantees the subject as the bearer of self-evident knowledges and truths about one's "inner" self.

A dialogic reading strategy, on the other hand, works to disarticulate these knowledge-power relations and validity claims from their presumed source in authorial consciousness, as well as the institutional procedures that reproduce the continuity between this and the individual reader's personal encounter with the text. Monologic reading practices entail the strong insulation of writing from reading and from their social agents. Dialogic practices disarticulate the strong insulation of these categories and attempt to rearticulate them to the field of practices that constitute both readers and writers. A dialogic reading disarticulates the strong insulation between authorial consciousness (producer) and reproducers in which reading agents, practices, and texts are positioned to regulate who may make and transmit *which* meanings and practices, and *how*. A critical social semiotics is therefore committed to both asking and seeking answers to the important question posed by Lemke (1983b: 159): Who is doing what to whom with this text? And how? What social interests are maintained or contested in this text, or through its intertextual relations? What social practices are reproduced or challenged by the relations between the discursive practices and the copatterned meaning relations in texts?

Bernstein (1986a: 9) develops the concept of *recontextualizing rules* in the following terms: "Pedagogic discourse then is a principle that removes a discourse (de-locates) from its substantive practice and context, and re-locates that discourse according to its own principle of selective re-ordering and focussing." As with the distributive rules, the recontextualizing rules will be formulated here in relation to both producers and reproducers. On the production side, the narrative text is itself a recontextualizing principle that "selectively appropriates, re-locates and re-focusses other discourses to constitute its own order and orderings" (Bernstein, 1986a: 9). I referred in chapter 5 to the way in which literary texts transform (recontextualize) social discourses and intertextual meaning relations and functionally integrate these to their own (con)textual principles. Thus heteroglossic relations between voices so integrated entail processes of both the disarticulation of this discursive "raw" material from other contexts and the selective rearticulation of these to the functional purposes of its own ordering and positioning principles. On the reproduction side, the pedagogic discourse "embeds a discourse of competency (skills of various kinds) into a discourse of order in such a way that the latter always dominates the former" (Bernstein, 1986a: 9). Bernstein calls the former the *instructional discourse* and the latter the *regulative discourse*. The first refers to the application and iteration of specific procedures and rules by virtue of which reading agents with specific competencies are produced. The formulation and application of these competencies transforms (recontextualizes) the (narrative) text according to a higher-order principle of regulation whereby the competencies acquired signify "the dominant principles of a given society" (Bernstein, 1986a: 10). It will be clear that this use of the term *competence* has nothing to do with the normative and asocial notion of internalized linguistic rules in transformational-generative grammar (e.g., Chomsky, 1965).

The discursive apparatus or formation that enacts the rules mentioned above functions to produce an a priori "truth," namely, the autoconstitutive subject of the unitary, rational individual. The iteration of these rules and procedures results in determinate strategies for the formulation, classification, interpretation, and transmission of the hegemonic sociodiscursive order. This works according to techniques for the codification of "rules of order, relation and identity" (Bernstein, 1986a: 10), which are the preconditions for the making and remaking of particular (inter)textual meanings and their validity claims. Nabokov's own formulation of artistic creativity and the two critical accounts cited above thus produce/reproduce the author/narrator's consciousness as "imitations," "representations," and "portrayals" of subjective experience, conceptualized both in terms of an "interior" of thoughts and emotions and an "exterior" of artistic perceptions, which are in turn united with the autoconstitutive subject of knowledge. These "rules of order, relation and identity" are not derivable, as I have insisted all along, from the text per se; they are derivable from the social relations of production of technocratic capitalism in and through the transmission and acquisition of specific social meaning making practices and moral and pedagogic competencies.

Bernstein's *evaluation rules* "distinguish two modalities of theories of instruction, one oriented to the logic of transmission and one oriented to the logic of acquisition" (Bernstein, 1986a: 15). The first of these, Bernstein points out, "privileges *performances* of the pedagogic discourse, the latter will privilege *competencies* of the acquirer." In the present context, the first can be taken to refer to the valorized space-time of narrative syntagmatic structure itself, whereby the paradigmatic (systemic) association and recontextualization of categories in syntagmatic structure can copattern with preceding (past) forms in some still larger syntagm through their paradigmatic associations with past values (see chapter 5). Similarly, actually occurring categories in the syntagm can anticipate future states and values according to the same valorized space-time. In this way, textual values are enacted and confirmed through their paradigmatic recontextualization with signifiers of past, present, and future (Thibault, 1986b: 9–10). These values are thus condensed within the internal spatiotemporal ordering of the textual syntagm. Further aspects of this process were discussed in chapter 5 in connection with the identity/difference dialectic. Bernstein's second distinction here refers to the modalities of reproduction of those discursive rules and procedures through which reading competencies are defined and evaluated by the training of acquirers in the selective activation and iteration of these same rules and procedures. The three-way distinction Bernstein makes between *distributive rules, recontextualizing rules,* and *evaluative rules* can be assimilated to Foucault's concept of discursive formation. This distinction provides an alternative to Foucault's reliance on cognitive-instrumental reason because of its inclusion of other axiological orientations and their validity claims. A discursive formation is a macrosocial construct that selects, integrates, orders, and positions enunciative fields (orders of meaning or intertextual formations) in socially and historically specific typical patterns. It is an analytical approximation of some ensemble of social and discursive practices. Bernstein calls his pedagogic device "a grammar for producing specialised messages, realisations, *a grammar which regulates what it processes*" (Bernstein, 1986a: 16; emphasis in original). It is then parallel to Foucault's *enunciative function,* which is defined as the principles that put into operation a given *enunciative field*. However, Foucault is less clear about what the "grammar" in the above sense of the typical patterns of use and modes of deployment of these enunciative fields might look like. Foucault is clear about the systemic nature of the regularity in dispersion of the thematic formations and social activity-structures that comprise a given discursive formation, but he is less explicit about the precise principles by which a given discursive formation, to use Bernstein's words, "regulates what it processes." Bernstein's distinction between distributive rules, recontextualizing rules, and evaluative rules can be reconstituted at the macrolevel of discursive formation in order to hypothesize and approximate more clearly just what the ordering and positioning (regulating) principles of such a grammar might look like. What is processed by this grammar can be analytically reconstituted at the analytical level "below" in the form of the social semiotic coding orientations. These, as we have already seen, regulate and distribute the differential access of social agents to meanings, texts, social situations, and even whole discourse genres at still lower levels. Thus the linking of the social semiotic codes to still higher-order discursive formations is an important step toward analytically reconstructing the micro/macro link from text to discursive formation via the intermediate levels of semantic register-type, intertextual formations, and the system of social heteroglossia.

In the previous chapter, I distinguished between a Coding Orientation A and Coding Orientation B. This is not to be equated with Bernstein's distinction between the elaborated and restricted coding orientations. The distinction I made in chapter 7 is more closely aligned with the one Bernstein (1986a: 7) makes between the *elaborate coding orientation* and the *elaborate code*. The latter embodies explicit principles of self-reflexivity concerning the praxis of their own elaborated coding orientations. The discursive practices that produce and reproduce the kinds of social meanings I have analyzed here hardly encompass Bernstein's elaborated/restricted distinction. What is encompassed is the differential operation of recognition and realization rules, which are specialized, I would argue, to the distinction between an elaborated coding orientation (A) and an elaborated code (B). The former is articulated in and through the contextual relations *between* the authorial and critical texts we examined above. The latter (i.e., B) is articulated, in the present context, by a critical social semiotic theory that attempts to disarticulate and rearticulate the elaborated coding orientation in ways that lead to the deconstruction of its principles and the articulation of their transformative potential. These operate differential recognition and realization rules, which entail differential principles of classification and framing. They are dependent, as we saw in chapter 7, on the kinds of control of categories (classification) and the kinds of control of interactions (framing) that are enacted in and through their consistent semantic frames and copatterned textual realizations. The relevant classification and framing principles may be summarized as follows:

Strong Classification

1. The author is the producer of the artistic creation; the critic/reader is reproducer/consumer, is evaluated as competent and incompetent reader according to usually implicit modalities of textual use.
2. Narrator-I is centered locus of knowledge-power in text.
3. Narrator-I is continuous with authorial I, seen as origin of subjective aesthetic experience.
4. Narrator and characters "represent" sociopsychological essences.
5. The textual world is a coherent unity, which derives from authorial creativity and subjective experience.
6. This textual unity and form evoke aesthetic and affective responses in reader, where the reader is constituted within the phenomenological horizon of the mutual becoming of text and reader.
7. There is strong insulation of the categories of the outer world of the economy, the marketplace, and administration and the inner world of spiritual and aesthetic values; reification of cultural experience through identification with inner, intrinsic values of abstract, universal Man disjoined from social practice.
8. There is strong insulation of social/political from aesthetic, thus disjoining function of text from its form in ways that produce a bourgeois "aesthetic distanciation" from material, practical urgencies (Bourdieu, 1979: 36–42).

Strong Framing

1. The social injunction to talk/write about one's subjective encounter with the text is predicated on the assumption of the text as the mediating point for the unfolding of a totally subjective reading experience, seen as morally and personally enriching.
2. The institution and authority of the official reproducers (e.g., education and mass media) in pedagogic practice is the voice for the dissemination of the "unthinkable" as the "thinkable."
3. Critical practice is preselected from legitimating discourses of representation, textual autonomy and authority, "individual" creativity.
4. There is strong insulation of the categories of writer, critic, reader, and text.

Strong framing and strong classification are specialized to a monologic mode of contextualization in which the strong insulation of categories and agents and the strong framing of interactional practices give voice to meanings and practices that articulate and maintain the hegemonic knowledge-power relations and validity claims as seen in their deployments of the dominant distributive, recontextualizing, and evaluative rules in the macrolevel social relations of the discursive formations in which they occur. Weak framing and weak classification are specialized to a dialogic mode of contextualization in which the weak insulation of categories and agents and the weak framing of interactional practices attempt to disarticulate both the principles of control that govern strong framing and strong classification in the elaborated coding orientation and to rearticulate the potential for transformation of their classification and framing principles as embodied in the self-reflexivity of the practices of the elaborated code. This means that the text and its producers and reproducers can be repositioned in regard to their macrosocial relations in ways that can voice potential alternative relations among texts, realizations, and positioned-practices through changes in the knowledge-power relations and validity claims involved (see chapter 7).

The analysis in chapter 6 of the differential semantic orientations that voice the Van/Humbert and Ada/Lolita discourses enables the concept of social semiotic coding orientation to be linked to specific types of semantic relations and their copatterned textual realizations and distributions. In other words, the codes can be analytically reconstituted in relation to the microlevel of actual texts in ways that Bernstein does not actually achieve (see chapter 7) but that are, nevertheless, implicit in his notion of the text as the making visible of social practices in a material form. This allows us to see more clearly how the coding orientations order and position (inter)textual meaning relations and the system of social heteroglossia in specific texts as voicings of particular positioned-practices in the social semiotic system. This is the only valid strategy, I would argue, for relating macrolevel hypotheses about power-knowledge relations and validity claims in the social formation to the thematic and actional semiotic in which they are enacted and realized. Macrolevel accounts on their own are not grounded in actual textual productions and social occasions of discourse. Macrolevel social analysis is disjoined from the microlevel such that it has no means of specifying how the higher-order or more global hypotheses concerning patterns of domination and control are articulated in practice. Microanalysis that is disjoined from the macrolevel cannot on its own theorize the more global systems of connections and disjunctions that relate one social situation-type, social activity-structure type, or textual production to others. Microlevel descriptions on their own, however subtle their insights may be in a specific contextual domain, are unable to theorize their relations to wider social relations and functions (see Lemke, 1985a; Wertsch and Lee, 1984).

The highest or most macrolevel concept in this book is Foucault's concept of discursive formation. This is an analytical construct that assembles and relates the various practices and meanings into a system of interacting subsystems. It is a conceptual and analytical framework for organizing relations at lower systemic levels into more global patterns, whose systemic regularities define the discursive formation. It is, in the present analysis, a means of integrating the three notions discussed from Bernstein into a model of the ways in which global patterns of hegemony and domination are articulated. At the level below are the social semiotic coding orientations, which regulate the production and distribution of the material and semiotic resources of the social formation, as well as the differential access of social agents to them. The codes regulate the forms of social consciousness, yet the concept of code needs to be articulated to the still higher-order discursive formations in order to conceptualize the relations *between* coding orientations in a more integrated framework. Our third level consists of the coactional and cothematic intertextual formations in which the system of social heteroglossia in the social formation is constructed. Intertextual formations are constructed and maintained by the alignments and oppositions of specific intersections of these intertextual resources. These are the textual voicings of sociodiscursive positioned-practices or discursive subject positions. Thus the codes at the level above differentially access social agents to these intertextual resources and the heteroglossic system of voices in ways that articulate a constant metastable dialectic of system-maintaining and system-changing relations among social meaning making practices. Voice is a textual concept whose specific semantic intersections articulate some positioned-practice in the social formation. Thus the concept of voice links with the next level down, the semantic register-types and discourse genres, which connect heteroglossic relations of cothematic and coactional meanings to the social situation-types in which they are typically enacted in and through their textual productions. In this way, the semantic level of register links heteroglossic relations to semantic patterns and their realizations in actual texts and social occasions of discourse. Thus the link from text to discursive formation is constructed through the dialectical reconstitution of a number of intermediate levels of analysis that have previously been disjoined in separate domains of inquiry (Lemke, 1985a). These relations have been schematized in Figure 8.1.

Semiotic Praxis and Social Responsibility

At the conclusion of chapter 4 I referred to Volosinov's concern for the exercise of responsibility in the use of the "word" in connection with Habermas's conception of critical practice. Throughout this study I have frequently referred to concepts such as "levels of relations" and "strategies of punctuation." All social meaning making—including our own theoretical practices—entails the typing or the

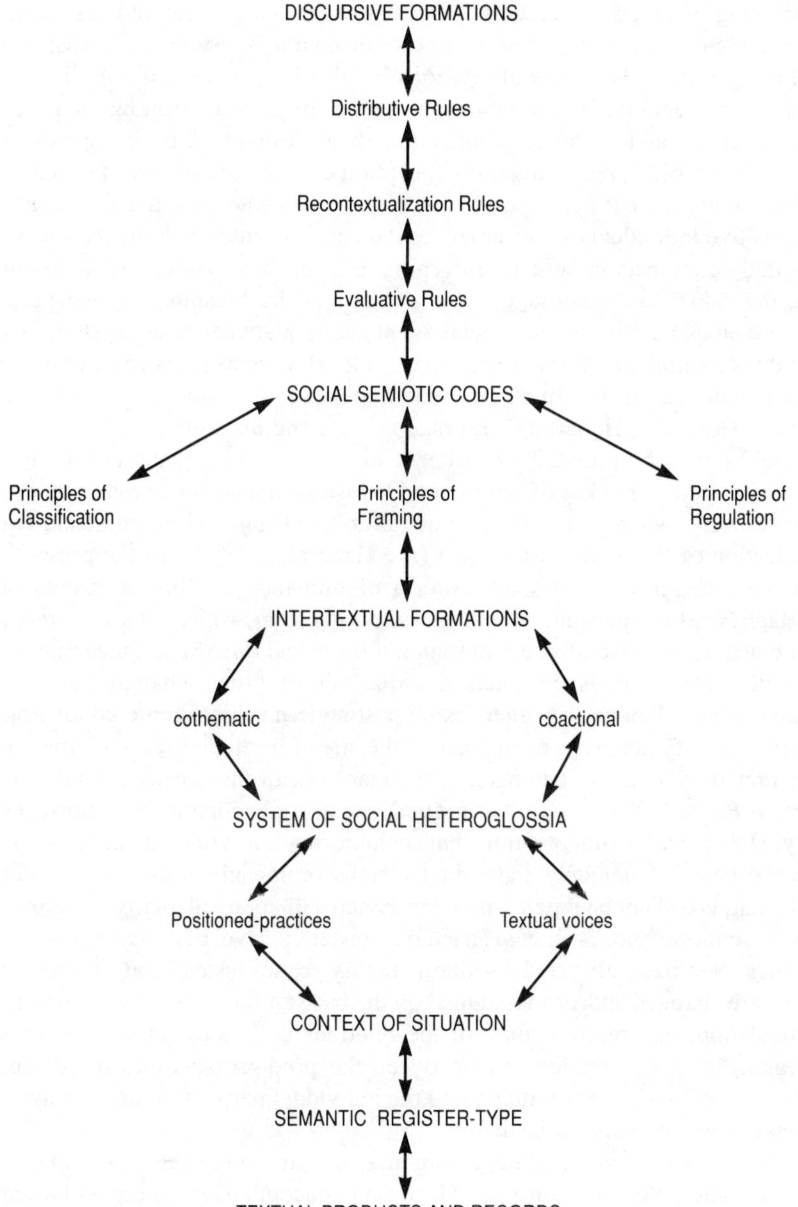

Figure 8.1. Rearticulating the macro/micro links; intermediate levels of analysis

mistyping of levels of relations involving contexts, power, and responsibility. The reduction of the subject to an effect of discourse is just one such epistemological mistyping of the levels of relations involved, as is the reifying discourse of "mind" in cognitive psychological accounts of *social* meaning making. The former enacts an ideologically functional disjunction of the social agent from the discursive subject, rendering this conception useless for a theory of social change while, at the same time, appearing to oppose or negate the unitary, rational, and acquisitive individual of consumer capitalism. The latter disjoins the social from the individual in an Imaginary mistyping of levels in ways that fail to account for the individual as constituted in and through social meaning making practices. How then can the individual social agent act on and change the system of social meaning making practices or some part of it? Habermas proposes a critical practice founded on his profound critique of cognitive-instrumental models of social action. However, Habermas's rational criteria and his attempt to define an ideal speech situation, founded on criteria of "mutual understanding" rather than success-oriented models of action, tend to assume transcendent rather than immanent criteria, whereby critical practice is able to transcend instrumental reason's reification of the modernist project (see Habermas, 1985). In the present study I have frequently emphasized criteria of immanence. This does not entail a metaphysical or speculative conception of this term, which was so perceptively critiqued by Gramsci, but a material and historical one. Social meaning making practices enact a constant metastable dialectic of system-changing and system-maintaining relations and practices. A postmodern subject-centered ideology has tended to reify language or the text as the site of particular subjectivities, which are immanent *in* texts. The result is a metaphysic of the decentered subject without, as Preve (1984: 61–73) has argued, either social identity or historical memory. However, I do not presume that social formations are maintained or changed on the basis of uniquely individual actions or meanings that, if uniquely individual, could not be typed within the systems of contextualizing relations of the social semiotic. Nor is change enacted solely at the level of abstract social collectivities. Neomaterialist social semiotic theory argues instead that systems of relations are changed and/or maintained on the basis of the constant articulation, disarticulation, and rearticulation of the relations both between systems of social meaning making practices and between the prediscursive and the discursive. These processes are not reducible to the individual per se although the individual social agent participates in them.

Gramsci's conception of hegemony may be returned to here. In chapters 7 and 8 I have attempted to reconstitute Gramsci's conception within the social semiotic conceptual framework. Gramsci understood the centrality of this concept to the whole process of social production and reproduction. He frequently used macrolevel concepts such as "nation," "people," "state," and "class"; however, he was a more subtle dialectician than many of his macrolevel commentators appear to appreciate. Gramsci was also concerned with the theoretical and political significance of language and linguistic change in the struggle between opposing hegemonic principles. His interest was in language as a dynamic historical social process rather than as a static and normative abstraction:

> The history of languages is the history of linguistic innovations; these innovations are not individual (as happens in art) but they are of an entire social community that has innovated its culture, that has "progressed" historically: naturally even these become individual, but not of the individual-artist, rather of the *complete* determined historical-cultural-individual-element.
>
> In language, too, there is not parthenogenesis, that is, language that produces other language, but there is innovation through the interferences from different cultures, and so on; this happens in many different ways and furthermore it happens for entire masses of linguistic elements, and in a molecular fashion (for example: Latin as "a mass" innovated the Celtic of the Gauls, and, on the other hand, it influenced German "in a molecular fashion," that is, lending single words and forms, etc.). Interference and "molecular" influence can occur in the same bosom of a nation, among different stratum, and so on; a new ruling class innovates as "a mass"; the jargon of the professions, and the like, that is, of particular societies, innovate in "a molecular fashion." The artistic judgment in these innovations has the character of "cultural taste," not of artistic taste, that is, for the same reason for which brunettes and blondes are liked and aesthetic "ideals" change, linked to determinate cultures. (Gramsci, [1918] 1977g: 262–63; my translation)

Gramsci here relates "molecular" processes of heteroglossia and hybridization to the semogenic resources of the social semiotic system in ways that link microlevel ("molecular") processes to partial hierarchies of higher-order meaning relations. Thus individual, including artistic, innovations occur, as Lemke (1988b) also points out, on the basis of *historically unique* innovations and molecular combinations that then ramify at more global levels throughout the system of relations. A social semiotic praxis must attempt to articulate this process of hegemonic-counterhegemonic struggle on all levels in the relevant system of relations. Gramsci well understood the links between human agency, social and historical processes, and linguistic practice in ways that are enormously suggestive for social semiotics. A critical social semiotics works to maintain the vital self-reflexive links between theory and practice. This means that the theorist cannot afford to construct an Imaginary and unarticulated opposition between theory and the objects of the theory. Theory must become part of praxis and praxis part of theory. Critical social semiotics must articulate its own relations to and functions in the meaning making practices of which it is a part. And these meaning making practices must in turn act back on theory to change it and hence to make it continually socially and politically relevant in specific domains of social practice. Gramsci understood that macrolevel patterns of domination and hegemony as well as microlevel patterns of social interaction and their patterns of realization are social and historical constructions, which can be contested and struggled over for the articulation of opposing hegemonic principles. Social meanings are not fixed, determinate, or mutually agreed upon but are made, unmade, and remade by competing articulating principles. We must be careful, however, not to interpret this back into the hegemonic terms of technocratic and consumer capitalism. It is not a question of a reified, differentially defined plurality of subject positions. Critical social semiotics can work toward the following goals: (1) to articulate those social meaning making practices that can intervene in and potentially change the metastable dialectic of system-maintaining and system-changing relations and practices; (2) to build a neomaterialist social semiotic praxis into the socially and historically defined project of those social and discursive practices committed to the contestation of limiting and repressive practices and social ideologies; and (3) to construct a self-reflexive praxis that can specify the local and global connections and disjunctions among interaction subsystems and that can articulate intelligent and responsible hypotheses about where, when, and how to intervene in patterned social meaning making on any given level in the social semiotic system.

This does not presuppose a global or totalizing formal theory, but a critical social semiotics of action, a praxis whose own meaning making practices can be hybridized with other social meaning making practices to permit their new joint or hybrid contextualization dynamics to disarticulate and rearticulate the typical relations of complementarity and homology between the material exchanges in the prediscursive and the semiotic exchanges in the discursive. The disarticulation or deautomatization of their typical relations of homology through the "unhinging" of the seemingly fully automatized mappings of the one onto the other implies the potential for "new" interactional practices and social meanings to be voiced. Whether their articulation succeeds in ramifying more globally across the system of social meaning making practices is a historical question that no theory can predict. All theories, however, inevitably take part in the play of praxis, enacting either the stabilizing social discourses through which the system of disjunctions is maintained or the potentially destabilizing discourses that resist and potentially alter these (Lemke, 1984c: 99–104). This potential must be articulated in socially specific domains of practice, whose hybridizations with a critical social semiotics of action can recursively generate not only analytical representations of the joint metastable contextualization dynamics that are involved, but also self-reflexive representations of the levels of power and responsibility these entail. It is only in this way that we can begin to construct an ethics that is freed from every metaphysical and absolutist doctrine of the individual:

> Man is to be conceived as a historical block of purely individual and subjective elements and of common elements and objectives and materials with which the individual has an active relationship. To transform the external world, and relationships in general, means to potentiate one's self, to develop one's self. That ethical "improvement" is purely individual is illusion and error: the synthesis of elements that are constitutive of individuality is "individual," but it [individuality] does not realize itself and does not develop without an activity toward the outside, which modifies external relationships, from those in the direction of nature to those in the direction of other men to varying degrees, in the various social groups in which one lives, right up to the widest relationship, which embraces all of humankind. For this reason, it can be said that man is essentially "political," since the activity for knowingly transforming and managing other men realizes his "humanity," his "human nature." (Gramsci, 1977d: 42; my translation)

Such an ethics recognizes that the semiotic resource systems (e.g., the lexicogrammar) mesh with the rational and critical potential of our social meaning making practices, and in ways that do not reduce the latter to the category of "transcendental consciousness" (Habermas, [1985] 1987b: 326). The uncoupling of the resource systems from the social action systems artificially separates grammar, meaning, and text, which are, accordingly, seen as only contingently and externally related to each other. This would fail to grasp Whorf's (1956a: 108) point that "language is a system, not just an assemblage of norms." The lexicogrammatical and text-building resource systems build in more possibilities, including unrealized ones, than does the norm, which affirms and typifies already preexistent traditions and ways of making meaning (Coseriu, 1973: 150). The reduction of the resource systems to cognitive-instrumental norms rationalizes semiotic form and function as a technical-utilitarian "tool" for the domination of both inner and outer nature. On the other hand, a nonmetaphysical ethics of human social meaning making recognizes that communication is a world-making ecosystem in which agents move, manage their relationships with one another, and pass from one experience to another, and which "provides an interpretative key to many human problems and phenomena" (di Giovanni, 1988: 91). Nevertheless, it is important not to enact a second uncoupling, which both Habermas's concept of communicative rationality and the poststructuralists in their different ways effect. In this regard, Preve (1984: 78) interestingly notes that Habermas's attempt to reconstruct a communicative rationality (an anti-postmodern one) occurs on substantially the same "linguistic terrain" as that of the poststructuralists. The neomaterialist framework of social semiotics insists on the dialectical duality of the material (prediscursive) and the social semiotic (discursive) dimensions of social reality. The complex and asymmetrical relations of complementarity between the two, and the relations of production and the social division of labor with which these complementarities are intertwined mean that the one cannot be uncoupled from or reduced to the other. These relations of complementarity constitute and are constituted in and through the unequal access to and distribution of both material and social semiotic resources, the asymmetric power-knowledge relations between social agents, and the relations of struggle and antagonism between social groups.

Such an ethics does not speak for the rights of the social agent qua property-owning and -consuming individual. Nor does it reduce to the cognitive-instrumental aporias of subject-centered reason. It is an ethics of the social agent's right to participate in both the typical and atypical intersections and articulations of social meaning making practices in ways that recognize and sustain the rights of social agents to construct meanings and practices that can give voice to yet-to-be-voiced human social possibilities.

Note

1. Threadgold makes the following pertinent observation on Halliday's semantically oriented systemic-functional grammar: "Arguing against the Derridean deconstructionist critique that linguistics imagines that we recover from discourse a 'fixed and stable meaning,' he [Halliday] suggests that it would be a very impoverished theory of discourse that expected to do this but counters:

> 'We *do* recover from discourse . . . a complex and indeterminate meaning . . . The reason it is hard to make this process explicit is that we can only do so by talking about grammar: and to do this we have to construct a theory of grammar: a *grammatics* . . . a designed system, a metalanguage' (Halliday, 1987: 145).

Then to paraphrase Halliday, its terms become 'reified' . . . and we confuse our *grammatics* (the categories, or labels we borrow from extra-linguistic experience in order to describe the *for us* ineffable experience of language itself (Halliday 1983) with the *real* grammar (language)" (Threadgold, 1989; emphasis in original).

Appendixes

Appendix 1

The analysis is coded for major, minor, elliptical, and nonfinite clauses; embedded clauses are not separately coded (see Halliday, 1985: 62-63). Clause complexes are designated by arabic numerals; constituent clauses that comprise a given clause complex by lower case letters.

Lolita Textual Excerpt (Nabokov, 1959: 60–61); Clause Rank Segmentation

1a Under my glancing fingertips I felt
1b the minute hairs bristle ever so slightly along her shins.
2a I lost myself in the pungent but healthy heat
2b which like summer haze hung about little Haze.
3a Let her stay,
3b let her stay . . .
4a As she strained
4b to chuck the core of her abolished apple into the fender,
4c her young weight, her shameless innocent shanks and round bottom, shifted in my tense, tortured, surreptitiously labouring lap;
4d and all of a sudden a mysterious change came over my senses.
5a I entered a plane of being
5b where nothing mattered,
5c save the infusion of joy brewed within my body.

6a What had begun as a delicious distension of my innermost roots
6b became a glowing tingle
6c which now had reached that state of absolute security, confidence and reliance
6d not found elsewhere in conscious life.
7a With the deep hot sweetness thus established and well on its way to the ultimate convulsion,
7b I felt
7c I could slow down
7d in order to prolong the glow.
8 Lolita had been safely solipsized.
9a The implied sun pulsated in the supplied poplars;
9b we were fantastically and divinely alone;
9c I watched her, rosy, gold-dusted, beyond the veil of my controlled delight,
9d unaware of it,
9e alien to it;
9f and her lips were apparently still forming the words of the Carmen-barmen ditty
9g that no longer reached my consciousness.
10 Everything was now ready.
11 The nerves of pleasure had been laid bare.
12 The corpuscles of Krauze were entering the phase of frenzy.
13a The least pressure would suffice
13b to set all paradise loose.
14a I had ceased
14b to be Humbert the Hound,
14c the sad-eyed degenerate cur clasping the boot
14d that would presently kick him away.
15 I was above the tribulation of my ridicule, beyond the possibilities of retribution.
16a In my self-made seraglio, I was a radiant and robust Turk,
16b deliberately, in the full consciousness of his freedom, postponing the moment of actually enjoying the youngest and frailest of his slaves.
17a Suspended on the brink of that voluptuous abyss
17b (a nicety of psychological equipoise comparable to certain techniques in the arts)
17c I kept repeating chance words after her—barmen, alarmin', my charmin', my carmen, ahmen, ahahamen—
17d as one talking
17e and laughing in his sleep
17f while my happy hand crept up her sunny leg

17g as far as the shadow of decency allowed.
18a The day before she had collided with the heavy chest in the hall and
18b 'Look,
18c look!'–
18d I gasped–
18e 'look
18f what you've done,
18g what you've done to yourself,
18h ah, look!';
18i for there was,
18j I swear,
18i a yellowish violet bruise on her lovely nymphet thigh
18k which my huge hairy hand massaged
18l and slowly enveloped–
18m and because of her very perfunctory underthings, there seemed
18n to be nothing
18o to prevent my muscular thumb
18p from reaching the hot hollow of her groin–
18q just as you might tickle
18r and caress a giggling child–just that–and;
18s 'Oh, it's nothing at all,'
18t she cried with a sudden shrill note in her voice,
18u and she wriggled,
18v and squirmed,
18w and threw her head back,
18x and her teeth rested on her glistening underlip
18y as she half-turned away,
18z and my moaning mouth, gentlemen of the jury, almost reached her bare neck,
18@ while I crushed out against her left-buttock
18# the last throe of the longest ecstasy man or monster had ever known.

Ada Textual Excerpt (Nabokov, 1969: 86–87); Clause Rank Segmentation

1a It was the children's first bodily contact
1b and both were embarrassed.
2a She settled down with her back to Van,
2b resettled
2c as the carriage jerked,
2d and wriggled some more,

2e arranging her ample pine-smelling skirt,
2f which seemed
2g to envelop him airily, for all the world like a barber's sheet.
3 In a trance of awkward delight he held her by the hips.
4a Hot gouts of sun moved fast across her zebra stripes and the backs of her bare arms
4b and seemed
4c to continue their journey through the tunnel of his own frame.
5a 'Why did you cry?'
5b he asked,
5c inhaling her hair and the heat of her ear.
6a She turned her head
6b and for a moment looked at him closely, in cryptic silence.
7a (Did I?
7b I don't know
7c –it upset me somehow.
7d I can't explain it,
7e but I felt
7f there was something dreadful, brutal, dark, and yes, dreadful, about the whole thing.
8 A later note.)
9a 'I'm sorry,'
9b he said
9c as she looked away,
9d 'I'll never do it again in your presence.'
10 (By the way, that 'for all the world,' I detest the phrase.
11 Another note in Ada's late hand.)
12a With his entire being, the boiling and brimming lad relished her weight
12b as he felt it
12c responding to every bump of the road
12d by softly parting in two
12e and crushing beneath it the core of the longing
12f which he knew
12g he had to control
12h lest a possible seep perplexed her innocence.
13a He would have yielded
13b and melted in animal laxity
13c had not the girl's governess saved the situation
13d by addressing him.
14a Poor Van shifted Ada's bottom to his right knee,
14b blunting

14c what used to be termed in the jargon of the torture house 'the angle of agony.'
15a In the mournful dullness of unconsummated desire he watched
15b a row of izbas straggle by
15c as the *calèche* drove through Gamlet, a hamlet.

Appendix 2

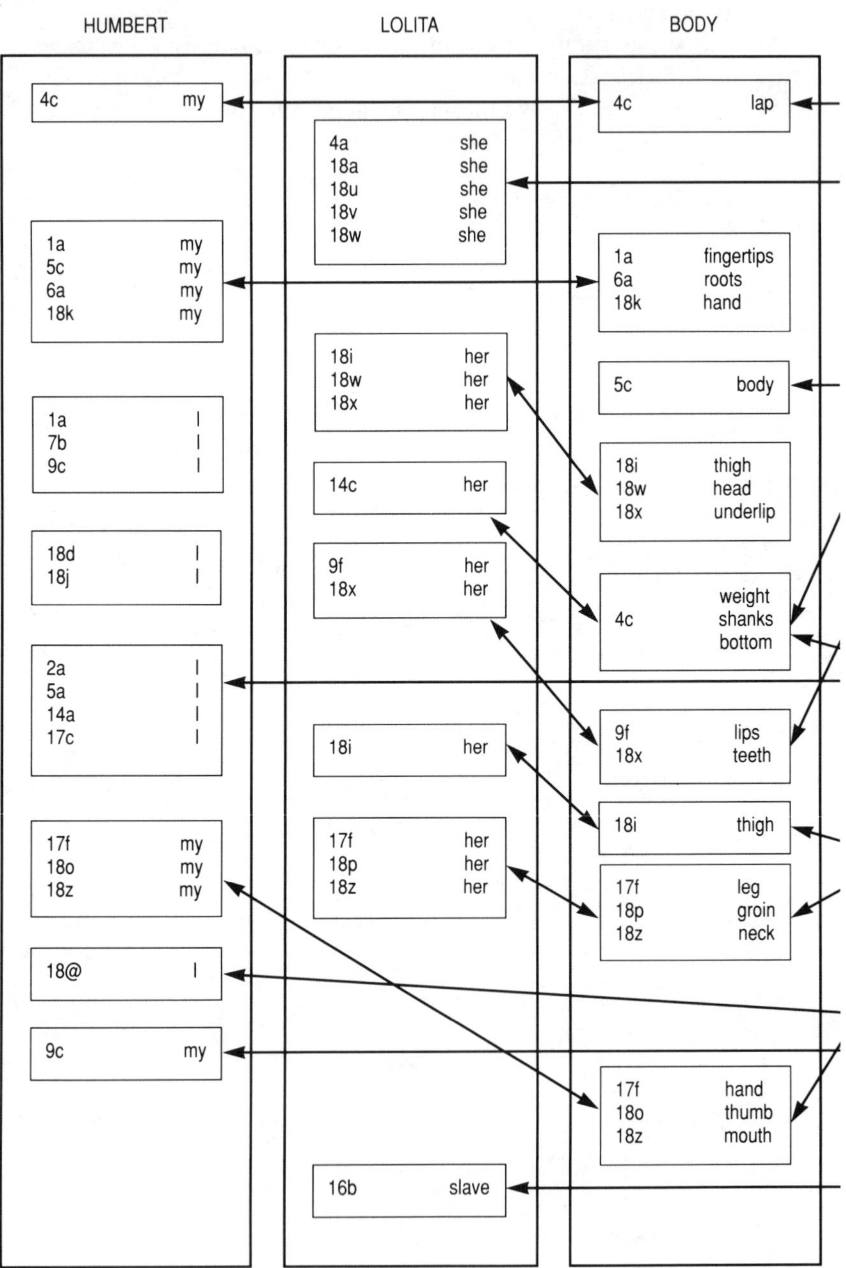

Appendix 2. Lexical Chain Interaction Analysis: *Lolita*

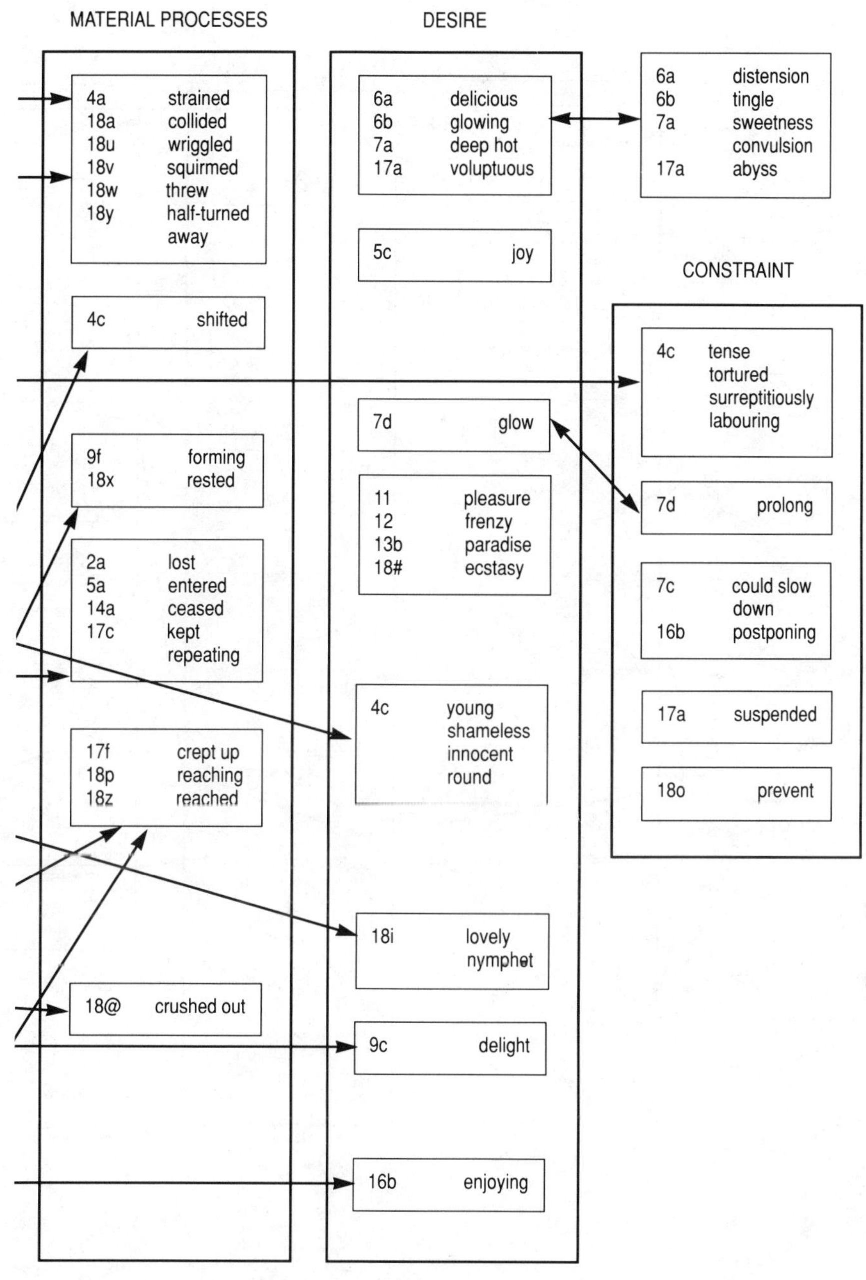
MATERIAL PROCESSES
DESIRE
CONSTRAINT
4a strained
18a collided
18u wriggled
18v squirmed
18w threw
18y half-turned away
4c shifted
9f forming
18x rested
2a lost
5a entered
14a ceased
17c kept repeating
17f crept up
18p reaching
18z reached
18@ crushed out
6a delicious
6b glowing
7a deep hot
17a voluptuous
5c joy
7d glow
11 pleasure
12 frenzy
13b paradise
18# ecstasy
4c young shameless innocent round
18i lovely nymphet
9c delight
16b enjoying
6a distension
6b tingle
7a sweetness
convulsion
17a abyss
4c tense tortured surreptitiously labouring
7d prolong
7c could slow down
16b postponing
17a suspended
18o prevent

Appendix 3

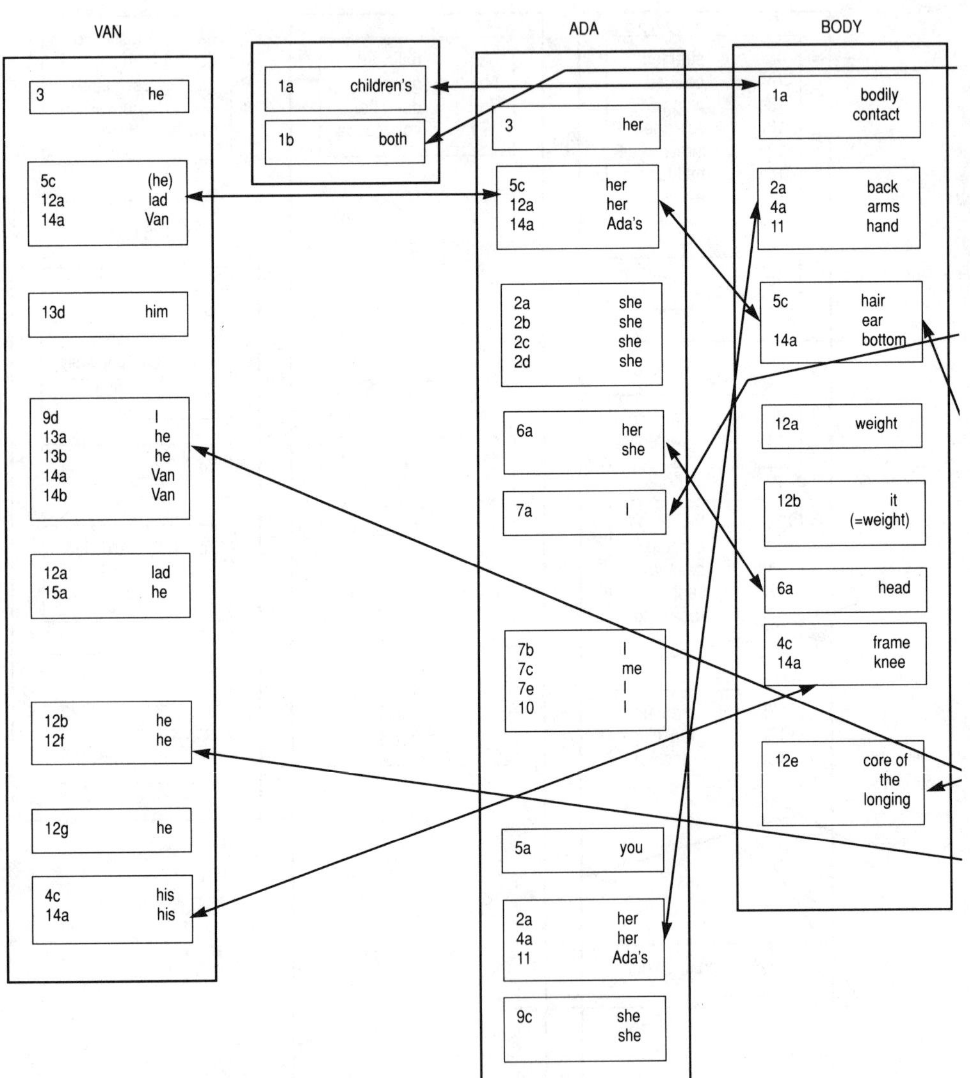

Appendix 3. Lexical Chain Interaction: *Ada*

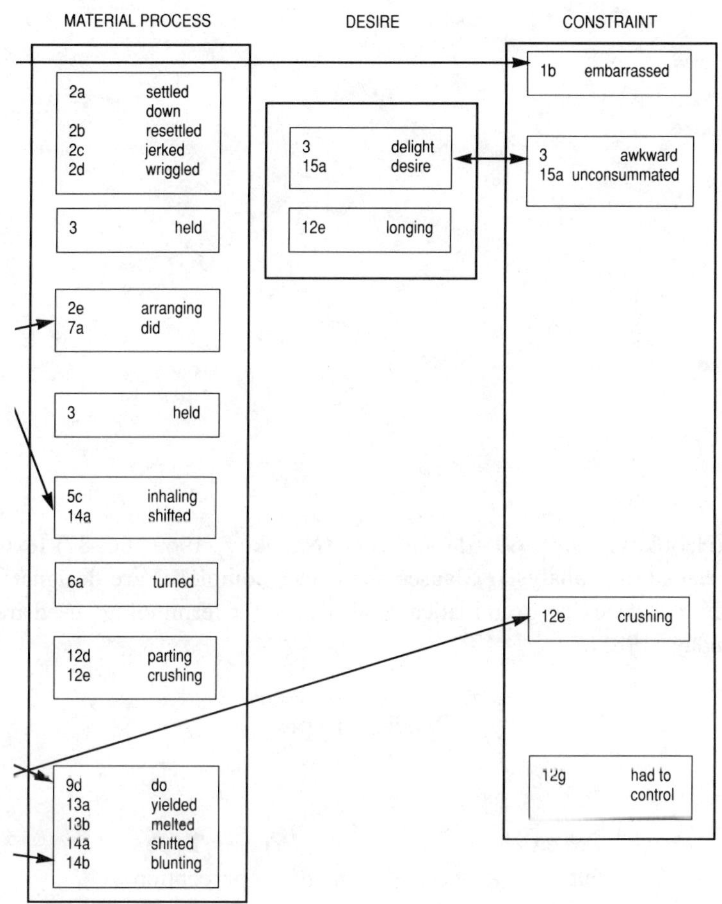
MATERIAL PROCESS
DESIRE
CONSTRAINT
1b embarrassed
2a settled down
2b resettled
2c jerked
2d wriggled
3 delight
15a desire
3 awkward
15a unconsummated
3 held
12e longing
2e arranging
7a did
3 held
5c inhaling
14a shifted
6a turned
12e crushing
12d parting
12e crushing
12g had to control
9d do
13a yielded
13b melted
14a shifted
14b blunting

Appendix 4

Lolita (Nabokov, 1959: 60–61) and *Ada* (Nabokov, 1969: 86–87) textual excerpts; clause rank analysis. Clauses and clause complexes are designated as in Appendix 1. The lexico-grammatical analysis and the terminology used are based on Halliday (1985).

Process Types

Lolita

Clause	Token	Process Type
1a	felt	mental : perception
1b	bristle	material : action
2a	lost	material : action
2b	hung	material : action
3a	stay	material : action
3b	stay	material : action
4a	strained	material : action
4b	to chuck	material : action
4c	shifted	material : action
4d	came over	material : action (metaphorical)
5a	entered	material : action (metaphorical)
5b	mattered	relational : attributive

5c	brewed	material : action (metaphorical)
6a	had begun	material : action
6b	became	relational : identifying
6c	had reached	material : action
6d	found	material : action (nonfinite)
7a	established	material : action (nonfinite)
7b	felt	mental : perception
7c	slow down	material : action
7d	to prolong	material : action (nonfinite)
8	had been	relational : attributive
9a	pulsated	material : action
9b	were	relational : attributive
9c	watched	behavioral : action
9d	minor clause	
9e	minor clause	
9f	were forming	material : action
9g	reached	material : action (metaphorical)
10	was	relational : attributive
11	had been laid	material : action
12	were entering	material : action
13a	would suffice	relational : attributive
13b	to set	material : action (nonfinite)
14a	had ceased	material : action
14b	to be	relational : identifying (nonfinite)
14c	clasping	material : action (nonfinite)
14d	would kick	material : action
15	was	relational : attributive
16a	was	relational : identifying
16b	postponing	material : action (nonfinite)
17a	suspended	material : action (nonfinite)
17b	minor clause	
17c	kept repeating	behavioral : action
17d	talking	verbal (nonfinite)
17e	laughing	behavioral : action (nonfinite)
17f	crept	material : action
17g	allowed	behavioral
18a	had collided	material : action
18b	look	behavioral : action
18c	look	behavioral : action
18d	gasped	behavioral : action
18e	look	behavioral : action
18f	've done	material : action

18g	've done	material : action
18h	look	behavioral : action
18i	was	existential
18j	swear	verbal
18k	massaged	material : action
18l	enveloped	material : action
18m	seemed	relational : attributive
18n	to be	relational (nonfinite)
18o	to prevent	material : action (nonfinite)
18p	reaching	material : action (nonfinite)
18q	tickle	material : action
18r	caress	material : action
18s	's	relational : identifying
18t	cried	verbal
18u	wriggled	material : action
18v	squirmed	material : action
18w	threw	material : action
18x	rested	material : action
18y	half-turned	material : action
18z	reached	material : action
18@	crushed	material : action
18#	had known	mental : cognition

76 clauses; 13 nonfinite; 3 minor:

action	material	= 45 (9 nonfinite)
	behavioral	= 10 (1 nonfinite)
mental		= 3
verbal		= 3 (1 nonfinite)
relational		= 11 (2 nonfinite)
existential		= 1

Ada

Clause	**Token**	**Process Type**
1a	was	relational : identifying
1b	were	relational : attributive
2a	settled down	material : action
2b	resettled	material : action
2c	jerked	material : action
2d	wriggled	material : action
2e	arranging	material : action (nonfinite)
2f	seemed	relational : attributive

2g	to envelop	material : action (nonfinite)
3	held	material : action
4a	moved	material : action
4b	seemed	relational : attributive
4c	to continue	material : action (nonfinite)
5a	cry	behavioral : action
5b	asked	verbal
5c	inhaling	behavioral : action (nonfinite)
6a	turned	material : action
6b	looked	behavioral : action
7a	Did	behavioral : action (elliptical)
7b	don't know	mental : cognition
7c	upset	mental : affection
7d	explain	verbal
7e	felt	mental : perception
7f	was	existential
8	minor clause	
9a	'm	relational : attributive
9b	said	verbal
9c	looked away	behavioral : action
9d	'll do	material : action
10	detest	mental : affection
11	minor clause	
12a	relished	mental : reaction
12b	felt	mental : perception
12c	responding	behavioral : action (nonfinite)
12d	parting	material : action (nonfinite)
12e	crushing	material : action (nonfinite)
12f	knew	mental : cognition
12g	control	material : action
12h	perplexed	mental : cognition
13a	would have yielded	material : action
13b	melted	material : action
13c	saved	material : action
13d	addressing	verbal (nonfinite)
14a	shifted	material : action
14b	blunting	material : action (nonfinite)
14c	used to be termed	relational : attributive
15a	watched	behavioral : action
15b	straggle	material : action
15c	drove	material : action

49 clauses; 8 nonfinite; 2 minor; 1 elliptical:

action	material	= 22 (6 nonfinite)
	behavioral	= 6 (2 nonfinite; 1 elliptical)
mental		= 8
verbal		= 4 (1 nonfinite)
relational		= 6
existential		= 1

Both texts make extensive use of action process types (i.e., material and behavioral processes). Furthermore, the proportion of mental, verbal, relational, and existential process types is low in both texts. Overall, material and behavioral action processes occur in the semantic environment of nontransitive Actor-Process or Medium-Process ideational-grammatical relations. When transitives do occur, it is mainly in the semantic environment of either Humbert or Van as semantic Actor or Agent rather than Lolita or Ada. The foregrounding of nontransitive process types emphasizes, in both texts, the linear sequencing of narrative actions and events. However, there is little suggestion that narrative participants act on other participants except in the restricted semantic environment already referred to.

Human Participants

Lolita

Clause	Token
1a	my, I
1b	her
2a	I, myself
2b	Haze
3a	her
3b	her
4a	she
4b	her
4c	her, her, my
4d	my
5a	I
5b	–
5c	my
6a	my
6b	–
6c	–

6d	–
7a	–
7b	I
7c	I
7d	–
8	Lolita
9a	–
9b	we
9c	I, her, my
9d	–
9e	–
9f	her
9g	my
10	–
11	–
12	–
13a	–
13b	–
14a	I
14b	Humbert the Hound
14c	the sad-eyed degenerate cur
14d	him
15	I, my
16a	my, I
16b	his, his
17a	–
17b	–
17c	I, her, my, my
17d	one
17e	his
17f	my, her
17g	–
18a	she
18b	–
18c	–
18d	I
18e	–
18f	you
18g	you, yourself
18h	–
18i	her
18j	I

18k	my
18l	–
18m	her
18n	–
18o	my
18p	her
18q	you
18r	–
18s	–
18t	she, her
18u	she
18v	–
18w	her
18x	her, her
18y	she
18z	my, gentlemen of the jury, her
18@	I, her
18#	man, monster

Ada

Clause	**Token**
1a	the children's
1b	both
2a	she, Van, her
2b	–
2c	–
2d	–
2e	her
2f	–
2g	him
3	he, her
4a	her, her
4b	–
4c	his
5a	you
5b	he
5c	her, her
6a	She, her
6b	him
7a	I

7b	I
7c	me
7d	I
7e	I
7f	–
8	–
9a	I
9b	he
9c	she
9d	I, your
10	I
11	Ada's
12a	his, the boiling and brimming lad, her
12b	he
12c	–
12d	–
12e	–
12f	he
12g	he
12h	her
13a	he
13b	–
13c	the girl's governess
13d	him
14a	Poor Van, Ada's, his
14b	–
14c	–
15a	he
15b	–
15c	–

The *Lolita* text contains sixty-eight nominal groups referring to human participants. Thirteen of these directly encode the speaking role of Humbert in the first-person pronoun *I*. Lolita is referred to only three times as addressee with the second-person pronouns *you* and *yourself*. There are eight occurrences of third-person pronoun tokens which directly encode Lolita as a character in the narrative. Thirteen nominalizations metaphorically encode the fictive speaker of the text as a deictic of possession in the nominal group (e.g., ***my** glancing fingertips, **my** innermost roots*); a further thirteen nominalizations similarly encode Lolita as character (e.g., ***her** abolished apple, **her** lovely nymphet thigh*). Those metaphorically encoding the speaking-I tend to refer to the character's actions and desires with respect to Lolita; those referring to Lolita tend to refer to her body as object or goal of these actions and desires (e.g., ***her** shameless innocent shanks,* ***her** left-buttock*). There are three instances of proper names and seven instances of nominalizations that refer to the speaker/narrator in the third person. A further nominalization refers to the intradiagetic addressee (i.e., *gentlemen of the jury*).

The *Ada* text contains forty-five nominal groups referring to human participants. Fifteen of these directly encode the character roles of Van and Ada in the third person. There are thirteen nominalizations that metaphorically encode these same character roles as deictics of possession in the nominal group (e.g., ***her** ample pine-smelling skirt,* ***his** own frame*). As in the *Lolita* text, there is the same tendency for these to encode Van as acting and desiring subject (e.g., *the boiling and brimming lad*) and Ada as goal of Van's actions and desires (e.g., *her weight*). Overall, this tendency is less pronounced than in the *Lolita* text, becoming more so in clauses 12a through 14a. The major difference between the two texts has to do with the encoding of the speaker in the first-person pronoun. This is totally skewed in favor of Humbert's narrating and confessing roles in the *Lolita* text, whereas it is confined to Ada's dialogic interruption in the *Ada* text. There are four nominalized participants and four proper names. Ada is encoded eight times as speaker by the first-person pronoun *I;* once as first-person Senser in the first-person pronoun *me;* and once as addressee in the second-person pronoun *you.* All these occur in Ada's dialogic interruption (i.e., clauses 7a to 10).

Tense

Lolita

Clause	**Token**	**Tense**
1a	felt	simple past
1b	bristle	nonfinite
2a	lost	simple past
2b	hung	simple past
3a	let . . . stay	simple present
3b	let . . . stay	simple present
4a	strained	simple past
4b	to chuck	nonfinite
4c	shifted	simple past
4d	came over	simple past
5a	entered	simple past
5b	mattered	simple past
5c	brewed	simple past

6a	had begun	past-in-past
6b	became	simple past
6c	had reached	past-in-past
6d	found	nonfinite
7a	established	nonfinite
7b	felt	simple past
7c	could slow down	modal operator
7d	to prolong	nonfinite
8	had been solipsized	past-in-past
9a	pulsated	simple past
9b	were	simple past
9c	watched	simple past
9d	–	
9e	–	
9f	were	simple past
9g	reached	simple past
10	was	simple past
11	had been laid	past-in-past
12	were entering	present-in-past
13a	would suffice	modal operator
13b	to set	nonfinite
14a	had ceased	past-in-past
14b	to be	nonfinite
14c	clasping	nonfinite
14d	would kick	modal operator
15	was	simple past
16a	was	simple past
16b	postponing	nonfinite
17a	suspended	nonfinite
17b	–	
17c	kept repeating	present-in-past
17d	talking	nonfinite
17e	laughing	nonfinite
17f	crept	simple past
17g	allowed	simple past
18a	had collided	past-in-past
18b	look	present
18c	look	present
18d	gasped	simple past
18e	look	present
18f	’ve done	past-in-present
18g	’ve done	past-in-present

18h	look	present
18i	was	simple past
18j	swear	nomic present
18k	massaged	simple past
18l	enveloped	simple past
18m	seemed	simple past
18n	to be	nonfinite
18o	to prevent	nonfinite
18p	reaching	nonfinite
18q	might tickle	modal operator
18r	(might) caress	modal operator
18s	's	simple present
18t	cried	simple past
18u	wriggled	simple past
18v	squirmed	simple past
18w	threw	simple past
18x	rested	simple past
18y	half-turned	simple past
18z	reached	simple past
18@	crushed	simple past
18#	had known	past-in-past

Ada

Clause	**Token**	**Tense**
1a	was	simple past
1b	were	simple past
2a	settled down	simple past
2b	resettled	simple past
2c	jerked	simple past
2d	wriggled	simple past
2e	arranging	nonfinite
2f	seemed	simple past
2g	to envelop	nonfinite
3	held	simple past
4a	moved	simple past
4b	seemed	simple past
4c	to continue	nonfinite
5a	did . . . cry	simple past
5b	asked	simple past
5c	inhaling	nonfinite
6a	turned	simple past

6b	looked at	simple past
7a	Did	simple past
7b	don't know	simple present
7c	upset	simple present
7d	can't explain	modal operator
7e	felt	simple past
7f	was	simple past
8	–	
9a	'm	simple present
9b	said	simple past
9c	looked away	simple past
9d	'll . . . do	future
10	detest	simple present
11	–	
12a	relished	simple past
12b	felt	simple past
12c	responding	nonfinite
12d	parting	nonfinite
12e	crushing	nonfinite
12f	knew	simple past
12g	had to control	modal operator
12h	perplexed	subjunctive
13a	would have yielded	modal operator
13b	(would have) melted	modal operator
13c	had not . . . saved	subjunctive
13d	addressing	nonfinite
14a	shifted	simple past
14b	blunting	nonfinite
14c	used to be termed	simple past
15a	watched	simple past
15b	straggle	nonfinite
15c	drove	simple past

Both excerpts predominantly select the simple past as the primary tense in each clause. This emphasizes the foregrounded concern with the narration of actions and events, reinforced by the occurrence of these tense selections in the semantic environment of predominantly material and behavioral process types. The semantic orientation of these selections is toward the construction of a fictive narrative situation. The occurrence of nonfinite elements is worth noting. Of the seventy-six tokens in the *Lolita* text, thirteen are nonfinite. Similarly, the *Ada* text has some forty-seven tokens, of which eight are nonfinite. This is, overall, a minor pattern. However, their occurrence in the environment of nontransitive action process types further reinforces the relatively indeterminate semantic status of many of the selections that realize Van/Humbert discourse. Nonfinite elements are indeterminate with respect to primary tense, modality, and polarity, thereby contributing to the lack of semantic explicitness of many of the processes associated with Van/Humbert discourse in both passages.

Experiential Metaphor

Lolita

Clause	Token
1a	my glancing fingertips (verbal classifier)
4b	her abolished apple (verbal classifier)
4c	my tense, tortured surreptitiously labouring lap (verbal classifier)
4d	a mysterious change came over my senses (material process incongruently encodes mental process)
5a	I entered a plane of being (material process incongruently encodes mental process)
5c	the infusion of joy (derived verbal noun)
6a	a delicious distension (derived verbal noun)
6b	a glowing tingle (verbal classifier)
7d	the glow (underived verbal noun)
9a	the implied sun (verbal classifier)
"	the supplied poplars (verbal classifier)
9c	my controlled delight (verbal classifier)
9f	her lips were still forming the words (material process incongruently encodes verbal process)
9g	consciousness (nominalized abstraction)
15	ridicule (derived verbal noun)
"	retribution (derived verbal noun)
16a	my self-made seraglio (verbal classifier)
"	consciousness (nominalized abstraction)
18r	a giggling child (verbal classifier)
18x	her glistening underlip (verbal classifier)
18z	my moaning mouth (verbal classifier)

Ada

Clause	Token
1a	the children's first bodily contact (underived verbal noun)
2e	her ample pine-smelling skirt (verbal classifier)

3	delight (underived verbal noun)
9d	your presence (nominalized abstraction)
12a	the boiling and brimming lad (verbal classifier)
12e	the longing (derived verbal noun)
15a	unconsummated desire (verbal classifier, underived verbal noun)

The two texts show a high degree of nominalization of verb processes. This is a form of grammatical metaphor (Halliday, 1985: chap. 10), whereby verbal processes are metaphorically (or incongruently) encoded as nominals. This process of nominalization means that the semantics of these verb processes is more abstract, less iconic with respect to the transitivity relations of the verb processes they metaphorically encode. There is therefore a lack of precise indexical specification of their process-participant relations. This would not be the case were these nonmetaphorically (or congruently) encoded as verbal processes and nominal participants in the ideational-grammatical semantics of the clause. Some examples of this pattern include verbal classifiers in the nominal group (e.g., *my **glancing** fingertips, my **controlled** delight*), derived verbal nouns (e.g., *the **infusion** of joy, **ridicule***), and nominalized abstractions (e.g., ***consciousness***).

Clause Complex Relations

Lolita

Clause	**Clause Complex Relation**
2a	
	hypotactic elaboration
2b	
4a	
	hypotactic elaboration
4b	
	paratactic extension
4c	
	paratactic extension
4d	
5a	
	hypotactic enhancement
5b	
	hypotactic enhancement
5c	
6a	
	paratactic extension
6b	
	hypotactic elaboration
6c	
	hypotactic elaboration
6d	

7a
paratactic extension
7b
expansion : idea
7c
hypotactic elaboration
7d
9a
paratactic elaboration
9b
paratactic extension
9c
paratactic elaboration
9d
paratactic elaboration
9e
paratactic enhancement
9f
embedding
9g
13a
hypotactic elaboration
13b
14a
hypotactic elaboration
14b
hypotactic elaboration
14c
hypotactic elaboration
14d
16a
hypotactic elaboration
16b
17a
hypotactic elaboration
17b
paratactic extension
17c
hypotactic enhancement
17d
paratactic extension
17e
hypotactic enhancement
17f
hypotactic enhancement
17g
18a
paratactic extension
18b
paratactic extension
18c
locution : quote
18d
locution : quote
18e
hypotactic elaboration
18f
paratactic extension

18g
paratactic extension
18h
hypotactic enhancement
18i
hypotactic locution (report)
18j
hypotactic elaboration
18k
paratactic extension
18l
paratactic elaboration
18m
hypotactic elaboration
18n
hypotactic elaboration
18o
embedding
18p
paratactic elaboration
18q
paratactic extension
18r
paratactic extension
18s
paratactic locution
18t
paratactic extension
18u
paratactic extension
18v
paratactic extension
18w
paratactic extension
18x
hypotactic enhancement
18y
paratactic extension
18z
hypotactic extension
18@
hypotactic elaboration
18#

Ada

Clause **Token**
1a
paratactic elaboration
1b
2a
paratactic extension
2b
hypotactic enhancement
2c
paratactic extension
2d
paratactic elaboration
2e
hypotactic elaboration

2f
4a
paratactic elaboration
4b
hypotactic elaboration
4c
5a
paratactic locution
5b
hypotactic extension
5c
6a
paratactic extension
6b
7a
paratactic extension
7b
paratactic elaboration
7c
paratactic elaboration
7d
paratactic extension
7e
hypotactic idea (report)
7f
9a
paratactic locution (quote)
9b
hypotactic enhancement
9c
paratactic extension
9d
12a
hypotactic enhancement
12b
embedding
12c
hypotactic elaboration
12d
paratactic extension
12e
hypotactic elaboration
12f
hypotactic idea (report)
12g
hypotactic enhancement
12h
13a
paratactic extension
13b
hypotactic enhancement
13c
hypotactic elaboration
13d
14a
hypotactic extension
14b
hypotactic elaboration

14c	
15a	embedding
15b	hypotactic enhancement
15c	

Paratactic clause complex relations entail relations of equal status between two clauses in a clause complex. The two clauses are able to stand independently of each other. Hypotaxis involves relations between clauses of unequal status, whereby one element is dependent on the other (see Halliday, 1985: 195). Paratactic clause complex relations may contribute to linear narrative sequencing, whereas hypotactic relations have to do with complex relations of qualification and interdependence between clauses. There is then less emphasis on linear, additive sequencing and more emphasis on abstract logical relations. In the two texts, parataxis tends to occur in the environment of Ada/Lolita as semantic Actor. Hypotaxis occurs more strongly in the environment of Van/Humbert as semantic Actor. These amount to no more than tendencies rather than rigidly defined distinctions. In general, hypotaxis occurs more frequently in clauses associated with Van/Humbert.

Modality and Modulation

Lolita

Clause	Token	Modality/Modulation
1a	felt	indicative : certain/subjective : explicit
2a	lost	indicative : certain/subjective : explicit
2b	hung about	indicative : certain/objective : explicit
3a/b	stay	imperative
4a	strained	indicative : certain/objective : implicit
4c	shifted	indicative : certain/objective : implicit
4d	came over	indicative : certain/subjective : implicit
5a	entered	indicative : certain/subjective : explicit
5b	mattered	indicative : certain/objective : implicit

5c	brewed	indicative : certain/objective : implicit
6a	had begun	indicative : certain/objective : implicit
6b	became	indicative : certain/objective : implicit
6c	had reached	indicative : certain/objective : implicit
7b	felt	indicative : probable/subjective explicit
7c	could slow down	modulation : oblique/permission : ability
8	had been solipsized	indicative : certain/objective : implicit
9a	pulsated	indicative : certain/objective : implicit
9b	were	indicative : certain/subjective : explicit
9c	watched	indicative : certain/subjective : explicit
9f	were apparently	indicative : probable/objective : implicit
9g	reached	indicative : certain/objective : implicit
10	was	indicative : certain/objective : implicit
11	had been laid	indicative : certain/objective : implicit
12	were entering	indicative : certain/objective : implicit
13	would suffice	modality : oblique/probable : implicit
14a	had ceased	indicative : certain/objective : implicit
14d	would kick	modality : oblique/probable : implicit
15	was	indicative : certain/objective : implicit
16a	was	indicative : certain/objective : implicit
17c	kept repeating	indicative : certain/objective : implicit
17f	crept up	indicative : certain/objective : implicit

17g	allowed	modulation : obligation/objective : implicit
18a	had collided	indicative : certain/objective : implicit
18b/c	look	imperative
18d	gasped	indicative : certain/objective : implicit
18e	look	imperative
18f	've done	indicative : certain/objective : implicit
18g	've done	indicative : certain/objective : implicit
18h	look	imperative
18i	was	indicative : certain/objective : implicit
18j	swear	indicative : certain/subjective : explicit
18k	massaged	indicative : certain/objective : implicit
18l	enveloped	indicative : certain/objective : implicit
18m	seemed	modality : probable/objective : explicit
18q	might tickle	modality : probable/subjective : implicit
18r	(might) caress	modality : probable/subjective : implicit
18s	's	indicative : certain/objective : implicit
18t	cried	indicative : certain/objective : implicit
18u	wriggled	indicative : certain/objective : implicit
18v	squirmed	indicative : certain/objective : implicit
18w	threw	indicative : certain/objective : implicit
18x	rested	indicative : certain/objective : implicit
18y	half-turned	indicative : certain/objective : implicit

18z	reached	indicative : certain/objective : implicit
18@	crushed	indicative : certain/objective : implicit
18#	had known	indicative : certain/objective : implicit

Ada

Clause	**Token**	**Modality/Modulation**
1a	was	indicative : certain/objective : explicit
1b	were	indicative : certain/objective : implicit
2a	settled down	indicative : certain/objective : implicit
2b	resettled	indicative : certain/objective : implicit
2c	jerked	indicative : certain/objective : implicit
2d	wriggled	indicative : certain/objective : implicit
2f	seemed	modality : probable/objective : implicit
3	held	indicative : certain/objective : implicit
4a	moved	indicative : certain/objective : implicit
4b	seemed	modality : probable/objective : implicit
5a	cry	interrogative
5b	asked	indicative : certain/objective : implicit
6a	turned	indicative : certain/objective : implicit
6b	looked at	indicative : certain/objective : implicit
7a	Did	interrogative
7b	don't know	indicative : certain/objective : implicit
7c	upset	indicative : certain/objective : implicit

7d	can't explain	modulation : permission/ability/ subjective : explicit
7e	felt	modality : probable/subjective : explicit
7f	was	indicative : certain/objective : implicit
9a	'm	indicative : certain/objective : implicit
9b	said	indicative : certain/objective : implicit
9c	looked	indicative : certain/objective : implicit
9d	'll do	modulation : willing/subjective : explicit
	never	modality : frequency : categorical
10	detest	indicative : certain/subjective : explicit
12a	relished	indicative : certain/objective : implicit
12b	felt	indicative : certain/objective : implicit
12f	knew	indicative : certain/objective : implicit
12g	had to control	modulation : obligation/objective : implicit
12h	perplexed	subjunctive
13a	would have yielded	modality : probable/subjective implicit
13b	(would have) melted	modality : probable/subjective : implicit
13c	had not saved	subjunctive
14a	shifted	indicative : certain/objective : implicit
14c	used to be	indicative : certain/objective : implicit
15a	watched	indicative : certain/objective : implicit
15b	straggle by	indicative : certain/objective : implicit
15c	drove	indicative : certain/objective : implicit

Note: Dependent clauses do not independently select for Mood, which is contained within the semantic scope of their independent clause.

Interpersonal Lexis

Lolita

Clause	Token	Interpersonal Meaning
1a	my *glancing* fingertips	interpersonal epithet : desire
2a	the pungent but *healthy* heat	interpersonal epithet : desire
4c	her *young* weight	interpersonal epithet : desire
	her *shameless innocent* shanks	interpersonal epithet : desire
	my *tense, tortured,* surreptitiously labouring lap	constraint
5c	the infusion of *joy*	connotative lexis : desire
6a	a *delicious* distension	interpersonal epithet : desire
6b	a *glowing* tingle	interpersonal epithet : desire
7a	the deep hot sweetness	interpersonal epithet/connotative lexis : desire
	the ultimate convulsion	interpersonal epithet/connotative lexis : desire
7d	the glow	connotative lexis : desire
18i	her *lovely nymphet* thigh	interpersonal epithet : desire
18p	the *hot* hollow of her groin	interpersonal epithet : desire
18z	my *moaning* mouth	interpersonal epithet : desire
18#	the longest ecstasy	interpersonal epithet/connotative lexis : desire

Ada

Clause	Token	Interpersonal Meaning
1b	embarrassed	connotative lexis : constraint
3	a trance of awkward *delight*	connotative lexis : desire
7f	something dreadful, brutal, dark	connotative lexis : constraint

12a	the *boiling and brimming* lad	interpersonal epithet : desire
12e	the core of the *longing*	connotative lexis : desire
13b	animal laxity	interpersonal epithet/connotative lexis : desire
15a	the mournful dullness of *unconsummated* desire	constraint

There are very few instances in the two texts where modality or modulation are realized in the verbal group. The main semantic orientation is toward the certain or "high" end of the modal scale (Halliday, 1985: 337). This is reflected in the predominance of declarative clauses in the indicative mood. The predominance of declarative clauses in the environment of action process types and simple past tense reinforces the emphasis on the sequencing of narrative actions and events. However, the low incidence of modality and modulation reinforces the predominantly noninteractive mode. The focus is on objects and participants rather than on their (modal) evaluations of verb processes. Both texts demonstrate a strong tendency toward interpersonal and attitudinal epithets in the nominal group, as well as lexis that connotes interpersonal attitudes, evaluations, and subjective viewpoint. Thus modality is not restricted in its realization to the verbal group but is prosodically interwoven throughout the structure of the clause (Halliday, 1985: 169). The use of interpersonal lexical epithets in the nominal group further enhances the overall focus on deverbal states and their modification.

Theme

The analysis of choices of Theme at clause rank may be summarized as follows:

Lolita:	
experiential	64
interpersonal	8
textual	28
Ada:	
experiential	35
interpersonal	2
textual	16

Of the sixty-four experiential themes in the *Lolita* excerpt, thirteen refer to the first-person pronoun of the narrator; thirteen are circumstantial elements, which frequently contain rank-shifted nominal groups; and a further thirteen are nominal groups. The *Ada* excerpt contains five Themes referring to the first-person pronoun of Ada as speaker in her dialogic interruption; four are circumstantial elements; and a further five are nominal groups. The principal difference between the two texts, as far as the use of experiential Themes goes, has to do with the different distributions of the first-person and third-person pronouns. This is reflected in Humbert's explicit first-person narration, whereas the narrator-I is less explicit in the *Ada* excerpt. Both texts confirm the extensive use of thematized circumstantial elements and nominal groups, many of which contain extensive pre- and postmodification of the Head element. In semantic terms, these factors are interpreted as further reinforcing the tendency to deverbal states rather than actions. The pronounced use of thematized circumstantial elements gives prominence to attributes, qualities, and spatiotemporal relations rather than actions, events, and participants. Some examples from both texts are: *under my glancing fingertips, deep hot sweetness* (Lolita), *in a trance of awkward delight, with his entire being,* and *in the mournful dullness of unconsummated desire* (Ada). The overall proportion of textual Themes is similar in both texts. Furthermore, both texts tend to use the same kinds of textual themes, for example, coordinating conjunctions such as *and, as,* and so on, and *wh-* relatives. The low incidence of interpersonal Themes in both texts further confirms the overall tendency toward a noninteractive mode.

Bibliography

Bibliography

Althusser, Louis. [1970] 1971. "Ideology and ideological state apparatuses (notes towards an investigation)." In *Lenin and Philosophy and Other Essays*. Trans. Ben Brewster, 127–86. London and New York: New Left Books.

Anderson, M., J. Deely, M. Krampen, J. Ransdell, T. Sebeok, and T. von Uexkull. 1984. *A Semiotic Perspective on the Sciences: Steps toward a New Paradigm*. Victoria University, Toronto: Toronto Semiotic Circle Monographs, Working Papers and Prepublications, No. 5.

Austin, J.L. 1962. *How to Do Things with Words*, ed. J. O. Urmson. London: Oxford University Press.

Bakhtin, Mikhail. [1929] 1973. *Problems in Dostoevsky's Poetics*. Trans. R. W. Rotsel. Ann Arbor: Ardis.

——.1981. "Discourse in the novel." In *The Dialogic Imagination: Four Essays by Mikhail Bakhtin*. Trans. Caryl Emerson and Michael Holquist, 258–422. Austin and London: University of Texas Press.

Banfield, Anne. 1973. "Narrative style and the grammar of direct and indirect speech." *Foundations of Language* 10, 1–39.

——.1978a. "The formal coherence of represented speech and thought." *A Journal for Descriptive Poetics and Theory of Literature (PTL)* 3 (2): 289–314.

——.1978b. "Where epistemology, style, and grammar meet literary history: The development of represented speech and thought." *New Literary History* 9 (3): 415–54.

Bateson, Gregory. 1973. *Steps to an Ecology of Mind*. London and New York: Granada.

——.1973a. "The cybernetics of 'self': A theory of alcoholism." In Bateson, 1973: 280–308.

——.1973b. "Cybernetic explanation." In Bateson, 1973: 375–86.

——.1973c. "Style, grace and information in primitive art." In Bateson, 1973: 101–25.

——.1973d. "A theory of play and fantasy." In Bateson, 1973: 150–66.

——.1973e. "Redundancy and coding." In Bateson, 1973: 387–401.

Beaugrande, Robert de. 1978. "Information, expectation, and processing." *Poetics* 7/2: 3–44.

——. 1980. *Text, Discourse, and Process: Toward a Multidisciplinary Science of Texts*. London: Longman.

Benveniste, Emile. 1966. *Problèmes de linguistique générale, 1*. Paris: Gallimard.

Bernstein, Basil. 1971. *Class, Codes and Control*. Vol. 1, *Theoretical studies towards a Sociology of Language*. London and Boston: Routledge & Kegan Paul.

——. 1972. "Social class, language and socialization." In *Language and Social Context*, ed. Pier Paolo Giglioli, 157–78. Harmondsworth: Penguin.

——. [1975] 1977. *Class, Codes and Control*. Vol. 3, *Towards a Theory of Educational Transmissions*. 2nd ed. London and Boston: Routledge & Kegan Paul.

——. 1982. "Codes, modalities and the process of cultural re-production: A model." In *Cultural and Economic Reproduction in Education: Essays on Class, Ideology and the State*, ed. Michael W. Apple, 304–55. London and Boston: Routledge & Kegan Paul.

——. 1986a. "On pedagogic discourse." To appear in *Handbook for Theory and Research in Sociology of Education*, ed. J. Richardson. Westport, Conn.: Greenwood Press.

——. 1986b. "Elaborated and restricted codes: An over-view 1958–1985." To appear in *Handbook in Socio-linguistics and the New Science of Language*, ed. Annol, Ditmar, et al.

Bourdieu, Pierre. [1972] 1977. *Outline of a Theory of Practice*. Trans. Richard Nice. Cambridge and London: Cambridge University Press.

——. 1979. *La distinction. Critique sociale du jugement*. Paris: Editions de Minuit.

Bronzwaer, W. J. M. 1970. *Tense in the Novel: An Investigation of Some Potentialities of Linguistic Criticism*. Groningen: Wolters-Noordhoof.

——. 1975. "A hypothesis concerning deictic time-adverbs in narrative structure." *Journal of Literary Semantics* 4: 53–72.

Broughton, John M. 1981. "Piaget's structural developmental psychology. Part 5. Ideology-critique and the possibility of a critical developmental theory." *Human Development* 24: 382–411.

Buckley, Walter. 1967. *Sociology and Modern Systems Theory*. Englewood Cliffs, N.J.: Prentice-Hall.

Bühler, Karl. 1934. *Sprachtheorie: Die Darstellungsfunktion der Sprache*. Jena: Fischer.

Callinicos, Alex. 1989. *Against Postmodernism: A Marxist Critique*. Cambridge: Polity.

Callon, Michel, and Bruno Latour. 1981. "Unscrewing the big Leviathan: How actors macro-structure reality and how sociologists help them to do so." In *Advances in Social Theory and Methodology. Toward an Integration of Micro- and Macro-Sociologies*, ed. K. Knorr-Cetina and A. V. Cicourel, 277–303. Boston and London: Routledge & Kegan Paul.

Chafe, Wallace. 1970. *Meaning and the Structure of Language*. Chicago and London: University of Chicago Press.

Charniak, E. 1977. "A frame PAINTING: The representation of a commonsense knowledge fragment." *Cognitive Science* 1: 355–94.

Chateaubriand, François René de. [1826] 1926. *Atala. René, les aventures du dernier Abencérage*, ed. Fernand Letessier. Paris: Garnier.

Chilton, Paul. 1983. "Self-critical linguistics." *Network*, no. 5: 34.

Chomsky, Noam. 1965. *Aspects of the Theory of Syntax*. Cambridge, Mass.: MIT Press.

Colby, Benjamin N., and Lore M. Colby, 1981. *The Daykeeper: The Life and Discourse of an Ixil Diviner*. Cambridge, Mass., and London: Harvard University Press.

Coseriu, Eugenio. 1973. *Lezioni di Linguistica Generale*. Turin: Boringhieri.

——. 1981. *Sincronia, diacronia e storia. Il problema del cambio linguistico*. Trans. Paola Mura. Turin: Editore Boringhieri.

Culler, Jonathan, 1983. *On Deconstruction: Theory and Criticism after Structuralism*. London: Routledge & Kegan Paul.

Derrida, Jacques. [1967] 1974. *Of Grammatology*. Trans. Gayatri Chakravorty Spivak. Baltimore and London: Johns Hopkins University Press.

——. 1978. "Structure, sign, and play in the discourse of the human sciences." In *Writing and Difference*, Trans. Alan Bass, 278–93. London and Henley: Routledge & Kegan Paul.

Descartes, René. [1637] 1963. "Discours de la méthode." In *Oeuvres Philosophiques*, vol. 1. Paris: Garnier.

Downes, William J. 1978. "Language, belief and verbal action in an historical process." *UEA Papers in Linguistics* 8: 1–43.

Durkheim, E. 1964. *The Division of Labor in Society*. New York: Free Press.

Eco, Umberto. 1976. *A Theory of Semiotics*. Bloomington and London: Indiana University Press.

——. 1980. "Two problems in textual interpretation." *Poetics Today* 2/1a: 145–61.

——. 1984. *Semiotics and the Philosophy of Language*. London: Macmillan.

Ellis, Jeffrey. 1984. "Some speculations on language contact in a wider setting." In *The Semiotics of Language*, vol. 1, *Language as Social Semiotic*, ed. Robin P. Fawcett, M. A. K. Halliday, Sydney M. Lamb, and Adam Makkai, 81–104. London and Dover, N.H.: Frances Pinter.

Fabbri, Paolo, and Sbisà, Marina. 1982. "Modelli (?) dell'analisi pragmatica." *Ideologia, Filosofia e Linguistica*, 595–622. Atti del Convegno Internazionale di Studi Rende (CS), September 15–17, 1978. Società di Linguistica Italiana: 19/II. Rome: Bulzoni.

Fillmore, Charles. 1968. "The case for case." In *Universals of Linguistic Theory*, ed. E. Bach and R. T. Harms, 1–88. New York: Holt, Rinehart & Winston.

——. 1977. "The case for case re-opened." *Syntax and Semantics* 8: 59–81.

Firth, J. R. 1957. *Papers in Linguistics 1934–1951*. London and New York: Oxford University Press.

——. 1968. *Selected Papers of J. R. Firth*, ed. F. R. Palmer. London: Longman.

Foucault, Michel. 1971. "The discourse on language." Trans. Rupert Swyer. *Social Science Information*, April 1971, 7–30.

——. [1969] 1974. *The Archaeology of Knowledge*. Trans. A. M. Sheridan Smith. London: Tavistock.

——. [1976] 1978. *The History of Sexuality*. Vol. 1, *An Introduction*. Trans. Robert Hurley. Harmondsworth: Penguin Books.

——. [1984] 1986. *The History of Sexuality*. Vol. 2, *The Use of Pleasure*. Trans. Robert Hurley. New York: Vintage Books.

Frow, John. 1986. *Marxism and Literary History*. Oxford: Basil Blackwell.

Galimberti, Umberto. 1983. *Il corpo. Antropologia, psicoanalisi, fenomenologia*. (Con un saggio di Eugenio Borgna [with an essay by Eugenio Borgna]). Milan: Feltrinelli.

Genette, Gérard. 1972. *Figures III*. Paris: du Seuil.

Giovanni, Parisio di. 1984. *Il mondo sommerso della comunicazione. L'ingresso in casa di riposo*. Montesilvano: Edizioni dell'Istituto di Ricerca sulla Comunicazione.

——. 1988. "The prospect of a psychology of communication." *Schemi di Lavoro. Rivista di comunicazione umana/Journal of Human Communication* 12: 65–101.

Grabes, H. 1977. *Fictitious Biographies: Vladimir Nabokov's English Novels*. The Hague and Paris: Mouton.

Gramsci, Antonio. [1918] 1972. "La lingua unica e l'Esperanto." In *Il Grido del Popolo*, February 16, 1918. Reprinted in *Scritti Giovanili: 1914–1918.* Turin.

——. 1977a. "Storicità della filosofia della prassi." In *Il materialismo storico e la filosofia di Benedetto Croce,* 115–18. (New integrated edition). Turin: Editori Riuniti.

——. 1977b. "Note per una introduzione allo studio della grammatica." In *Letteratura e vita nazionale*, 247–57. (New integrated edition). Turin: Editori Riuniti.

——. 1977c. "Il linguaggio, le lingue, il senso comune." In *Il materialismo storico e la filosofia di Benedetto Croce*, 29–32. (New integrated edition). Turin: Editori Riuniti.

——. 1977d. "Che cosa l'uomo." In *Il materialismo storico e la filosofia di Benedetto Croce,* 32–42. (New integrated edition). Turin: Editori Riuniti.

——. 1977e. "Concetto di 'ideologia'." In *Il materialismo storico e la filosofia di Benedetto Croce*, 57–59. (New integrated edition). Turin: Editori Riuniti.

——. 1977f. "La proposizione che 'la società non si pone problemi per la cui soluzione non esistano già le premesse materiali'." In *Note sul Machiavelli sulla politica e sullo stato moderno*, 100–102. (New integrated edition). Turin: Editori Riuniti.

——. 1977g. "Linguistica." In *Letteratura e vita nazionale*, 258–64. (New integrated edition). Turin: Editori Riuniti.

Habermas, Jürgen. [1981] 1984. *The Theory of Communicative Action*. Vol. 1, *Reason and the Rationalization of Society*. Trans. Thomas McCarthy. London: Heinemann.

——. 1985. "Modernity–an incomplete project." In *Postmodern Culture*, ed. Hal Foster, 3–15. London and Sydney: Pluto Press.

——. [1985] 1987. *The Philosophical Discourse of Modernity: Twelve Lectures*. Trans. Frederick Lawrence. Cambridge: MIT Press.

——. 1987a. "On the obsolescence of the production paradigm." In Habermas, 1987: 75–82.

——. 1987b. "An alternative way out of the philosophy of the subject: Communicative versus subject-centered reason." In Habermas, 1987: 294–326.

——. 1987c. "Some questions concerning the theory of power: Foucault again." In Habermas, 1987: 266–93.

——. [1967] 1988. "On the methodology of the general theories of social action." In *On the Logic of the Social Sciences*. Trans. Shierry Weber Nicholson and Jerry A. Stark, 43–88. Cambridge: Polity.

Halliday, M. A. K. 1969. "Options and functions in the English clause." *Brno Studies in English* 8: 82–88. Reprinted in *Readings in Systemic Linguistics*, ed. M. A. K. Halliday and J. R. Martin, 138–45. London: Batsford, 1981.

——. 1973. "Linguistic function and literary style: An inquiry into the language of William Golding's 'The Inheritors'." In *Explorations in the Functions of Language*, 103–43. London: Edward Arnold.

——. [1961] 1976a. "Categories of the theory of grammar." In *Halliday: System and Function in Language*, ed. Gunther Kress, 52–72. London: Oxford University Press.

——. [1966] 1976b. "Lexical relations." In *Halliday: System and Function in Language*, ed. Gunther Kress, 73–83. London: Oxford University Press.

——. 1978. *Language as Social Semiotic: The Social Interpretation of Language and Meaning*. London: Edward Arnold.

——. 1979. "Modes of meaning and modes of expression: Types of grammatical structure and their determination by different semantic functions." In *Function and Context in Linguistic Analysis: A Festschrift for William Haas*, ed. D. J. Allerton, Edward Carney, and David Holdcroft, 57–79. Cambridge and London: Cambridge University Press.

——. 1981. "Types of structure." In *Readings in Systemic Linguistics*, ed. M. A. K. Halliday and J. R. Martin, 29–41. London: Batsford.

——. 1982. "The de-automatization of grammar: From Priestley's *An Inspector Calls*." In *Language Form and Linguistic Variation: Papers Dedicated to Angus McIntosh*, ed. John Anderson, 129–59. Amsterdam: John Benjamins.

——. 1983. "On the ineffability of grammatical categories." In *The Third LACUS Forum 1983*, ed. Alan Manning, Pierre Martin, and Kim McCalla, 3–18. Columbia, S.C.: Hornbeam Press.

——. 1985. *An Introduction to Functional Grammar*. London: Edward Arnold.

——. 1987. "Language and the order of nature." In *The Linguistics of Writing*, ed. D. Attridge, A. Durant, N. Fabb, and C. MacCabe, 135–54. Manchester: Manchester University Press.

Halliday, M. A. K., and Ruqaiya Hasan. 1976. *Cohesion in English*. London: Longman.

Halliday, M. A. K., and J. R. Martin, eds. 1981. *Readings in Systemic Linguistics*. London: Batsford.

Hammersley, Martyn, and Paul Atkinson. 1983. *Ethnography: Principles in Practice*. London and New York: Tavistock.

Harré, Rom. 1983. *Personal Being. A Theory for Individual Psychology*. Oxford: Basil Blackwell.

Harris, Roy. 1981. *The Language Myth*. London: Duckworth.

Hasan, Ruqaiya. 1973. "Code, register and social dialect." In *Class, Codes and Control*, vol. 2, *Applied Studies Towards a Sociology of Language*, ed. Basil Bernstein, 253–92. London: Routledge & Kegan Paul.

——. 1978. "Text in the systemic-functional model." In *Current Trends in Textlinguistics*, ed. Wolfgang Dressler, 230–46. Berlin: Walter de Gruyter.

——. 1980. "The texture of a text." In *Text and Context: Aspects of Language in a Social Semiotic Perspective*, M. A. K. Halliday and R. Hasan, 43–59. Sophia Linguistica, Working Papers in Linguistics, no. 6. Tokyo: Sophia University.

——. 1984. "Coherence and cohesive harmony." In *Understanding Reading Comprehension*, ed. J. Flood, 181–219. Newark, Del.: International Reading Association.

——. 1986. "The ontogenesis of ideology: An interpretation of mother-child talk." In *Language Semiotics Ideology*, ed. E. A. Grosz, Gunther Kress, M. A. K. Halliday, and Terry Threadgold, 125–46. University of Sydney: Studies in Society and Culture, no. 3.

——. 1987a. "Directions from structuralism." In *The Linguistics of Writing*, ed. D. Attridge, A. Durant, N. Fabb, and C. MacCabe, 103–23. Manchester: University of Manchester Press.

——. 1987b. "The grammarian's dream: Lexis as most delicate grammar." In *New Developments in Systemic Linguistics, vol. 1, Theory and Description*, ed. M. A. K. Halliday and Robin Fawcett, 184–211. London and New York: Frances Pinter.

Henriques, Julian, et al. 1984. *Changing the Subject: Psychology, Social Regulation and Subjectivity*. London and New York: Methuen.

Hirst, Paul. 1976. *Social Evolution and Sociological Categories*. London: Allen & Unwin.

Hirst, Paul, and Penny Woolley. 1982. *Social Relations and Human Attributes*. London and New York: Tavistock.

Hjelmslev, Louis. [1943] 1961. *Prolegomena to a Theory of Language*. Trans. Francis J. Whitfield. Revised English edition. Madison and London: University of Wisconsin Press.

Hodge, R., and G. Kress. 1979. *Language as Ideology*. London and Boston: Routledge & Kegan Paul.

Hollway, Wendy. 1984. "Gender difference and the production of subjectivity." In *Changing the Subject*, Julian Henriques et al., 227–63. London and New York: Methuen.

Hunter, Ian. 1982. "The concept of context and the problem of reading." *Southern Review* (Australia) 15 (1): 80–91.

Hymes, Dell. 1981. *"In Vain I Tried to Tell You": Essays in Native American Ethnopoetics*. Philadelphia: University of Pennsylvania Press.

Israel, Joachim. 1979. *The Language of Dialectics and the Dialectics of Language*. Brighton: Harvester Press.

Jakobson, R. 1960. "Linguistics and poetics." In *Style in Language*, ed. T. A. Sebeok, 350–77. Cambridge, Mass.: MIT Press.

Jameson, Fredric. 1981. *The Political Unconscious: Narrative as a Socially Symbolic Act*. London: Methuen.

Keller, Rudi. 1985. "Towards a theory of linguistic change." In *Linguistic Dynamics: Discourses, Procedures and Evolution*, ed. Thomas T. Ballmer, 211–37. Berlin and New York: Walter de Gruyter.

Kosok, Michel. 1976. "The systematization of dialectical logic for the study of development and change." *Human Development* 19: 325–50.

Kress, Gunther. 1985a. *Linguistic Processes in Sociocultural Practice*. Deakin University, Victoria: Deakin University Press.

——. 1985b. "Discourses, texts, readers and the pro-nuclear arguments." In *Language and the Nuclear Arms Debate: Nukespeak Today*, ed. Paul Chilton, 65–87. London and Dover, N.H.: Frances Pinter.

——. 1987. "The social production of language: History and the structures of domination." To appear in *Discourse in Society: Functional perspectives*, ed. Peter Fries and Michael Gregory. Norwood, N.J.: Ablex.

Labov, William. 1972. *Language in the Inner City*. Philadelphia: University of Pennsylvania Press.

Lacan, Jacques. [1956] 1968. *Speech and Language in Psychoanalysis*. Trans. Anthony Wilden. Baltimore and London: Johns Hopkins University Press.

Lee, Benjamin. 1985. "The semiotic mediation of ontology." In *Semiotic Mediation: Sociocultural and Psychological Perspectives*, ed. Elizabeth Mertz and Richard J. Parmentier, 99–128. New York and London: Academic Press.

Lemke, Jay L. 1983a. "Classroom communication of science." Final report to the National Science Foundation (U.S.A.). Available as *Research in Education* (ERIC Clearinghouse microfiche/hardcopy) ED 222 346.

——. 1983b. "Thematic analysis: systems, structures, and strategies." *Recherches Sémiotiques/Semiotic Inquiry* 3 (2): 159–87.

——. 1984. *Semiotics and Education*. Victoria University, Toronto: Toronto Semiotic Circle Monographs, Working Papers and Prepublications, no. 2.

——. 1984a. "The formal analysis of instruction." In Lemke, 1984: 23–62.

——. 1984b. "Action, context, and meaning." In Lemke, 1984: 63–93.

——. 1984c. "Making trouble." In Lemke, 1984: 94–150.

——. 1985a. "Textual politics: Heteroglossia, discourse analysis, and social dynamics." School of Education, Brooklyn College, City University of New York. Mimeo.

——. 1985b. "Ideology, intertextuality, and register." In *Systemic Perspectives on Discourse: Selected Theoretical Papers from the Ninth International Systemic Workshop*, ed. J. D. Benson and W. S. Greaves, 275–94. Norwood, N.J.: Ablex.

——. 1988a. "Discourses in conflict: heteroglossia and text semantics." In *Systemic Functional Approaches to Discourse: Selected Papers from the 12th International Systemic Workshop*, ed. J. D. Benson and W. S. Greaves, 29–50. Norwood, N.J.: Ablex.

——. 1988b. "Towards a social semiotics of the material subject." In *Sydney Association for Studies in Society and Culture, Working Papers*, vol. 2, nos. 1–2, 1–17. Sydney: University of Sydney.

Locke, John. [1690] 1965. *Two Treatises of Government*. London: New English Library.

Longacre, Robert E. 1974. "Narrative versus other genre." In *Advances in Tagmemics*, ed. Ruth M. Brend. Amsterdam and London: North-Holland.

Lo Piparo, Franco. 1979. *Lingua intellettuali egemonia in Gramsci*. Rome and Bari: Laterza.

MacCabe, Colin. 1979. "On discourse." *Economy and Society* 8 (3): 279–307.

Malinowski, B. 1923. "The problem of meaning in primitive languages." Supplement 1 in *The Meaning of Meaning*, C. K. Ogden and I. A. Richards, New York: Harcourt Brace and World.

——. 1935. "An ethnographic theory of language." Part 4 of *Coral Gardens and their Magic, 2*. London: Allen & Unwin.

Martin, J. R. 1981. "How many speech acts?" *UEA Papers in Linguistics* 14–15: 52–77.

——. 1984. "Mode chapter." In *English Context: Register and Genre* (manuscript). Department of Linguistics, University of Sydney. Mimeo.

——. 1985a. "Process and text: Two aspects of human semiosis." In *Systemic Perspectives on Discourse: Selected Theoretical Papers from the Ninth International Systemic Workshop*, ed. J. D. Benson and W. S. Greaves, 248–74. Norwood, N.J.: Ablex.

——. 1985b. *Factual Writing: Exploring and Challenging Social Reality*. Deakin University, Victoria: Deakin University Press.

——. 1986. "Grammaticalising ecology: The politics of baby seals and kangaroos." In *Language Semiotics Ideology*, ed. E. A. Grosz, Gunther Kress, M. A. K. Halliday, and Terry Threadgold, 225–67. University of Sydney: Studies in Society and Culture, no. 3.

—— 1987. "Exporting systemic grammar: Ideology, genre and register in functional linguistics." Department of Linguistics, University of Sydney. Seminar paper.

——. 1988. "Grammatical conspiracies in Tagalog: Family, face and fate—with regard to Benjamin Lee Whorf." In *Linguistics in a Systemic Perspective*, ed. J. D. Benson, M. Cummings, and W. S. Greaves. Amsterdam: John Benjamins.

Marx, Karl, and Frederick Engels. [1846] 1969. "Feuerbach. Opposition of the materialistic and idealistic outlook." Chapter 1 of *The German Ideology*. In *Selected Works in Three Volumes*, vol. 1, 16–80. Moscow: Progress.

——. [1848] 1969. "Manifesto of the Communist Party." In *Selected Works in Three Volumes*, vol. 1, 98–137. Moscow: Progress.

——. 1976. *Collected Works*, vol. 5. London: Lawrence & Wishart.

Mason, Bobbie Ann. 1974. *Nabokov's Garden: A Guide to* Ada. Ann Arbor: Ardis.

McKellar, Bruce. 1988. "The place of socio-semiotics in contemporary thought." In *Language Topics: Essays in Honour of Michael Halliday*, vol. 2, ed. Ross Steele and Terry Threadgold, 523–48. Amsterdam: John Benjamins.

Merleau-Ponty, Maurice. [1942] 1983. *The Structure of Human Behavior*. Trans. Alden L. Fisher. Pittsburgh: Duquesne University Press.

Minsky, Marvin. 1975. "Frame-system analysis." In *Thinking: Readings in Cognitive Science*, ed. P. N. Johnson-Laird and P. C. Wason, 335–76. London and Melbourne: Cambridge University Press.

Mouffe, Chantal. 1979. "Hegemony and ideology in Gramsci." In *Gramsci and Marxist Theory*, ed. Chantal Mouffe, 168–204. London: Routledge & Kegan Paul.

Mukarovsky, Jan. 1977. *The Word and Verbal Art: Selected Essays by Jan Mukarovsky*. Trans. and ed. J. Burbank and P. Steiner. New Haven and London: Yale University Press.

Nabokov, Vladimir. [1955] 1959. *Lolita*. London: Weidenfeld & Nicolson.

——. 1969. *Ada or Ardor: A Family Chronicle*. London: Weidenfeld & Nicolson.

——. 1973. *Strong Opinions*. London: Weidenfeld & Nicolson.

Nietzsche, Friedrich. [1886] 1980. "Jenseits von Gute und Böse." In *Sämtliche Werke, kritische Studienausgabe in 15 Bänden*, vol. 5, ed. Giorgio Colli and Mazzino Montinari. Berlin and New York: Walter de Gruyter.

Painter, Clare. 1984. *Into the Mother Tongue: A Case Study in Early Language Development*. London and Dover, N.H.: Frances Pinter.

Parsons, Talcott. 1964. *Social Structure and Personality*. Chicago: Free Press.

Pateman, Trevor. 1981. "Linguistics as a branch of critical theory." *UEA Papers in Linguistics* 14–15: 1–29.

Pêcheux, Michel. [1975] 1982. *Language, Semantics and Ideology*. Trans. Harbans Nagpal. London: Macmillan.

Peirce, C. S. 1974. *Collected Papers*. Vols. 1 and 2, ed. C. Hartshorne and P. Weiss. Cambridge, Mass.: Harvard University Press.

Pike, Kenneth. [1954] 1967. *Language in Relation to a Unified Theory of the Structure of Human Behaviour*. 2nd ed. The Hague: Mouton.

Preve, Costanzo. 1984. *La teoria in Pezzi. La dissoluzione del paradigma teorico operaista in Italia (1976–1983)*. Bari: Edizioni Dedalo.

Prigogine, Ilya. 1976. "Order through fluctuation: Self-organization and social systems." In *Evolution and Consciousness: Human Systems in Transition*, ed. Erich Jantsch and Conrad H. Waddington, 93–133. Reading, Mass.: Addison-Wesley.

Prodi, Giorgio. 1977. *Le basi materiali della significazione*. Milan: Bompiani.

Reddy, Michael J. 1979. "The conduit metaphor – a case of frame conflict in our language about language." In *Metaphor and Thought*, ed. Andrew Ortony, 284–324. Cambridge and London: Cambridge University Press.

Rosch, Eleanor. 1977. "Classification of real-world objects: Origins and representation." In *Thinking: Readings in Cognitive Science*, ed. P. N. Johnson-Laird and P. C. Wason, 212–22. London and New York: Cambridge University Press.

Rossi-Landi, Ferruccio. 1973. *Ideologies of Linguistic Relativity*. The Hague and Paris: Mouton.

Said, Edward. 1985. "Opponents, audiences, constituencies and community." In *Postmodern Culture*, ed. Hal Foster, 135–59. London and Sydney: Pluto Press.

Saussure, Ferdinand de. [1915] 1983. *Course in General Linguistics*. Trans. Roy Harris. London: Duckworth.

Schank, R., and R. Abelson, 1977. *Scripts, Plans, Goals, and Understanding*. Hillsdale, N.J.: Erlbaum.

Silverman, David, and Brian Torode. 1980. *The Material Word: Some Theories of Language and Its Limits*. London and Boston: Routledge & Kegan Paul.

Silverman, Kaja. 1983. *The Subject of Semiotics*. New York and Oxford: Oxford University Press.

Silverstein, Michael. 1979. "Language structure and linguistic ideology." In *The Elements: A Parasession on Linguistic Units and Levels*, ed. Paul R. Clyne, William F. Hanks, and Carol L. Hofbauer, 193–247. Chicago: Chicago Linguistic Society.

——. 1980. "The three faces of 'function': Preliminaries to a psychology of language." In *Proceedings from a Working Conference on the Social Foundations of Language and Thought*, ed. M. Hickmann, 17–38. Chicago: Center for Psychosocial Studies.

——. 1981. "The limits of awareness." Austin, Texas: Southwest Educational Development Laboratory, Sociolinguistic Working Paper, no. 84.

——. 1985a. "The functional stratification of language and ontogenesis." In *Culture, Communication and Cognition: Vygotskian Perspectives*, ed. James V. Wertsch, 205–35. Cambridge and London: Cambridge University Press.

——. 1985b. "Language and the culture of gender: At the intersection of structure, usage, and ideology." In *Semiotic Mediation: Sociocultural and Psychological Perspectives*, ed. Elizabeth Mertz and Richard J. Parmentier, 219–59. New York and London: Academic Press.

Sinnott, Jan Dynda. 1981. "The theory of relativity: A metatheory for development." *Human Development* 24: 293–311.

Sohn-Rethel, Alfred. 1978. *Intellectual and Manual Labour: A Critique of Epistemology*. London: Macmillan.

Therborn, Göran. 1980. *The Ideology of Power and the Power of Ideology*. London: Verso.

Thibault, Paul J. 1984. "Narrative discourse as a multilevel system of communication: Some theoretical proposals concerning Bakhtin's dialogic principle." *Studies in 20th Century Literature* 9 (1): 89–117.

——. 1986. *Text, Discourse, and Context: A Social Semiotic Perspective*. Victoria University, Toronto: Toronto Semiotic Circle Monographs, Working Papers and Prepublications, no. 3.

——. 1986a. "Introduction." In Thibault, 1986: i-v.

——. 1986b. "System and process in a textual syntagm: The social semiotic construction of gender." In Thibault, 1986: 1–25.

——. 1986c. "The cognitive hypothesis: a critical comment." In Thibault, 1986: 26–43.

——. 1986d. "Thematic system analysis and the construction of knowledge and belief in discourse: The headlines in two Italian newspaper texts." In Thibault, 1986: 44–91.

——. 1986e. "The literal meaning hypothesis: A critical comment." In Thibault, 1986: 92–100.

——. 1986f. "Knowing what you're told by the Agony Aunts: language function, gender difference, and the structure of knowledge and belief in the personal columns." In Thibault, 1986: 101–52.

——. 1986g. "Metaphor and political oratory in Ronald Reagan's acceptance speech." In *U.S. Presidential Election 1984: An Interdisciplinary Approach to the Analysis of Political Discourse*, ed. R. M. Bollettieri Bosinelli, 149–68. Bologna: Pitagora Editrice.

——. 1988. "An interview with Michael Halliday." In *Language Topics: Essays in Honour of Michael Halliday*, vol. 2, ed. Ross Steele and Terry Threadgold, 601–27. Amsterdam: John Benjamins.

——. 1989a. "Genres, social action and pedagogy: Towards a critical social semiotic account." *Southern Review* (Australia) 22 (3): 338–62.

——. 1989b. "Grammar, technocracy, and the noun: Technocratic values and cognitive linguistics." *Sixteenth International Systemic Congress*, Helsinki, June 12–16, 1989. To appear in *Recent Systemic and Other Functional Views on Language*. Trends in Linguistics: Studies and Monographs, ed. Eija Ventola. Berlin and New York: Mouton de Gruyter.

Thibault, Paul J., and Theo van Leeuwen. Forthcoming. "Grammar, society, and speech acts: Renewing the connections." Unpublished manuscript.

Threadgold, Terry. 1986a. "Semiotics–ideology–language." In *Language Semiotics Ideology*, ed. E. A. Grosz, Gunther Kress, M. A. K. Halliday, and Terry Threadgold, 15–60. University of Sydney: Studies in Society and Culture, no. 3.

——. 1986b. "The semiotics of Volosinov, Halliday, and Eco." *American Journal of Semiotics* 4 (3–4): 107–42.

——. 1987. "Rossi-Landi's higher dialectical level: Alienation, relativity and ideology." *Il Protagora, anno xxviii*, January-December, IV Series, 81–98. For Ferruccio Rossi-Landi, ed. Susan Petrilli.

——. 1988. "Changing the subject." In *Language Topics: Essays in Honour of Michael Halliday*, vol. 2, ed. Ross Steele and Terry Threadgold, 549–97. Amsterdam: John Benjamins.

——. 1989. "Language as social semiotic: A grammatics for a cryptogrammar." Chapter 18 in *Modern Semiotics/Nyere Semiotik*, ed. Jorgen Dines Johansen and Svend Erik Larsen. Odense, Denmark: Odense University Press.

Urwin, Cathy. 1984. "Power relations and the emergence of language." In *Changing the Subject*, Julian Henriques et al. 264–322. London and New York: Methuen.

van den Daele, Leland D. 1974. "Infrastructure and transition in developmental analysis." *Human Development* 17: 1–23.

——. 1975. "Ego development in dialectical perspective." In *The Development of Dialectical Operations*, ed. Klaus F. Riegel, 129–42. Basel and Munich: Karger.

Volosinov, V. N. [1930] 1973. *Marxism and the Philosophy of Language*. Trans. Ladislav Matejka and I. R. Titunik. New York and London: Seminar Press.

——. [1929] 1980. "La costruzione dell'enunciazione." In *Il linguaggio come pratica sociale*, ed. Augusto Ponzio, 95–133. Bari: Dedalo.

Wertsch, James, and Benjamin Lee. 1984. "The multiple levels of analysis in a theory of action." *Human Development* 27: 193–96.

Whorf, Benjamin Lee. 1956. *Language, Thought and Reality: Selected Writings of Benjamin Lee Whorf*, ed. John B. Carroll. Cambridge, Mass.: MIT Press.

——. [1941] 1956a. "The relation of habitual thought and behavior to language." In Whorf, 1956: 134–59.

——. [1936] 1956b. "A linguistic consideration of thinking in primitive communities." In Whorf, 1956: 65–86.

——. [1938] 1956c. "Some verbal categories of Hopi." In Whorf, 1956: 112–24.

Wilden, Anthony. [1972] 1980. *System and Structure: Essays in Communication and Exchange*. 2nd ed. London: Tavistock.

——. 1981. "Semiotics as praxis: Strategy and tactics." *Recherches Sémiotiques/Semiotic Inquiry* 1 (1): 1–34.

Indexes

Name Index

Subject Index

Theory and History of Literature

Volume 44. Daniel Cottom *Social Figures: George Eliot, Social History, and Literary Representation*
Volume 43. Michael Nerlich *The Ideology of Adventure, Volume 2*
Volume 42. Michael Nerlich *The Ideology of Adventure, Volume 1*
Volume 41. Denis Hollier *The College of Sociology*
Volume 40. Peter Sloterdijk *Critique of Cynical Reason*
Volume 39. Géza von Molnár *Romantic Vision, Ethical Context: Novalis and Artistic Autonomy*
Volume 38. Algirdas Julien Greimas *On Meaning: Selected Writings in Semiotic Theory*
Volume 37. Nicolas Abraham and Maria Torok *The Wolf Man's Magic Word: A Cryptonymy*
Volume 36. Alice Yaeger Kaplan *Reproductions of Banality: Fascism, Literature, and French Intellectual Life*
Volume 35. Denis Hollier *The Politics of Prose*
Volume 34. Geoffrey Hartman *The Unremarkable Wordsworth*
Volume 33. Paul de Man *The Resistance to Theory*
Volume 32. Djelal Kadir *Questing Fictions: Latin America's Family Romance*
Volume 31. Samuel Weber *Institution and Interpretation*
Volume 30. Gilles Deleuze and Félix Guattari *Kafka: Toward a Minor Literature*
Volume 29. Peter Szondi *Theory of the Modern Drama*
Volume 28. Edited by Jonathan Arac *Postmodernism and Politics*
Volume 27. Stephen Melville *Philosophy Beside Itself: On Deconstruction and Modernism*
Volume 26. Andrzej Warminski *Readings in Interpretation: Hölderlin, Hegel, Heidegger*
Volume 25. José Antonio Maravall *Culture of the Baroque: Analysis of a Historical Structure*
Volume 24. Hélène Cixous and Catherine Clément *The Newly Born Woman*
Volume 23. Klaus Theweleit *Male Fantasies, 2. Male Bodies: Psychoanalyzing the White Terror*
Volume 22. Klaus Theweleit *Male Fantasies, 1. Women, Floods, Bodies, History*
Volume 21. Malek Alloula *The Colonial Harem*
Volume 20. Jean-François Lyotard and Jean-Loup Thébaud *Just Gaming*
Volume 19. Jay Caplan *Framed Narratives: Diderot's Genealogy of the Beholder*
Volume 18. Thomas G. Pavel *The Poetics of Plot: The Case of English Renaissance Drama*
Volume 17. Michel de Certeau *Heterologies*
Volume 16. Jacques Attali *Noise*
Volume 15. Peter Szondi *On Textual Understanding and Other Essays*
Volume 14. Georges Bataille *Visions of Excess: Selected Writings, 1927–1939*
Volume 13. Tzvetan Todorov *Mikhail Bakhtin: The Dialogical Principle*

Volume 12. Ross Chambers *Story and Situation: Narrative Seduction and the Power of Fiction*

Volume 11. Edited by John Fekete *The Structural Allegory: Reconstructive Encounters with the New French Thought*

Volume 10. Jean-François Lyotard *The Postmodern Condition: A Report on Knowledge*

Volume 9. Erich Auerbach *Scenes from the Drama of European Literature*

Volume 8. Mikhail Bakhtin *Problems of Dostoevsky's Poetics*

Volume 7. Paul de Man *Blindness and Insight: Essays in the Rhetoric of Contemporary Criticism* 2nd ed., rev.

Volume 6. Edited by Jonathan Arac, Wlad Godzich, and Wallace Martin *The Yale Critics: Deconstruction in America*

Volume 5. Vladimir Propp *Theory and History of Folklore*

Volume 4. Peter Bürger *Theory of the Avant-Garde*

Volume 3. Hans Robert Jauss *Aesthetic Experience and Literary Hermeneutics*

Volume 2. Hans Robert Jauss *Toward an Aesthetic of Reception*

Volume 1. Tzvetan Todorov *Introduction to Poetics*

Paul J. Thibault is Professoré a contratto at the Facoltà di Scienze dell' Educazione of the University of Verona, where he teaches a course on language and education. He has held teaching positions in linguistics, semiotics, and literary theory at Murdoch University (Western Australia) and the University of Sydney, and in English language at the University of Bologna. Thibault studied linguistics at the University of Newcastle and completed his Ph.D. at the University of Sydney. He is author of a monograph, *Text, Discourse, and Context: A Social Semiotic Perspective*, as well as articles on semiotics, discourse analysis, and linguistics.